John Brucato

A SICILIAN
in
AMERICA

An Autobiography

by

John Brucato

A SICILIAN IN AMERICA

Published by
Green Hills Publishing Company
Millbrae, CA 94030

Book Production by
Quali-Type, Inc.
Livermore, CA 94550

ISBN 0-9635292-0-X

To my dear wife Joan,
for her patience . . .
and understanding.

Acknowledgments

Grateful acknowledgment is made to my dear and long time friend Alessandro Baccari, for his brilliant, generous and dedicated guidance in making this book possible.

To Kathy Baccari for her valued assistance and her constant encouragement in every step of the way.

To Pansy Tom for her long and arduous task in the preparation of the manuscript.

To Jack Russell for the benefit of his editorial knowledge and his confidence in the value of the manuscript.

Also By John Brucato

❦

- **The Farmer Goes To Town (1948)**

❦

- **War Comes To The Farmlands**

  A series of nine articles appearing in the old San Francisco
  News in 1942, depicting the plight of the small family
  farmer trying to survive during wartime.

Table of Contents

Introduction

One of the most beautiful islands in the world is the island of Sicily, one of the 20 regions of Italy. Some of the most beautiful and interesting people inhabit this ancient and unusual land. When you have a Sicilian for a friend he is your friend for life.

Here is an unusual and incredible story of a Sicilian American, John Brucato, who has lived a full life filled with accomplishments, never easy and mostly against odds, sometimes insurmountable odds.

In this book, he will take you through his many involvements, before, through and after the World War I era, the Bootleg and the Tin Pan Alley days, the Charleston period, the Depression and onto the present day. He will relate the many happenings, his uncanny description of events, sometimes witty, always factual.

Brucato is at home with the wealthy, the powerful, the politicians, but he is happiest with the common people, the "little guys" and most of all — his family. He boasts about his "American family" and the many relatives he left behind in Sicily, which he calls his "Italian family." His love of them and their love of him is his greatest satisfaction. "This is my wealth," he would say, "my family."

His life has been a challenge, whether in business, government, in civic life or in the many enterprises he initiated, fighting tirelessly and with conviction, and at all times for the benefit of the community. He fought for just causes, spurning wealth for his principles, but most of all, trying to overcome the Mafia stigma, with good deeds.

His experiences, his narrations, his many anecdotes, all on a low key basis will give the reader a fascinating and enjoyable "inside" on this man's productive and exciting life.

Now in his middle octogenarian years he remains active in his community, serves on many boards and continues to think young and aggressive, despite a few minor physical ailments that come with old age. He reasons that your "second" life begins at 65 which he calls the "youth of old age." And as you continue through the Golden years, middle age begins at 85 and you are really old when you pass 95.

Alessandro Baccari
A Friend

Foreword

How does one go about fighting to eliminate the stigma of the Mafia that seems to be attached to those of Sicilian birth, or Sicilian roots?

Perhaps, in this book, "A Sicilian in America," I may have lighted a candle, a small candle but a light that could spread. Another candle, another light. Soon there could be many lights and eventually the illumination from these many candles, these many lights will be like Times Square at night, like Las Vegas with its night time illumination, all brought about by a lot of little people like myself lighting a candle.

It is long past due, that this movement starting at the Grass Roots, the Sicilian Grass Roots, spreads this illumination, this Gospel, not according to Matthew or John, but the Gospel of Rebellion, not a rebellion against our glorious country, America, but a rebellion against those Mafia bastards who have maligned the good name of Sicily and those with Sicilian roots.

We have to defeat these *Mafiosi* and those of Sicilian roots who glorify the Godfathers, the Goodfellas and the many films and books that make them wealthy at the expense of their countrymen.

This would be a grass roots revolution to be brought about not with weapons but by good deeds and publicizing of the many, many accomplishments and contributions of Sicilians to the world, their country, their state and their local communities. The battle has just begun and it is up to you and me who have Sicilian roots.

Perhaps the fault lies with we of Italian or Sicilian descent. We have been too complacent. What I have gathered, however, is that there has been an "awakening,": and that we are angry. We are fed up with being depicted negatively, by the media, as criminals, bigots or buffoons.

We want the media to show the many positives of life in their communities. We want to bring out the contributions we have made, the good things, the constructive things, the humanitarian, the many, many aspects of our heritage that are just the opposite of what they depict and we want that change now.

The greatest offenders are television and the motion pictures where we are always the "Bad Guys," the mob, the Mafia princesses and everything that has a violent background. Is this what the viewers really want? If that is so, then we are really sick and God help us all.

Those Italian American writers, actors, producers whose works perpetuate these stereotypes are not excused. The lure of riches may be hard to resist but they too, must be held responsible.

From the time Italians began arriving on our shores in large numbers in the 19th century, the media has linked them to criminality. That, despite the figures of the U.S. Dept. of Justice, that fewer than one-tenth of one percent of Italian Americans are involved with organized crime. Consider that there are more than 25 million Americans of Italian descent who are proud of their family oriented values, their hard constructive work and their many, many achievements that helped make this country so great. Add to this number the many millions in addition that have intermarried and do not bear Italian names but are proud of their Italian roots.

We say _basta_, enough! We want to be treated as an equal part of the American mosaic, maintaining our proud ancestral roots and participating fully and fairly in the fabric of American life, and I say _damn_ those of Italian origin who have richly capitalized on the defects of that infinitesimal few who give us a stigma that we must bear on our shoulders and on our children's shoulders.

The Author

Sicilian born John Brucato arrived in America at the age of 4, together with his family in 1909. He was reared in the Bensonhurst section of Brooklyn. After graduating from the College of Agriculture at Farmingdale, Long Island, he went west to continue his viticultural studies at the University of California at Davis.

Following a tour of duty as a farm hand and farm manager, he became a Food & Drug inspector in New York City. He later went west and did creditable work with the California State Department of Agriculture.

Later, he operated his own vineyard in the Alexander Valley (before it became famous) in Sonoma County and with the repeal of the infamous Prohibition Amendment, he and his two brothers operated a successful bonded winery for 18 years in San Francisco, until the untimely death of his older brother and the resultant sale of the winery.

He became manager of the Agriculture and Land Division of the San Francisco Water Department making millions of dollars for his beloved city in the leasing of its far-flung properties owned by the city.

With a food shortage during World War II, he successfully organized the Victory Garden program which resulted in over 70,000 "back yard" gardens in the city.

In order to assist the family sized farmers who had difficulty selling their crops, during wartime, he organized the famous San Francisco Farmers' Market which became the "Grand Daddy" of the more than 180 farmers markets organized throughout California as Certified Farmers' Markets.

He served and serves on many boards and commissions in various capacities — civic, business, fraternal and many other activities, all to the benefit of others with no financial gain for himself. He always felt that whatever he was involved in was his way of paying back to his adopted country, America, in many small, many big ways.

John Brucato at age four in 1909.

Chapter 1

The Early Years

As I look back at my life, I must say that it was a difficult, interesting and rewarding life. When one lives for more than 87 years, he lives through a lot of history.

During my lifetime, I lived through two World Wars, plus the Korean and Vietnam Wars, the Prohibition and bootleg period, two Depressions, the Charleston and jazz period, and the births of the automobile, the airplane, and the front-wheel drive.

As a young immigrant, I witnessed discrimination and integration, and I was always in search of the "American Dream."

I was born in Sicily on May 12, 1905 in the city of Palermo. My parents were strong-willed, affectionate people. I was blessed to have them and two wonderful brothers, Frank and Peter, and Frances, a gracious sister.

My father, Francesco Antonio Brucato, and his brother, Peter *(Zio Pietro)*, and their father before them were in the business of exporting lemons from Sicily. My father's office, packing sheds and lemon groves were located near the town of Cefalú, about thirty miles east of Palermo where we lived. But as time passed like in so many places, farmland disappeared and Cefalú became urbanized.

The business was quite prosperous until a worldwide depression struck with all its fury in 1908. Europe, particularly Sicily, was economically hard hit by its impact. His main outlets were the New York and London markets.

As Italy suffered, Sicily suffered more so. It lacked industry and natural resources, and the majority of the population was

3

illiterate. Characteristic of most depression periods, the rich seemed to be getting richer while the poor got poorer. The wealthy truly lived the good life as they had their country *villas* and fashionable *palazzos* in the city. The majority of the Sicilians were *contadini* (peasants) who struggled greatly to survive. My family was best described as middle class, which, during this time, was scarce.

Sicily was and still is one of the world's most beautiful islands with a history that goes back thousands of years and a culture marked by the many foreign invaders throughout the centuries. Its exquisite architecture stands as a symbol of outside influence. There are Phoenecian, Greek and Roman ruins, and temples and buildings of the Byzantine, Norman, Arab and Gothic periods.

As one gets older, the memory of one's youth becomes easier to recollect. Things that happened yesterday or last week become difficult to remember. As I close my eyes, I see so clearly the Sicily of my youth.

In the cities of Palermo, Messina and Catania, there were fashionable parades in a select quarter of the city on Sundays. In Palermo, this section was called the *quatro canti* (four corners), made famous as Garibaldi's tent headquarters from where he planned the campaign to defeat the Bourbons who ruled Sicily and Naples for many years. (Garibaldi, at a later date, completed the conquest of most of Italy handing "the keys of the kingdom" to Vittorio Emanuele in Rome.) Each Sunday, families of the nobility would show off their finery as they strolled about greeting each other while the peasants looked on not with envy, but amusement. The automobile was just in its infancy and as yet had no place in the Sunday ceremony called *La Passegiata* (the walk). I would guess at that period that besides attending the opera, it was the best show in town.

Another important part of Sicilian social life which I remember so well were the sidewalk *cafes* and pastry shops where one could have a *cafe espresso* (coffee), *gelato* (ice cream), *cannoli* (pastry), and a few *biscotti* (biscuits) in the company of friends. And now that I am a "big boy," I am happy to say that this activity is still part of a Sicilian's daily routine.

The Arabs invented ice cream, but it was the Sicilians who immortalized it.

The *Palermitanis* are a friendly and gracious people. This was the families' day out and they really made the most of it.

It was a wonderful era, but no longer possible due to the

The city of my youth — Palermo. Villa Roma as seen from Julius Caesar Square.

My father (holding a prickly pear) and friends enjoying a Sunday outing at Cefalú (near Palermo) where he had his lemon packing plant — 1905.

advent of the automobile. How I enjoyed my *gelato* as a little boy. In fact, the memory is so profound that on each trip I have taken to Sicily (ten), part of my reason for going was to relive these memories.

My best pal at the time was my *nonno* (grandfather), Nino Gallo, my mother's father. It was he who developed the "Sicilian sweet tooth" in me.

Other things that pop up in my memory of that time was that of the street sweepers who would go about pushing a cart with a broom and shovel. Their main job was to pick up the bundles of garbage tossed out of the windows by the housewives every morning. It was the custom of the times and as I look back, quite an unsanitary one. How I would laugh when a bundle of garbage would come sailing out of the window and on a number of occasions, a near-miss of some innocent passerby minding his own business.

Another vivid sight comes to mind, which I recall with fondness. The milkman would pass by in the early morning with his three or four cows and several goats. Residents from their second and third floor balconies would lower baskets with pitchers, along with notes indicating how much milk was needed and the exact amount of *lira* currency. The herdsman proceeded to milk a cow or goat and fill up the pitchers with fresh, warm milk. The housewives would then haul up their baskets, exchange a few words with the milkman, say *ciao* and *arrivaderci* until the next time. The warm, foamy milk was passed through a filter and boiled so that it would be safe to consume.

This same pattern applied to the other vendors whether they were the breadman, the fishman, the butcher or whoever had anything to sell. Who needed supermarkets in those days when home delivery was the key to marketing success?

My mother often spoke of the family home. She described what today would be considered a condominium. It was a spacious seven-room home occupying the entire second floor as we would describe it in America. However, in Italy, the second floor is the *primo piano* (first floor). The ground floor is known as the *pian terreno*.

The floors were all of Italian marble making the hot summers cool. In the winter months, the floors were covered with rugs to generate warmth. The main rooms had floor-to-ceiling windows.

While there was running water in the house, the drinking

water came from a public fountain nearby. The palatable sparkling water was collected daily and stored in earthen jars.

It was a comfortable home with a large kitchen, which was considered the most important room in a Sicilian home, and a large balcony overlooking the street. Most of the entertainment was done in the kitchen because it was so spacious.

All "live-in" buildings had a *guarda porta* (custodian), who served as the building's security guard and maintenance man. In the event you were without your key, you could not enter unless you saw the *guarda porta*. I remember his name as Lorenzo, a friendly man who loved children and had six of his own.

The family records note that I was born in my mother's family home on the *Via Francesco Crispi* overlooking the beautiful bay of Palermo on the marina, a most attractive parkway.

Because of the city's affinity to the sea, Palermo has always been called *La Conca D'oro* (the Golden Shell). A chain of mountains surround the city — the most famous being *Monte Pellegrino* where the Shrine of Santa Rosalia, the patron saint of Palermo, attracts thousands of pilgrims every year. In the distance is the village of Monreale situated on a mountain top and famous for its cathedral with priceless mosaics and a gigantic painting on its spacious ceiling of the *Padre Eterno* (Eternal Father) looking down on the congregation with his outstretched arms — surely one of the man-made wonders of the world.

I was the youngest in my family, the *bambino* (the baby). I was pampered and spoiled by my parents, brothers and sister. As I look back, I can honestly say that I really enjoyed the pleasure of their attention. I miss them greatly. In remembering them, I pray often to the good St. Francis who not only is the patron saint of Italy, but the saint whose motto of life, "Lord, make me an instrument of Thy peace," played a strong influence on us Brucatos. My parents handed down his teachings to all their children.

Through generations of Brucatos, the first son was always named Francesco. How proud my father was of his name and so was my brother, Frank. In a strange way, I can admit now that I was always a little envious of not being named Francesco.

I owe so much to my parents who throughout my life nourished me with love and understanding. They certainly knew how to use discipline to develop my talents.

I will always remember my father with his picturesque handle-bar moustache. He must have spent a great deal of time trimming and waxing that facial fixture, although I know that "Pop" was not a vain person. He had a love for the outdoors and was quite a hunter who enjoyed roaming the dry Sicilian countryside in search of his prey. Most of the time, as I remember, it was a rabbit or two.

My mother was an extraordinary woman, the catalyst for all our family activities, the personification of strength and gentleness. Like my father, she, too, was proud of her name, Rosalia, especially since Santa Rosalia was the patron saint of Palermo. How she enjoyed people. Her greatest passion was history. I truly believe that it was from her that I acquired my deep interest in history, geography, and my deep respect for my fellow man. "Mama" was always cool, calm and collected. Never once did she ever display the Sicilian temperament — shouting one minute, affectionate the next.

I shall never forget the family doctor who performed the major surgery on my knee. His name was Giuseppe Di Lorenzo. Dr. Di Lorenzo took care of my family for several decades. He was a soft-spoken man who wore glasses and had a thick moustache that gave him a decided look of authority and dignity.

Before my family was to embark to the New World in 1909, I developed a large swelling on my right kneecap. It was so serious and painful that Dr. Di Lorenzo decided on immediate surgery. As to what caused this unusual swelling, I did not know. The surgery was performed at home. Hospitals were not the place to go in those days. The only time a person wound up in a hospital was when there was no other hope for survival. It was generally recognized as "the end." For that reason and also for the fact that hospitals generally lacked the necessities that we have today (sanitation was practically unknown), my home became the hospital. The dining room table was used to perform the operation. It was a sturdy, well-built table made from the best Sicilian walnut.

Dr. Di Lorenzo enlisted the aid of several members of my family for the purpose of holding me down, so I wouldn't move during the surgery. There were no anesthetics in those days. Several blankets were laid out on the table covered by a sheet for me to lie on. Water was boiled and clean cloths were made available. The operation was a huge success, thanks to the surgical skills of Dr. Di Lorenzo.

Post-operative care included going to the beach often to bake my knee in the hot sand. A month after the surgery, my mother took me to Mondello, a resort area near Palermo where she buried my knee in sand. The Palermitani would spend their summers in Mondello bathing in the Mediterranean Sea. The Mondello Pavilion was famous all over Europe and attracted many Scandinavians, Germans and English who wanted to escape the rigid northern European winters.

What I also enjoyed was the old Sicilian custom of sipping a small glass of marsala wine immediately after coming out of the water. It made no difference how warm the temperature was, and it was usually quite warm. The idea was that the sip of marsala was an "insurance" against catching cold. At the tender age of four, I really enjoyed my sip of marsala while I had to spend most of the afternoon baking my knee in the hot sand.

The operation delayed our planned trip to America, but not for long. America, the promised land, became the goal of my parents. My father would say years later when asked why he came to America: "It was time to start a new and better life."

I have a photo of when I was four which my grandchildren today seem to enjoy because I had long, curly hair. I would generally go along with their teasing by telling them what a beautiful child I was. This, of course, put me on the receiving end, but who cares. We would always wind up with a few laughs.

Prior to leaving for America, my father took me to a barber who expertly shorn all of my long, curly locks of hair. My mother cried for a week saying, "My poor *bambino*. He is no longer a child. His beautiful curls are gone."

My father booked passage for us on the *Giuseppe Verdi*, one of the better transatlantic steamships out of Naples for New York. Passage on ships were at a premium. It seemed that all of Europe wanted to come to America. There were just not enough ships.

To reach Naples from Palermo, the family took the overnight *postale* (mail boat). One could go by rail, but it took too long and seldom ran on time. The *Giuseppe Verdi* was crowded with human beings all striving to get to America. These immigrants were not lazy people. They wanted work of any kind, which their own country could not supply them. They had families and little or no money, borrowing where they could or using up their life savings and whatever assets they possessed in order to make this drastic change in their lives.

The majority of those aboard traveled in steerage where they were packed like a can of sardines. The lack of sanitation was unbelievable. What they brought aboard was what they ate — dried salame, bread, biscuits and cheese. It was sad to see mothers picking lice from the heads of their children. Unfortunately, it was a period in time when there was little or no regulations concerning health and sanitation. The toilet facilities were indescribable. The body stench and vomiting from those who suffered seasickness added to the unbearable conditions. It was survival. This situation, as I learned at a later date, was similar and quite common on ships from all nations carrying immigrants to the ''promised land.''

We were fortunate to get a stateroom in second class. There were six of us and we still had to make room for two more people. Crowded as it was, we were at least able to eat in better conditions even though the food was not very good.

After a rather rough ten days at sea, we reached Ellis Island in New York Harbor. For my parents, passing beneath that most beautiful of all ladies, the Statue of Liberty, was the greatest thrill in their lives. The steerage passengers with identification tags pinned to their garments got off at Ellis Island to be inspected by the health doctors and nurses, while second and first class passengers went through their quarantine inspection aboard ship.

We were met at the pier by my favorite uncle (my mother's brother), Roberto Gallo, who operated a successful custom house brokerage business in Manhattan. He found us a home in Bensonhurst, one of the better sections of Brooklyn. This was ideal for me as we would be only a few blocks from Gravesend Bay which, at that time, contained a sandy beach where I could go to bake my knee. The rent was less than $40 a month. It was a three-story woodframe house with a huge lot, which eventually became our vegetable garden. Everybody in those days had vegetable gardens, and raised rabbits and chickens. The house was heated by a coal furnace in a huge, deep and spacious basement. The basement would be used to store at least three tons of coal and a supply of firewood. There was also room for several barrels of wine and lots of storage space for root vegetables and general items. The furnace would be started about mid-October and ran constantly until May. It required about two tons of coal a month to heat this huge house by steam. Pop would bank the fire at night and being the first to get up, he would shake the ashes and add a few shovels of coal until they became red hot. He would then add more coal, enough to keep the house warm until evening when another few shovels of coal would be needed. Once a week, we would lift the full barrel of ashes up the five steps and roll it out to the sidewalk for the city's sanitation department trucks to pick up.

I acquired my "green thumb" from my father. We grew enough tomatoes to sun dry into tomato paste that would be converted into our winter supply of tomato sauce. I was my father's assistant in the garden. We grew all kinds of vegetables. This is where I developed my liking to gardening. (This period could have been the planting of a "seed" that eventually grew into my agricultural future.)

When school opened in the fall (the first fall), Frances, Frank, Peter and I registered and began our American education at Public School 163 in Bath Beach. We had to walk ten blocks to school as there were no school buses back then. It was quite a long walk in the cold, wintry snow.

Mary E. Lynch, an attractive, tall but stern spinster, was the perennial principal of PS 163. She was like a "Lady Solomon" responsible for such a polyglot assortment of Italians, Jews, Irish and Poles. (There were very few Hispanics or Blacks at that time.) This was the make-up of our neighborhood. It was easy to make friends inasmuch as were we not all immigrants?

One teacher would teach all subjects in one classroom. The teachers were all women, with the exception of two men. Mr. Moore taught shop while Mr. McDermott taught English. Discipline had to be tight considering the nature of the pupils. When a student became a problem, he was sent to Mr. Moore or Mr. McDermott. He would generally receive a cuffing or a few slaps on the knuckles with a heavy ruler. There was no P.T.A. in those days and very few complaints from the parents. We were living in a tough society that only respected discipline.

Peter and I became very close in our grammar school days. We learned how to handle our fists by necessity, and we did quite well. There were always fist fights during recess or lunch period. When more than one was involved, Peter and I would fight back-to-back and challenge our attackers to come forward.

We learned four languages in our growing-up period. We spoke our Sicilian dialect and Italian at home, English at school, and "Brooklynese" in the streets. Up to this day, I still have a little "Brooklynese" in my speech.

For breakfast on a school day, we would have either hot chocolate or half-coffee, half-milk, bread, butter and jam, and sometimes cooked oatmeal. The dry, packaged cereals (like Cornflakes) were just beginning at that time. Our school lunch was packed in a small lunchbox consisting of a peanut butter and jelly sandwich and a hard-boiled egg. Mother would give us five cents to spend for lunch. There were generally pretzel, pickle and halvah vendors (all Jewish) outside the schoolyard. I would spread my purchases in this fashion: two cents for a pretzel, two cents for a kosher pickle, and the last cent for halvah, a delicious Jewish candy.

There were no playgrounds in those days. We played in the streets. Other than an occasional appearance of a horse and wagon or one of those new Model-T Fords, there was no traffic to disturb us. Everyone had rollerskates. We all played hockey in the summertime and ice hockey in the winter. The ice skates were clamped to our shoes and strapped to our feet. Baseball and football were also popular in the sandlots, and when the weather was right, we swam in Gravesend Bay. During the cold winters, it was sleighs, snowballs and snow forts.

We had no supervisors, playground directors, or playgrounds. Almost everyone participated in some sport or another unless he was ill.

The city's famous underground subway system spread out into the suburbs (we were suburban in those days) except Brooklyn and Queens where the subways were elevated. Thanks to "Honest John Hylan," mayor of New York City, the subway fare never changed. You could ride anywhere in the five boroughs of New York for a nickel.

Coney Island was not too far away. Everyone went there on weekends and especially on hot summer days. They would roast and suffer in the unventilated trains in order to get to Coney Island to cool off. There would be millions of New Yorkers on the crowded beaches getting sunburned, dipping or swimming in the garbage-polluted waters.

New York City's garbage came in the following manner: it would be hauled out to sea in huge barges and dumped into the ocean 12 miles out. With the change of tides, the garbage would float back towards the beaches at high tide. No one seemed to mind. With one hand, you propelled yourself when swimming while the other hand was used to push the garbage aside. After refreshing in the waters of Coney Island, the return trip would be hot, humid, and smelly of body odors, kosher pickles and garlic breath. It was a way of life. After all, you've just spent a day at Coney Island mingling with the crowds, had a hot dog (generally smothered with mustard or sauerkraut), corn-on-the-cob, popcorn, a few bottles of beer or sasparilla. You felt you had a good time. New Yorkers are indeed a strange breed.

Before I finished grammar school, my mother, Frances, Peter and I made a return trip to Sicily. My father and Frank stayed behind. It was 1915 and World War I was in progress. Italy was neutral at the time, so we felt safe. My mother owned a condominium that was part of the family inheritance. During our absence, my aunt and her family, including my favorite grandfather, occupied the second floor of the building. It was located off the *Via Roma* and almost across the way from Palermo's famous *Hotel de le Palme.* At that time, the area was strictly residential.

Peter and I went to the Salesian School of Don Bosco for a month. Because we were *Americani*, the usual struggle for survival took place as always when young boys of 10 to 15 years of age are together. They fought us the "Italian way." Peter and I fought the "Brooklynese way," back-to-back, full of control of our well-educated fists. After the second day, we were "accepted" — after the others received bloody noses, black eyes, and a few swollen jaws.

My grandfather was my idol. Everyday, Peter and I would go with him in a *carozza* (horse-and-buggy taxi) to the *vucerria* (open-air farmers market) where everything was sold. *Vucerria* translated in English is "the place where they (the vendors) shout." If you ever heard a Sicilian shout in an open-air market, you will realize why they all want to be opera singers.

Of course, the treat came at the conclusion of the shopping — a real Sicilian *cannoli.* Peter and I were usually good for two apiece, plus a dish of *gelato.*

I always enjoyed the table scene at dinner time. Grandpa Gallo was a most lovable man, a historian and a retired engineer. He was a strict disciplinarian, especially at the table. His philosophy was that there should be no talking during dinner. It was a place to eat. The talking came after the dessert. This rule was faithfully carried out.

It was the time of year when lentils were plentiful. They were my grandfather's favorite dish. Of course, you must realize that lentils, like any kind of bean, produces gas in your system.

When you eat a lot of lentils, it would be necessary to emit the gas or you would become slightly bloated. We had lentils three nights in a row. One evening during dinner, those gathered around the table were enjoying their dish of lentil soup. As silence remained supreme, Grandpa Gallo (probably uncontrolled) emitted a blast of gas that sounded like a mild celebration of the Fourth of July. While we all remained quiet in respect to him and continued our dinner, he would in a soft voice be heard to say (after each blast), *"Alla faccia dei nemici della Santa Chiesa,"* which meant, "In the face of the enemies of the Holy Church."

We had to cut our summer vacation short as Italy was about to declare war against Germany and join the Allies. We left Naples on the *Cristoforo Colombo* for New York. Prior to reaching Gibraltar while we were in the Mediterranean and everyone was promenading on deck after supper, a frightening incident occurred. Out of the dark, black waters, a light was seen. Suddenly, we realized it was a submarine — a German submarine. Italy was still neutral, but nevertheless, the sub pulled alongside and signaled that they were coming aboard. After a brief period, the boarding crew left with their prisoner. He was a German who was defecting and trying to flee to America.

Brooklyn looked mighty good to us. Frances graduated from Bay Ridge High School and went to work for the Italian Consulate. She was proficient in Italian, English, Spanish, and some German. Frank never finished high school. He went to work as the family finances were none too healthy. Peter graduated from New Utrecht High School and started his career as a custom house broker working for our uncle, Robert A. Gallo.

How I ever graduated from high school, I will never know. All Brooklynites are rabid baseball fans from the age of three to 99. When the baseball season started, I believe I spent more time at Ebbetts Field when the Dodgers were at home, than I did in high school. I was not alone in this respect. The word "fanatic" was derived from the Brooklyn fan. We never cared whether they won or lost. If they happened to win, they would be cheered. If they lost, they were bums *(dose Brooklyn bums)*.

The big game was when the New York Giants played the Brooklyn Dodgers whether it was at the polo grounds or at Ebbetts Field. It was always like a World Series. So keen was the rivalry. They called it the ''Nickel World Series,'' because that was what it cost by subway to go to either field.

One of my father's main goals after settling in New York was to see to it that each of his children received a good education. The family decided that I was to be given the opportunity to get a college education. These were not easy times, especially since my father's lemon exporting business was practically wiped out by a government embargo on Sicilian lemons in order to protect the new fledgling lemon producers in California controlled by the newly formed Sunkist Citrus Cooperative.

Despite this problem, the decision was made that Giovanni (that's me) was to go to college.

Chapter 2

The College Years

My father wanted his children to be college educated. This was not possible because of the serious Depression affecting the New World. He had suffered greatly in his lemon exporting business but nevertheless it was possible for one, the youngest son to get a college education.

He would say, "In Sicily this would not have been possible, but in the New World, everything is possible."

My ambition was to have a career in the field of agricultural sciences. In Farmingdale, Long Island, a new agricultural college had come into being. It was called the New York State Institute of Applied Agriculture; otherwise known as the College of Agriculture, and in short, the New York Aggies. The college was ideally located about 35 miles from the city in an area largely agricultural and famous for its Long Island potatoes, cauliflower, and the many pickle and sauerkraut farms. It had an outstanding faculty and this is where my father felt I should go.

The college was small, located on 500 acres and about two miles west of the appropriately named town of Farmingdale. Three hundred students attended the college — nine of whom were girls who domiciled in a spacious cottage called the Mott House while the boys lived in two large dormitories. Besides the living facilities, there were five other buildings used for teaching purposes including agronomy, horticulture, sciences, animal husbandry, and general miscellaneous subjects.

Of the 300 students, 75 were Federal Board students (veterans of the just-ended World War I), while another 25 were Baron De Hirsch students who came from underprivileged

Jewish families. Most of these students did not stay with agriculture. They generally wound up in the Catskill Mountains in New York State, which was famous as a Jewish vacation resort area. They ran boarding houses featuring fresh, farm vegetables which were usually purchased at the wholesale markets.

My first roommate was a Jewish lad from the Bronx. His name was Louis Nadelbaum, but I will always remember him as Louie. One time, we found ourselves with a free weekend. Louie suggested that we go to the city where there was a dance and some kind of celebration in the synagogue in his old neighborhood. I said, "Louie, how can I get in? You know I am not Jewish." To this, he replied, "Don't worry. I will get you in." When we arrived at the synagogue, the rabbi was at the door checking in the people. He looked at me and passed me in with a welcome smile. When he came to Louie, he said, "I am sorry, no Gentiles allowed." I often wondered after that incident whether you begin to look like those you associate with.

I went out for football. It was the first season for this fledgling college. I had played a lot via the neighborhood sandlots and really enjoyed the game. I made the varsity in spring training and prepared myself for the coming fall season. Our coach, Ward Brennan, was well-known and experienced. He made his reputation at Fordham University as a player and coach.

In those days, there was no huddle. The quarterback was in complete command and called the signals with little or no help from the bench. You played offense and defense with no "special teams." The only time you had any relief was if you were injured, exhausted, or played a lousy game.

I started the season at left halfback. The forward pass was in its infancy and seldom used. Football was a power game. Most of our plays were through the line and around the ends. I was fast and made substantial gains, especially around the ends. During the first year, we played out of our class — Fordham University, New York University, and some of the other leading eastern colleges. It was no wonder we lost every game, but to our credit, not by much. We were outmanned and short on substitutes. As Coach Brennan often said, we had guts and most importantly, we lost with dignity, fighting to the bitter end. It was certainly a well-deserved compliment.

During the second season, we performed the opposite by

winning every game except one. We should have beaten St. Stephens College, but we lost because our team was ridden with the flu. We had gone up the Hudson River in upstate New York to play this team on their home ground during a blizzard. It was impossible to keep the field clear of snow. Everytime I carried the ball, my face would be smothered in the deep snow after being tackled. We ran out of manpower and the most unbelievable thing happened. St. Stephens loaned us one of their men, who, incidently, played a good game.

Three seasons did something to me. I learned how to lose with dignity, and how to win and be gracious in victory. I believe that trait followed me throughout my life.

I was deeply involved in my studies, performing well in every subject but chemistry. My fellow chemistry students and I felt that Professor Sloat was rather difficult to understand and equally hard in discussing a point with him. We had taken our final exams in his class and felt that we would be rather fortunate if we came near a passing grade. Fate always seems to intercede and sometimes solve difficult situations. It so happened that a group of us, including six who had taken their finals in chemistry, took off after dinner to do some ice skating at the "Clay Pit." It was the old swimming hole in the summer which made an ideal ice skating rink during the winter when it froze over. We were surprised to find Professor Sloat and some of the faculty already enjoying the skating on the smooth, glassy-like ice. Lo and behold, we heard a loud noise. The ice started to crack and who fell through the ice but Professor Sloat. He went down and fortunately, he came straight up without hitting his head on the ice and managed to hold onto the edge of the ice. I was closest to him and crawled on my belly towards him to grab his hand. Two others held onto my legs and somehow we managed to get the good professor out. We had a big bonfire going, wrapped him in a blanket, thawed him out and carried him to his room where we put him to bed. Three days later, we received our grades. Somehow we were not really surprised when those of us who participated in the rescue learned not only had we passed, but we had received a score of ninety-eight percent.

In my junior year, I changed roommates. His name was Larry Malone, a real nice guy. He came from a wealthy New York family. I don't believe Larry ever did a stroke of work in his life. Nevertheless, he was strong as an ox and became a top tackle on the Aggie football team. His folks would come down in their Stanley Steamer (deluxe automobile) and sometimes we would take a long weekend trip.

About eight of the members of the team became close-knit friends. We were always together. With such a frisky group, we got involved in a lot of mischievous pranks just for the hell of it. If we were ever caught, we would have been called "juvenile delinquents." One night when we had some time on our hands, we decided to have a party. Our football season had just ended with a well-earned victory. We had all the ingredients (food and beverages) for a big midnight snack, so we invited all the members of our victorious squad to join us. Someone said, "We have no ice cream." That was no problem. Some of us went into the night towards the mess hall. We managed to get inside and spotted a ten-gallon can of ice cream. Great, just what we wanted. The party was going well until we opened the ice cream container and discovered that it was chocolate. That was a big disappointment. One of the "burglars" decided to go back and leave a note saying, "Thanks for the chocolate. Please have strawberry next week. Signed, The Goo Goos." The story doesn't end here.

The next day was Sunday — the day they always served ice cream. The chef came out of the kitchen to address the diners. He sadly removed his chef's hat and said, "Last night, some culprits broke into the refrigerator and stole the ice cream that was to be served today." He hesitated and then continued, "Fortunately, we do have a small quantity of ice cream available which we will serve only to our football heroes." I believe some of us suffered a slight case of indigestion. I know I did.

One of my favorite subjects was entomology. Before completing this course, it was necessary to have a complete collection of most of the insects in the area. On weekends, some of my "goo goos" joined me in scouring the fields chasing butterflies with our big butterfly nets. A lot of this chasing occurred near some of the nearby highways. We often wondered what passing motorists thought when they saw a dozen grown men chasing butterflies in all directions with their oversized nets.

Before graduation, I received a most unusual proposal. In 1923, Albert Johnson, president of the college, had signed a contract with the new Bolshevik government in Moscow. When the Bolsheviks overthrew the Czar of Russia and assumed power, there was a great deal of confusion there. The new government wanted some agricultural experts to help them start up their so-called "Five-Year-Plan" to modernize their agriculture. They called on A.A. Johnson. He selected six of the seniors, including me, to join him. After much deliberation, I decided that my future was in California. I was not too sure about this new Communist regime. Johnson did go to Russia with six of his graduates. Included in this group was one of my good friends, "Duke" Mischenko, a Russian. We read about Johnson's success in one of the New York magazines. I also kept in close contact by mail with the group for about two years. After that, I never heard from them again. I wrote numerous follow-up letters, but to no avail. I wonder what would have been my fate had I joined them?

Chapter 3

On to California

In 1924, my application for post-graduate studies at the University of California Davis, College of Agriculture was accepted. I was to start in September.

During the summer months, I had an opportunity to work on a farm in the state of Maine. It was part of the Piel family's 2,000-acre estate. The chance came about when Oswald Piel, a classmate of mine, invited me to journey to Maine for a visit. At that time, the Piel family owned and operated one of the largest breweries in New York. When we arrived at the farmhouse, I couldn't believe how beautiful the area was. It was located in the central part of Maine near Moosehead Lake. Most of the land was untouched by human occupation as it was thousands of years ago. Part of the land was virgin timber and mostly pine trees. It was truly a primeval forest with an abundance of birds, along with deer, elk, moose, bears, foxes and mountain lions.

What the Piel family referred to as a farmhouse was a 14 room mansion, which they used for summer vacations. Adjacent to it were several guest houses and a lodge to accommodate the caretaker and hired help. So large was this acreage that the main highway from Portland to Quebec passed through the property.

When the Piels asked me if I would be interested in working during the summer as general farm manager and herdsman for their livestock, I was delighted, for it gave me an opportunity to make some money before going west to attend graduate school. My quarters were small but beautiful and I was happy to have my meals with a wonderful middle-aged German couple who were the caretakers for the estate. I always enjoyed German food and I really did justice to the sauerkraut, pigs knuckles, and all the German delicacies, particularly the sausages.

The herd consisted of four Guernsey and two Jersey milking cows, and a ferocious-looking Guernsey bull that eventually became my pet. There were four draft horses, 60 laying hens, and an abundance of barnyard fowl. I would rise at 5 a.m. in the morning, brush down the cows, fill the feed troughs, and commence my hand-milking. Enough milk was kept for household use while the remainder went into butter and cheese. By 7 a.m., a hearty breakfast awaited me. There was not a lot of work to do as the hay was not yet ready. Other than take care of the animals, I had a lot of free time on my hands. I believe I read every book that was in the family library concerning the American Revolution. It fascinated me to retrace Benedict Arnold's expedition through the wilds of Maine on his way to attack Quebec.

Since I was in the center of one of the greatest hunting and fishing areas in the state, I became attached to nature studies and committed to the preservation of the environment, both for humans and animals.

The Piels came up often and I enjoyed their gracious company and generosity. Three days before my departure, one of my former Aggies, Richard Burns, came up to the farm to visit and together we hitchhiked back to New York via Quebec and Montreal. There was no problem getting rides in those days. The dangers in hitchhiking had not yet begun.

From Jackman, Maine, we followed the highway to Quebec enjoying immensely the "old town" known as the French Quarter where everyone spoke French and marveled at the development and diversity of the architecture in the new section of the city. From Quebec, we traveled along the St. Lawrence River until we reached Montreal, another majestic city. Our days and nights were filled with true friendship as we shared our dreams and hopes of what the future might bring us. It was a time in my life where I can truthfully say that I learned the meaning of contentment.

Each step of the way was full of colonial history as we went on to Lake Champlain, Lake George, Saratoga, Albany, down through the Hudson River Valley to New York and finally, home to Bensonhurst. My friend and I believed that we entered a time machine and were but early American explorers carrying out the task of the pathfinders. After a week's stay at home with my family sharing with them the memories and joy of my summer adventure and basking in the warmth of their love and attention, I took the Overland Limited to San Francisco.

The five-day journey across America made me realize how beautiful and big this continent of ours was. I arrived at the Oakland depot on August 18 where I was met by my brother, Frank. It was an emotional reunion, for I am proud to say I have always been close to my brothers and sister. After a moment of tear-filled eyes and smiles, he put my luggage in his 1923 Chevrolet touring car. (The sedan had not come into being at that time.) Although it wasn't a warm day, Frank was determined to keep the top down as we motored onto a ferryboat to cross the bay to San Francisco. We disembarked at the Ferry Building and from there, we drove to his bachelor home in the Bayview District. The first thing he wanted me to see when we got there was his backyard garden where, with typical Sicilian pride, he pointed to his two lemon trees loaded with lemons and the cactus plants which produced those delicious, juicy grenade-shaped fruits called the *ficcu d' india* that are a must in every Sicilian garden.

The following day, Frank drove me to the Davis campus to register and start my activities in graduate school where I was to specialize in viticulture, hoping someday to operate my own vineyard.

In 1924, U.C. Davis was strictly an agricultural college. The enrollment consisted of approximately 600 male and 9 female students. Today, it is no longer an agricultural college, but a major university. In my time, there were two dormitories, a science, horticulture, and agronomy building, and a general purpose building which included administration. There was also a cow barn, a horse barn, and poultry and hog buildings. The college insisted that all agricultural students serve one month at each of the animal facilities. This was part of the overall education known as "applied agriculture."

I will always remember my first month's assignment to horse barn duties. In addition to cleaning the stables, we had to load the horse manure onto a truck, hand-shovel and spread this valuable organic manure over the fields as fertilizer. We followed the same procedure with the cow and bull barn. It was a common joke to mention that you were "on your way to the cornfields." Nonetheless, this interesting subject came under the heading of "applied agriculture." We, of course, took this in stride and indeed made it fun.

One of the main reasons for my arriving two weeks before the semester began was that I had been invited to try out for the varsity football team. Since they had my athletic record, they welcomed me with open arms. I made the varsity as a running back — left halfback to be exact — and played five games before a shoulder separation knocked me out for the remainder of the season.

I enjoyed my viticulture courses studying under one of the most famed experts in the wine and viticultural world, Professor Bioletti.

It wasn't long before I was invited to join the Tau Beta fraternity. The initiation ceremony was held in the college auditorium. There were about 70 in attendance. It was my turn to go up on stage and go through a certain ritual. Everyone knew that I came from Brooklyn, so they took advantage of my "Brooklynese" accent. The popular song at that time was, "I'm Jealous of the Birdies in the Trees."Naturally, I couldn't say "bird." I could only say "boid." One fellow had a big paddle in his hand while the other said, "Now sing that part again." When I came to "boid," I would receive a well-aimed paddle on my fanny. If I was paddled once, I believe I must have been paddled more than a dozen times. Nevertheless, I was the hit of the initiation ceremonies and my fanny was a rosy red color. I personally enjoyed the ceremonies very much.

I moved into the fraternity house situated on the campus and met some real wonderful guys. I became extremely close friends with Joseph Perelli-Minetti. His father was considered one of the highest authorities on wine in California. He was the head wine consultant for the University of California and was involved in the upgrading of California wine at the time. Just about the time I was completing my tenure in graduate school, Joe's father passed away. Joe had one year to go to get his degree. The Perelli-Minetti family owned about 600 acres of choice vineyard, apple and prune orchards south of Healdsburg in Sonoma County. He asked me if I could consider managing his family ranch since I would be completing my graduate studies within a month. Once again, the opportunity prevailed and I looked forward to the challenge. I was elated as it was quite a timely proposition and I happily accepted.

Joe's mother, Jeanne, was of French and Italian descent. She warmly accepted me into the family. My home was a one-room cabin near the main house and each day, I would take my meals with the family. Mrs. Perelli-Minetti was an excellent cook as was Grandmother Perelli-Minetti who was also living there. One of her cooking specialties was homemade bread baked in an outdoor Dutch oven. She made a special black bread that was practically a meal in itself.

There were two farmhands who worked under my supervision. They were remarkable oldtimers from the Tuscany region of Italy. No chore was impossible for them to handle. Like all former *contadini* (peasants), they had a wonderful sense of humor and constantly sang while they worked. It was their way of life, and the singing seemed to help pass away the time and somehow lighten their load.

I had a young black stallion at my disposal and used to ride it when I would be working on the 100-acre Gravenstein apple orchard about a mile from the main ranch. At times, however, I would have a small problem with the horse. Being a stallion, the rather young and frisky animal would get excited when he spotted other horses in the pasture. I learned in a hurry never to ride the stallion when there were horses grazing in this particular pasture, but there were certain times when I had to go through as it was a shortcut. I must say that this became the wildest ride imaginable.

The Perelli-Minettis were quite popular. They also had a big family of cousins and relatives. On weekends, they seemed to come from all over northern California just to visit or barbecue. They were fun people and very family-oriented, so they were welcomed with open arms.

In the history of California winemaking, the Perelli-Minetti name is well-respected. Today, a branch of the family operates a successful winery in the San Joaquin Valley producing millions of gallons of wine.

After almost a year on the ranch and with the return of Joe, who just graduated from the College of Agriculture at Davis, I had to make a decision as to what I would do next. The times were not good, and while I had an excellent agricultural education with a lot of farm managerial experience, I questioned whether or not this was the time to own and operate my own ranch. One has to remember that this was the unpopular Prohibition era and that wine could only be made and used for religious or medicinal purposes.

My brother, Frank, had been in California for several years, was established and doing fairly well as a produce broker. He was also a shipper of wine grapes for thirsty easterners who were clamoring for grapes to make their own wine for home consumption. The harvest season was beginning. Through the efforts of Frank, I went to work for Tom Porcaro, who was shipping a carload of wine grapes a day out of the Lodi and Fresno areas in the San Joaquin Valley. My duties were to go into the grape-growing areas to buy wine grapes from the various growers, paying cash upon delivery to the refrigerated cars at the railroad sidings. I did rather well working on a commission basis instead of on a salary because the volume was so substantial.

In the meantime, I had received a letter from Eddie Amendola of Gargiulo and Amendola, one of the biggest wholesale produce merchants on the New York market. At that time, my family rented the upstairs portion in the Amendola two-family home in Bensonhurst. He wrote to ask if I would join him in a Florida venture. His idea was to buy and ship out-of-season escarole and endive to the New York market during the winter months. The offer sounded appealing. In the fall, I would buy and sell wine grapes from California, and in the winter, I would ship escarole and endive from Florida. During the summer, I was free to explore other avenues. I wrote Eddie back informing him that I wanted in on the deal and would be returning to New York in ten days. We had a month before the Florida season began, so like many young sprouts, we decided to live it up in New York. The style of dress in those days was a derby, a topcoat with a velour collar, spats, and a cane. Generally, our evenings were spent in a speakeasy joint gulping down the most awful "rot gut" booze imaginable (I guess after a time we became immune to it) and went home. We followed a routine where we would expel the liquid poison by means of putting two fingers in our mouths, producing a cleansing effect on our abused insides. Being a student of Roman history, I remember that the fun-loving Romans always followed this procedure after a night of high living. There were special places called a vomitorium to take care of this famous Roman pastime. We had a perfect spot to eliminate our bootleg intake. Mrs. Amendola had two rose bushes on each side of the walkway going towards the front steps. I don't know why we favored only one side, the right. Eddie had a small Boy Scout shovel that he kept hidden in a bush close by. This was used to dig a small hole and cover it when we completed our little chore.

This went on for some time. A year later, Mrs. Amendola approached me and said, "John, with all your knowledge and schooling in growing things, why are the two rose bushes on the right side looking so healthy and full of roses while the two rose bushes on the left side were just normal." She looked at me and said, "I don't understand it. I give the same treatment to all the roses." I don't believe I ever answered her question and I think that if she were alive today, she would still be puzzled.

Chapter 4

The Florida Land Boom . . . and Bust

We took off in Eddie's car for Florida. It was in the month of February. The southern states looked beautiful at this time of year and we really enjoyed the trip, stopping overnight in the picturesque and historic city of Charleston, South Carolina.

Our destination was Orlando situated in central Florida, noted for its oranges, grapefruit, out-of-season vegetables, swamps and alligators. New Yorkers would winter in Miami, Melbourne, and other warm spots on the Atlantic side of Florida, famous for its beaches and climate. We rented rooms in a boarding house. I purchased a second-hand Dodge sedan as we were not always together and I also had to have freedom of movement.

The attractions of Florida were not yet known to the outside world. They thought of the state as a mosquito haven with hot, sultry summers, and other than agriculture, there was little else to offer and practically no industry.

We represented several wholesale commission merchants, principally Gargiulo and Amendola in New York's produce market. There was a lively demand for the escarole and endive mostly by Italians and those of Mediterranean extraction. As we progressed, we were shipping an average of one carload a day. My fee or commission came to about $50 a day, which was considered good money in the middle 1920s. We were quite satisfied with our income. In the meantime, Florida's budding real estate boom broke out in all its fury. It all started when two wealthy tycoons from Miami secretly purchased thousands of acres of bare land of which quite a bit was swamp land, and sold off lots for a proposed subdivision. Then came the unscrupulous developers who also laid out their proposed subdivisions. The news stories made headlines in the cold midwest and northern states. They told of the attractions of the Florida climate, swimming in the warm waters of the Atlantic, the palm trees, and the opportunities in owning your own home in Florida. The targets were retirees and senior citizens. Their plan was highly successful. They came out of the frigid north in dribbles. Then, it became an avalanche. Lots that sold for $100 one week were selling for $200 the next. People gathered in hotel lobbies, bars, and street corners talking real estate. Prices continued to double and triple with no end in sight. The boom spread from Miami to quiet and peaceful Orlando. It reminded me of the Gold Rush in 1849. As time passed, it became the biggest real estate boom ever seen in this country.

I began to ask myself, "What am I doing here making a measly $50 a day when millionaires were sprouting up overnight?" I decided to become a sales agent for the Mount Plymouth Land Company. (The nearest mountains were in Georgia.) The Mount Plymouth Development was laid out in rather clever fashion. The streets were staked as were the hundreds of lots. The business area was also identified by stakes where the post office, bank, city hall, and a dozen other public buildings would be. There was a swampy area that in time would be a lake with a marina. An old rusty dredge sat in the mud for future use. They did build one house, a very attractive looking "model" with all the furnishings and a spacious living room. This is where the sales pitch was to be made. The policy was not to have more than a dozen prospects at a time. There were many sales sessions during the day.

My job was to pick up the new arrivals from the arctic northern states at the various hotel lobbies. My Dodge sedan held five passengers. When I delivered my five prospects to the furnished home, they would be greeted, offered soft drinks, sandwiches and cookies, and then turned over to the professional "spellbinder," who was usually a back country preacher. The sales pitch would last about a half-hour. Whatever he would say created no problem. These people came down and seemed quite anxious to buy lots. Generally, nine out of ten prospects bought and paid hard cash (no checks).

I would make three trips a day and was paid in cash at the close of the day. While I was rather cool to this way of making a living, I couldn't help notice the land values doubling and tripling. Everybody was buying lots and everybody was talking money. I was somewhat like the dog on a bridge with a bone in his mouth. He saw the reflection in the water and wanted that bone, too. I finally succumbed to the idea of becoming a millionaire. I, too, wanted some of that money. Perhaps I was a bit naive. I sure was not satisfied with the income from shipping escarole and endive. I was now in another world, so it seemed to me. Eddie felt the same way, too. We temporarily parted. He went to work for another developer. We did get together in the evenings, however, to compare notes.

I began to put my earnings directly into land. On paper, I was rich like everyone else. If you ever saw a boomtown with money flowing like water, this was it. I had actually reached a point where one evening I lit my cigar with a one dollar bill. I would say, "What the hell. I am now a millionaire." Again, I'd say how naive I was. How naive we all were. Like all good things, they came to an end, and what an end it turned out to be.

One morning, a story appeared in the Miami and Orlando newspapers stating that a large block of land was sold at a much lower price than going sales. The next morning, several more tracts were sold at "sacrifice" prices, then more and more. Were the "big boys" unloading, taking their profits and moving onto other pastures? People became scared and some began to sell. At first, it was a trickle and suddenly, there was a panic. It was like a run on the bank. How could a thing like this happen?

Two weeks later, you could not sell your property for any price. Who would want it? The owners would be stuck for taxes and assessments. I found myself in the same position as were my friends, many from New York and those who I got to know during my real estate adventure. Overnight, I realized that I was now broke. My only asset was my second-hand Dodge that played an important role in building up my land empire. I had to sell my car to pay for my train fare back home with a few dollars to spare. My misery was my own secret. The only thing I told my family was that I was heading back to California after a few days of rest. It was really great to relax in my pleasant surroundings with the warmth of family and old friends.

My problem was that I did not have the money to pay for my train fare to California. My salvation would be, once I reached the Golden State, that I would seek out an old family friend who operated a successful cannery in Riverbank in the San Joaquin Valley. His name was Larry Zerillo. I would work in the cannery during the tomato canning season. That would take me to the fall wine grape harvest, which would put me back on my feet. But where was I going to get the money for the train ride? I was ashamed to admit my predicament. Everyone thought I had done quite well with the escarole and endive business. No one knew that I went belly up in the Florida land boom.

Chapter 5

My Passport To Hell -
The *S.S. Walter Luchenbach*

Strange things happen when you least expect it. I ran into an old sailor friend of mine whom I had not seen in years. Over a couple of beers and after learning of my predicament and desperate need to get to San Francisco, he suggested that I "ship out." He told me that he had a friend on the *S.S. Walter Luchenbach* who was loading cargo for San Francisco. I went to see this friend who, after a brief introduction, looked me over carefully and signed me on as a "wiper."

I went through a 20-day period in my life that I will always remember till my dying day. A wiper is the lowest job on a ship. The *Walter Luchenbach* was an oil burner, and my job was to keep wiping oil and just about everything else in the bowels of that ship. It was hot work, insufferably hot. I worked in my shorts and occasionally would seek relief by going to the ventilator, which was a hollow pipe that drew the outside air into the engine room. This was great, except that the hot tropical air coming down through the so-called ventilator was hotter than the temperature in the working area.

The other "joy" of working my way over was our living quarters, and living it was. It was alive with bedbugs and cockroaches. This situation, of course, was not conducive to a good night's sleep. Most of the crew slept on deck.

We left New York in late June and after two days, we were in the tropics. It was a 20-day trip through the Caribbean, the Panama Canal, and up the Pacific Coast to San Francisco. Fortunately, I had the company of three very nice young men. They were college boys working their way to San Francisco during their summer vacation. They, too, did not care to sleep in their assigned quarters. As one of the young men remarked, "I have no desire to compete with all that activity (the bedbugs and roaches)." There would be sudden rain showers as does happens in the tropics, so we would move over under some shelter and continue our nocturnal sleep *al fresco*.

I did not care to eat the food that was served to us. Here again, we had to compete with such living things as maggots and other nondescript crawling bugs. About the fourth day, we capitulated to what was being served. Hunger does strange things, especially when it comes to survival. We ate the food and managed to survive.

I believe we were a bit before our time. By that, I mean that it was before the advent of the unions which, thank God, changed the course of navigation, the treatment of men who manned the ships, particularly the freighters. I could now say, "God Bless the maritime unions."

We had one break during this long arduous voyage when we went through the Panama Canal. The crew was permitted to go up on deck. It was glorious like the Resurrection, but so short-lived. It lasted only eight hours and then it was back down into the hole. The last nine days were almost unbearable. I had burns on my arms, legs and back from touching the hot metal in the course of my wiping. At one time, I felt so depressed that I said to myself that if I died and went to hell, it could not be worse than what I had been going through here. Fortunately, I did not die, so I did not know what hell would be like. Instead, I lived to see the beautiful Golden Gate of my beloved San Francisco. You have no idea what Heaven looked like on that beautiful July morning. The fog was there to greet me, to refresh me, and to bring to an end this most unusual experience.

I was approached suddenly by one of the officers who wanted to know what I was doing on deck when I should have been attending to my duties in the boiler room. I quickly responded that I was through and that I was getting off when we docked in San Francisco. I had company, the three college students and four others who had the same idea. With a red face and a loud commanding voice, the officer practically shouted, "You can't quit. If you do, you will forfeit your pay!" To this, one of the students replied, "Shove it!" My reply was a little different. My grandfather had a solution when you were in a difficult situation and had to make a decision. It sounds good and is most effective when it is said with a true Sicilian dialect — *Ah fan gul!*

I left whatever I owned on the ship. I didn't care to infest San Francisco with the living, crawling vermin that I knew had invaded my belongings. I had $65 in my possession. From the dock, I telephoned Frank, my brother. He was surprised to hear my voice. I said, "Frank, this is Willie Happaday (that was the name I used when I signed up aboard ship). I mean, this was Willie Happaday. Please come and pick me up." It was quite a reunion. Being the youngest in the family, I was always the favorite *picciriddu* (little boy). I spent one hour in the tub and under the shower. Frank prepared a plate of ravioli, fresh spinach, garlic bread, a thick sirloin steak, some pastry, wine, and a *cafe expresso*. I felt like the prodigal son. It was nice to be with my brother again. It was a typical foggy day. Again, I thank God for that health-giving fog.

After some relaxation and conversation, I telephoned our old family friend, Larry Zerillo, who operated a highly successful tomato processing plant in Riverbank near Modesto. Glad to hear my voice, he said, "Come down as soon as you can and ask Mateo to pick you up." Mateo Monterosso was working for Larry at that time and happened to be in San Francisco for a few days goofing off. He was a most likable person, young, and full of fun. He had worked in almost every trade including bootlegging, and anywhere else where he could make a dollar, honest or otherwise. Mateo did the cooking for the Zerillo family and was a handyman in and around the cannery.

I found a room in Riverbank with cooking facilities and went to work in the cannery. The tomato harvest was now in full swing. My job was to check the farmers' trucks at the time of unloading. I assisted the state cannery inspector who would check every load and practically every box in order to maintain the Health Department's high quality standards. At other times, I moved empty and full boxes, and made sure that there was sufficient help on all the belts to keep everything moving.

Mateo and I became good friends. One day, Zerillo was entertaining some eastern buyers and as an old California custom, they wound up with a typical Italian home-cooked meal. I was not eating regularly as by the time I got home, I was too exhausted to do any cooking. Mateo did all the shopping and because of this sumptuous spread, he would generally have a good portion of the leftovers to fill his own well-stocked kitchen. When you are tired and hungry, certain "voices" tell you where you can find something good to eat. This particular voice urged me to crawl through Mateo's unlocked window and discreetly help myself, which I did. The next night when I opened my refrigerator, I found to my surprise that it was completely empty. There was a printed note stating, "A THIEF SHOULD NEVER STEAL FROM ANOTHER THIEF." The following night, Mateo met me at the door with a big smile on his face. He said, "John, I hope I taught you a lesson." Following this, he took me to the best restaurant in Modesto and treated me to a gourmet dinner. (How can you be angry with a guy like that?)

At the end of the tomato cannery season, I again teamed up with Tom Porcaro, shipped a lot of wine grapes to the eastern markets, and eventually took the Overland Limited to New York and Bensonhurst. My family was always glad to see their wandering son. I never told them about my Florida real estate adventure. The only one who knew about it was Frank, and some years later, my other brother, Peter.

One of my college friends from Farmingdale called one day and wanted to know if I was interested in a seasonal job with the New York State Division of Forestry in the campaign to eradicate the gypsy moth in upstate New York. Inasmuch as it was a seasonal winter job, I became interested and eventually found myself involved in trying to keep the gypsy moth from invading New York. Massachusetts was heavily infested with this voracious pest that could wipe out a forest in short order. The battle line was drawn along the New York, Massachusetts and Connecticut borders. It was an all-out war as each village, town and section was thoroughly mapped out. Our job was to spot the yellow clusters of eggs generally found underneath the limbs or trunks of trees. When a discovery was made, we would call in the spray squad who went right to work to eradicate this most dangerous pest. It was interesting, healthy outdoor work, and while the winter was a cold one, it did not seem to bother me since I always would think of the hell I went through on the *Walter Luchenbach*.

It was back to Brooklyn, still planning someday to go back to California to own and operate my own vineyard. The time was not yet ripe. I was hoping that soon the Prohibition Law would be repealed so I could make my move. The movement for repeal was getting stronger. Al Smith and Congressman Fiorello La Guardia were the leaders in the drive to repeal this obnoxious Prohibition Law that everyone seemed to be violating as a way of life. The speakeasy was the hub of our everyday social life. It was about this time that I became closely associated with my brother, Peter, and his many friends.

Peter and Anthony Triola were close friends. Along with his younger sister, Josephine, we became part of a fun-loving group. We decided to purchase a Packard Twin Six, a real gas guzzler, but who cared. Everyone was working. There were six partners and a one-sixth partnership was not too costly. As time went on, I found myself getting closer to Josephine. We decided that perhaps one day, we would be married. My problem was that I did not have a steady job.

The Triola family originally came from Messina in Sicily. Their customs, food and dialect were totally different from the *Palermitani* who occupied the opposite, or western, portion of Sicily. The Messinisi culture had a predominantly Grecian background while Palermo was Arabic, Norman and Spanish. Of course, in the melting pot of the New World, these differences had little value. Shortly after I became a food and drug inspector, Josephine and I were married in the Church of Our Lady Help of Christians in Bensonhurst. It was a typical Italian wedding with lots of guests, food, and dancing.

Chapter 6

The Food and Drug Inspector

Throughout my life, I seemed to be blessed by being in the right place at the right time. I wanted to get married and I didn't have a steady job. So what occurred, thanks to one of my former Aggie college chums, was that I learned there was going to be a civil service examination for the position of a food and drug inspector for the New York City Board of Health.

There were 30 positions open. These were not new jobs; they represented positions formerly held by 30 food and drug inspectors who wound up at Sing Sing, the Federal Penitentiary on the Hudson River in Ossining, New York. They were all convicted in a scandal that rocked New York City. It was the famous milk scandal in which the inspectors were guilty of bribery in permitting adulterated milk and milk products to be sold. Not only were the inspectors sent to jail, but many owners of quite a number of milk distributors in the city as well.

It was difficult to buy a good bottle of wholesome milk in New York. They not only skimmed the cream from the milk, but water was actually added. The inspectors just looked the other way while their pockets bulged with bribery money. The adulteration also involved butter, cheese and ice cream.

New York City, as the largest city in the nation, consumed a lot of milk and milk products. The tragedy of this situation was that it led to many infant deaths. At that time, most of the milk in the congested areas and neighborhoods was sold in bulk cans of approximately 40 gallons. It was dispensed by ladling the milk out to a customer's container with a long handled dipper. This caused another health problem in that the long handled dippers were seldom cleaned. It resulted in unwashed hands which held the contaminated handles, increasing the bacteria count — the primary cause of infant illness and death.

I applied for the position, passed the necessary qualifications, and started studying for the examination. I wanted this job in the worst possible way. With this steady job, I could get married. The day the examination arrived, there were 310 qualified applicants. I said my usual "Hail Marys" and sat down to take the test at 8:15 a.m. The examination was completed at 4:30 p.m. I did not even take a lunch break because I was too involved. It was a written examination and I wrote exactly 29 pages in order to answer the many questions. I left feeling that I had no doubt flunked. My mind was dazed from the lengthy test.

Two weeks later, I received a registered letter indicating that my score was 890 out of a possible 1,000. It also stated that I placed number one on the list of candidates taking the test. I practically fell off my chair. I couldn't believe it, eventually reasoning that perhaps what I wrote in those 29 pages must have either confused them or I was a lot smarter than I thought.

I was assigned to the lower east side of Manhattan. This was the hotbed area of corruption involving the adulteration of milk and milk products. We operated in a systematic way. Two days a week, I would be on the job during the early morning hours when the milk trucks were making their deliveries to the retail stores. I would take samples of the bulk milk in the cans for butter fat content. Two were kept for our laboratories and one sample was given to the driver. All samples were sealed, numbered and properly identified.

One day a week was devoted to taking samples for bacterial count. All samples for butter fat and bacteria were immediately delivered to our labs. The other days would be left to general inspection. Anyone working as a food handler was required to have a food handler's card. We would also inspect the premises for health code violations including sanitation and proper handling of food products. When the laboratory released the test results, we would be notified with details as to whether there was a case for adulteration or bacterial defect. I would then write up an FFA (Facts for Arrest), cite the violator, and see him in court in about two weeks. The violators were as numerous as the "sands on the seashore" so to speak. We spent considerable time in court. The judges were quite severe in handing out the punishment, which resulted in heavy fines. The third violation meant suspension of the offender's license

Mom in front of our family home in Bensonhurst with our 1927 Hudson sedan — 1928.

My sister, Frances, at age 32.

John Brucato at age 25 in front of his Bensonhurst home — 1930.

My beloved father, Frank A. Brucato.

with a possible prison term.

After about six months, things calmed down and we achieved fairly good control and great improvement in the quality of dairy products. (Butter tubs had been set in water to increase the weight. Cheese and ice cream had been sold with insufficient butter fat. This was now almost a thing of the past.)

Several times, we would stage "nocturnal raids" on some of the suspicious pasteurizing plants and on a few occasions, we actually caught the culprits with a hose adding water to the milk. Of course, they wound up in jail.

I really enjoyed my job. It was exciting and I felt I was accomplishing something worthwhile.

New York City had a large Jewish population. During some of the Jewish holidays, all caps on milk bottles were kosher and printed entirely in Jewish. The hundreds of Jewish dairy stores closed. So great was the Jewish influence in the city that a Jewish holiday or holy day meant an almost complete shutdown of business and traffic.

I became friendly with a group of rabbis in the lower east side where they "held court" (on a cold winter day) sitting around a pot belly stove in one of the kosher dairy stores. Because of my frequent inspection visits, I gradually became accepted. I joined them in sipping kosher cherry wine, and partook in a few matzo balls, some gefilte fish and unleavened bread.

I was promoted and assigned to the pasteurizing plants, and wholesale butter, ice cream and cheese establishments. During the Jewish holy days, I noted that the rabbi had to be present in the pasteurizing plant. It made the milk kosher and all milk caps indicated that you were drinking kosher milk. Along similar lines, I was invited to visit one of my former Baron de Hirsche Aggie friends who went up to the Catskill Mountains in upper New York supposedly to farm. He was operating a successful kosher boarding house for vacationing Jewish families.

I happened to be present when they were butchering some cows for their meat. The rabbi was there examining the entrails and stamping his approval on three of the four animals butchered. The fourth was declared unclean as there were pieces of baling wire in his stomach. Bale hay is held together with baling wire and evidently, a piece was swallowed by the cow. Without any hesitation, I heard the rabbi say of the unclean cow, "Sell this one to the Gentiles."

I was on this job for about four years and was on my way up as far as promotions were concerned. In the meantime, Prohibition was about to be repealed. The public had had enough of this hypocracy that made criminals out of ordinarily law-abiding citizens. There was a complete defiance of the Prohibition Amendment and it was about time to tell the "Drys" to get lost. These developments rekindled my desire to follow through with my first love — a vineyard and orchard of my own in God's country, Sonoma County. I had a month's vacation coming to me, so we decided to go to California and find me a vineyard.

Chapter 7

Alexander Valley - The Vineyard Years

Ever since my graduate days, I always had a dream of returning to California. In fact, I can say that it was my lifelong dream to own my own vineyard. It has been seven years since my last visit to California. I sincerely believed that my future was here. I always had the words of Horace Greeley in the innermost recesses of my mind: "Go west, young man. Go west."

While safe and secure in my position of food and drug inspector, I was not satisfied. I wanted to be my own man, so I kept encouraging my brother, Frank, to see what he could find for me. He had been in business in the Golden State for the past 10 years. It was his letter to me indicating that there were now several choice vineyards for sale. This was 1932. The Depression was still in full force, and perhaps this would be the time to buy a vineyard at a reasonable price. I was excited at the possibilities and so together with my wife, Josephine, we took the Overland Limited from New York to San Francisco.

There were no major airways at that time and the mode of travel was principally by train. It required four-and-a-half to five days for the cross-continental trip. We slept in a comfortable pullman car for four nights. This was my fifth trip and it was Josephine's first. While traveling on the train, I made the acquaintance of Charlie Sandoval, the dining car's maitre d', a rather scholarly gentleman. During our many conversations, I inquired as to the noticeable difference in price between the ham and eggs in the dining car and the ones served in the coffee shop. My point was that the price in the dining car was twice as much as that in the coffee shop; yet, they were the same in every respect. Sandoval gave me a mischievous look and in his soft modulated voice said, "John, I am surprised at your ignorance. You see, in the dining room, we serve with cloth napkins and tablecloths. And of course, we also serve parsley. That makes the difference." (I should have never asked.) Over the years, I have made it a habit to always ask for parsley whenever I dined.

Frank was there to meet us when we arrived at the Oakland depot. We crossed over on one of the bay's colorful ferryboats. I shall never forget when Josephine saw the beautiful skyline of San Francisco from the bridge of the Southern Pacific ferryboat. After a few days of rest at Frank's home, we drove up to Rio Nido, a vacation resort near Guerneville on the Russian River in Sonoma County where we picked up an old family friend, Sil Oliva, who had located a 75-acre ranch near Healdsburg.

The Oliva family at that time had great political influence in San Francisco. His brother, Gus, served for years as the city's Honorary Chief of Protocol. Whenever celebrities arrived with the likes of Charles Lindbergh, Babe Ruth, the Prince of Wales, just to mention a few, Gus was on hand to greet them.

The Gus Oliva legacy involved two things — the first being the annual Easter egg hunt in Golden Gate Park for children. Eggs were filled with money from $1 to $100. The event cost Gus more than $25,000. The second was whenever someone made the rank of captain or lieutenant in the San Francisco Police Department, Gus presented him with a solid gold star. Today, these badges are historical keepsakes. If you wanted to get anything done in San Francisco or Sacramento, you had to see Gus Oliva.

There were four brothers in the Oliva family. The other two were Albert and David. While Sil and Gus were the politicians, Albert ran the business while David attended Stanford University where he was a star athlete. The Olivas were in the wholesale produce business in the old Washington Street produce district. They had a lucrative business supplying the better restaurants, hotels and steamship lines. At one time, they were the largest shareholders in the Bank of Italy (later, the Bank of America). They were comfortably wealthy until the Depression practically wiped them out. As a matter of fact, they were cleaned out completely. Gus never got over it and was constantly in the news media involved in many a fast deal. He eventually became a sorry case.

Sil came out in good shape and opened the Exposition Fish Grotto on Fisherman's Wharf, one of the better and most popular restaurants on the wharf, made himself a bundle of money and earned a good reputation. After chatting with Sil's attractive wife, Louise, we took off for Alexander Valley. Frank drove the Chevrolet while Sil, Josephine and I enjoyed the scenery and the many vineyards as we passed through Sonoma county's famous wine country. As we entered Alexander Valley, my heart started to pump heavily with anticipation. Once we got to the ranch, I immediately fell in love with it. Everything I dreamed of was there. Approximately 60 acres were in full bearing wine grapes while five acres had beautiful French and Imperial prunes. Another five acres were committed to a mature Gravenstein apple orchard. There was also a hay field and two acres, which served as a family orchard with quite a variety of fruits and an unbelievable Italian vegetable garden that made my mouth water. It was a good, modern well-kept ranch totaling 75 acres.

The six-room house was fairly well-built, but it needed a new roof, some fixing-up and a paint job. To top it off, there was an old two-story winery building built of stone on the property. It was truly a historic building. This, however, was for the future and had great potential inasmuch as we were still in the Prohibition period. And last, but not least, there was a well-built barn equipped with stalls for horses and cows, and if all that was not enough, the sale included a four-wheel Fordson tractor and some miscellaneous equipment.

Actually, it was a beautiful ranch. From the front porch, we had a view of Mt. St. Helena and breathtaking panorama of the adjacent mountains. There was also a live, flowing creek that emptied into the Russian River two miles south. A naturally deep, pool-like lake made an ideal swimming hole, and a diving board and clean, sandy beach completed this most surprising part of the property. The contour of the land was quite variable as you went from one hill to the other along narrow dirt roads. I got the feeling that this was really exciting and rather interesting. The water supply was unbelievable. There were two springs at a higher altitude which kept a 2,000-gallon redwood tank full at all times. The water was crystal clear and almost sparkling.

I felt I was buying a vineyard and a vacation resort. The price was right, so we decided to buy the ranch. I paid $12,000 for this beautiful ranch. Sil and Frank enthusiastically agreed that this was the right place for me. I took possession of the ranch on June 6, 1932. I sent Josephine back to Brooklyn to close out our affairs. She was to return in September at which time, I had hoped that I would have the ranch house ready for occupancy.

I kept thinking that inasmuch as we were still in the Prohibition era, I felt we could do well either shipping the wine grapes to the New York market where there was a good demand for home winemaking, or to the North Beach and Mission districts of San Francisco where there was a large Italian and French population anxious and willing to make their home-made wine from Sonoma County grapes. I submitted my resignation as a food and drug inspector and settled down to take over my new duties, chores and responsibilities as a ranch owner.

Josephine arrived safely in New York and proceeded to make preparations for the family to return to Alexander Valley in September. Arrangements were made for her brother, Anthony, to drive my 1931 Chevrolet touring passenger car carrying Josephine, my mother, mother-in-law, my two year-old son, Jackie, and my pit bulldog, Terry. Anthony built a protective rail or siding on one of the running boards which would provide the dog with his perch, so that he could ride comfortably on the 3,000-mile transcontinental trip.

In the meantime, I had a lot of work to do on the ranch. The house reconstruction was to be supervised by Frank. He came up to the ranch every Friday night, worked all day Saturday from sunup to sundown, while Sunday was a day of rest, a real Italian feast day. He was not alone. He had three able friends — Tony Durso, a painter; Frank Rocca, a carpenter; and Mateo Monterosso, a jack-of-all-trades. The weekends were like a circus. Everyone knew what had to be done. Frank Rocca had a beautiful Neopolitan voice. He would be on top of the roof working and singing away with unbelievable energy and talent. The more he sang, the harder he worked. Tony Durso was on the quiet side. He was just having a good time as was Mateo.

Frank did the supervision and the cooking. There was always that Sunday *cioppino* with a pasta special and all the goodies that generally go with a sumptuous Italian meal. Dinner started at 1 p.m. and would last until 4 p.m. They were very efficient by cleaning, washing and packing up before heading back to San Francisco by 5:30 p.m. This was repeated every weekend for six consecutive weeks. They completed the house, had a helluva good time, and made a lot of friends with my neighbors.

A Portuguese woman who lived nearby kept house for me while her husband, Francesco, was my steady all-around employee and hired hand. Frank would come up every weekend with a ton of food, which was stored in my perfect storeroom carved into the hillside. It always maintained a steady cool temperature.

We had good neighbors. The Puccinelli family was on one side, and the Massoni and Belli families were on the other. They were northern Italians from Tuscany and knew the wine grape-growing business. We made many friends up and down the famous valley. It seemed that they really enjoyed visiting with us and of course, the wine flowed like water into our glasses. It was an old neighborly California custom and we really enjoyed it.

We did not have a lock on any of our doors. There were never the problems that we face today. When I think of how we are now locked, barred and living in a fortress-like situation in Millbrae, I think of my Alexander Valley days and say to myself, "What the hell has happened to our way of life?"

Francesco, my Portuguese neighbor, became my right-hand man as time passed. He did just about everything. He ran the Fordson tractor, cultivated, overhauled everything that was mechanical including my Chevrolet, my $10 one-ton Ford truck, the engines, pumps, and the tractor. The pay scale in the valley in 1932 was 25 cents an hour. I paid Francesco 30 cents an hour which was all that I could afford. He was satisfied and seemed to enjoy the work. He was really a workaholic. On Saturdays, I gave him a bonus — a gallon of red wine which he relished. Sometimes, I would give him two gallons. He never drank during the working day, only on weekends. Sometimes on Monday, he had a shaky start, but after an hour or so, he was in full control.

My ranch was situated at the southern half of Alexander Valley at the junction of the Knights Valley Road going to Calistoga and Chalk Hill Road which led to Santa Rosa. The valley did not become famous until the late 1960s and '70s. Today, it is probably the best-known, quality-producing wine grape region and the most prestigious in California. During my time, Alexander Valley, south of "Jim Town" or Goodale's Corners, contained some grape land, lots of prunes, hops and hay fields. My vineyard contained the following wine grapes —

zinfandel, petit syrah, carignane, and *alicante bouschet.* The grape mostly in demand during the Prohibition era was the *alicante bouschet.* This variety today is the least desirable and least valuable because of its heavy, dark red color. It is used mostly for blending lighter wines.

The Italian trade during Prohibition demanded the *alicante.* It was also known as "Dago Red." While the price of wine grapes ranged from $30 a ton for *zinfandel, petit syrah* and *carignane,* the *alicante* fetched $150 dollars a ton and up on both the New York and San Francisco market. How times have changed considering today's price range from $250 a ton to over $1,000 a ton depending on the variety, while no one wants the *alicante* at any price.

Since it was June when I took over the ranch, I lost no time in cultivation immediately. There was a good growth of wild mustard between the rows of the vineyard and the orchard. The mustard was disked under and made a wonderful organic combination when mixed with the soil. It was the ideal organic fertilizer. While Francesco performed this operation, I did my first sulfering, especially on the *carignanes* because they were subject to mildew. There was no irrigation in this area at that time inasmuch as the abundant winter rainfall supplied sufficient ground moisture to produce a good crop. Today, practically everyone irrigates to increase production. (We did not have the improved irrigation systems and equipment available today.)

The prunes required little care as opposed to the grapes and therefore, produced much-needed revenue. The Gravensteins, while producing high-quality apples with large sizes and good crops, were difficult to sell. They were an early apple harvested during late July and August, and perhaps one of the best flavored and juiciest of all apples. Evidently, there was too much competition from the abundant soft fruits during this time of year, especially from the peaches, apricots and plums. I shipped my first 300 packed boxes of apples through the Blue Goose commission merchants to be auctioned on the New York market, receiving a bill for freight charges and a "zero" for the shipment. What a start for this new venture. No one paid cash for a farmer's produce. You either sold the apples on consignment or at a public auction. The following year was an improvement. I was able to sell to a few retail stores, roadside stands and wherever else I could for cash.

I purchased a Ford one-ton truck for $10. Someone on Fitch

Mountain in Healdsburg was cleaning house after a divorce settlement. I heard about this auction and attended the sale. No one wanted the truck. The auctioneer looked at me and said, "Mister, do you want the truck?" I told him I was interested, but couldn't make up my mind. At this point, he glanced at his watch and beckoned me to come closer. "Mister, have you got $10 on you?" I said, "Yes." "Please, give me the $10 and take the truck. Here are all the papers. I want to go home. It has been a long day." I needed a truck and this was it. It had all hard rubber tires, a flatbed that would be good for my hauling, and other heavy work. I just about made the ten miles back to the ranch. Francesco looked it over, spat the chewing tobacco out of the left side of his mouth, and went to work overhauling the engine. I don't know how much baling wire he used to hold the various parts together, but by the time he was finished, I had me a first-class truck, although it never went more than 15 miles per hour. But who cared about the speed? Life traveled at a much slower pace in those days.

September came and the "Okies" returned safe and sound, but rather tired. Terry, our pit bull, had red rings around his eyes from exposure to the weather while riding on the Chevrolet's running board. Jackie, my son, broke all records drinking Coca Cola in lieu of milk during the eight-day trip. My mother went to live with Frank in San Francisco while my mother-in-law stayed with us for awhile. My father remained in New York and came west later as would Peter, who eventually joined Frank and I in the champagne business.

I purchased a Guernsey cow so that we would have our own milk and butter. We called her "Abondanza", which means "plenty." She indeed lived up to her name producing 15 to 18 quarts of milk a day. I had a centrifugal cream separator that removed the cream so that we could make our own butter and ricotta cheese. The skim milk was fed back to another acquisition, a piglet. This young pig was to be butchered at about 300 pounds, a gala affair every winter when neighbors joined together in helping to butcher their pigs on a cooperative basis. Thus, we had porkchops, various specialized cuts, and lots of sausage. Times have changed. There doesn't seem to be this kind of cooperation today.

To complete my livestock inventory, we added a dozen laying Leghorn hens, a few Rhode Island reds for meat, and my last acquisition, a horse. My faithful steed was used primarily to ride around my little "fiefdom" on my early morning inspection tour.

It was the kind of life I always dreamed of. The problem was that we were still riding out the big Depression and no one was making any money. Many of the farmers and orchardists were facing bankruptcy. We were living in the Hoover administration. Our illustrious president was in no mood to help the farmers. The situation was nationwide and it was not only agriculture that was suffering. The light at the end of the tunnel was the growing agitation against the unpopular Prohibition Amendment, which made our nation of law-abiding citizens a nation of law violators. Most everyone drank the "rot gut" that was offered in the speakeasies. It was patriotic to thumb your nose at the Prohibition Amendment and the "Prohi" law enforcers.

The Al Smiths and the Fiorello La Guardias were a rising breed in fighting this unjust law. We, in the wine grape-growing business, looked forward to the repeal of the Prohibition Amendment to the Constitution and getting a decent price for our grapes. Our hopes were in the forthcoming election in which we (and many others) were praying that Franklin D. Roosevelt, with his promises for relief, would unseat our do-nothing incumbent, Herbert Hoover.

In the meantime, foreclosure of valuable farms and orchard properties were daily occurrences. Some of my neighbors and friends were on the verge of losing their farms and homes. I believe this period was one of the turning points of my life. I got involved in trying to help people survive and fought against injustices wherever they occurred. The story of my future life will bear this out.

I made the acquaintance of Wilford Howard, president of the Farmers Protective League. This was an "ad hoc" group of farmers who decided to band together to protect themselves from the injustices of the times, particularly the possible foreclosures facing them. There was a militant Roman Catholic priest from Sebastopol, a large Gravenstein apple-growing area, who became associated with Wilford. Many of his parishioners in Sebastopol were in trouble. Father Charles Phillips decided that before he could save their souls, he had better save them from losing their livelihood and their homes.

Wilford Howard and Father Phillips asked me to join them in organizing the many troubled ranchers and begin meeting at some central location. I felt that this was the kind of challenge that would get me involved in helping my neighbors.

My two sons, Peter (left) and Jack — 1942.

The wonderful Brucato boys — Frank, John, and Peter — 1949.

I said, "Count me in. How about meeting at my place?" It seems that I had the ideal spot — under my fig tree. There was an immense fig tree in my garden. The branches were spread out like an octopus. The outer branches, with their heavy leaves, came right down to the ground.

The enclosure was like a large room. There was a long table that sat 20 people comfortably and if we had to squeeze them in, 30. During the heat of the day (80 to 100 degrees-plus in the summer), the "room" was cool and comfortable. On one end was a small brick barbecue, an ice box, a dish and pot cabinet, a sink with a faucet which gave us our clear spring water, and a ten-gallon barrel of red wine complete with a spigot. No one drank white wine in those days. Any stranger who passed by was always welcome to a glass of cool spring water or wine. This was the old California hospitality of the times. It was a good custom.

This was where we held our strategy meetings and dedicated ourselves to solving the problem of foreclosures, which affected all of us. We were all in the same boat so to speak and it was here that our battle cry spelled out the words, "WE WILL FIGHT TOGETHER." We had an immediate problem. One of Father Phillips' friends in Sebastopol was a Methodist minister, the Reverend Richard Case, who owned and operated a 40-acre family Gravenstein apple orchard. The holders of the deed of trust were foreclosing on him. The Reverend Case could not meet his mortgage payments inasmuch as his apple crop did not bring in enough money to meet his obligations. His problem now became our problem as the scheduled foreclosure was to take place on the steps of the Santa Rosa City Hall in two weeks.

At one time, we had 40 farmers' meetings at the fig tree sanctuary. Franklin D. Roosevelt was overwhelmingly elected president. Herbert Hoover was gone. We decided that we must act fast now. We sent hundreds of telegrams to Roosevelt and all the newly elected Congressmen and Senators who we thought could help, particularly those from California.

The foreclosure was to take place on Saturday morning at 11 a.m. on the steps of the Santa Rosa City Hall. Hundreds of farmers were in attendance. At 10:45 a.m., we received a telegram which was given to Wilford Howard. It was read aloud and stated simply that there was an immediate moratorium on all farm foreclosures. The telegram was signed by Henry Morgantheau, the new Secretary of the Treasury. The hundreds of farmers attending the foreclosure shouted with glee. There were tears on the wrinkled faces of those rugged farmers when the news was announced. It was at this juncture that Wilford Howard stood up straight and in his loud, commanding voice proclaimed, "Everything is going to be all right boys. Let's go home and tend to our crops." Father Phillips hugged the Reverend Case as tears ran down their cheeks. If ever there was an ecumenical movement, this was the place to start. Much to my surprise, I found myself surrounded by the farmers, Wilford Howard, the Reverend Case and Father Phillips, all seeking to shake my hand, pat my back, and hug me. Unanimously, they said, "We shall never forget your fig tree sanctuary." I practically froze and despite my goose bumps, I managed to smile and reciprocate my feelings. This was the first time in my life that I was ever in a situation so historical as this.

With Roosevelt's victory came the repeal of the Prohibition Amendment. The big moment was now upon us. Our hopes for the future were never brighter. We looked forward to higher prices for our wine grapes and a reopening of the long-closed wineries. The sad part of this narration was that these wineries and those who went into the wine business were their own worst enemies.

A few established wineries continued in the business during the Prohibition period. Some of them, Concannon, Wente Brothers, Christian Brothers, and a score of others, operated under government permits to produce and sell for sacramental and medicinal purposes, and for the wine vinegar trade. The problem was that millions of gallons of what was once good wine remained in storage during the many years of Prohibition. These wines were sealed in huge tanks by the Alcohol Tax Bureau and eventually released by the government upon the repeal of this unpopular amendment. In the meantime, the wines slowly deteriorated and developed a high acidity and vinegary taste. They should have either been distilled, dumped or converted into wine vinegar. With greed and disregard for the public and future of the wine industry, these individuals proceeded to filter and bottle their so-called California wine and flooded the retail outlets. The public reaction was immediate. After the first sampling of these wines that were unfit for human consumption, it was "thumbs down" on California wine. The public turned to the European imports and for all purposes, the infant California wine boom died at birth. As one prominent wine wholesaler remarked, "The baby did not really die at birth. It was actually an abortion.''

There was no wine institute at the time. The wine and grape industry suffered and went through a long paralyzing period. Eventually, some of the old-time family wineries got together and formed an organization of wine owners called The Wine Institute. All the legitimate wineries signed up. They developed strict quality rules that were aimed to produce high-quality California wines that would be governed and controlled under the highest quality standards. It was survival or else. It took a few years and as quality improved, a tremendous promotional program got underway and eventually succeeded.

The price of wine grapes dropped dramatically. The best *zinfandels* brought $15 to $25 a ton. It was quite a comedown from what we expected. It was going to be a long pull for both the wineries and the vineyards. I believe it could be best described that the grape growers had guts, lots of guts, and as Wilford Howard told us on the steps of the Santa Rosa City Hall, "All right boys, let's go home and tend to our crops.''

We lived somewhat of a good life. Joe Montara stopped in to see us every two weeks. He sold salame, sausage and cheese. On those days, we welcomed these salesmen and made them feel at home. When Montara arrived, we sat under the fig tree, poured a glass of wine, ate cookies and gossiped about the news of the day. We also had a weekly fish peddler and a baker who passed by twice a week and received the same treatment.

We did our grocery shopping at Goodyear's Store in Jim Town. Once a week, we would shop at Cerri's in Healdsburg. He carried a full line of Italian groceries and other goodies.

When the prunes were ripe, they were handpicked from the prepared ground and placed into lugs (field boxes). From there, they were hauled to our dipper near the barn where the prunes were dumped into a wire basket, immersed into a hot lye solution (lye cracks the skin) for one minute and then spread on a tray. The trays were hauled to the nearby dry yard to dry in the sun for a week or two. If the weather was threatening, they would be stacked one on top of the other. The next process was to stack the trays for a four-to-five-day ''sweating'' period and then haul them to a special bin in the barn for storage until after the grape harvest or early winter when they would be sold. The Imperial prunes were larger than the French prunes and commanded a higher price.

One night, my horse got into the prune bin as the door was probably left open. The more prunes he ate, the more water he drank. I found the poor creature in the morning still alive, but greatly bloated. By the time the veterinarian arrived, my faithful steed had passed onto his horse heaven or wherever good horses go.

We always had visitors every weekend. I don't believe we ever had time to be lonely. My son, Jackie, was always with me when I went into the fields. I was never one to use foul words or swear. When my truck got stuck in the mud or some other minor mishap, I generally used my one and only swear word, "Goddamn it." One day, we had some visitors from San Francisco. Some of the gals wanted to go out in the fields and pick some wildflowers. Jackie, Josephine and I joined their expedition. Jackie, showing his hospitable nature, picked a lupine, a poppy, and began to say, "Here's a little flower. Here's another pretty flower. Here's a goddamn pretty flower." Of course, they all knew where he received his "informal" education.

At grape harvest time, I cleaned out a portion of the old winery building, putting in about seven cots and toilet facilities for some of the expected grape pickers. The harvest started in September. It was the hottest time of the year. When the sugar content in the grapes reached 20 percent sugar, it was time to pick the grapes. Fortunately, the four main varieties did not all mature at the same time. However, when the harvest began, we had to be ready and moving.

I had already signed contracts with various wineries. One year, I sold to Petri at their Sebastopol winery. I also sold to Italian Swiss Colony in Asti, Sebastiani in Sonoma, and Louis Martini in the Napa Valley.

Generally, we had plenty of pickers among our own neighbors. The itinerants would come and go. They were never reliable, but I gave everyone a job. Pickers were paid by the field box or lug, which weighed about 25 to 30 pounds. Each lug was marked with the identification tag of its respective picker. The lugs would be picked up at the end of the rows and recorded. They would then be loaded on my $10 Ford flatbed truck and hauled to the packing shed where they would be reloaded on a five-ton truck ready to go to the winery.

The supervision of the harvest operation was a tedious job as I had to watch the pickers and the boxes, and look ahead to the next field ready for harvest. Although it was hard work, the harvest was a joyous time. The neighbors, all good friends, chatted and sang as they worked each day.

One year, I decided to sell to individuals from San Francisco instead of to the wineries. Frank knew many old-time Italians from North Beach who made their own wine. They came to see me and bought me out completely, knowing that my district produced good wine grapes. They made their own private deals by saying, "I'll take this hill" or "I need four tons of *zinfandel* and one ton of *alicante*" and so on. What was really great was that the buyers paid me in advance. The terms were "Cash. F.O.B. Ranch." The trucking charges were paid on arrival.

I had a good, reliable trucker who hauled ten tons on his semi-truck. He knew North Beach and where the buyers lived. One hot day, we finished loading about 3 p.m. and the truck took off for San Francisco. Jackie and I hopped into the Chevrolet and went into Healdsburg. As we were approaching a sharp turn in the road near Jim Town, I noticed a commotion ahead. There was a prune orchard where the road took an L-turn. I said to Jackie, "My gosh, it looks like somebody lost part of their load." As we got closer, I remarked, "Gee, I feel sorry for that poor guy whoever he is." "Daddy, Daddy," said my quick-witted son. "That's our truck!" It sure was our truck. Evidently, the ropes holding the lugs of grapes were loosened and when the sharp turn was negotiated, about 30 lugs of *zinfandels* hit the gravel and dirt in the prune orchard. The temperature had reached 106 degrees in the shade. To show how neighborly these people in the valley were, six men immediately began shoveling the grapes back into the boxes, eventually reloaded the truck, and tied the lugs securely for its journey to San Francisco.

Six months later, I met two members of the Beviacqua family. They had purchased four tons of my hillside grapes. We had a nice chat and before leaving, the elder Beviacqua looked at me in the eye and with his Genovese smile, he said, "John, we made some good wine, a really good, excellent wine. Next year, I want six tons, but please, when I buy that hill again, I only want the grapes. You keep the hill." When my neighbors had shoveled the grapes into the boxes, some of the gravel was mixed in. When gravel goes through the crusher, it makes a helluva lot of noise and the crusher comes to a halt.

The repeal of the Prohibition Amendment made it possible for us to set up a winery operation in San Francisco. We had long planned that this would be a family operation involving three families — Frank's, Peter's and mine. Frank was knowledgeable in all phases of wine production. I had studied

California methods of the wine business while Peter ran the office. We decided that since no one else was producing naturally fermented-in-the-bottle champagne, this would be our specialty field. We had a friend, Dr. Attilio Musco, who was a top winemaker and had much experience in Tuscany as a champagne specialist. With Dr. Musco in our employ, we decided that Peter, who was in New York in the custom house brokerage business, together with my favorite uncle, Roberto Gallo, who was ready to retire, come west to join our new enterprise. Frank and I would be involved in production and sales.

The time had come that Josephine, Jackie and I would move to San Francisco to be closer to our new venture. It was an exciting decision to make and our planned goal over the many years was now becoming a reality. The ranch operation was under control. I divided my time between Alexander Valley and the Brucato Winery. My father, who retired from his produce business, joined us and went to live with my mother and Frank in a five-room flat on Bay Street near Mason in North Beach. Pop came up to the ranch on weekends and did some gardening to keep busy. He did not like being idle in his retirement, so he enjoyed puttering around on the ranch.

I hired a reliable couple, the Pestones, who were oldtimers from the Piedmont region of Italy. They occupied a fully-equipped, two-room outer building so that our home was free for our use. I went up to the ranch on weekends and returned each Monday morning during normal operations. At harvest time or when certain phases required my full attention, my stay was longer. This went on for two years until I decided to sell the ranch in order to concentrate all my efforts on the San Francisco winery operation. My decision was based on the premise that there was no money in wine grapes. The market never got off the ground. The good times did not begin until about eight years later when California wine finally came into its own, thanks to the Wine Institute.

I did not have a crystal ball at the time. Had I been able to predict the future, I would not have sold this beautiful vineyard. I doubled my money when the sale was made, but it was a far cry from today's prices. Alexander Valley became a prime choice wine grape-producing region with top quality wine production. The French and the Europeans moved into Alexander Valley during the high inflation period. The area was finally discovered. My property today would be worth a million dollars with several pluses.

The purchaser of my ranch was the managing editor of the *San Francisco Examiner*, Bill Wren. He immediately pulled out about half of the vineyard and turned the land into a horse and cattle ranch. My home was completely demolished as if it were never there. He did, however, convert the old stone winery building into a beautiful deluxe home. He, too, did not have a crystal ball. In fact, his home burned to the ground leaving only the original stone walls. I never did see Bill Wren again.

I have passed by the old homestead several times in the past few years. Memories and a warm tear or two have been shed. I really loved that place. I think of how hard I worked and enjoyed every bit of it, the fall and winter prunings, the cultivation and ground chores in the spring, and the beautiful and rewarding harvest during the hot summer and early fall. I would pinch myself and come out of my dream. Yes, it did happen. I did what I always wanted to do — have a vineyard of my own.

At times, it was quite a struggle to make ends meet, but in the final analysis, I must say that we led a good and interesting life. I met my challenge and felt that now was the time to move on to a new one. I was part of our new winery, reunited with my brothers, Frank and Peter, and with my parents in the background. How I loved my family. In these exciting moments of change, I had only to look ahead. And what the hell! In the words of the immortal Giuseppe Garibaldi, *"Sempre avanti!"* (Always go forward).

Chapter 8

Naturally Fermented in the Bottle

Our champagne business began to look quite promising. The quarters in the old Zellerbach building were becoming a bit cramped. Real estate in those days was in the doldrums. We found what we really wanted at the corner of Sansome and Broadway Streets (855 Sansome Street) in San Francisco. We purchased two adjacent buildings — one facing Sansome Street with three floors, a spacious basement and an elevator; the other facing Broadway Street. It was previously used as a seed warehouse, making it ideal for wine storage tanks. The building was vacant for some time and the price was right.

We became U.S. Bonded Winery #3810, operating under the name of West Coast Vintners Company. We immediately started our fermentation process after transferring our equipment from the Zellerbach building. While waiting for our first production, a portion of the winery was set aside to produce a ''sparkling'' or so-called carbonated wine. This brought us some ready cash.

In the interim, we became acquainted with Fred Abruzzini, who was manager of the famous Beringer Brothers Winery in St. Helena. We entered into a contract with the winery to produce some of their initial Beringer Sparkler. This was shortly after the repeal of the Prohibition. We produced several hundred cases for Abruzzini, which also brought in some needed cash. There is a photograph in Beringer's sampling room showing our crew, which included Frank and I dressed in a protective fencing mask, rubber apron and heavy gloves. At the same time, we produced some sparkling wine for the old Covick Winery in Rutherford in the Napa Valley.

Alberto "Shorty" Saveri was our all-around man. He was only five feet tall, but was strong as an ox. He claimed his strength came from a steady diet of garlic in all his foods. Shorty came from Pisa in the Tuscany region of Italy. He was an unusual person, constantly smoking those twisted Petri brand Toscano cigars. He was never sick in his life and could move a full barrel of wine with the greatest of ease.

Our workers were old-time families from the North Beach section of San Francisco. There were mothers, daughters, sons, cousins, aunts and friends. Annie Zanca was the leader, the one who took charge when we were not around. She would stop working a half-hour before lunch and take over the kitchen chores. One of the working tables was converted and prepared for the "family" lunch. Annie always prepared a pasta with her own Sicilian tomato sauce. There was always a variety of food available, be it fish, meat or when we were really busy, plain hero sandwiches stuffed with salame, cheese, mortadella and a lot of the trimmings that made up a nourishing meal. Sometimes, or I should say quite often, guests stopped in and were welcomed to lunch with the workers. Here again, everything was "family."

Labels were put on the bottles by hand as were the corks, wiring and tin foil that were applied to the champagne bottles. The bottles would then be cleaned, wrapped in tissue paper, packed in either wooden or cardboard boxes, and properly stenciled. In those days, there was little or no mechanization in the wineries. That came later. The long working tables were situated between rows of wine storage tanks made from either oak or redwood. These tanks held from 5,000 to 20,000 gallons. We had a capacity of more than 100,000 gallons.

In the production of champagne, the company purchased three or four varieties of white wines suitable for the proper champagne blending. When this blending was achieved, we added the grape yeast and other ingredients to bring about a so-called secondary fermentation from the one year-old wine. We followed the old French procedure of the inverted bottles on the racks followed by scheduled turning and shaking by hand every three days. This forced the sediment to settle and eventually cake on the cork. The bottles were then transferred into a low freezer tank where just the necks were frozen. By a simple ejection of the cork, the sediment caked on the cork was forced out by the effervescence or gas while the ice held back the liquid. Each bottle was then filled to its proper level, recorked with a new cork, and placed in bins for aging. They were constantly inspected for impurities and other levels. This was how champagne was made and called "naturally fermented in the bottle."

During the early years in the champagne business, one of the biggest problems was the lack of new champagne bottles. They always say that the Genovese are shrewd, wise and know how to make a buck or two. I should mention that the scavenger companies in California were controlled by those who emigrated from Genoa. They were smart enough to realize that the Prohibition era was about to come to a close. Years before repeal of this unpopular amendment, they began to accumulate wine and champagne bottles. They set up several huge washing and sterilizing plants where the collected bottles were placed in storage awaiting the resurrection of the wine business. They also realized that the big glass companies were starting to manufacture champagne bottles.

It must be said that while the fermentation process is taking place inside the champagne bottles, there develops a great deal of pressure equal to seven atmospheres. Many of the new champagne bottles were poorly made. They had imperfections and quite a few exploded as the inside pressure developed in the bottle. It sounded like bombs going off.

As an aside to this narrative, I remember a young chap by the name of Alessandro Baccari. During his summer vacation while attending Santa Clara University, he was put to work by Frank turning and shaking bottles. (Al was wearing his own fencing mask inasmuch as he was an inter-collegiate fencing champion.) Suddenly, there was a series of explosions that really put the fear of the Lord in our temporary employee.

Those of us in the champagne business were approached by some of our Genovese scavenger friends who convinced us that the sterilized bottles in storage were now available at about half the price of the faulty new bottles. Inasmuch as the scavenger bottles were made in Europe and already tested by their former contents, it did not take too long for them to begin supplying us with what was now considered a safe champagne bottle. (No wonder some of the wealthiest Italians are of Genovese extraction.) Eventually, the Owens-Illinois Glass Company and others improved the quality of their champagne bottles. In the meantime, our Genovese friends had a few bonanza years when they actually laughed their way to the bank — the Bank of America — which, incidently, was founded by another Genovese, A.P. Giannini.

During the late spring, we were busy with the fermentation process. The summer was usually devoted to bottling and labeling. The big rush was from October through the Christmas season. We employed 15 to 20 people during this busy period. We had no problems with our help. When there was a rush order to get out, they seemed to really pitch in and work. We considered them as our family and treated them as such.

Peter, although managing the office, also helped when labeling or packing was required. We all did what had to be done. Frank, Peter and I were managers, shipping clerks, bottlers, labelers and floor sweepers. There were no rules or regulations.

In the early years, a high portion of our business was with some of the major wineries. We were very proud that the champagne we produced was in good demand. The unusual was that we never received cash from the wineries. It was all by pre-arrangement. Everyone was short of cash and so were we. It was an even exchange of goods. They wanted our champagne and we wanted their wine. It was referred to as the barter system. A classic example involved a telephone call from Augustus "Gus" Sebastiani, owner of the Sebastiani Winery in Sonoma. He said that he was shipping a carload of wine to New York and would be picking up 50 cases of Champ D'or to be included in the shipment. Louis "Louie" Martini requested 50 or 100 cases of champagne as would the Italian Swiss Colony, Petri and Scatena wineries. In turn, we requested certain types of white wines that would be suitable for our champagne-making. It was a wonderful arrangement. Everyone was building inventories while supplying their customers. It was a situation made necessary in rebuilding California's reputation for good wines in order to offset the horrible, almost total destruction of the wine business due to the greed and shortsidedness caused by those who dumped their unfit wines on the market after the repeal of the Prohibition Amendment. While the Wine Institute was formed to build up quality and establish standards, we all realized that it would take time, lots of time, to restore California's reputation to where it once was.

The barter system was not only restricted to our winery friends, but covered a much wider field. We had lots of fishermen friends at Fisherman's Wharf. They came to the winery with huge sacks of crab, rock cod, salmon or whatever was caught outside the Golden Gate. In return, we gave them gallons or demi-johns of wine as an exchange. What do you do with a 90-pound sack of crab or fish? (There were other fishermen who followed the same procedure.) Peter divided the fish or crab between our three families and the other families who worked for us. Of course, there was also enough held back for the daily luncheons and the big Friday *cioppinos.*

It was truly a wonderful era. We had friends in the olive oil, cheese and salami-making business, and several others who enjoyed our wine and champagne as we enjoyed their products. I don't want to leave out a bakery, macaroni factory, and other similar establishments. Then, there was De Simone's Grocery Store on the corner of Bay Street and Columbus Avenue where large quantities of our wines and champagnes were sold. Our three families had open accounts with Frank De Simone. It was groceries for wine, a beautiful arrangement. Peter and De Simone sat down every three months and squared accounts. They always seemed to balance.

There was a similar agreement with Gibson's Butcher and Grocery Store at the corner of Bay and Hyde Streets. I believe the Gibsons were in that location since the beginning of time. Frank and the family lived in the upper flat owned by the Beviacqua family just two houses away from Gibson's Market.

One of the most unusual arrangements was with the Malcewicz brothers, Frank and Joe. They were both former professional heavyweight wrestlers. In fact, Joe was a world champion wrestler for many years and was known as the "Utica (New York) Tiger." The two brothers were wrestling promoters who held the wrestling franchise for northern California. They held monthly wrestling matches at the Civic Auditorium and later at the Cow Palace. My brother, Frank, made a deal with them which gave us a "box" with eight or more seats in exchange for the equivalent value of wine or champagne. We soon became regular wrestling fans. We invited our friends and clients to the bouts. It was rather exciting, and they always put on a good show. We got to know quite a few wrestlers who visited the winery together with one of the Malcewicz brothers whenever they were in town prior to their bouts. They enjoyed a glass or two of our sherry wine.

We became friends with the reigning champion at that time, Renato Gaddini. He was very popular and always drew standing-room only crowds. The fans yelled *"Forza Gaddini"* and to the delight of everyone, he obliged by squeezing his headlock on his opponent just a bit tighter. We really enjoyed

Man Mountain Dean. There was also the Mexican favorite, Pedro Gomez, the Masked Marvel, and Gorgeous George.

There is one incident which took place that I will never forget. The main event was between Renato Gaddini and Pedro Gomez. This was a sellout crowd. The Cow Palace was equally packed with rabid Italian and Mexican fans. Naturally, the Mexican fans were rooting for their hero, Pedro Gomez. The box next to ours was occupied by 12 people of Mexican descent. One of the fans was a buxom woman, rather attractive and holding an infant who slept through all the previous bouts. The event was announced. When Pedro Gomez, the challenger, was introduced the Latinos went wild. In the meantime, the infant, whose name I learned later was Manuelo, suddenly came to life. After such a good, long sleep, it was natural to wake up hungry. The usual way to inform one's mother is to cry and cry he did. We became somewhat concerned. Of all the times, this infant was to start bawling now? As it turned out, there was no problem for the mother. She opened her blouse and soon Manuelo was nourishing himself with his mouth attached to the welcome nipple that was part of a well-formed, exposed breast. The excitement increased and every once in a while, the mother jumped up and down while still breast-feeding. Suddenly, Renato Gaddini got his famous headlock around Pedro Gomez's neck. The crowd was yelling, *"Forza Gaddini,"* and the noose was drawn tighter. The Mexican fans retaliated by yelling, "No! No! Give it to heem!" The intensity was so great that while the mother was jumping up and down like a yo-yo, poor little Manuelo lost his grip on the once-cherished nipple and began to cry. No problem for the mother. She secured the connection time after time while Manuelo probably wondered, "What the hell is going on here?"

Finally, Gaddini pinned Gomez to the mat. The referee tapped Gaddini three times, the match was over and Gomez was beaten. In the meantime, the excitement in the adjacent box subsided. There was nothing left to cheer about. Manuelo finished his dinner and quickly went back to sleep.

Hollywood was noted for its big parties. It was a heavy champagne-drinking community. We had an inside track with one of the big buyers who catered to the Hollywood elite and seemed to like our champagne. This contact was made possible because of our relationship to the Three Stooges who were riding high in the entertainment world at the time. Moe Howard and his two brothers went to school with us in

Brooklyn. Moe and my brother, Frank, became close friends. When the Three Stooges became famous, they were regular visitors at the winery when they came to San Francisco. When Frank and I made our annual trip to Hollywood shortly after the Christmas holidays to collect some bills and goof off, we were Moe's guests at his palatial home in Beverly Hills. Through him and his brothers, we built up a lucrative Hollywood outlet for our champagne. In their private lives, it is to be noted that the Stooges were real, serious people. They lived normal, quiet lives, but when on stage and before the cameras, all hell broke loose with their zany antics.

Our principal business was in New York and the eastern cities while our private label route accounted for one-fourth of our business. One of our interesting outlets was Frankie De Goff's Club Deauville on lower Sutter Street in San Francisco. De Goff made his money during the bootleg era and successfully operated his popular nightclub for many years. In fact, it was the place to go on Saturday night with long lines of customers waiting to get in. We sold De Goff 30 to 40 cases of champagne a week. Like all successful operators, the crowded quarters encouraged De Goff to seek a larger nightclub. He did just that and took over a three-story building on lower O'Farrell Street and spent huge sums of money on the most elaborate furnishings. Frankie De Goff wanted to go big time. Opening night was a huge success as almost all of San Francisco turned out for the gala event. Floodlights and traffic jams led to this new ''super nightclub of nightclubs.'' I guess that it must have been just curiosity, because each succeeding week thereafter, the crowds were conspicuous by their absence.

The O'Farrell Street building was just too big. It was scary. No one likes to go into a huge arena-like nightclub. People like to be crowded. There is a feeling of intimacy in a small place while in a large, spacious nightclub, the customer gets the feeling of loneliness. I always believe that it is better to pack them in, let them wait, and never worry or think of expansion. The old Tadich Grill in the financial district of San Francisco is a classic example of being highly successful while remaining small and hard to get into.

Frankie De Goff eventually went into bankruptcy. A few years later, he opened a dive called the Streets of Paris. It was a downstairs basement on lower Mason Street in the heart of the Tenderloin. Where at one time De Goff attracted the cream of San Francisco society, he went to the opposite extremes with his Streets of Paris.

With the passing years, our champagne became popular in the eastern states. During the Thanksgiving holidays, the big seller was sparkling burgundy. It seemed that turkey and sparkling burgundy made a good combination. We also produced pink champagne, but I'll never know why. There was never enough demand to make it profitable. Our big break came during the filming of one of Charles Boyer's scenes showing him at the bar with a glass of pink champagne in his hand. With an empty champagne glass, he was demanding more pink champagne. This scene involved much drinking with the noted actor repeatedly saying, "I will have another glass of 'ze pink champagne.' "

We had some 200 cases of pink champagne in storage gathering cobwebs. The public's reaction to the bubbly pink was such that in two days, we moved out the entire inventory and since we were the only winery that had the pink champagne on hand, we did a lively business for several years to come. It is strange how one thing leads to another. We found that during the filming of the various drinking scenes, the genuine product was never used. To film one scene alone where the actor is ordering a drink, it is generally repeated many times to achieve perfection.

One day, we had a visitor from Hollywood who was interested in having us produce the imitation or "fake" champagne which was non-alcoholic. The result was a lucrative arrangement where we supplied the type of drinkable champagne needed for this purpose. For this, a portion of the winery was set aside and removed from the bonded premises. The liquid involved was distilled water with a slight, sweet flavor. Inasmuch as certain scenes involved the opening of nine to twelve bottles to get the perfect shot, you could imagine what would happen to the actor who supposedly had to drink the champagne. A slight carbonization was added and the bottle was then dressed like a genuine champagne bottle. The nice thing about selling this so-called champagne was that no federal or state taxes were involved, and no complicated forms needed to be filled out.

The winery became a meeting place for people from all walks of life resulting in lasting friendships. Frank was greatly involved in the opera world as I was involved with the San Francisco Farmers Market. Before Gaetano Merola started the San Francisco Opera Company, we had the San Carlo Opera and many visiting opera stars via the concert route. One of the early visitors to the winery was Tito Schipa, the world-famous lyric tenor. During his stay in San Francisco, he was a steady visitor to the winery as well as my mother's home where he enjoyed her *lasagne*, especially when she made it with her Sicilian tomato sauce. We would joke about his liking her tomato sauce because Schipa, being Neopolitan, readily admitted that her sauce was the best. (Neopolitans claim to make the best pasta and sauce in Italy.)

Another of our close friends was Tom Porcaro, a very popular San Franciscan who was a long-time family friend from Brooklyn with origins in Sicily. He had a palatial home with spacious, landscaped grounds on a hillside in the town of Ross in Marin County. Porcaro was a successful businessman dealing in imported Italian food products and a prime shipper of wine grapes to the eastern seaboard. During the Prohibition era, he purchased the old-time Montebello Wine Company in San Francisco, located at 24th and Folsom Streets. There was a big demand for wine used for sacramental and medicinal purposes. There was also a good demand for wine vinegar. He realized the potential of this market.

There were millions of gallons of vinegary wines that were in storage during the long Prohibition era. Most of the wineries with this non-descript wine were up against a stone wall. They were short of cash and didn't know what to do with their unsalable product. Procaro purchased large quantities of this so-called "wine." After proper inspection and a release from the Treasury Department (later the Alcohol Tax Unit), he paid a ridiculously low price and took possession. He had a successful process in which he produced a high-quality wine vinegar which was readily received in the eastern seaboard markets where they paid a good price and got a good wine vinegar. Tom Porcaro made himself a bundle of money. He became a major distributor for our champagne.

Porcaro gave big parties over the weekends at his attractive home in Ross. While he was of Sicilian birth, his wife, Enrichetta, came from Florence in Tuscany. She was a most gracious hostess and an excellent cook combining the best cuisine of Sicily and Tuscany. His first wife died following a long illness. They had three beautiful daughters, the eldest of which won a beauty contest that almost propelled her into stardom in Hollywood. After their father remarried, the three girls went back to Sicily to visit relatives. It so happened that each met and married local businessmen in Palermo.

My wife, Joan, and I met two of the girls, Pinella and Maria, on one of our many visits to Palermo. My octogenarian cousin, Franca Columba, arranged the meeting at her beautiful park-like villa in Mondello, a famous seaside resort on the blue Mediterranean near Palermo. We enjoyed seeing them after so many years and thanks to Franca's gracious hospitality, we reminisced a bit about the past and this unexpected reunion.

The Baccari family in San Francisco were our close friends, particularly Frank's. Alessandro Baccari, Sr. was a world-famous photographer, especially for his work with the San Francisco Opera Company, its stars, and the city's upper echelon. His wife, Edith, was a perfect "madonna" in one of the photos taken by her husband, and could have been taken for the real Mona Lisa. Baccari was also an artist and a successful playwright. His great gift to San Francisco was the annual Baccari Vintage Festival. This event was highly publicized and its participants included many Hollywood stars and other talented people. It was strongly supported by the California wineries. Judging from the huge quantities of luscious wine grapes in the rotunda of San Francisco's famous city hall, one got the impression that this could have been a winery rather than a city hall.

Frank took a liking to young Alessandro Baccari and became his godfather. He nicknamed him *"Scugnizzo,"* a common expression in Naples for a street urchin.

Opera great Gaetano Merola was not only an outstanding conductor, but he had an unusual gift in discovering opera stars of the future. The list of his discoveries were many. Amongst them was Florence Quartararo, a local girl who reached the heights in the opera world, married and retired.

Then, there was Livia Marracci, another local soprano. She was a frequent visitor to the ranch and winery, and at one time, we thought she and my brother, Frank, would tie the knot. Livia eventually married a wealthy oil man from Bakersfield and disappeared into the sunset.

Another local find was Josephine Tumminia, a brilliant and attractive woman who also married and disappeared. It seemed that there was no big money to be made by singing in the opera at that time.

Speaking about discovery of talent, I remember the day when Joseph Brocia, a prominent New York food broker who was a close friend of the family and who made frequent trips to San Francisco, brought with him a young, attractive and very talented lady. She came from Bari, a city on the Adriatic Sea. When she arrived in New York, she was more like an attractive peasant girl just in from the country. She was "consigned" to Brocia's care. With her came another young lady, her traveling companion. Brocia, knowing of Frank's involvement with the opera world, particularly his close relationship with Gaetano Merola, wrote to him and requested that he make all the local arrangements on their arrival in San Francisco. After resting for a day following the long, five-day transcontinental train trip, Frank introduced Licia Albanese to Merola. The first and only audition did it. He immediately realized that he had a future star on his hands. His judgement was not only correct, but Licia Albanese eventually became one of the top sopranos of the opera world. Wherever she sang, it was standing room only. She not only became the hit of the San Francisco Opera, but also the New York Metropolitan Opera House, *La Scala* in Milan, and all the cities of the world where opera was appreciated. Merola saw to it that Licia received the best accompanist and the best of everything that would help glamourize his latest find. She became very popular in San Francisco. She was wined and dined on Nob Hill, Hillsborough, and every place where society reigned. Licia not only had tremendous talent, but beauty, charm, and a warm personality. She stayed at the Palace Hotel and spent whatever free time she had at my mother's and at my home where she was family. She later married a New Yorker and for many years, she continued to be the toast of the opera world.

Every week, one of the opera stars took over and prepared a special dish from their native land. Stella Roman and Licia Albanese were in all their glory. There was at least a dozen or more from the opera company singing, laughing and enjoying the freedom from their routine activities. Frank always presided to see that nothing went wrong. Peter was his backup.

For over 15 years, the Friday *cioppino* luncheons at the winery attracted individuals from every walk of life. The limit was 30. We invited judges, politicians, businessmen, news media, athletes, and close friends. Frank and Peter occasionally did the honors on one Friday while the next Friday belonged to Joe Alioto's father (who was a partner in one of the wholesale fish companies), followed by Vince Quartararo, another prominent fish broker. The Aliotos and Quartararos supplied the fish while we supplied the beverages and other necessities.

The winery became the melting pot and meeting place of many people, particularly on Fridays, a tradition we carried on for the 18 years that we were in business.

It was a rather select group, and being invited was a cherished honor. There was nothing formal about all this. Everyone sat down on a bench. The long tables between the wine tanks were covered with Italian-style tablecloths and several types of wine were placed on the table (mostly red wine). It was convenient to remove their coats, roll up their sleeves and put on a "*cioppino* jacket," inasmuch as the right way to eat a *cioppino* was with bare fingers, assisted by a chunk of Italian bread from one of North Beach's famous Italian bakeries (Whoever heard of French bread?). The bread, of course, was to sop up the juicy and tasty *cioppino* sauce that smothered a large assortment of fresh-cooked crab, oysters, clams, prawns and the basic fish which was either a rock cod, striped bass or whatever was in season. All this conglomeration was cooked in the sauce which was generously flavored with garlic, basil, parsley and other tasty condiments. It was a place where everyone let their hair down, so to speak, ate, and enjoyed the conversations. At no time was business of any nature discussed.

Perhaps I could best describe the *cioppinos* by referring to Dick Nolan's column in the May 25, 1970 issue of the *San Francisco Examiner* entitled, "Vintage City Hall." He stated, "Wasn't it only a week or so ago when we kid reporters shut down the City Hall beat and trooped off for a three-hour luncheon at the Brucato Brothers Winery?"

"Let's see, there was dapper Dick Chase from the *News*, Benny Kline, Chief Administrative Officer Thomas Brooks, and Joe McCann from the Police Department who drove Brooks' Cadillac. The Brucato winery was one of those North Beach family businesses you scarcely see around any more . . . Lunch at the winery was an occasion worth closing down the City Hall beat . . . When these occasions occurred, we usurped the authority to declare ourselves a holiday, key City officials were alerted and put on notice that they could reach us at the Brucato winery only if the City Hall dome caught fire."

"The Brucato winery made good wine and on luncheon days, John and his brothers would set up the tables in the midst of the bottling machinery and wine tanks . . . Chase of the News, who was considered the dean of the City Hall reporters, would take the occasion to remind us. 'You guys had better enjoy this because you will never have a better job in the newspaper business . . . and we will never forget the old brick winery that was so cool and sweet-smelling with the Brucato boys fussing around urging everybody to try this and a little of everything. They were magnificent hosts.' ''

Our winery was more than a winery. It was an institution. Celebrities and people who made San Francisco great were some of the visitors. Sports figures like Joe DiMaggio, Lefty O'Doul, Tony Lazzari, Ernie Lombardi, and so many others became our guests and friends. Gaetano Merola, Alessandro Baccari, Sr., Mayor Angelo Rossi, Earl Warren, Montgomery Street businessmen, financiers like A.P. Giannini, and countless others were no strangers to us. They all stopped in to chat, enjoy a sip of sherry or marsala, and went their way. It was like a gathering of people in the ''who's who'' category. We were a low-key family people. We loved people and they loved us. It was our way of life.

Jumping ahead of my narrative, Frank, a long-time bachelor, married Raffaela Caiati, who happened to be Gaetano Merola's niece. The wedding reception took place at the winery and over 400 guests attended. Frank made his own wedding cake since he was a master pastry chef amongst his many other talents. This was a four-tier *cassata*, a Sicilian specialty. The guests all agreed that it was a masterpiece. It really was.

Six months later, my beloved brother died of a heart attack. His passing affected us all so greatly that it put a pall on the operation of the winery. But saddest of all, he did not live to see his daughter, Barbara, who was born six months after his death. Licia Albanese became Barbara's godmother. At the tender age of two, Licia used her in a special scene in *Madame Butterfly*. After the third year, she decided that Barbara was getting a bit too heavy to hold in her arms, so that was the end of Barbara's career in the opera world. Licia was so devoted to Frank that every season after registering at her usual Palace Hotel, she was driven to the Golden Gate National Cemetery where he was buried. She also continued to visit my home in the Sunset district of San Francisco just to relax and be with ''family.''

Many years later when Licia was semi-retired doing only concerts and occasionally an opera, she sang at the opera house with a relatively unknown tenor named Luciano Pavarotti. The opera was a sellout as she and Pavarotti were at their best.

My good friend, Joseph Alioto (then mayor of San

Wedding reception for my brother, Peter and his wife, Marie — 1940.

The West Coast Vintners Co. in San Francisco.

Two "hired hands" at the winery — Joe DiMaggio and Lefty O'Doul — 1938.

Francisco) called asking Joan and I to join him at the Sunday Golden Gate Park concert. I had not seen Licia for several years. Joe suggested that as an old-time friend, it would be nice for me to present the "keys to the city" not only to Licia Albanese, but to Luciano Pavarotti as well. We drove to the mayor's home in Pacific Heights, enjoyed several cocktails, and then accompanied him to the park concert in his chauffeur-driven limousine. When I saw Licia in her dressing room preparing for her concert, she jumped up and gave me a warm hug and an Italian-style greeting — a kiss on both cheeks. Joan and I were introduced to Pavarotti, who had a scarf around his throat to protect his delicate vocal cords from San Francisco's famous fog. There was an overflow crowd of over 20,000 people in Golden Gate Park to hear the concert and see for themselves who this fellow Pavarotti was. At intermission time, the mayor gave a short talk and introduced me as a long-time friend of Licia's.

Following another year of concert work, the great Licia Albanese went into retirement at her estate on Long Island, while Pavarotti ascended to greater heights and became a living legend with his magnificent tenor voice and dynamic personality.

About this time, the process of champagne in bulk had arrived. Instead of the naturally fermented-in-the-bottle champagne, it was now made in large tanks and called, "naturally fermented, bulk process." There were many variations according to the different processes that constantly kept improving. We did well and eventually, the naturally fermented-in-the-bottle champagne became a major part of our business.

We had a lot of help from Joe Vercelli, an old-time vineyardist and winemaker. He operated a small winery near Healdsburg, not too far from my ranch. Joe later became manager of the ailing Italian Swiss colony winery in Asti, made a big success and retired. He was called out of retirement to take over Souverain, another winery located near Geyserville, and brought it back to its prime. In my estimation, "Little Joe" as he was called, was one of the real old-time wine experts and knew the wine business from top to bottom. He was very personable and you always felt that it was a privilege working for him or just knowing him.

We sold our champagne under three labels — *Champ D'or, Palais Royale,* and *Charlemagne.* One of our major outlets was via the private label. This involved wineries, restaurants, and estate-minded individuals who wanted their own private labels.

Perhaps at this point, as I look back over the years reminiscing about certain people and events, I cannot overlook our long relationship with Montgomery Jackson. He never liked his first name, so we always called him Jackson. Since the opening of our winery, Jackson, who was in the shipping and freight forwarding business, stopped in every morning on his way to his office nearby. Our tax-paid room was always open for possible retail sales. There were three 5-gallon barrels of sweet wine equipped with a spigot (faucet) for sampling and social purposes. The barrels were labeled, "Port," "Sherry," and "Muscatel." Jackson would stop in, say hello, converse in his broad Australian accent, discuss the weather, pour himself a glass of sherry, gulp it down, say goodbye and go on his way. This routine went on for many years. We liked him and he liked us. We actually set our clocks by his arrival. It was always 8:10 a.m., never one minute earlier or later.

There came a time, however, when Jackson either forgot to say hello, or for some unknown reason, he just came in, gulped down his sherry and was on his way. An out-of-the-ordinary occurrence such as this became noticeable. We began to wonder what was wrong. It reached the point where Jackson had to be taught some manners, especially respect. One morning, Peter substituted the barrel of sherry with wine vinegar, leaving the sherry label on. We generally started working at 8 a.m. The entire crew and my two brothers awaited in anticipation from a concealed observation point. In came Jackson at exactly 8:10 a.m., picked up his glass, opened the spigot until the glass was full and gulped it down. This time, he screamed. His eyes were bulging red, and just as fast as he gulped down the wine vinegar, he spit it out. Jackson, picking up his hat from the floor, stormed out the door and disappeared into the street. We never saw him again. Sorrowfully, we all later agreed that we missed him. Perhaps there is a lesson to be learned here. It is an old Italian proverb that says, "Always sip your wine. Never gulp it down."

Now in the peace and quiet of my garden in Millbrae, pleasant memories are recalled that bring forth instances that happened during these unforgettable winery years. I think of today's traffic gridlock and the almost insurmountable attempt to park a vehicle in downtown San Francisco. I think of the fact that we had no problem parking our three Chevrolets, the employees' cars, the trucks, those of the many customers, visitors, and neighbors around Broadway and Sansome Streets who never saw a parking meter or a meter maid.

The matter of security seldom concerned us. There was little fear of muggings, pickpocketing, or disorderly conduct. I speak in generalities. It was a different world then during the years between 1934 and 1952. What gave us the feeling of safety and security, perhaps, could be attributed in part to the two husky, handsome policemen who had the map of Ireland spread over their masculine faces. Shamus O'Rourke and Dennis Reilly covered the beat in the winery area in addition to Broadway and what was once the notorious Barbary Coast. They were tough as nails, but had hearts of gold. Anytime there was a problem on their beat, Shamus and Dennis were on the spot and took over. If there was fighting or disorder, they first attempted to settle things in an orderly fashion. If that didn't work, their well-educated fists went into action. They never maimed anyone, but they beat the hell out of them until order was restored. There was respect for law and order as long as these two sons of Ireland were around. They stopped in to see us during some time of the day, chatted with us and sipped a small sherry before going on their way.

One day, we were all working feverishly to complete a large order that was to be picked up for shipment. Everyone, including my father, pitched in as time was running short. In the meantime, there was a completed lot of 52 cases of champagne that was awaiting pick-up by another trucker. We expected them later in the day, but they happened to arrive much earlier. These 52 cases weighing 65 pounds each had to be loaded right away. Shamus and Dennis appeared for their daily sip of sherry. Sizing up the situation, they waved Frank, Shorty and I away, took off their hats and coats, rolled up their sleeves and in no time, had the truck loaded and away. It was Shamus who approached me with that red faced map of Ireland and those twinkling eyes and said, "John, this will cost you two sips of your sherry wine." No wonder I was always fond of the Irish.

Then, there were the two Little Sisters of the Poor. Sister Veronica, age 92, accompanied the driver in the broken-down Model-T Ford truck and paid us her weekly visit on Saturday morning. (Everyone at that time worked five-and-a-half days; that is, up to 1 p.m. on Saturday.) This was Frank's private deal.

Since the early winery days, this was a weekly occurrence. He had about eight gallons of port wine ready for her. The Little Sisters of the Poor gave each patient at their Lake Street home a glass of port wine every afternoon. (I guess we would call it a coffee break today.) Sister Veronica told us that the old folks treasured this daily treat — perhaps the reason why some of the old folks at the home lived to the ripe, old age of 90 or 100. She also confessed that she, too, enjoyed her daily sip.

The Hotaling Warehouse was several blocks from the winery. It was one of the largest whiskey warehouses in northern California. Hotaling, himself, visited us every once in a while, enjoying his sip of sherry wine and going about his business, which was generally at the bank to deposit some of his millions. There was a little poem written about him. It had to do with the 1906 San Francisco earthquake when most of the downtown area was reduced to ashes. One of the few buildings that survived was the Hotaling Warehouse, which was loaded to the roof with the latest shipment of scotch whiskey that had just arrived from Scotland. Thus, the poem:

"They say the town was rather frisky.
Why did the Lord burn down the churches
and save Hotaling's whiskey?"

Directly across the street from our office was a popular bar called The Black Cat, and a three-story hotel. It was a lesbian bar that attracted some of the best dressed and attractively attired women. They drove up in expensive cars — no Fords or Chevrolets — and spent several hours meeting their friends in this most unusual location. We happened to know what was going on inasmuch as they, too, enjoyed our *Champ D'or* champagne.

We also had two high-powered, German-made binoculars that were put to good use by some of our friends who enjoyed watching the "Passing Parade" from our office window. One day, while getting out of my car, a young, attractive woman leaving the bar to get to her car which had been parked next to mine, met me eyeball-to-eyeball and pleaded with me to keep her secret. She happened to be a neighbor of mine on Thirtieth Avenue with a fine family of two boys and a girl. I quickly assured her that her secret would be kept provided that I did not see her around this notorious bar again. A year later, she gave birth to a fourth child and we never saw such a happy family.

By this time, my eyes become heavy and sleep falls upon me, a very refreshing sleep. I awaken to the chirps of the many robin red-breasts and the rubbing against my knees and legs of my neighbor's cat, Midnight. In the meantime, I hear the voice of my wife, Joan, informing me that the *lasagne* is getting cold. It is time to get back to reality.

Chapter 9

Invited To Run For
The Board of Supervisors

Candidates for the November 1949 supervisorial election were lining up in early July. Many prominent people were either being mentioned or had already thrown their hats into the ring. At that time, amongst many other responsibilities, I was busy managing an ongoing winery in San Francisco with Peter.

One day, I received a telephone call from Steve Mana, a prominent San Francisco attorney who practiced law in North Beach together with his brother, Lawrence, who later became a Superior Court Judge, and John B. Molinari, who later became Presiding Judge of the State Court of Appeals. Steve was representing a non-profit organization known as the Volunteers for Better Government. It was originated by the Junior Chamber of Commerce. This group's function was to primarily seek out and completely finance candidates for the Board of Supervisors. The money was raised from some of the most outstanding and prestigious business firms in San Francisco. The selectee was assured of at least $20,000, which was a sizable sum at that time, plus the benefit of a high-geared campaign.

Steve informed me that I was their top selection. Naturally, I was flattered and the temptation to accept was rather exciting. When I first got involved in the promotion of the Victory Garden Program during war time, I pledged to myself that I did not want to run for any political office. As time went on, I found myself heavily involved in dealings with politicians because of my civic activities, and I drew the line as far as becoming a politician.

Arthur Caylor, in his well-read column in the *San Francisco*

News, wrote about the forthcoming supervisorial race. He stated, "The incumbents on the Board of Supervisors may be up against some strong talent that may knock off two or three incumbents. Who can tell? For example, John G. Brucato is teetering on the edge. His build-up from the Victory Gardens, his Angel Island achievement, and the Farmers' Market make him a dangerous candidate. He even has some very strong people who wish to contribute to his campaign fund."

I believe I would have accepted, but declined due to the reorganization of the family winery since Frank's passing. Steve Mana put my decision on hold for two months hoping that I would change my mind, which I didn't. Harold Dobbs was eventually selected and was elected to office. Later on, they endorsed George Christopher, who later became one of San Francisco's mayors.

Shortly after, an unfortunate incident happened. Peter had a heart attack and we rushed him to the emergency hospital. He recovered from this only to have a series of minor attacks. The doctor suggested that we get out of the business for Peter's sake. Rather than run the winery alone and because of the close relationship I had with both my brothers, we decided to sell the winery.

In the meantime, I was informed that there was a civil service examination for the position of superintendent of the agricultural and land division of the San Francisco Water Department. Ben Kline, who was the assistant administrative officer to Thomas Brooks at the time, suggested that I take the exam as the job was a timely one for me and right up my alley. The timing was perfect. We were in the process of selling the family-operated winery after 18 successful years. I took the exam and came out number one. It was the thirteenth day of the month, the seventh month of the year, and my examination paper was numbered 13. (There was a 29 there someplace, but at any rate, I always use these numbers when I play roulette or keno.)

The Weibel family was our rival in the champagne business, and also started out and struggled along for many years in a basement on Clay Street in San Francisco. The family then purchased its present winery in Mission San Jose. They became very successful and today are considered one of the top in their field, producing a high-quality bulk process champagne. Fred Weibel, Sr. eventually passed the business onto Fred, Jr. after his "retirement." (The Swiss Germans never retire.) We dealt with them over the years and we could never find a nicer Swiss German family than the Weibels.

Fred Weibel, Jr. became interested in two of our bulk process champagne tanks. They were a little on the "shorts," but they needed the tanks, so we made a deal. It was arranged that we took the equivalent in champagne to the value of the tanks. We were once again back to the barter system. It worked out fine for us inasmuch as we sold the champagne to some of our former customers, making a small profit on each sale.

The sale was consummated on August 20, 1952. We helped the Weibels when they were struggling and today, with a third generation Weibel at the helm, they have risen to the heights. Besides greatly enlarging their Mission San Jose plant, they now operate a large vineyard and winery near Ukiah in Mendocino County. Their tasting room is one of the most attractive in the wine industry. Every time I visit the Weibel Winery in Mission San Jose, I get a nostalgic feeling when I walk into the production room and see my former tanks at the entrance. These tanks made good champagne for the Brucato family and now they made a superb champagne for the Weibel family.

On October 1, 1952, I assumed my duties as manager of San Francisco's "Baronial Empire," a fiefdom covering 64,000 acres of water department lands in San Francisco, San Mateo, Alameda and Santa Clara Counties.

Peter, my beloved brother, died in 1956, leaving me as the last of the clan.

Chapter 10

San Francisco's Baronial Empire

The following is the inscription on the Sunol water temple that serves as a motto of which the San Francisco Water Department tells the story of this taken-for-granted commodity — water.

> "I will make the wilderness a pool of water,
> and the lands, springs of water — the
> stream whereof shall make glad the City."

Tall cottonwoods flanked the water temple gracing Willis Polk's architectural jewel, which was inspired after the classic temple of Vesta in Italy.

I remember during the first week on the job, I had to visit and inspect the water department lands in Sunol. I found myself standing before this classic design and marveling at the blend of man's creation and God's creation of the land. As I walked within the temple, I sensed the beauty of Greek, Roman and Egyptian influence in a simple design, and a history of man's civilization immortalized in Polk's design. It merged two separate traditions — a graceful Greek-inspired interior and a mode of construction invented in the near east 1,000 years earlier, but used mainly for fortifications until the Romans developed its potentialities.

As an amateur historian, I became extremely interested in each area where my work took me. Sunol fascinated me. Preliminary investigation allowed me to learn that its history dated back to 1787 and that it was named after Don Antonio Sunol, an adventurer who deserted his ship while it was berthed in

San Francisco Bay. He was 21 years of age at the time. During that year, he married a beautiful girl named Dolores Bernal of San Jose.

It was an area rich in history. Along with the Bernals and the early settlers were Don Jose Noriega, Don Roberto Livermore, Manuel Mendoza, the Silvas, and the many Portuguese and Spanish Mexicans who settled in this fertile area. The Bernals had large Spanish land grants given to them because of their service to the Spanish Crown. The Bernal land grant covered 100 square miles, quite a fiefdom. These early pioneers lived a good life as they raised cattle and sheep, grew lots of hay, and grain. There were no traffic jams or polluted air in those days. Many lived to a ripe, old age.

As the years passed during my tenure of duty for the water department, I witnessed the exodus of the Portuguese and the old Spanish families. In the '60s and '70s, cattle brought high prices and good grazing land in California was at a premium.

I made some wonderful friends in the Sunol Valley. One of the strongest friendships was with the many Mendoza families. All farmed independently and were good ranchers. Oh, how I recall when the neighbors joined each other and assisted in the roundups and branding of their cattle. This neighborly spirit always thrilled me. My mouth still waters when I think of the juicy, thick steaks that were served after the round-up was completed, those beans, and the many goodies that were washed down by generous servings of red and white wine.

With the gradual passing of these pioneer oldtimers (circa 1975) came the Texans and southern California cattlemen. Grazing land that brought $12 an acre jumped to $25 and more. Poor, brushy land that couldn't be given away for $3 brought $15 per acre. After all, it was a case of demand. It became a somewhat crazy situation and quite a few of these high bidders bit the dust a few years later when beef prices tumbled.

The Sunol Valley is one of the most beautiful valleys in California. It is part of the massive land holdings of the San Francisco Water Department in Alameda and Santa Clara Counties. Two reservoirs, the Calaveras and San Antonio, and the Sunol Filter Galleries are integral parts of the San Francisco water system. From this area, approximately 20 percent of the city's water supply originated.

When the city acquired the Spring Valley Water Works in 1930, the land acquisition included 37,000 acres in Alameda and Santa Clara Counties, and 23,000 acres in San Mateo

County. The use of these lands was strictly limited. They were primarily watershed or water protective lands. The primary use was for water production.

More than 200 miles of rights of way and isolated parcels, including the 500 acres of well fields in Pleasanton and numerous miscellaneous parcels made up the water department empire. The San Mateo holdings of 23,000 acres, being part of the Crystal Springs and San Andreas watershed, were never available for leasing. The one exception was the Crystal Springs Public Golf Course, which was leased to a private operator and returns over $250,000 per year to the water department on a percentage basis. Some minor use of this watershed include equestrian, 4-H clubs, and related uses.

Approximately 30,000 acres of the Sunol Watershed Properties are in grazing. This use was compatible to watershed operations. These lands were good, fair and poor. The income from grazing was the highest per acre in northern California. The rental rates ranged from $6 per acre to $11 per acre (1970 prices). The rates were based on how much feed the land would produce. On good grazing land, one cow or animal "lived" on five acres. Much of the land was brushy, rocky or steep and in various areas required 30 or more acres to support one animal.

The original lessees inherited from Spring Valley were primarily old stock Portuguese. They were good cattlemen, rents were low, but the life was good. As time went on, the oldtimers disappeared. One of our oldest tenants, Manuel Mendoza, 80, rode the range on his modest 260-acre leasehold. At one time, he grazed several thousand acres. In 1970, Mrs. Rose Thomas (nee Mendoza), aged 84, was the oldest lessee, grazing over 900 acres.

The breed of cattlemen now paid higher prices. A particular type of cattleman was the contractor, the mortician, the industrialist, who, in order to obtain certain leases, greatly outbid the conventional cattleman. While this was fine for the city, it was an unhappy occasion for the cattleman.

More than 35 years ago, I "inherited" the Sunol Valley, an arid, thistle-infested valley of over 2,000 acres. The primary income was from a poor quality hay raised on share crops and some fair grazing.

Taking the meaning from the inscription on the Sunol Water temple and putting it into practice, a gradual, steady transformation began to take place. Objections from management became more and more apparent. "We are in the water business. The land use was secondary." Despite the frustrations of working under such a policy, hundreds of acres were converted into lush strawberry, vegetable, and nursery crop leases. The berries yielded from $125 to $150 per acre per year, while vegetable and nursery crops produced $65 to $100 per acre per year rental (pre-inflation prices) to the city.

One heavily infested field of thistles containing 90 acres yielded a grazing rental of less than $800 per year. Converted to strawberries, the city's rental income jumped to over $21,000 per year, remained as a model agricultural development, and was visited by leading agriculturists from all over the state, including students from various agricultural colleges.

Perhaps one of the most interesting characters I encountered was John Perata. It is interesting to note that he was a mortician. In fact, he was part-owner of one of the biggest mortuaries in northern California, Valenti, Marini and Perata, located in San Francisco's North Beach district in what was, and still is, one of the most colorful parts of San Francisco. Until recent years, it was heavily populated by his fellow Italians.

Many is the time John conducted a funeral service from his mortuary, escorted the body for the Requiem Mass or service to Saints Peter and Paul Church, the Italian Cathedral of the West, dashed back to his car parked closeby, and headed straight out to his cattle ranch in Sunol. What a sight it was to see him moving about the range still dressed in his funeral pinstripe trousers and long charcoal mourning coat, along with his constant companion, an unlit El Roi Tan cigar in his mouth.

At times, John telephoned me to meet him at the coffee shop in Sunol. I liked him. He was a very interesting man. Inasmuch as I, too, was a cigar smoker at the time, he would hand me one of the five cigars he always carried in his pocket. We both decided to skip the coffee as we had some respect for our insides.

John enjoyed being a cattleman and I must say I really enjoyed his company. I will always cherish in my memories the sight of John Perata when he rode a horse, a very skinny, half-starved horse that reminded me of the "Tales of the Wayside Inn" when Ichabod Crane rode his scrawny horse on the road to Tarry-Town on the Hudson River.

Then, there was Coleman Foley, as Irish as Irish can be. He had the luck of the Irish. He owned about 500 acres of the poorest grazing land that could hardly support a score of nanny goats. His land happened to be along Vallecitos Road north of Sunol on the way to Livermore. Along came General Electric which decided that it wanted to buy some of Foley's land for its nuclear reactor site. The land was bought at the astounding price of just a shade less than $1 million, an unheard of price during those pre-inflation days.

Coleman Foley couldn't read or write, but he was so smart that he pyramided his newly acquired "grubstake" into a very profitable cattle and grain empire. He also acquired a bank in the San Joaquin Valley. Foley was a staunch Democrat and a great admirer of President John F. Kennedy, another Irishman who made good. When Kennedy, then-Senator, inaugurated his "Food for Freedom" drive to assist the earthquake victims in Greece, Foley donated a carload of grain in Kennedy's name. Because of his humanitarian gesture, he received a personal invitation from Kennedy to attend his Presidential inauguration. Foley went all out for this event. He outfitted himself with longtail formal attire and an appropriate stove pipe hat, and took off for Washington, D.C. where he was personally received by President Kennedy.

Foley and I became close friends. I leased him several hundred acres of water department lands and it was my joy to see this Son of Erin grow bigger and bigger in the cattle world. One day, while we were having lunch in Livermore, he confided in me that he was going to take a wife. He did it the old-fashioned way. She was a picture bride — that is, some of his Irish relatives in Ireland sent him a photo of his bride-to-be. His relatives assured him that she was a good housekeeper, and that she was strong and worked hard in the fields. She was also capable of raising a family, a large family.

Everything went quite well for Foley. His new bride arrived. She was 20 years younger than Foley, worked hard, obeyed orders and raised for him a typical large Irish family. Coleman Foley was a rare breed.

Perhaps what made Sunol famous in the early days was Joaquin Murietta, the famous bandit who hid out there. He held court in a well-protected grove of prickly pears. These prickly pears grew in a somewhat hollow area, were 15 feet tall, and spread out in such a way that a natural "room" was carved out of the grove for his protected use. I made up my mind that I was going to preserve this unusual grove for two reasons: the first being that it was Joaquin Murietta's hangout; the second being that because I was of Sicilian origin, the fruit of the prickly pear brought frothing at the mouth in anticipation of devouring this most healthy and delicious fruit.

Luther Burbank, a famous botanist among his many achievements, developed a "prickless" pear. These pears, of course, did not have the Burbank touch. They were full of small spines which gave the handler a rather itchy feeling. (Any experienced prickly pear lover placed the fruit in a bucket of water, thereby removing most of the troublesome spines.)

Early history books relate how the early navigator explorers coming around the Horn and up the South American and Mexican coasts cast anchor, went ashore, and partook of the fruit of the prickly pear. Inasmuch as scurvy was a common problem amongst the crew on these long voyages, the prickly pear cured it. It is to be noted that this semi-tropical fruit, which grows abundantly in California, is quite high in Vitamin C and contains many beneficial elements for the human system. The San Jose area still ships prickly pears in huge quantities to the New York and eastern cities where the fruit is relished and in demand by those of Mediterranean extraction.

The Southern Pacific Pipeline Company informed the Water department that it was coming through the Sunol properties with a huge underground pipeline to transport gas from Livermore to San Jose. This proposed pipeline would go through the prickly pear grove and completely destroy it. I immediately objected to water department management, which passed the buck to the Public Utilities Commission (they approve water department leases). Evidently, no one wanted to get involved in this prickly matter. I made a strong presentation before the PUC at their following Tuesday meeting. Although they were sympathetic to my plea, I felt their final decision would be a negative one. I then suggested a meeting at Sunol for the purpose of inspecting other properties and at the same time, inspect the grove and perhaps sample some of the fruit. The commission very seldom turned down this type of meeting. The Sunol water department headquarters also included a picturesque grape arbor seating 40 people with barbecue and other facilities used to entertain government and other officials on city business. The five commissioners and an assortment of management personnel were just about to complete their well-barbecued steaks and beans when I suddenly appeared with a tray of well-ripened prickly pears. I went through the art of properly cutting the skin in such a way that it exposed the grenade-shaped fruit, and suggested to Commissioner Eddie Baron to partake of the fruit. After some questionable reluctance, he picked up the fruit, took a small bite, hesitated, then looked at me and asked for more. By the time this episode was completed, everyone present had their fill and expressed their complete approval of the prickly pear.

At Tuesday's Public Utilities Commission meeting, the commission unanimously approved Southern Pacific's proposal — only on the condition that they bypass the prickly pear grove. This condition no doubt raised some eyebrows amongst the Southern Pacific officials present. It did cost them more money by going around instead of through the grove. I felt that not only did I save a historic landmark, but I also preserved a source of one of my favorite fruits, the prickly pear. And, oh yes, I am sure Joaquin Murietta would have been pleased at this decision.

During my regime, I changed the face of the Sunol Valley from hay and grazing into a more picturesque and profitable use. The change included strawberry fields, large-scale tomato and truck crop plantings, nurseries, Christmas tree farms, and increased acreage of walnut orchards. The biggest revenue producer was the Santa Clara sand and gravel lease along Calaveras Road.

Alameda Creek was an annual headache for the water department. During the season of heavy rains, the overflow from the Calaveras Reservoir picked up momentum through Alameda Creek and caused damaging and costly floods. The Army Corps of Engineers were constantly building levees and dredging this troublesome waterway. In my humble and practical solution, we entered into a long-term lease with the gravel company. Steve Dorsa, a large-scale gravel operator from Santa Clara County, assumed the lease as the highest responsible bidder. He was later joined by Dick Humphries, former head of another large sand and gravel company. One of the major conditions of the lease was the constant dredging of Alameda Creek. This and the normal gravel excavations produced a handsome revenue to the city. We were on a royalty basis, so much per ton. The other condition was that the excavations eventually become man-made lakes, properly landscaped for future recreational use.

One of our large-scale achievements was the vineyard lease of 2,000 acres to Almaden Vineyards. The area selected by them surrounded the new San Antonio Reservoir. Jack Fisher, vice-president of Almaden, received the enthusiastic endorsement of the Almaden hierarchy. They planned to plant 1,000 acres at first in three different areas or blocks. They also planned to erect a small winery for crushing only, so that the grapes would require little hauling at harvest. The problem here was that all this happened in July of 1969, which was less than a year before my retirement at age 65. I put the package together so that whoever succeeded me would have no problem in following through to the benefit of the city and lessee.

The ground was prepared for planting. The timetable called for the first plantings in 1970, covering 450 acres, followed by 550 acres in 1971. Unfortunately, this promising and outstanding development died in the hands of an incompetent management.

Jack Fisher and Almaden Vineyards could no longer put up with management's procrastination, indecision and complete bureaucratic incompetence. They finally broke their lease, paid a penalty for this action, and went to greener pastures in San Benito County where they now farm a 2,000-acre vineyard. Their departure was a big loss to the city, but no one seemed to care. I was gone and Sunol happened to be in left field.

Several prestigious wineries were also interested in planting a vineyard on our Sunol properties. The most prominent included Wente Brothers and Concannon Vineyards from nearby Livermore Valley, known for its high-quality wine grapes and wines.

Cresta Blanca, Mirassou and many others watched the progress of Almaden Vineyards. They could not understand the indifference and lack of cooperation from the San Francisco city officials. Some of them told me after I retired that the water department officials felt a sigh of relief. It was an unbelievable fact that the water department did not want their properties developed. For 21 years, I heard the same old story — "We are in the water business. Nothing else matters."

General Arthur Frye, while he was manager of the water department, was the strongest obstructionist. One of his widely publicized remarks was, "I want to see this land returned to grazing."

While I was manager of the land division, I was able to make progress despite the roadblocks, delays, and stupid, ignorant opposition. Perhaps the reason they got into so much trouble later on was because of their incompetence and lack of decision.

The incredible stories of the Sunol Golf Course scandal, the rape of the city's million dollar walnut orchard, the Pleasanton industrial park fiasco and others are based on facts and carefully preserved notes and records. To paraphrase a prominent winery official who was interested in leasing Sunol Valley land, "I guess you just can't do business with San Francisco."

On the lighter side, I must insert a little anecdote concerning poison oak. When I operated my 75-acre vineyard up in Alexander Valley in Sonoma County before the repeal of Prohibition and through the 1930s and 1940s, one of the constant problems was the annual eradication of poison oak which was quite prevalent in that area. As we all know, poison oak can be troublesome and quite itchy to say the least.

The Puccinelli family were my neighbors. They, too, had the poison oak eradication problem. We all worked together helping each other out on a neighborly basis. Puccinelli revealed the secret to me as to how to avoid catching poison oak, especially when you handle it and particularly when you burn it — the worst time to catch the itch.

"Pooch," an oldtimer from Genoa, told me to do what he learned from the old country — drink two glasses of wine before breakfast. Evidently, the soothing effects of the wine would generate through your pores and develop a natural resistance to the poison oak. Doing this before breakfast was not too difficult a task, or was it a task? After all, I was in the habit of drinking one big glassful of grapefruit or orange juice before breakfast. So what was the big difference? One was the fruit of the tree, the other was the fruit of the vine.

I never caught poison oak nor did Puccinelli. I always remembered this episode and offered my solution to anyone who was a victim of poison oak. The problem of poison oak came up constantly over the years at the Farmers' Market. Because of the relationship between the many farmers and their customers, the question of how to prevent catching poison oak was often asked. (The farmers were supposed to be experts on such matters.) I discussed the problem with some of our oldtimers, but did not get too far. My version was never taken seriously. The big break came, however, during the spring of 1963. It was during my stewardship as manager of the San

Francisco Water Department's "baronial empire" covering 64,000 acres in four Bay Area counties. I made millions of dollars for the city by leasing its lands without interfering with its primary uses as watersheds for our local reservoirs. I had the reputation of leasing everything that brought additional revenue to the department.

The story broke in the *San Francisco Chronicle* and the *San Francisco Examiner* on June 5, 1963. All sorts of headlines appeared such as "Sure Cure for Poison Oak" or "City Itches for More Cash" and on and on. The Crystal Springs Reservoirs in San Mateo County were protected by 23,000 acres of watershed lands. Hundreds of acres along Canada Road south of Pulgas Temple were heavily infested with poison oak. The city did very little to eradicate this obnoxious plant, and you couldn't blame them.

There was a nursery outfit in Belmont that approached me on the possibility of gathering poison oak on a commercial basis. Two brothers owned the company known as Higgins and Higgins (God Bless the Irish). The Higgins brothers had an arrangement or permit with us (the city) for the gathering of teasel heads, cattails and other weeds growing on the water shed. They were in the business of drying and selling these weeds to other nurseries and floral shops for decorative purposes. We charged them a minimal rental of $200 per year. We were actually reluctant to collect this fee, for, were they not keeping the weeds down on a part of the watershed? Of course, my first question was, "How can you gather poison oak without catching it?" "Very simple," replied one of the brothers. "Our workers drink wine before their breakfast . . . and probably have a snort or two during the day." "Eureka!" I screamed. "Puccinelli was right."

Their method of gathering involved a crew of 8 to 12 Mexican laborers. They cut and baled the poison oak, then loaded them onto a truck. My next question was, "What the devil do you do with it?" The answer was that it was sold to medical laboratories, which were developing cures and preventatives for poison oak and other uses. The Higgins brothers made 12¢ a pound. The price varied depending on the number of laboratories in the business, which I later learned was a competitive business.

Well, the "what you may call it" hit the fan when I presented the proposal to the city's Public Utilities Commission for their approval at the weekly meeting in the city hall. When something as unusual as this came before such an austere body of five commissioners with reporters in attendance to cover the happenings at the meeting, it resulted in a field day, particularly for the news media. Generally, the PUC meetings were rather dull. There were usually 20 to 30 items on the agenda — most of them routine items covering millions of dollars for city expenditures which involved pipelines, roadways, power, water production, and the like. The news stories hit the Associated Press wires and all the other national and international news services. We had a lot of laughs, and although I was on the receiving end explaining this new city involvement, I believe I came out in good shape. The ones who really enjoyed this unrehearsed show at the PUC meeting were the two brothers, Higgins and Higgins. After the meeting, they couldn't hold back their exuberant feelings. "Thanks, John, for putting us on the map."

Two weeks later, the Higgins brothers called me to again express their appreciation. "We have been swamped with phone calls." I understood they hired three more people at the nursery to handle the new business that was generated by the widespread publicity.

The Farmers' Market capitalized on this new event. Various circulars were handed out. We emphasized, however, that this was not a sure cure or preventative. It was effective on some and ineffective on others. We suggested that people try it out. After all, wine is considered a food. We also suggested, "Sip the wine. Don't guzzle it."

Chapter 11

The Sunol Valley Golf Course Scandal

Dr. Saul Leider, a nationally known golf course expert who was a dentist by profession, was interested in finding a golf course site on the city's vast water department property in Alameda County. He operated a number of golf courses in California, but one which became very profitable was the popular Rinconada Golf Course near Santa Cruz. He was also the guiding light of his brother's operation of the Crystal Springs Golf Course, which was leased from the city and located on the watershed in San Mateo County.

One day, Dr. Leider and I began a cooks tour of possible sites. There was no question in his mind when he decided upon a 600-acre pasture and hay field as the right location. "Here it is, John. We will look no further." The property was adjacent to the water department's million dollar walnut orchard, separated by Alameda Creek and looking eastward over the Sunol Valley floor with its picturesque rows of strawberry and vegetable fields, tree farms, and its rolling hills — a view which was simply breathtaking. The land was rented to the Mendoza family and used for grazing cattle. Most of it was infested with thistles and considered poor grazing land. The rental received by the city from the Mendozas was $4,500 a year.

The projected revenues from this future golf course complex with a possible investment of $5 million or more was rather attractive. Less than a year later, Dr. Leider passed away. He did not live to see his dream come true. The idea and the seed had been planted. I had hoped and long-dreamed of such a development. In the meantime, I called in experts to inspect and report on the possibilities of this future recreational site.

91

All came to the conclusion that this location was ideal for a golf course.

Following Dr. Leider's untimely demise, a very personable, knowledgeable and wealthy self-made man who had a reputation of getting things done, appeared on the horizon — Raymond W. Morrow. He teamed with Clark Glasson, a well-known professional expert on the development of golf courses. Together, with James Brasil, a deputy city attorney, we put together a proposed golf course lease for the purpose of leasing the site to the most responsible and highest bidder. The usual procedure in leasing water department lands or any city property was to first obtain approval of the manager; in this case, the water department. Following this, it must then be approved by the city attorney, then the manager of Public Utilities, who submits the proposal to the Public Utilities Commission for its endorsement. The water department would then recommend that the lease be awarded to the highest and most responsible bidder, who must supply a Faithful Performance Bond to protect the city after the lease is awarded. Of the several bids received, the commission awarded the lease to Ray Morrow and Clark Glasson.

Prior to the commencement of construction of the golf course, Frank Ivaldi, a prominent East Bay contractor, joined Morrow and Glasson. At the time, Ivaldi had a limited partnership as owner of the Oakland Raiders professional football team.

The lease was written for 42 years with renewal options, and covered 280 acres of this gently, rolling terrain. On this property were three small man-made lakes or reservoirs that were stocked with fish. As time progressed, Ivaldi became the spokesman and prime mover in the development of the property. The plan called for two public 18-hole golf courses, a swank Mediterranean-style clubhouse with a restaurant, a coffee shop, several attractive bars, conference rooms, a banquet hall with a dance floor, and a pro shop with ample lockers. In addition, there were to be picnic and swimming areas, a golf driving range, and just about everything that would round out a complete recreational complex. The lakes, in addition to fishing, were to supply the water for irrigation, while the drinking water would be supplied by the water department. The two courses were to be lined with palm trees that came from the Imperial and Coachella Valleys in southern California. Both courses would be illuminated for playing at night.

Perhaps the principal reason for Frank Ivaldi's involvement and enthusiasm was that he envisioned the complex as the future home training camp for the Oakland Raiders. Wayne Valley, the head man for the Raiders at that time, gave the project his blessing as did Scott Stirling, the Raiders' general manager. Their combined feeling was that the team would be training within its primary drawing area, and that the weather was excellent and superior to their present training camp in Santa Rosa. It was an ideal place. Ivaldi's plan was that he would give each interested player a piece of the action. For example, Jim Otto, all-pro center for many years, might want to invest in the skeet shoot concession or any other facility available.

Construction was proceeding at a rapid pace. I suggested to Ivaldi that he lease an additional adjacent 500-acre parcel of grazing land. He could obtain this parcel by a permit, paying the going rental and keeping the present tenant on the land with his cattle, and at a future date, include the parcel in his master lease, of course, at a much higher rental. The 500 acres were ideal for all types of recreational use and would help make the Sunol Valley complex an all-around, all-purpose recreational spa. (This was eventually accomplished.)

In April of 1968, the Sunol Valley Golf Course was opened to the public. The beautiful clubhouse building with its many banquet facilities, luxurious interiors with its Mediterranean-style decor, blossomed out in all its glory. Under Ivaldi's direction, the first annual P.G.A. Invitational Golf Tournament, a $50,000 prize affair, gave Sunol a great deal of good publicity attracting other major tournaments, particularly one with many star-studded Hollywood celebrities and superstar athletes. Sunol was now on the map; so successful and widespread was the promotion.

It was interesting to see the many San Francisco officials and politicians who turned out in droves to take advantage of this new facility on city-owned land. Many of them resorted to maps to find out where Sunol was and how to get there. This area, at least for the time being, was no longer out in left field.

The P.G.A. Golf Tournament attracted over 150 golf pros who thoroughly enjoyed this new golf course, particularly the illuminated night playing which turned out to be a first in the golf world. The project, in the early years, was a moneymaker. In the second year of operation, the San Francisco Water Department grossed over $150,000, which was big money in those days. It was nice going and the future seemed bright as time went on. Today, the city nets over $350,000 per year.

Frank Ivaldi eventually bought out his two partners. He needed to expand or in other words, to complete his vision of an all-around recreational facility that included a hotel-motel complex. He put in most of his money and some of his family's cash in order to get the project off the ground. Ivaldi brought in new partners on a limited-partner basis. The new partner was an American-Hawaiian group headed by Bob Lee. Development costs were estimated at over $3 million, which attracted national attention. The ambitious and thoroughly researched plan called for a 150-room hotel-motel complex, development of the adjacent free-flowing Alameda Creek with a dam and lake for complete aquatic recreation, hiking and equestrian trails, picnic and barbecue areas, along with the training camp for the Raiders which included a regulation football field. The project would provide a substantial increase in revenues to the city as opposed to the $4,500 yearly rental obtained from the Mendoza family for grazing their cattle. It was quite a dream and quite an undertaking. All we needed was the official approval of the city's Public Utilities Commission.

The existing 280 acres devoted to the two golf courses were to be combined with 330 acres of the adjacent hay field now held by Ivaldi's water department permit. The total complex covered 610 acres. While all these promising projects were taking place, there appeared a "fly in the ointment" in the person of James K. Carr, the new manager of the San Francisco Public Utilities empire, which controlled the activities of the city's Municipal Railway, the Hetch Hetchy Water and Power System, the San Francisco Water Department, the San Francisco International Airport, and the Bureau of Light, Heat and Power. Carr, who formerly served as undersecretary of the Interior in Washington, came to San Francisco at the request of then-Mayor Jack Shelley, formerly in Congress for many years representing San Francisco. He and Carr were long-time friends. (Mayor Shelley seemed to favor having retired army generals head up various San Francisco departments together with bureaucrats like Carr. He later did appoint five retired army generals.)

Jim Carr assumed complete command. Nothing could be done without his approval. He held considerable weight in the Democratic Party and made no bones in exercising his authority, which was tremendous. His influence over his superiors and members of the Public Utilities Commission was incredulous. He acted at will, had considerable charm, and twisted any criticism into a personal asset.

The Sunol Valley Golf Course modifications sat on Carr's desk for a long time and appeared to be hammered down with spikes, big spikes. He appeared to be lukewarm to the proposal. It seemed that Carr followed his own policy of not approving a project unless he played a big part in it. He had been of late under severe criticism by the local press for his many actions and inactions concerning the operations of city agencies.

We shall digress from the golf course project for a moment and simply relate to some of the incredible actions that generated from his overactive, fertile and scheming mind. I will dwell on a very important development which affected my few remaining years prior to my retirement.

Carr came up with an unbelievable plan. He wanted to combine the operation of the agencies under his control under three so-called czars. He wanted to build a utility empire with himself as a self-proclaimed czar. So great was his power that the five commissioners, his political superiors, sat back and did nothing. He never submitted any detailed organizational plan for public review. He proceeded on his own plan to organize all the properties under a land or property czar. Of the other two czars, it was hinted that one would have jurisdiction over the Municipal Railway and the other would control the airport. The Hetch Hetchy and water department had not yet entered into his scheming mind; only the land division covering the water department and Hetch Hetchy properties, the land holdings of the Municipal Railway, and the properties under the airport. They were to be lumped under one czar for property management. Fortunately for the city and the taxpayers, Carr did not get past the first czar as we shall see.

I was left hanging on the vine. I had eight major lease projects that were held in obeyance until the new czar for property management came on the scene. No one could figure Jim Carr out. He seemed to have a high respect for me and our meetings were always cordial. I could have liked the guy, but circumstances made this impossible.

One of Mayor Jack Shelley's latest appointments was another one of his retired army generals, Arthur Frye, who assumed the position of manager of the San Francisco Water Department and became an immediate ''boss'' General Frye wasted no time in taking command of the water department and informed his staff that they had just about joined the army. There were many discussions at the weekly staff meetings. He was smart enough, however, to realize that this was a different ballgame, so he gave in a little and changed his ways. I received a memo from General Frye that I was to put all my lease matters on hold until the arrival of the new director of property management. I strongly objected, stating that major lease modifications needed immediate solutions. While causing financial problems to our lessees, the city, in the meantime, was not getting the projected large-scale revenues that were hanging fire for a long period of time.

We had many disputes. I was trying to do my job in a business-like manner and attempting to bring in more revenue, while the General got his nose out of joint if I did not follow his army routine that he insisted should be followed. He was rather cold and merciless in his dealings with the many city lessees. He never understood that a lessee who paid a substantial rent and abided by the terms and conditions of his lease was actually a member of the city family. At least that was the way I treated my tenants, big or small.

At one time, General Frye accused me of bringing in too much business. "Who are you working for?" he asked once. I replied, "Art, I am working for the city through you as my superior, and I do not intend to be downgraded to a position of inertia." The strange thing was that the situation went on for the first three months. He really respected me because I fought for everything that I thought was in the best interest of San Francisco. As a matter of fact, everytime we had an exchange of this kind, the General calmed down and said, "Come on John. Let's go and have a cup of coffee," and we did.

The news media did not let up on Jim Carr's inertia and indecision. They were anxiously waiting for the appointment of the new director of properties, "Czar Number One." Dick Nolan, the *San Francisco Examiner's* investigative and city hall reporter, nicknamed the proposed three czars as the "Three Bears." Everyone at the city hall thought that I would be selected as Carr's new director of the Land Management Bureau, since I was credited with converting the desert into a Garden of Eden, bringing in millions of dollars from land and agricultural leases that once bore thistles and poor grazing, low-income properties. They were now high-yielding agricultural, recreational, commercial and industrial developments.

However, this was not the case. With less than two years before my retirement, and much to everyone's surprise, James Carr announced the appointment of John C. Lilly as the new property manager of the city's public utilities department. He glowingly stated that Mr. Lilly had extensive managerial experience in public administration and a broad background in government. (As time went on, it was learned that John Lilly quit as head of West Bay Rapid Transit before it went belly up.) Without taking the time to even say "hello," I found myself placed in the role of John Lilly's instructor.

After 21 years of a successful career as land manager of San Francisco's vast land holdings, I suddenly began to feel the twist of the blade being applied to me — first slowly, then forcefully and perhaps rather ruthlessly. I felt that I did not deserve the kind of treatment I was receiving at John Lilly's hand. I was prepared to accept the inevitable, but not as to what was beginning to unveil. I also realized that I had a paper pusher on my hands. He could not make up his mind even on small, unimportant matters. After I showed him where everything was (including the bathrooms), going into detail concerning the various properties, procedures, unfinished business, and answering questions about many irrelevant matters, I was about fit to be tied . . . tied up tight. It was exasperating.

The first event that took place, or I should say Lilly's first move, was the evacuation of my office to a new location — a desk and a chair in the far corner space formerly occupied by some filing cabinets. He then hired another stenographer and a clerk. "*Mama Mia,*" I said to myself. "Here comes the paperwork and God Bless the Sicilian Navy."

Jim Carr held up the Sunol Valley Golf Course lease proposal for six months, awaiting the arrival of his new "land czar." Frank Ivaldi, in the meantime, was sweating it out together with his partners. Every day of delay was costing him money, lots of money. It was also costly to the city. They were losing the anticipated revenue from this new complex. I did my best to calm them down. I said, "Frank, you are no longer dealing with me. I am the new office boy, so be patient. I am sure Mr. Lilly will act very soon." How naive we all were. John Lilly began to write up his objectives. He told me that the Ivaldi matter would have to wait. I said, "John, we have been waiting for this matter to move. We are talking about millions of dollars of future revenue to the city. It should have your top priority." To go into the many details, the voluminous reports that generated from Lilly's active, but impractical mind would require a month of Sundays to reach a decision, and that was rare.

These unbelievable and incredible developments were best explained by Dick Nolan, the able investigative reporter for the *San Francisco Examiner*, in his column of September 5, 1969.

John Lilly's major fault was his negative approach to everything that he faced. The simplest proposals became major problems to him. He always had to have "a survey, a study, and more information." Lilly was a perfectionist, not a businessman. He was never able to reach a conclusion except on insignificant matters.

My fact sheets on every lease proposal were completely ignored. I believed that he had one big item on his mind, and that was to get rid of me. I was too successful, too businesslike, not perfect enough and I did not procrastinate or vacillate. The atmosphere in my small cubbyhole, which was supposedly my office, became unbearable. This little Sicilian boy was not going to lose this fight.

Lilly told my secretary, Ann Radovan, that from now on she was to show him everything I gave her to type before she started on it. Four different secretaries were hired in the first six months while he was in office. He created an atmosphere of espionage, distrust and confusion by trying to get Rita Worthington, my former secretary who was now one of his, to spy on me. He took her out for coffee, and whatever he did or said caused her to ask Civil Service for a transfer, complaining of being overworked due to voluminous, unnecessary typing. Rita developed a nervous breakdown and came to me for help and advice. I suggested that she hang on as I was about to blow this whole unusual and uncalled-for situation wide open.

The "shizer hit the fan" when Lilly took it upon himself to go after Eli Leider, lessee of the Crystal Springs Golf Course (one of our successful golf course leases), who was a very cooperative tenant. He did not like Eli. The Leiders were eagerly awaiting a modification of their lease in which they were to invest heavily in the reconstruction of the clubhouse and other improvements which would have greatly increased the city's revenue. Lilly had been sitting on this proposed modification as he did with several other major leases. He raised the roof at the city hall after his personal inspection of the Crystal Springs Golf course premises in which his son took numerous photographs of petty items. The matter broke out in the news media. The Health Department, in the meantime, gave the Leider family a clean bill of health. The so-called violations were not of Leider's doing, but rather, it was due to the many inconveniences caused by the highway realignment project, which made a mess of a portion of the golf course.

That was enough for me. I decided that the time had come for the powers that be at city hall to decide between John Lilly and John Brucato. (At this point, I must inject that Joseph L. Alioto succeeded Jack Shelley as mayor of San Francisco.) I sent a letter to James K. Carr on October 16, 1969, which best describes my feelings at the time.

''I have reached the point where I can no longer continue under the jurisdiction of John Lilly.

The operation of my office has reached an intolerable and impossible situation with no hope in sight for relief. This man is a survey specialist. Routine matters become monumental tasks to the point where important matters are sidetracked because too much time is spent on items of lesser importance.

I inherited 42 calendar items that General Frye held back for the past year awaiting the establishment of this new bureau. Most of these are routine and should have been disposed of instead of becoming major time-consuming issues.

I have tried to tell Mr. Lilly that his concern should be on one or two big deals and permit me to dispose of all of this unfinished business.

This morning I could not contain myself any longer. After he had agreed on all the items contained in the proposed walnut orchard lease, he handed me a seven page list of questions pertaining to this lease (most of which he has in his 'package') that would take weeks to to answer.

I told him that this was another 'survey' and that I have 'had it.'

Jim, I don't want to do anything to hurt you and particularly Joe Alioto. This man is going to embarrass both of you. He just doesn't have it and I cannot continue in this fashion and jeopardize my health any longer.

I have put in too many years building up this Division. I will not sit idly by and see all this destroyed because of this man.

I have no alternative but to go all out and expose this situation unless something is done.

I have put in a call to the Mayor's office. I would strongly suggest that this matter be discussed with you and the Mayor."

I did speak to Mayor Alioto about this cancerous problem. I strongly emphasized to the mayor that there would be trouble on the Sunol Valley Golf Course matter, the walnut orchard modification, the Pleasanton Industrial Park complex, and a few others, explaining that these projects were dying on the vine and could affect his administration.

When Jim Carr heard about my contact with the mayor, he blew his proverbial top. I was quickly summoned to his office at city hall. When I arrived, General Jack Crowley was present. Carr, red in the face and screaming at the top of his lungs, accused me of insubordination. My Sicilian blood rushed to my head. I couldn't take it anymore. I didn't give a damn.

The shouting on both sides was heard all over the second floor of the usually quiet and dignified atmosphere of this seat of city government. Fortunately, General Crowley stepped in just in the nick of time. Carr was exhausted and sat down. He didn't expect the reaction that he got from this hot-blooded Sicilian. After he caught his breath, he looked at me straight in the eye and strangely remarked, "John, what the hell are we fighting about?" To this, I replied, "I really don't know. You did not give me a chance to say hello when I entered that door." General Crowley had two double scotches and handed one to each of us. The battle ended in a draw . . . or was it my victory?

Carr's attitude had completely changed. He said, "John, you win. I will take the necessary steps to relieve John Lilly of his duties. He has some vacation time coming, but as of now he is through." Then, he made a statement that was almost as incredulous as it was laughable. After the second drink, he, with a serious face, said, "John, I will promote you to Lilly's job with the title of deputy director and an increase in pay." Was that my victory? As manager of the agriculture and land division, I now became deputy manager of the PUC properties. Why not manager?

My Sicilian blood again began to come to a slow boil, but I held back and with these words, I said, "Thanks a lot Jim. You realize that I now have only six months to go before my retirement? You could have given me this job three years ago. What do I say? Better late than never?"

Jim Carr did not fire John Lilly. He gave him a chance to resign, which he did. Again, Dick Nolan, the *San Francisco Examiner's* investigative reporter, most ably stated the facts in his column of December 26, 1969. (Carr was gradually less effective by his many costly mistakes).

With time running out on me, I put together all the unfinished business that had been held up by bureaucratic inertia so that my successor would have no problems. All he had to do was just follow through. Jim Carr let loose of the Sunol Valley Golf Course proposal that was gathering dust, lots of dust, on his desk. Deputy City Attorney James Brasil was instructed to proceed in drafting a new lease that would make the Sunol Valley Golf Course complex perhaps one of the most interesting and exciting recreational developments in California, including facilities for the Oakland Raiders' professional football training camp and headquarters.

An article dated January 8, 1969 by Russ Cone, city hall reporter for the *San Francisco Examiner*, best describes this long awaited development. The fat was now really in the fire. How fast this would move remained to be seen.

My 65th birthday would be on May 12th. My final days as manager of the land division was May 31, 1970. They gave me a retirement party at Caesars Restaurant on Bay Street and another party at the prestigious Press Club on Polk Street.

The unfinished business began under the auspices of Frank Loskay, who was a right-of-way agent for the city's real estate department. It was not to be a good deal for the city. The new manager of the land division was a top right-of-way man who was an expert in his field, but as subsequent events will show, he knew little or nothing of land management and agriculture.

The story of the management of the land division was an unfortunate one for San Francisco. It was incredible how fast situations developed, starting with Faithful Performance Bonds on the city's leases. They permitted these vital and necessary bonds to expire and failed to renew them. These bonds protected the city against rental delinquency, and carried out the many and various provisions of the leases. This involved the Sunol Valley Golf Course lease, the city's valuable walnut orchard lease, and many other important leases.

The first rental delinquency affected the Sunol Gardens, involving 150 acres of choice row crop vegetable lands. Sunol Gardens was a long-time lessee and operated by George Goodale, who was also a buyer for Lady's Choice, a popular brand operating out of Oakland. Because of the nature of this type of farming, the accepted method of collecting rent was to get a crop assignment from the cannery in which Goodale had a contract. The vegetable grower had all his investment in the crop or crops he was growing. The general practice in agriculture was that the cannery loaned the farmer money and was paid when the crops were delivered to the cannery. In this respect, we received a signed crop agreement. When the vegetables were delivered to the cannery, payment was received.

Evidently, management did not understand this standard procedure. They held three meetings with Goodale. They should have listened to Al Spotorno, my former agricultural assistant, who was now working under him. Goodale had a perishable crop in the ground. It would be some time before the harvest. He eventually was forced into bankruptcy and walked out of his lease. The stupidity of all this was that management had permitted the Faithful Performance Bond to expire. If this bond had been renewed, the city's rent would have been realized. The abandoned 150 acres developed into a crop of noxious weeds that was a menace to adjacent vegetable fields. To add insult to injury, the water department was forced to disk up the land, all 150 acres that is, at a cost of $10 per acre. They had to repeat this operation two more times, bringing the cost to the city of $4,500, plus the loss of $12,750 in rent, and a vacant parcel of land - all of this because the management did not or refused to understand what a crop assignment was all about.

The valuable walnut orchard lease was lost because of their complete ignorance of agriculture and a personal dislike of the lessee. The Sunol Valley Golf Course did not get their lease modification, and time became a serious problem.

Frank Ivaldi began to fall back on his rental payments. Everything gradually began to fall apart. He was now $75,000 delinquent in his rent. The city could not enforce the collection because, again, the Faithful Performance Bond was not renewed. In the meantime, the bonding company would not renew Ivaldi's bond unless he was removed from the delinquency list. The situation became chaotic. No one seemed to know what to do.

I received a call from General Crowley, who replaced Jim Carr as manager of utilities. He suggested that we have lunch together. I liked Jack Crowley, so I accepted his invitation to meet at the Officers Club at Fort Mason. He told me "he needed me." Would I be willing to serve in an advisory capacity for him (at no pay inasmuch as I was on city pension)? My reply was, "If you make my appointment official, I would be very happy to assist you." Mayor Alioto approved this unusual action after the PUC unanimously voted my appointment in this capacity. It was brought out at the commission meeting during a discussion concerning me that during the 21 years of managing this vast land empire, my rental delinquency rate averaged four-tenths of one percent per year. Very few real estate concerns could match this figure.

My first assignment commenced on June 23, 1971. This concerned Almaden Vineyards, which filed a request to bow out of their vineyard lease covering 1,000 acres, plus the building of a winery. Almaden was not very happy with the treatment they were receiving from Frank Loskay and General Frye. They had high hopes during my regime, but all this had changed after my retirement. Jack Fisher, Almaden's vice president who had jurisdiction over the vineyard development, had already notified the city that they were through. We agreed to meet with Fisher at the Almaden headquarters in Los Gatos. General Crowley, together with Jack Christiansen, the newly appointed director of finance for the PUC, picked me up at my home. We met with Fisher at Almaden on July 10, 1971. Our meeting was enjoyable since it was a four-and-a-half hour lunch. He agreed to rescind his letter of cancellation and everyone was rather delighted, at least for the time being. The sad part was that Almaden cancelled their lease one-and-a-half years later. Fisher said he had had enough. He could no longer carry on under the present water department management. Almaden paid the penalty for cancellation and walked away. San Francisco really missed the boat as they would do many times more.

My next assignment came on July 29, 1971. I was to meet with the Sunol Valley Golf Course executives concerning their rental delinquency. They owed the city $75,000. I met with Frank Ivaldi, Bob Lee, who was head of the Hawaiian partners,

Art Pretzer, their attorney, Bob Johnson, and others. We discussed their problem in depth. Their main point was that they needed their lease modification approval, which had now been pending for over two years. They stressed the fact that this was necessary in order for them to refinance their recreational complex, making it possible to construct the hotel and make other improvements. They also needed this approval so that the Ivaldi family could recoup their original cash investment of over $2 million, which made the golf course possible.

I had no problem working out an arrangement that would be acceptable to the city. They gave me a $15,000 check payable to the San Francisco Water Department and a promissory note for $60,000. General Crowley gladly accepted their proposal and said he would turn everything over to his new director of finance, Jack Christiansen.

If the PUC management moved along on this latest development, there would not have been the Sunol Valley Golf Course scandal. I kept saying to myself, ''What the hell happened to Ivaldi's proposal?'' What did Jack Christiansen do with it? Apparently, someone (quite mysteriously) put it on the back burner and it ''got lost.'' My inquiries were to no avail. I did all I could do. They wanted me to help them and I did. It then slowly dawned on me that I was wasting my time. Did I not have 21 years of frustration, procrastination, and incompetent superiors? Why should I add more years to this? I was not trying to break any records involving patience, so I informed General Crowley that I had reached the end. I had too many other and more important matters to take care of.

In the meantime, things began to happen — big things. Frank Ivaldi's group was now trying to get someone to buy out their lease. They had to find either a new partner or group with sufficient finances, or sell out and recoup their investment. An excerpt from a feature story appearing in the *San Francisco Chronicle* dated July 13, 1975 somewhat gives you an idea of the developments.

> ''From 1967 until he retired in early 1970, John Brucato kept a sharp eye on Sunol and the city received $140,000 from the Sunol Golf Course. A substantial increase was generated the following year.
>
> But, once he was gone through retirement, jurisdiction of the property was taken over directly by the PUC.

Arthur H. Frye, Jr., manager of the City Water Department, who would normally administer the watershed lands, was instructed to leave the supervision of the Sunol Golf Course to the PUC staff. The PUC staff got excuses from Ivaldi. He made no rent payments between May 1970 to April 1971. By June 1972, there were 'rumors' of 'skimming' without recording it on their books.

By January 1974, Ivaldi's back rent was around $250,000.

At this point, Joseph Anthony Romano appeared and set up an office at the Golf Course, with a partner, Niel Nielsen, a one-time Lockheed engineer.

Romano and Nielsen said they were wealthy real estate operators, each holding over $3,000,000 worth of stock in a company, which later turned out to be unregistered. Romano gave the PUC a check for $306,000 to clinch the lease agreement. The check, however, turned out to be pure rubber. It bounced.''

After a series of legal and financial maneuvers, it came out that Romano was a well-known gangster from Buffalo, New York, with a long police record. He, in the meantime, invested over $200,000 for improvements in the clubhouse, including new furnishings, rugs, and many other additions. These improvements have been the only upgrading to this beautiful clubhouse building to date (March 1985). Romano was now out $200,000. Ivaldi's lease was restored to him by the PUC. The commission credited the $200,000 spent to Ivaldi's debt of $350,000.

The county grand jury, after hearing 40 witnesses, recommended that the three top PUC officials be fired. (This never came about.) The Sunol Valley Golf Course scandal made major headlines in the news media for over two years.

A Honolulu-based group headed by Stephen Bartholomew handed Jack Christiansen a certified check for $100,000 as a down payment, hoping to get the scandal-ridden golf course lease. Welton Flynn, president of the PUC, complained that Christiansen had not given the commission all the facts involved. Romano seemed to be the most unconcerned individual in this whole scenario. He retained Jack Fahey, a well-known Bay Area attorney. For some unknown reason, Romano seemed to be enjoying the spotlight during the long grand jury hearings. The $100,000 check was returned to Stephen Bartholomew. This deal could have saved the golf course inasmuch as the Hawaiian group was well-financed and had considerable experience in recreation. Romano's attitude concerning his questionable background was publicly stated at a press conference. He said, "I paid my debt to society and my past is behind me." I don't believe he received much sympathy for this statement.

It is well to note Dick Nolan's well-read column in the *San Francisco Examiner* dated September 23, 1974 in summarizing this unbelievable city operation. He related how the city started off with a moneymaker and wound up with a big mess on its hands, attributed primarily to City Hall's ineptitude and bungling, and then asking, "What happened to the money?" He quoted Tony Romano, who, at one time, became the dubious possessor of the golf course lease — "This is a gold mine." Nolan then goes on to cite the city's failure to have the Faithful Performance Bond renewed, and why the rent was permitted to lapse. Continuing his line of questioning, the unanswerable one remained as to why the highly qualified and financially capable Japanese Hawaiian group was brushed aside in order to save Ivaldi's lease, and why Romano, with his bouncing checks, was permitted to continue the operation of this valuable golf course lease.

My part in these incredible happenings began on February 6, 1975 when I appeared before Thomas E. Kotoske, head of the U.S. Department of Justice's "Strike Force," who was investigating the golf course scandal. I supplied him and the Federal Criminal Grand Jury with all my records. They were amazed and thoroughly surprised that after my retirement, leaving what was a most successful and profitable city operation, that such a thing could happen. I was highly complimented by the Federal Grand Jury foreman and Thomas Kotoske.

I appeared before the San Francisco County Grand Jury and received a similar reaction. They were also starting an investigation of the city's walnut orchard. They could not understand how under my supervision the city was receiving from $70,000 to $80,000 a year on a percentage basis, while management could only realize $2,000 to $8,000 a year. This interesting narration is covered in another chapter concerning "The Million Dollar Walnut Orchard."

I always remained on good terms with General Crowley. In fact, some time before the golf course scandal came to an end (or did it?), he asked if I could find a good reliable, well-financed prospective lessee. I informed him that I would try to oblige.

Since my retirement, I became a land-use consultant, which exposed me to a large number of land brokers who could possibly find some good reliable prospects. I sent a number of dependable groups to see Crowley and also reactivated the Bartholomew group. We had several meetings with him, including James Morita, a Japanese Hawaiian who headed up the City Bank of Honolulu, and Robert Selway, who was president of Selco International, a highly respected international financing and development group. These people were ready to proceed with hard cash. They would buy out Ivaldi's interest and enter into a new lease arrangement with the city. Crowley was impressed, asked for and received a $100,000 certified check as good faith.

James Brasil, deputy city attorney, who worked with me in preparation of my various leases during the last ten years of my city servitude, was instructed to prepare a lease form. While the city had restored Ivaldi's lease to him, he still owed a substantial sum. They had cancelled Romano's lease and returned it to Ivaldi. There was a deadline for Ivaldi to bring his indebtedness to date — February 4th. He was vacationing in Hawaii at the time. Jack Christiansen kept after him to come up with the cash. Christiansen continued to extend the deadline. Crowley then informed him that there would be no further delays. "We have Bartholomew's certified check for $100,000. We can't keep them waiting much longer." When Ivaldi, through Christiansen, learned that this group with ready cash was about to take over his leasehold, he took the first plane out of Honolulu and presented Christiansen with an unknown amount upon his arrival in San Francisco. Ivaldi was now in, the Hawaiian group out.

Bartholomew was in the city attorney's office with James Morita cooling their heels for several hours, waiting for Jack Christiansen to complete the lease terms. Suddenly, a messenger appeared and returned the $100,000 certified check to an astonished Morita. They immediately tried to reach Crowley or Christiansen on the telephone. "They were not available" was the response. If you ever saw an angrier group of businessmen in action, they really gave vent to their feelings.

Out loud they shouted, "We were used. We have not been properly treated." The two men were amazed at the shabby treatment at the hands of these San Francisco public officials.

James Morita, who was a highly respected Japanese American businessman and banker, and had purposely flown out from Honolulu to close this deal, made a simple matter-of-fact statement in front of an array of newspaper reporters: "I would be reluctant to have any further dealings with the city of San Francisco."

A turnabout occurred in 1986. Ivaldi did improve the golf course and the banquet facilities. The income to the city also showed improvement.

There were many attempts to link Joseph Alioto while he was mayor to Sunol Valley. He was not the mayor at the time and did not hand the lease over to Ivaldi as had been narrated in this chapter. The Sunol Golf Course was awarded to the highest and most responsible bidder. In this respect, I must relate a very interesting event that took place before my retirement in 1970. It was one of many attempts by so-called "investigative" reporters and writers who were trying to find something on Mayor Joseph L. Alioto and his possible connections with the underworld, presumably because of his Sicilian extraction.

A damaging story appeared in *Look Magazine* written by two investigative reporters, Brisson and Carlson. (Brisson was actress Rosalind Russell's son.) It attacked Mayor Alioto and his alleged acquaintance with a certain underworld character, centering on a meeting held at the Nut Tree Restaurant near Vacaville. The story was highly volatile and stated that Mayor Alioto had mafia or underworld connections. He sued *Look Magazine* and after a long period of time was completely vindicated to the point that the publication eventually went bankrupt and out of business.

One day, I received a telephone call from Brisson saying that he was coming to my office with Carlson. His tone and manner were rather crude and quite commanding. I told him that he would have to make an appointment for the next day as I was tied up in an all-day meeting. He would not say what his purpose was in seeing me. When he realized he could not barge in on me at his pleasure, he became offensive and concluded that he would report me to the mayor, for after all, he was a public servant and a citizen has the right to inspect public records, etc. While keeping my cool and taking this unnecessary abuse, I said to him, "When you speak to the mayor, make sure you spell my name right." With this, he angrily hung up.

Two hours later, I received a telephone call from John DeLuca, the mayor's executive secretary. He said, "What did you do to that guy?" Then he laughed and said that I did the right thing. Brisson apologized to him for his brusque manners. DeLuca said that Brisson would be calling me for an appointment. At 4:30 p.m., he telephoned and in a rather subdued voice requested an appointment for 9 a.m. the next day. I replied by saying that I looked forward to meeting with both him and Carlson.

After introducing themselves (as though I didn't know who they were), they asked permission to look over the lease files. I asked if I could assist them, but they wanted to look through the files on their own. This was an improper procedure, but I decided to give them all the rope they wanted. They worked from 9:15 a.m. straight through the lunch hour. At about 3 p.m., I decided to intercede. I guess they were somewhat relieved when I offered my assistance as they seemed rather exhausted. I asked them what they were looking for. They finally broke down and said, "We want to know how Joe Alioto gave Santa Clara Sand and Gravel Company their lease and what conditions were made." I almost broke out in laughter and proceeded to pull out the entire file showing them that Alioto did not "give" Santa Clara Sand and Gravel Company anything at all as he was not mayor at the time. I then showed Brisson and Carlson the bid form that was mailed out to everyone who was interested in mining gravel on this public property. Santa Clara Sand and Gravel Company was the highest responsible bidder.

I continued explaining to the two men that my next procedure was to secure water department management and the city attorney's approval before placing the bid on the Public Utilities Commission's weekly calendar for final approval. You never saw two more frustrated individuals when they found out that they were on a wild goose chase. As they were getting ready to leave my office, I said, "You could have saved yourselves a lot of time if you had just told me what you were looking for in the first place." The two investigative reporters walked away, never looked back, and didn't even say goodbye.

Chapter 12

The Million Dollar Walnut Orchard

Who would ever think of a city such as San Francisco owning and operating a walnut orchard?

When San Francisco purchased the Spring Valley Water Company in 1930, they also inherited 100 acres of choice high-producing walnut trees in Alameda County. The orchard is situated over the Sunol filter galleries, which is a water-collecting underground basin contributing approximately five million gallons of pure crystal water daily into the Sunol Temple area, and eventually into the water system.

The main varieties of walnuts in this original orchard were the popular Franquettes, Mayettes, and Payne. This beautiful, mature orchard became part of my many responsibilities. I was immediately involved in a cumbersome civil service system that limited the farmer-like operation of the orchard. There were three civil service employees, all capable and experienced farmers. The problem was our bureaucratic set-up.

A farmer operating an orchard is sometimes forced to work late through the night and weekends when necessary. Under civil service regulations, our employees were limited to an 8 to 5 day. In other words, if they were irrigating and it was 5 p.m. on a Friday, the irrigation would stop and pick up on Monday at 8 a.m. This was applied to spraying, harvesting or any one of the many operations necessary or where weather, maturity, and other factors in which nature had to be served. We operated under this cumbersome procedure until 1959 when we were finally permitted to lease out the orchard to a capable and well-qualified operator.

The beautiful Sunol Valley contained a very rich

agricultural soil. We leased out many and various parcels for vegetable and nursery crops, strawberries, tree farms, and just about everything that could possibly be grown, including lots of hay and grain. The city received a good income in this regard as did the lessee.

We operated our own dehydrator, which consisted of a large corrugated-type building with a complete receiving, processing (drying and grading), and storage facility. We called it the "Nut House."

The harvesting, which began in early October, was a time of feverish activity and generally lasted until early November, depending on the season. We belonged to the Walnut Growers Association, a cooperative of walnut growers, and delivered our entire crop to its processing plant in Walnut Creek, and later to the main headquarters in Stockton. (Walnut Creek in the 1950s was a town of 1,800 people.)

We never had to be concerned about the sale of the walnuts as the association took care of that. We received partial payments until about April when final payments on the delivered crop were made. The city's Sunol walnuts were considered top quality. The association's score sheet year after year showed that our walnuts received the highest price based on the color of the walnut meat, the size, and the freedom from insect or bacterial damage. One year, the association's monthly bulletin (July 1956) headlined the city's orchard as "The Million Dollar Walnut Orchard."

As a result of good cultural management, it was visited by students from the many agricultural institutions and people from many parts of the world interested in the culture of walnuts. In other words, it was a showplace that we took a great deal of pride in.

In 1948, I welcomed a large-scale strawberry grower from San Jose into the city family. Joe Kiser wanted to lease 40 acres of land for growing strawberries. It involved about ten Japanese families. Each family would tend to his own plot of six acres. Strawberry growing is what you call "intensified farming." A family could live on six acres. At that time (1950s), row crop farming land was renting for $80 per acre and considered a good, reasonable price. Because of the intensity of the crop and the availability of plentiful water, we agreed on a negotiated rental of $100 to $150 per acre. Kiser was well-satisfied as was the city.

The area desired by Joe Kiser was a 40-acre parcel adjacent

to the city's walnut orchard. The strawberry varieties were principally Tioga and Lassen. They were high-producing berries recently developed at the University of California, Davis. We called them the "educated strawberries."

I had been planning to request a sum of money from the city to plant this particular 40-acre plot to walnuts. I needed about $15,000 to buy the necessary trees and cover the cost of planting the walnuts. We made a most unusual deal with Kiser. We would select the trees and he would buy them, plant them under our supervision, and take care of the walnut trees for five years, the life of his strawberry lease. Under this arrangement, he would grow the strawberries between the rows and pay us a nominal rent of $80 per acre. The trees, being small at planting, would become sizable after the fifth year. At that point, we would take over. In this fashion, we got our new orchard of 40 acres, Joe Kiser raised some profitable strawberries, and the Japanese growers made a good living. We planted Franquettes, Hartleys, and some Payne varieties, and we did not have to go to the city for a $15,000 to $20,000 appropriation.

I followed the same procedure in 1956 when we decided to plant another 60 acres of walnuts. My decision was based on the fact that walnuts were a profitable crop to the city. It was a clean operation and it also enhanced the beauty of this most beautiful Sunol Valley. In this regard, I would say that while the water department was collecting 5,000,000 gallons of water from below the surface of the Sunol filter galleries, my department was collecting a handsome revenue above the surface from the walnut crop. How could we lose? We had it both ways — from below and from above.

On another occasion, I was dealing with a vegetable grower, Bill Monahan, a young and handsome Irishman. He was a specialist who raised cucumbers for cucumber pickles and was under contract with Lady's Choice, a well-known processor located in Oakland. His main crop was kosher pickles. We joked a bit with Monahan. "Who ever heard of an Irishman raising kosher pickles?" We were told that Lady's Choice was considering a new label, "Monahan's Kosher Pickles."

Here, I saved the city another $20,000 (pre-inflation) which would pay for the cost of trees to plant the 60 acres. Monahan received a five-year lease. He would pay a nominal rental, grow the cucumbers between the newly planted rows of trees, and care for the trees under our supervision until the sixth year when we would take over. Again, we got the best of the deal.

Bill Monahan eventually went down to Mexico to farm, became a successful grower, married a cute Mexican girl, and as I learned many years later, he had six of the most beautiful dark-eyed children and was expecting the seventh.

By 1985, we had an unveiling of a huge, colorful redwood sign stating the history of the walnut orchard since its acquisition from Spring Valley Water Company.

Wayne Haas was the longtime manager of the Walnut Creek receiving plant for the Walnut Growers Association. He and Grant Burton, a large-scale walnut grower in the Danville area and a director of the Walnut Growers Association, were frequent visitors to our orchard in Sunol. Another prominent visitor was Gene Serr from the University of California, Davis, who was one of the world's best known experts on walnuts. We carried on a series of mutual experiments in the orchard, particularly in the control of walnut insect pests and diseases. Haas, Burton, Serr and I became fast friends. We met often to discuss mutual orchard problems.

I was frequently featured at the annual association meeting in Walnut Creek. One of the major problems in a walnut orchard is the control of aphids. Let the aphids go uncontrolled and the orchard would not survive. The latest development in the control of aphids was the strong pesticides that came into use. While they controlled the aphids completely, they also killed the beneficial insects that kept the harmful ones under control. These new, powerful insecticides upset the balance of nature.

We stuck to our usual applications of nicotine sulfate, a spray that controlled the aphids but did not harm the beneficial lady beetles. However, one day while I was discussing some problems with one of my Filipino farmers at the Farmers Market, he told me about a simple way of controlling these pesky aphids. He suggested the biological method of fighting nature with nature. The following week, he presented me with a gallon jar of live lady beetles. I turned them loose in a corner of the walnut orchard just as the aphids were beginning to emerge.

The following year, I noted the lack of aphids in my experimental corner of the orchard. I put in a requisition to buy seven gallons of lady beetles (coccinellidea) at $8 a gallon. The head of the city's purchasing department scratched his head and came over to see me. He said, ''John, what the hell is this? I have been the city purchaser for 13 years. I've never heard of this before." With sort of a hidden smile, I replied that if he'd never heard of anything like this before, there was always the first time. We got the beetles.

In two years, the aphids disappeared. We stopped spraying the orchard, saving about $6,000 a year. About every two years, I added several gallons more of lady beetles to invigorate our biological achievement.

I made a presentation on this unusual procedure at one of our annual meetings. I don't know how many growers adopted the lady beetles, but it was very well-received.

We were constantly fighting nature as farmers. There was an invasion of grasshoppers advancing on a wide front from the Livermore Valley. It must be understood that when grasshoppers attack, they destroy everything in sight. I was also thinking of the hundreds of acres of strawberries, peas, and other luscious crops raised by our tenants. It was war. What was I to do? As always, you go to the experts . . . but who were my experts? Of course, after much deliberation, I said, "My farmers at the Farmers Market." Here were a number of seasoned veterans who were constantly at war with nature's predators.

I called a meeting one Saturday morning involving eight of my close farmer friends. It was a council of war. The grasshoppers were attacking and we had to delay their advance long enough so that we could counterattack. This was the advice I received from my experts.

The situation at Sunol was well covered by the news media. There were headlines and concern. We were not alone. We had many neighbors who were in the path of the hungry grasshoppers. Planes with spray material stood by ready for the signal to attack. Turkeys by the hundreds became involved. They came up from the San Joaquin Valley, courtesy of two of my big turkey grower friends. Turkeys love grasshoppers. We called them our secret weapon. We systematically burned fields (about 15 acres) in the path of their advance. Then, nature came to our assistance. We had a cool spell. This slowed the grasshoppers' advance. In the meantime, the planes took off and sprayed wherever there was a heavy concentration.

It seemed that the unexpected was no longer a surprise. Thousands of blackbirds appeared from nowhere and furthering this unbelievable situation, hundreds of seagulls — yes, seagulls — came in to assist the blackbirds, the burning, the spray planes, and the turkeys. It was quite a battle and we emerged victorious.

Another unusual situation occurred in the walnut orchard. We found that the crows really enjoyed our choice walnuts. They were really smart. We observed the crows picking up a walnut (during the harvest season), flying a short way to one of our paved roads, dropping the walnut on the road, coming down to eat the meat from the broken shell, and returning for the next one. We couldn't complain about this trivial loss, although the crows numbered into the hundreds. They earned whatever they ate. The crows were our allies. They devoured many of the slugs and snails that could have been a serious problem. This was another way in which we were able to exercise biological control — nature against nature.

Problems with our civil service employees and the cumbersome bureaucratic procedures in the operation of a walnut orchard became so great that I decided the time had come to lease the orchard to a responsible, qualified and financially capable operator. We advertised for public bids in 1959, and our Public Utilities Commission awarded the lease to Bankhead and Sons.

Armand Bankhead had been our walnut-harvesting contractor for many years. He made sizable improvements to our dehydrator, brought in new equipment, and for the first season which ended in 1960, performed a complete mechanical harvesting operation for the first time on our crop. No more handpicking with stoop labor.

The irrigation system was improved, and Bankhead and his two capable sons began a long and satisfying partnership with the city. We received 52 percent of the delivered crop while he received 48 percent. We had to increase the capacity of the dehydrator inasmuch as the new 40-acre and 60-acre orchards were coming into full bearing. We had to double the capacity as we now had 200 acres of walnuts. Again, we went through another strange, bureaucratic procedure when I had to get approval from the finance committee of our Board of Supervisors. My requisition was for $50,000. There would be no problem under ordinary procedure; however, it turned out that this was not an ordinary procedure.

The finance committee was running late. They were going to take a supper break and return to the chambers of the city hall at 8 p.m. Supervisor Dan Gallagher was chairman of the finance committee. Ordinarily, he was a level-headed, seasoned, and much-respected supervisor. While Gallagher and his committee took their supper break, we all surmised that perhaps a few too many "snorts" had been imbibed by the respected supervisor.

There were ten heads of various city departments waiting to make their presentations. At this point, Gallagher decided that only half of whatever would be requested would be approved. The chief of police was sitting next to me. He needed $2,000 to purchase a new horse for the Golden Gate Park detail. Gallagher and his committee reviewed the request, banged the gavel and said, "Chief, you will get half the amount this year. Come back next year." The chief shook his head, sat down, and seemed a bit bewildered. Gallagher noted that Chief Ahearn had not left his seat. He looked at him and said, "Chief, do you have something else on your mind? What is the problem?" To this came an honest reply. "Supervisor Gallagher, I am trying to figure out which half of the horse I am going to buy?" Chief Frank Ahearn got his $2,000 for the whole horse. My item for $50,000 was cut in half. "Come back next year, John, and pick up the rest of it."

Bankhead did an outstanding job. He did everything in a farmer-like manner. The orchard prospered, and both the landlord and lessee made money. We had what was widely known as a "model orchard." At times, it resembled a classroom, judging from the many college and agricultural school students who made special field trips to Sunol. Bankhead planted an additional 37 acres of walnuts at his own expense.

I had to prepare a program for the gradual removal and replanting of the original 100-acre orchard planted by Spring Valley. In 1967, this orchard was 66 years old and would soon begin to show its age. I developed a gradual removal and replacement program to be done in stages of seven to ten acres a year. In the meantime, I was running out of time. I was retiring in less than two years. My assistant, Al Spotorno, was quite capable of carrying out this program when my successor would take over the jurisdiction of the orchard.

My successor turned out to be Frank Loskay. While he was a good right-of-way agent in the city's real estate department, he certainly was inexperienced in agriculture, in particular, a walnut orchard of 200 acres. The chain of events that took place after my retirement makes an unbelievable and incredible chapter.

Frank Loskay lost no time in creating obstacles to Bankhead's successful orchard operations. For some strange and unknown reason, he developed a personal dislike to Bankhead and his two very capable sons. There were bad feelings between them. The personal angle should have never entered into this worsening situation. Evidently, Loskay, completely ignorant in the operation of a walnut orchard, wanted an overall change.

The unforgivable error committed by Loskay was in permitting Bankhead's Faithful Performance Bond to expire. He took no steps in having it renewed. None of his superiors seemed to be aware of this matter, which left the city completely unprotected in the enforcement of the lease provisions. Bankhead had reached the point of utter discouragement. He finally decided that under the circumstances, he wanted out. His lease was officially cancelled as of March 1, 1976. To put it rather mildly, Loskay kicked the Bankheads out.

Six months passed by with absolutely no care for this beautiful model orchard. No one knew what was on Loskay's mind. His superiors did not seem to be concerned. What an incredible situation. The 37 acres of new walnut orchard trees planted by Bankhead at his own expense of over $36,000 were left unattended. The trees eventually perished.

Frank Loskay came up with a new lessee. His name was Louis Mangini, a grower and operator of the Mt. Diablo orchards near Brentwood in Contra Costa County. He was primarily a processor who dried walnuts on a commercial basis in his huge dehydrator for other growers at a fee. He was a very clever operator; that is, he made his own deal with the inexperienced Loskay. He realized that Loskay knew almost nothing about a walnut orchard, and that the orchard needed immediate attention.

The most unheard of and perhaps the most ridiculous terms were accepted by Loskay. The city was getting 52 percent of the crop from Bankhead. We had in process before I retired a new arrangement where Bankhead would have 60 percent and the city, 40 percent, because of his investment which included new farming equipment and his satisfatory performance. The new deal gave the city a measly ten percent for the first four years, going to 20 percent for the next six years.

The lease did not include the 37 acres planted by Bankhead. Mangini convinced Loskay that he should not include this acreage because it was not yet in production. This, of course, was the death sentence to this young, promising orchard.

Eventually, the city pulled out the dying neglected trees and lost a future-producing orchard. The criminality of the new arrangement did not include the necessary Faithful Performance Bond, which left the city absolutely helpless. Mangini was also not required to use the city's walnut dehydrator. This gave him complete control of the crop. He would harvest it directly from the field into his trucks where they were delivered to his own dehydrator in Brentwood, and dried and mixed with other nuts from other growers. No one had the unusual quality of the Sunol walnuts.

The city was at the mercy of Mangini. There was absolutely no way of keeping track of what left the orchard. When we operated the dehydrator during Bankhead's tenure, we had complete control. The walnuts were delivered to the dehydrator to be dried, and after the process was completed, they would be loaded on Bankhead's truck and weighed by a certified weighmaster, then delivered to the Walnut Growers Association.

At all times, we knew exactly what we had. It was the only business-like way to go. We were handling taxpayers' money and were responsible to see that the city received their just share. How Loskay convinced the managers of the water department, and the five members of the PUC that the city had a good deal with Mangini was beyond belief.

During the ten-year period of Mangini's lease, he made a lot of money. The city did not. He operated the orchard in a very unfarmer-like manner and did very little, except to harvest the crop. The only time the soil was worked over was prior to the harvest, so that when the nuts would drop, the mechanical harvesting machine could gather in the walnuts. He did very little pruning or spraying. Most of the time, the ground was overgrown with weeds. In spite of this gross neglect, Mangini harvested record crops year after year. He was that lucky.

The price of walnuts went to recordbreaking highs. There was a worldwide demand for California walnuts, and Mangini was literally "sitting in the saddle." No one knew how many tons of walnuts he harvested or how the reputed high-quality walnuts from the city's orchard were graded. Mangini did the grading at his home ranch where he also handled large quantities of walnuts from the growers in the Brentwood area. These were not noted for good quality. No one ever inspected the grading process just to see that the city's high-quality walnuts were not mixed with the Brentwood crop.

At the end of the season, Mangini sent the water department his statement with a check for the city's share. It read: "I received so much for the crop, I am enclosing the city's share." Great guns and little fishes . . . lots of little fishes. Is this the way to handle public property when a sloppy operator has full control? How did he ever get away with it? No Faithful Performance Bond, no supervision of his operations, and no control of the quantity harvested or graded. It seems that everyone knew that Mangini was taking the city for a ride.

Disease began to appear in the orchard, particularly blackline, which eventually kills the tree. A good farmer would immediately remove the infected tree, fumigate the soil, and replant with a healthy tree. The city should have stepped in to save the orchard. Where was management? No one seemed to understand or care.

With the bumper crops and high price of walnuts, the city's pitiful share was from $6,000 to $9,000 a year. Rumors circulated in the walnut world that Mangini was making a fortune from the city's walnut orchard. He surely had a sweetheart deal.

On April 29, 1975, Dick Nolan summarized the walnut orchard fiasco in his column entitled, "How Not to Farm." He pointed out how the city had an ideal lease arrangement with Bankhead and Sons, which performed in a very farmerlike manner, improving the orchard and giving the city a substantial return on its investment. He went on to describe how under the city's bureaucratic and unbusiness-like management, there was no Faithful Performance Bond to protect the city's interest and a complete lack of supervision, which resulted in a pitiful amount returned to the city as the "city's share." It was unheard of that the new lessee, Mangini Farms from Brentwood, actually received his lease without benefit of public bidding.

Robert Hollis, who wrote in the *San Francisco Chronicle* on September 15, 1974, wondered how the city received only $7,000 on a record crop of 124 tons. He further stated, "The decidedly less lucrative lease came to light yesterday during the financially ailing Sunol Golf Course investigations. The city was receiving $80,000 and more a year under the Bankhead lease, which was under strict control by previous management, and evidently under this new lease, the city not only lost control because there were no controlling instruments, but lost a pot of money besides."

During the closing days of the Sunol Golf Course Grand Jury investigation, I was called to testify before the county Grand Jury regarding the walnut orchard mismanagement investigation which had just started. They were baffled and wondered how, during my administration, the city did quite well financially and otherwise. Their problem was to decipher how the city got so little now ($7,000 a year) and had done so well before. They were moving fast towards indictments, but unfortunately for the city, the Grand Jury's term ended before they could complete the investigation. The succeeding Grand Jury did not follow through. They claimed it was too much of a "hot potato." Like the Sunol Valley Golf Course scandal, management and the city swept everything under the rug.

Mangini finished out his ten-year lease. In the meantime, the trees kept dying off in the 40-acre and 60-acre parcels. The main 100 acre parcel planted by Spring Valley in 1910 was in really bad shape. My plan for gradual removal of these old trees and subsequent replanting was never followed through. They had reached the stage of removal.

Mangini's lease expired on December 31, 1981. Prior to this expiration, there were others — many well-qualified, reliable and capable walnut growers — who became interested in the orchard, but no one in city government really gave a damn. There was no more beautiful and practical use of this portion of the Sunol Valley, which was then a thriving, picturesque and colorful walnut orchard. The city, however, leased the orchard to Armanino Farms. They would receive a high rental from the specialized chives and herb crops that Armanino was capable of producing.

I can never forget what Armanino did when they removed the old walnut trees on the original 100 acres planted by Spring Valley. If they were required to replace the trees, I could then forgive the mortal sin they committed. Eventually, Armanino took over the 40 acre orchard. The trees were also pulled out, replanted by chives, thyme, parsley, and other specialty crops. The city received a high rental, but the walnut trees were gone forever.

The fate of the remaining 60 acres, which I also planted in 1956, was now in the hands of a large-scale nursery grower. This orchard, too, was dying from blackline infection and the many large gopher holes. It was a sad, sad situation. There was no salvation unless an experienced operator came in immediately. The dying trees would have to be removed, the land had to be fumigated and replaced with new, healthy trees.

Spring Valley Water Company had lots of foresight. They knew how to make money and did. They also had an eye for beauty and recognized the fact that something beautiful had to tie in with the Sunol Water Temple. Their selection was a 100 acre walnut orchard. The fame of this productive beauty spot went far and wide. At the time, there were men of vision. I can't say the same for management that succeeded me.

Thus, ends the saga of San Francisco's Million Dollar Walnut Orchard. With a tear in my eye and sadness in my heart, I can only say, ''What a way to die!''

Epitaph:

In the peace of my garden, I received a telephone call. It was a sad, bitter, but factual call from one of my close friends living in Sunol. In short, I was told that the bulldozers had just completed the total eradication of the remaining 60 acres of walnut trees. I did not shed a tear, perhaps I was expecting this fateful moment. I was, however, overcome with a deep feeling of anger, unprecedented in my long and unusual life. It was an anger of bitterness that finally had to come. ''My walnut orchard, my million dollar walnut orchard was gone, gone forever.''

When I think of the thousands of visitors and particularly, groups of students that I entertained from all over the world during my 21 years that I managed this horticultural gem, who came to see this model of walnut orchards, labeled by the Walnut Growers Association as ''San Francisco's Million Dollar Walnut Orchard — I say with this unusual bitterness and sadness in my heart — ''Where were the environmentalists, the Sierra Club, the nature lovers and most of all the bureaucrats at the city hall, the water department management, where were they? And I say as loud as I can humanly say — ''Shame on you San Francisco, shame, shame, shame! ! ! !

Chapter 13

The Pleasanton Industrial Park Fiasco

One of the most beautiful residential areas in California is the city of Pleasanton. It was not a large community back in the 1960s and early 1970s. Now, it is a thriving, fast-growing city with industrial parks and commercial shopping centers. It, too, had growing pains like all cities which moved too rapidly.

Pleasanton was not always in this situation. Not too long ago, the biggest attraction in Alameda County was the county fairgrounds. For a short period of ten days or so, the city was packed with fair-goers, particularly those attending the ever-popular horse races, which was the main attraction and big moneymaker. When the fairgrounds closed at the end of this short season, they "rolled in the sidewalks" and everything went back to a quiet, easygoing farming community. If you lived on a higher level, you belonged to the prestigious Castlewood Country Club outside of the city limits.

The San Francisco Water Department owned a 520 acre parcel across the way from the fairgrounds along Bernal Avenue. There were a number of high-producing water wells on the land, which were part of the Spring Valley Water Company's holdings acquired by San Francisco in 1930. When I assumed management of the water department properties, Victor Lund of Pleasanton was the principal lessee.

Victor Lund raised a lot of hay from which the city received 25 percent of the crop. (Most leases ran for five years.) Along came the well-to-do nurserymen, Jackson and Perkins, who specialized in roses. They succeeded Lund and paid the city three times more than the hay lease. They planted the entire 520 acres in a field of roses of all colors. It was the most picturesque sight in the Livermore Valley.

We had a wonderful and profitable relationship for many years. They were a great asset to the city of San Francisco and to Pleasanton. At the expiration of their lease, Jackson and Perkins decided to move to Arizona primarily because of the labor problem. Due to the availability of cheap Mexican labor in Arizona, which was close to the Mexican border, it was not difficult to understand their position. They employed a lot of hand labor, which was costly and not available in the Pleasanton area.

The scene changed from hay to roses, and now to row crop tomatoes. Joe Seitz and his brother were one of the largest tomato growers in the area. They specialized in tomatoes for the canneries. Their lease agreement paid a higher rental to the city than the roses. The Seitz brothers farmed completely mechanical, but nevertheless, they employed many farm laborers. When their lease expired, they took off for Mexico to become tomato growers below the border.

We had no problem leasing the land. Not only was the soil deep and rich, but the well field supplied the irrigation water. (The unused wells were held in reserve in the event of an emergency drought or shortage of water.) There followed a succession of vegetable truck farmers. The difference now was that I held the leases down to short terms of two or three years. My reasoning was that I was thinking of a possible industrial park complex. Two railroads, the Southern Pacific and Western Pacific, ran parallel to our eastern boundary. Also, a freeway, Route 680, was being constructed, dividing our property where one-third would be east and two-thirds would be west of the freeway.

I convinced our water department management and the Public Utilities Commission that a study of the property together with the city of Pleasanton should take place as soon as possible because of changing times. The PUC authorized this comprehensive study, which included one of our city attorneys, our engineering staff, the planning department, and myself. Pleasanton supplied its city manager, attorney, planner, and a member of the city council. We met often during a one-year period and came up with a practical and attractive plan that received approval of the two communities. Now that we had a damn good plan, with some well-orchestrated publicity we attracted some very interesting proposals. The plan became effective June of 1961.

Eastman Kodak Company fell in love with the proposed park. There developed a shuttle of top Kodak officials from the headquarters in Rochester, New York, to Pleasanton and San Francisco. They required only 30 acres and proposed a long-term prepaid lease of $1,300,000 in cash. I would have been very happy to have Kodak come in for less. They were the catalysts and would have attracted many others of the same high-class caliber.

It looked promising. We were now ready to move along in developing this most interesting property, the Pleasanton Industrial Park. Then, there was the usual bureaucratic roadblock. It was our beloved manager of utilities, James K. Carr. He couldn't make up his mind and always hired experts, advisors or consultants at a great cost to the city. He was unbelievable the way he ran his public utilities empire.

Kodak, in this long interim, was being wined and dined by other nearby developing industrial parks. At the height of their desperation, they finally served notice on Jim Carr that they couldn't wait any longer. They went to San Ramon. What a letdown. What a tragedy. This scenario was repeated time and time again.

Something big and exciting happened. I received a telephone call from Robert Nahas, a prominent land developer in the East Bay who was responsible for the emergence of Oakland's downtown development. He was also a prime mover and later, head of the Oakland Coliseum complex. Bob and I became good friends, inasmuch as he was also a director of the East Bay Municipal Water District, our counterpart there. (He was a director of the Oakland Coliseum at the same I was a director of the Cow Palace. We managed to resolve our differences in scheduling events.)

It so happened that Nahas and his group had just purchased a 240-acre site along Bernal Avenue, across from our 520-acre industrial park parcel. The purchaser was the Great Southwest Corporation of Dallas, Texas. This company had developed one of the nation's largest planned industrial park complexes combining industrial and recreational use in Texas. It is today known as the Six Flags Over Texas, a family entertainment center which ranks on a par with Disneyland. They also developed a similar attraction in Georgia, the Six Flags Over Georgia.

Together with Nahas, we discussed and developed a proposal that was submitted to the Public Utilities Commission.

The Great Southwest Corporation planned to invest $20 million for the Disneyland-type development on the 240 acres across Bernal Avenue that they just purchased. They were definitely interested in a long-term lease on our 520-acre parcel on an "as is" basis for an industrial park. The detailed proposal submitted by Nahas to James Carr sat on his desk for a month.

Nahas, growing impatient, decided that perhaps it would be best to charter a plane and invite the officials of San Francisco and Pleasanton to Dallas in order to inspect their outstanding development and to give them an idea of what could be done on the city's property. We then received a letter from Angus G. Wynne, Sr., president of Great Southwest. Carr informed us through James Finn, his secretary, that he was ill and could not make the trip to Dallas. General Frye, manager of the water department, had a similar excuse. In the final analysis, I was told to represent the city.

There were five in the San Francisco contingent and 20 from Pleasanton, including its mayor and members of the city council. The excursion took place on Saturday, October 5, 1968. We left Pleasanton at 6:30 a.m. and returned at 10 p.m. It was a most exciting, enlightening and informative trip. Too bad the "ill" city officials missed the boat.

The *Pleasanton Times* headlined the development mentioning the proposed $40 million fun center and industrial park project. The city of Pleasanton went wild with enthusiasm. They now looked to their friend and neighbor, San Francisco, to get going.

San Francisco stood ready to make millions of dollars from this well-financed project in which the city would receive a handsome percentage of the gross income. I supposed Pleasanton, like Sunol, was also out in left field so to speak. Perhaps we would need another Sunol Valley Golf Course scandal to make our lethargic, well-paid city officials wake up.

I was at my wit's end, frustrated and ready to start screaming. What the hell is the matter with our city officials? It was rather difficult to find an answer to that question.

James K. Carr, as we found out later, deliberately held back any action on his part. He was waiting to appoint his new land czar, John Lilly. Carr was just unbelievable. He held up this most important project worth millions of dollars to the city, because he was "not ready." Lilly was eventually appointed by Carr as the new director of public utilities properties. I became second in charge. I was frantically trying to get this project going and was running out of time. I wrote a strong memo to my superior, General Arthur Frye, pointing out that the Texans were on the verge of throwing in the sponge. I received a brief note written on my returned memo to him stating that "all property matters were on hold until the new director comes on the job." Yikes! Great guns and little fishes! Or better still, "What the hell kind of management has been inflicted on San Francisco, the city that knows how?" Well, it came to pass. Great Southwest wrote a stinging letter complaining of their treatment by the city and went elsewhere with their millions to invest. Now the fun part began. I should rather say, the tragedy began to unfurl.

I retired in May of 1970. My successor, Frank Loskay, did nothing except to continue an agricultural tenant on the land raising hay and some vegetables at a nominal rent. The city of Pleasanton operated a sewage disposal plant adjacent to our proposed industrial park site. They were having trouble disposing of their effluent, or in other words, liquid sewage. Pleasanton was growing too fast and their sewage plant was not. They needed land on which to spray their effluent. As always, management became rather accommodating and agreed to turn over most of the property to Pleasanton, so they could dump their sewage on San Francisco's valuable land. After all, the land was idle and Pleasanton was not getting anywhere with San Francisco on the proposed industrial park. Why not resolve our sewage problem in this fashion? They kept increasing the land usage until October 22, 1974.

Resolution No. 74-0346 was unanimously approved by the Public Utilities Commission on October 22, 1974. This is how it read:

> "Authorizing the general manager of the San Francisco Water Department to execute a Land Use Permit to the city of Pleasanton for the purpose of: Conducting necessary operations for disposing of liquid sewage effluent . . . construction of holding ponds for said sewage at an annual rental of $18,065 per year."

The resolution further stated:

> "Mr. Frye introduced Mr. William H. Edgar, city clerk of Pleasanton, Mr. Floyd Mori, mayor, and Mr. Gene Dana."

They must have had one rip-roaring reception. I could picture the hidden glee in the eyes of the Pleasanton officials.

No doubt, they must have laughed out loud all the way home to Pleasanton. They must have also said, "The country hicks really gave it good to the city slickers." San Francisco had a pot of gold in its hands and let it slip away. They exchanged its millions of dollars of prospective revenue for a pittance and a land full of Pleasanton's sewage.

Again, I can only say, "What a way to die!" The story doesn't end here.

Many years have gone by. On February 25, 1986, a strange and unbelievable item appeared on the Public Utilities Commission's calendar as "Item 10," submitted by the general manager, Rudolf Nothenberg. It read:

> "Authorizing the General Manager of Public Utilities to negotiate and execute contracts for professional services in connection with the management of Water Department lands in Pleasanton, California, for an amount not to exceed $40,000 for the current fiscal year, commencing on February 25, 1986; and authorizing the Manager of Utilities to request an additional sum of $200,000 for the 1986-87 Water Department Capital Budget Request for the continuation of these services."

Then, on October 28, 1986, the Public Utilities calendar contained another eye opener requesting an appropriation of $375,000 for a plan to develop the Pleasanton properties. This was submitted by Douglas Wright, director of planning and development. Shortly after this outlandish request for the huge sum of $375,000, something new was happening. Not being able to get anywhere with San Francisco on the industrial park development and reaching the point where Pleasanton, could perhaps make an ideal land use for its rapidly growing city, it came up with a real dilly at San Francisco's expense. Could this latest idea on the part of Pleasanton be an act of revenge because of San Francisco's indecision, procrastination, or plain ignorance of the potential revenues and benefits that would have accrued to both communities?

Pleasanton was now sitting in the saddle. It had growing pains. How nice it would be to have some new park land, a golf course, and other light recreational usage — all at the expense of the city of San Francisco. This is how Rudy Nothenberg, the manager of public utilities, informed the commission that their valuable property in Pleasanton would greatly be downgraded if this move became a reality:

"Mr. Nothenberg said that the City of Pleasanton is recommending that Water Department property east of Route 680 be placed in an 'urban reserve' and that a moratorium be placed on development of the property for ten years. It is also recommended that Water Department property west of Route 680 be designated from Agricultural and Grazing to Park and Recreation for possible use as a public golf course. Both of these recommendations, if enacted, will have an adverse effect on the value of our property. A public hearing on this matter is scheduled for December 9 in Pleasanton to allow input from the property owners affected. Both Real Estate Department personnel and Commission staff will attend this hearing to oppose the moratorium and downzoning of this Water Department property."

Thus, ends the saga of what could have been a great achievement if it were not for the usual bureaucratic bumbling on the part of those who supposedly represent a great city — San Francisco. One of my close friends described this ongoing and prevalent situation as "bureaucratic constipation."

Chapter 14

The Proposed Cherry Valley Resort

San Francisco's huge water and power operations, in addition to the San Francisco Water Department's holdings, included the vast Hetch Hetchy System.

Situated in the High Sierra, the watershed lands covered hundreds of square miles, principally in Yosemite National Park and Stanislaus National Forest. By terms of the Raker Act, Congress permitted the development of this vast area for the purpose of San Francisco creating not only its own water supply, but for a good part of the Bay Area, particularly the peninsula. The city was also to share this water with the Modesto and Turlock irrigation district in the San Joaquin Valley.

The main reservoir is the Hetch Hetchy held back by the giant O'Shaughnessy Dam. There is another small reservoir, Lake Almanor. The city also produces power for its own use and sells the rest of the power to the Pacific Gas and Electric Company (PG &E).

Because of the increasing population, the far-seeing city officials at that time decided to expand its water-collecting area with the construction of the Cherry Valley Reservoir situated in the Stanislaus National Forest, one of the world's beauty spots.

This narrative deals with the Cherry Valley buildings and grounds. They were built in 1952 on forest land in the development and construction of the Cherry Valley Reservoir, later named Lake Lloyd in honor of one of San Francisco's great engineers who was the driving force in this huge undertaking. The buildings were erected in a rather attractive and luxurious style in order to make the resident engineers feel at home. This also accommodated the many visiting officials who eagerly came to see the site during construction. With the completion of the dam, everyone went home and the luxurious buildings were closed for many years. In fact, the Hetch Hetchy budget carries an item of $75,000 a year for maintenance of these buildings.

No one seemed to have any idea as to what to do. They were not the usual temporary building shacks. These were very well-built. The so-called "camp house" had a spacious kitchen, dining room, office, and rest areas. There were two attractive houses with four bedrooms and two baths, two duplexes with four bedrooms and four baths each, five well-built cabins, and several other usable buildings including a large garage and a spacious warehouse. Everything was in, including sewage, water, electricity, and practically every gadget found in a city home. The most attractive consideration was the location with a breathtaking view of Lake Lloyd and a most beautiful panorama of the Sierras.

Lake Lloyd is primarily used to generate power, unlike the Hetch Hetchy reservoir which is used only for drinking purposes. However, it is a mecca for boats and water sports. Although not publicized, the lake is generally crowded with sportsmen during the summer season.

Stanislaus National Forest maintains a huge camping ground complex closeby. The park officials would like to see San Francisco develop the Lake Lloyd site for public recreation. No one in the city would listen to their request.

Back in the early 1960's, the voters in San Francisco voted by large plurality for the merger of the Hetch Hetchy System with the San Francisco Water Department. One of the few great managers of the city's utility empire at that time was Robert W. Kirkwood, an able and business-like executive. He and I spoke the same language — we wanted to get things done.

Anticipating the merger of the two departments, Kirkwood assigned me to proceed and develop a possible use of Cherry Valley as a resort complex. I accepted, jumped in with both feet, and immediately contacted the Stanislaus National Park officials. Their enthusiasm over the possibilities far exceeded my expectations. They offered us a small, adjacent peninsula involving a $250,000 project to develop a marina for the launching and storage of boats with complete facilities if we would develop our resort complex.

The San Francisco County Grand Jury visits Hetch Hetchy once a year and remains two days to inspect this gigantic operation. They also visit and inspect all city properties, or as many as possible, prior to submitting their annual report on the "State of the City."

I was invited to meet them at Cherry. Included in this group of jurors was a member of the Swig family, and several prominent realtors and property developers. They saw and agreed with me as to the tremendous possibilities, particularly Swig, who envisioned a million dollar operation. He measured, analyzed, and came up with a plan. He also wanted to be considered when we would call for bids. I lost no time. The city attorney approved a proposed lease form in 1964. The next step was to submit it to the Public Utilities Commission for its approval.

At least 25 reputable and financially capable developers were ready to bid on the Cherry complex. With the assistance of the Park Service officials, the Swigs and others, we dubbed the project as the "Million Dollar Resort Proposal." It was very exciting and there was great anticipation. Then, the unexpected happened. Bob Kirkwood passed away. He was succeeded by James K. Carr. It took Carr some time to get going. He came to San Francisco fresh from the Department of the Interior in Washington where he was the undersecretary.

Jim Carr was a powerful Democrat who had lots of juice. Everything he did had a political smell. He had been appointed by Mayor Jack Shelley, a former Congressman from San Francisco who was also a powerful Democrat. Carr was in no hurry. He disregarded the time and effort that was put into the preparations that went into this project. He brushed aside the fact that many prospective bidders were waiting patiently to invest a lot of money to make this exciting resort development a reality.

Carr did not seem to be interested in the prospect of the city making a huge bundle of money on this valuable property situated in one of the most beautiful areas of the picturesque Sierra Nevada mountains, which many called the "Switzerland of California." He overlooked the fact that the city constructed a rather expensive campsite that was built at a great cost to the city, which was now laying idle for many years and cost the Hetch Hetchy System $75,000 of the taxpayers' money just for maintenance.

What eventually happened was unbelievable. Carr

dismissed the whole project by the wave of a hand and with an unusual simple statement: "Mayor Shelley may want to convert this into a day camp."

That was the end of the Cherry Valley Resort Proposal. The project remained idle until my closing years. I resurrected it and was hoping to have it leased before my retirement. In the meantime, John Lilly came aboard. He picked it up and made a detailed study consisting of about 30 pages. He was eventually fired and left the scene, I was gone, and Cherry Valley went back to resume its long sleep.

Charge another fiasco to our inept city officials. These episodes I have shared reveal the incredible lack of business practice or judgement in city government. What a shame!

Chapter 15

There Is Oil In Those Hills

The oldtimers living in the Sunol area were pretty foxy fellows. Most of them made their stakes in cattle. They never seemed to be satisfied and were always looking for greener pastures.

On my weekly visits to Sunol, I made it a point to meet with these wise men in a time-worn coffee shop on Sunol's one and only main street. The coffee, particularly the coffee pot, had seen better days. It took a cast iron stomach to survive the second cup.

Carl Zwissic, Vic Lund, and usually one of the Mendoza clan were my companions. We tried to solve the world's problems and wound up with the local happenings. There were lots of rumors that oil could be found in this particular area. Not too far away in the Livermore Valley hills, there were a few scattered wildcat wells in production. At that time, crude oil was going for $2.35 a barrel, which was a lot of money then. Compared to the high OPEC price of $35 per barrel during the oil embargo days of the 1970s and the price of $22 a barrel (1987 prices), it may not have seemed to be a lot of money. We will nevertheless confine this narrative to the era of $2.35 a barrel.

The thought of oil, like gold, is always a challenge and it is always exciting. As time went on, I was approached by agents representing a number of oil companies. I never go too far with them as my feeling was that they were only fishing or window shopping.

One day, Joe Covello, representing McCulloch Oil Corporation in Los Angeles, showed me some drilling tests that his company had completed in our immediate area. He came in with a discovery well near Livermore. At a depth of only 1,350 feet, the well pumped over 100 barrels per day of high gravity oil. They drilled a total of six wells averaging 100 barrels a day per well. The wells were relatively shallow. Over a period of two years from 1967 to 1969, the Livermore field produced over 250,000 barrels of crude oil.

After several meetings with Covello, he produced evidence after making more tests that there were oil deposits on the Perata grazing lease, the Bonita Park area, and two other locations — all on water department properties. He submitted a letter to me for my review in which he pinpointed the proposed sites his company was prepared to lease. Inasmuch as the land was leased for cattle grazing, Covello's proposal emphasized that there would be no interference with the cattle. He would pay a fee per acre at a much higher rental than for grazing. We would actually be receiving two rentals for the same acre. The exploratory lease would run for five years.

In the event of an oil strike, the city would receive one-seventh of the price paid for crude oil; the one-seventh royalty being 14.3 percent of 100 percent, giving us 14⅓ cents per dollar as our share. On this basis of 35 cents per barrel on 400 barrels per day, it would yield $50,460 per year.

Thanks to our Arab friends and their OPEC organization, the amount of the city's share would be most impressive when converting from 1968 figures to 1981 prices. With 400 barrels per day at $5.00 per barrel, the daily take would be $2,000 or $720,000 per year. Ten wells at this annual income would return at least $7,200,000 per year.

McCulloch was aiming for 40 wells. (I will not, at this time, translate this into numbers.) The area involved for each well would be less than half an acre. Naturally, I was quite thrilled and discussed this matter with General Art Frye, manager of the water department. To my surprise, this usually negative man beamed with excitement. I almost fell out of my chair when I saw his enthusiastic approval. I then suggested that we have a meeting at top level. I invited Covello to join us in Frye's office in San Francisco.

On April 4, 1968, James Saul, vice president and general manager of McCulloch Oil, and Joe Covello, contract lease agent, met with General Frye and myself. We discussed the proposal at length and agreed on a proposed lease arrangement to cover the 500-acre Perata lease and the Bonita Park area adjacent to this parcel. It was specifically agreed that the oil operation would not interfere with the grazing lease or any of the water department's activities on the land. If no oil was found, we would be guaranteed our $10 per acre or $5,000 a year. I figured, "What did we have to lose?" Deputy City Attorney James Brasil was instructed to prepare the necessary lease form.

In the meantime, for some strange reason, General Frye began to hesitate. The lease form had been signed and approved by Thomas O'Connor, the city attorney. The next step was for General Frye to submit the lease form with my fact sheet to the Public Utilities Commission through the general manager, James K. Carr. Frye sent a memo to Carr indicating that due to certain ramifications (whatever that meant), he would need more time for study. Time drifted by when James Saul wrote a letter to General Frye inquiring as to the delay. The PUC should have received the proposal on April 23, 1968 as scheduled. Saul waited until October 1, 1968.

Frye's classic letter to Saul on October 8, 1968 was typical of how bureaucracy operated in the city hall. It stated: "The matter has been under consideration by the city attorney and as soon as we hear from him in this regard, we will advise you accordingly." Over a long distance conversation with Joe Covello, he remarked, "In other words, I guess this is the kiss of death."

Tom O'Connor, the city attorney, was not holding up the lease. He had already approved and signed the proposal. I pressured General Frye to get his act together. He asked the city attorney to redraft the lease proposal and on October 28, 1968, Frye received the new lease form ready to go. (I did manage to have the royalty price to the city increased from one-seventh to one-sixth.) It was a beautiful lease containing all the necessary safeguards to the city. Then started the waiting period.

The fall season flowed into winter and then, it was spring. Two things happened on May 12, 1969. It was my 65th birthday and I was to retire on May 31st. The second incident made worldwide news. On May 12th, the Associated Press headlined a story out of New York, "McCulloch Soaring on a Sea of Oil." It was announced that McCulloch struck oil, lots of oil, on the north slope of Alaska. "The price of McCulloch oil stock rose 124 points yesterday on the American Stock Exchange," it was reported.

The story should end here, but it doesn't. In 1974, I received a call at home from General Crowley, who succeeded Jim Carr as manager of utilities. (Carr was eventually demoted to manager of the San Francisco Airport. After a short period, he resigned to become manager of the Sacramento Airport and subsequently retired.) He was interested in proceeding on a new oil lease. I said, "Fine, Jack. Why not go ahead?" He replied, "I don't have any file. No one seems to know where the file is." To this, I remarked, "The reason you do not have a file on this matter and many other matters is because General Art Frye, at his inception as manager of the water department, ordered all department heads to destroy all records over five years old because space was at a premium." At that meeting, I argued with Frye, refusing to destroy my records because "we are in the land business and records are never destroyed." Frye, fresh from his army days, commanded me to obey his orders. I certainly did not destroy records of my major leases — this is why I am able to write this story.

I did some soul searching and decided not to turn over any of my photocopied records to Crowley. I felt that he was on his way out and I just did not have any confidence in those who ran the water department and the public utilities at that time.

About a year later (1975), I met Joe Covello in San Francisco. He told me that he was still interested in an oil lease with the city, but "I felt that Saul and I had been burnt by the way we were treated by the city." His parting words were, "If you can get involved, I would certainly be interested."

Today, Joe Covello is president of the Central California Oil Company near Bakersfield and operates 30 high-producing oil wells. Again, San Francisco missed the boat.

Chapter 16

Cork Oak

The subject of cork oak goes back to the early years of my tenure managing the properties of the San Francisco Water Department in 1944. Since the harvesting of the first cork oak bark on that date, nothing further has been done.

Five hundred and fifty cork oak trees had been planted in the Pulgas Temple area near the Crystal Springs Lakes and have been taken care of by the operating division of the water department. They were in a fairly healthy state.

I write this chapter for the simple reason that the San Francisco Water Department had thousands of acres on its watershed lands that were ideal for the planting and growing of cork oaks. This would serve two purposes. Inasmuch as cork oak requires many years in order to harvest the mature cork bark, it is not for the immediate expectation of a cash crop; rather, it is for posterity. They are beautiful trees and are ideal for watershed planting, helping to retain the soil during periods of heavy rainfall. Furthermore, cork oak can be grown here just as it has been for centuries in Spain, Portugal, France, and North Africa.

There was a time during World War II when it was impossible for the United States to import cork from Spain or Portugal, the world's principal source of this valuable product. Some cork is grown in North Africa and France. The world's production is about 300,000 tons a year.

The United States is the biggest consumer of cork. We think of cork when we open a bottle of wine or champagne. What we don't realize is that it takes 15 years before the outer bark can be removed from the cork tree. It is then necessary to wait another four years for the second stripping and every four years thereafter.

The Spanish and Portuguese cork oak trees continue yielding their bark beyond 100 years. About 60 percent of the 160,000 tons of cork imported into the United States goes into insulation, while 30 percent goes for composition, inner soles, gaskets, life preservers, and many other products.

I became interested in the cork oak as a possible future source when I discovered a grove of 17 cork oak trees growing on a hill near our headquarters in Sunol. I also found three giant cork oak trees on one of our right-of-ways in Alameda County, and several large mature trees near our peninsula division headquarters in Millbrae. I reasoned that if these trees can be grown here, why should Portugal, Spain, and North Africa continue to enjoy this monopoly?

One of our nurserymen lessees, Noel Pennington from Belmont, was somewhat of an expert on cork oak trees. We made the acquaintance of George Greenan, an executive of Western Crown Cork and Seal Company, one of the country's biggest importers of cork for processing into wine corks and various kinds of cork seals. We became interested in the possibilities of developing a California source of cork oaks. Another enthusiast in our group was Woodbridge Metcalf, better known as Woody. He was the state forester with the State Division of Forestry at the University of California at Berkeley.

We learned that cork oaks were grown in scattered areas throughout California. Groves were found in Sonoma County, Roeding Park in Fresno, Butte County, Davis, and along California Drive in Burlingame. The biggest stand of cork oak trees was in Bidwell Park in Chico planted by the University of California in 1904.

The growing of cork oak trees is not a quick cash crop. It involved the planting and planning for the future. It was for posterity. We saw the future in planting watersheds as a prime example, visualizing over 5,000 acres of our watershed lands around the Crystal Springs Lakes in San Mateo County where the water department owned over 23,000 acres. About 8,000 acres could be planted on the water department's 36,000 acres in Alameda and Santa Clara Counties in the vicinity of the Calaveras and San Antonio Reservoirs.

Farmers and city folks who owned large tracts or estates could plant the trees in the unprofitable parts of their holdings and also on public lands. Western Crown Cork and Seal

Company agreed to put up a large sum of money to finance the planting of seedlings in areas controlled by the division of forestry.

In order to properly publicize this potential new industry, we decided that there was enough cork on the 25 or more mature trees growing on water department property to prove that cork could be grown and sold in California. I received the approval of water department management and the Public Utilities Commission to proceed in commercially stripping our trees and selling the cork through our normal channels.

George Greenan, Woody Metcalf, Frank Peters, my assistant, Noel Pennington, and I changed into overalls and went to work stripping our cork oak trees. This first-time event commenced on July 6, 1944. Metcalf and Greenan were experts. The first one we tackled was the 60 year-old tree in Millbrae. (The bark was stripped in such a way as not to harm the cambrium layer directly under the bark. This life-giving layer supplied nourishment to the tree.) We stripped the cork from a total of 21 trees. Some were not mature enough, but we were able to strip 2,000 pounds of salable cork.

We made history. The city purchasing department, which was responsible for selling whatever the city produced or didn't need, went through the customary procedure of advertising the cork that was to be sold. Bids were opened on July 17, 1944. The highest bidder turned out to be Western Crown Cork and Seal at 3½ cents a pound. Mind you, this was not an earthshaking income to the city. Regardless that the city's coffers were only enriched by $70 dollars, the historic significance was that it was the first native grown cork ever sold in America.

Over 100,000 cork oak seedlings (one year-old trees) were available. We received permission to use the rotunda of the city hall, where the water department sponsored an exhibit of some of the stripped cork and some very attractive displays. We had on hand 10,000 of the seedlings and emphasized that they should be grown for the future and planted in unused locations.

The city hall exhibit was so successful that we repeated it at the San Francisco Junior College (now City College of San Francisco). The interest taken by the students was remarkable. Everyone seemed to be most cooperative. They billed the exhibit as the San Francisco Water Department's "Educational Exhibit." Thousands of people came to visit this most unusual new curiosity. It was planned for two days, but lasted for one week. Thousands of seedlings were also given away.

My next step was to plant 1,200 seedlings near Pulgas Temple where the Hetch Hetchy and East Bay waters poured into the Crystal Springs Lakes. The problem here was that the water department operations division neglected the care of the trees. When John O'Marie became manager of the peninsula division, he immediately began to protect the growing trees from souvenir seekers and deer. I must say that the deer really enjoyed eating the tasty buds and new shoots. The problem was enormous. It was estimated by the Fish and Game Commission that more than 3,000 deer roamed the watershed, which was also their sanctuary. O'Marie constructed a deer fence around the cork oak plantation. Today, over 100 healthy trees survive and have now blended into this most picturesque area.

We did not become a cork-producing state on a commercial basis, but we did prove that California could produce high-quality cork. According to Western Crown Cork and Seal, the world's largest cork manufacturer, 2,000 pounds of cork purchased from the San Francisco Water Department were shipped directly to their Baltimore plant where it was turned into high-quality champagne corks. Who can tell? Perhaps someday when you open that bottle of California champagne, you may well be handling a California cork.

As an aside, I have stated how deer have a yen for cork oak buds. I had a similar situation on one of my nursery leases on our Sunol properties; only this had to do with gladioli. This particular grower raised ten acres of gladioli. He never figured that the numerous deer in that area favored his gladioli buds. They must have been rather tasty as almost three acres were consumed by the deer.

California law permits a grower to kill the deer that appear to be damaging his crops. The sticker here is that whatever deer he kills, he must report it to the sheriff of the county and deliver the deer to the nearest public institution where it could be consumed.

In the case of the gladioli grower, the Santa Rita Prison in Pleasanton was the recipient of the deer for consumption by the inmates. The nurseryman delivered one to three deer a day there. While venison was enjoyable as a main dish, there was a rather unusual problem. One day, I received a call from the warden informing me that some of the inmates were about to rebel. "No more deer meat, please!" "And just what brings this about?" I inquired. The warden replied, "The problem is, John, that the deer meat has a very strong gladioli taste.''

I don't know what our gladioli grower did about this, but I do know that the Santa Rita Prison inmates went back to their hamburger and beans with no complaints.

Chapter 17

70,000 Victory Gardens

Commitment and civic involvement has had much meaning to me. To work without commitment renders no satisfaction or pride of achievement. Not to contribute to society is an ungrateful way to go through life.

I remember how important this thought meant to me during the period of World War II. Food was considered one of the most important weapons of war. There was a shortage of food nationwide. Everyone was on rations and conditions were not improving. We were not only feeding ourselves, but our allies as well.

In the winter of 1941, a series of articles appeared in the *San Francisco News*, a then-prominent afternoon newspaper owned by the Scripps Howard newspaper empire. These articles appeared daily and concerned the growing of vegetables in your backyard or vacant lot. They were good articles, but the timing of their appearance was wrong. The stories advocated planting tomatoes, zucchini, stringbeans, and other warm weather crops that grew only during the summer months. It happened to be December.

This caught my immediate attention. How in Heaven's name can a responsible newspaper print such misinformation? I could have let it go and continued to take care of my winery business. I decided to call the city editor who turned out to be Charles Massey. I explained my feelings to him and he said, "Why don't you come in to see me so we can talk about it?" I accepted and was in his office at the old *San Francisco News* the following day.

Massey was rather impressed by our meeting, particularly

with my knowledge and agricultural education and background. Charlie, as he was called, suggested that I write a series of articles on "Victory Gardens." To this, I replied, "Give me a few days and we go." The series was entitled, "A Victory Garden Guide for San Francisco." It ran for six consecutive days with the response so great that Charlie suggested I get together with Louise Weick, the garden editor. That's how it all started. As a result, a War Garden Committee was formed to publicize the raising of vegetables in San Francisco.

In the meantime, I continued my writings with another series of articles describing the problems facing farmers raising food for the war effort. It was entitled, "War Comes to the Farmlands," and ran for five consecutive days in the *News*. These articles attracted wide attention and it did make it rather easy to form a good representative committee.

I heard from Clarence Lindner, publisher of the *San Francisco Examiner*. He offered the resources of his newspaper and assigned his garden editor, Oliver Kehrlein, to work with me. That was great. My brothers encouraged me to get involved.

Frank Clarvoe, managing editor of the *News*, called to say that the pages of his newspapers were available. His last words were, "Let's get going." I wanted a sponsor. I thought of Bill Carroll, the county agricultural commissioner, but he was too busy because he was shorthanded. It was suggested that perhaps the San Francisco Junior College, which had a horticultural division, could be of some help. This is where I met Harry Nelson, who was head of the horticultural division and had, at various times, written articles on growing vegetables at home. Harry and I hit it off immediately. We had much in common and spoke the same language — food.

Harry Nelson suggested that the president of San Francisco Junior College (later it became the City College of San Francisco), Archie Cloud, might be interested. In this respect, I believe I met one of the most fascinating and lovable persons ever. He was about six feet, six inches; I was five feet, eight inches. He had recently written a book telling how he stole the coveted axe from the Stanford University campus prior to the annual Big Game with the University of California at Berkeley. It became quite an issue between the two rival universities.

Dr. Cloud, without hesitation, agreed to sponsor the San Francisco Victory Garden Council. The headquarters was to be at the college and all the facilities, particularly the horticultural division with Harry Nelson, was to be at our disposal. He immediately named me chairman of the council.

We invited representatives of all the city's garden clubs, organizational service groups, labor groups, and any others willing to participate. At the meeting, they unanimously approved my chairmanship. We went to work and the garden editors were our outlets to reach the public.

Henry Budde, Sr., owner of the vast chain of neighborhood newspapers (later known as the *San Francisco Progress*), became one of our biggest backers. He was also on the Park Commission, and his influence, political and otherwise, played a large part in the success of the program.

The general feeling was that raising vegetables in San Francisco was not feasible. There was too much fog, sand, the summers were too cool, and many other objections. That was the challenge.

Since it was wartime, we became a part of the Civilian Defense Program. In this respect, I was to become associated with the city's leading politicians, educators, bankers, socialites, and people who were the acknowledged leaders of the Bay Area communities. Mrs. Alfred Ghirardelli, representing the Red Cross, Mrs. Clarence Coonan from the American Women's Voluntary Service, and many others offered their services. They were Max Leonard, agricultural commissioner from San Mateo County, agricultural editors from *Sunset Magazine*, and legions of interested people from every walk of life who became part of my team.

While in the process of formation, I was faced with my first major problem. I was to speak before the Utile Dulce Club at the Palace Hotel and had never addressed a group of more than ten people before this lightning bolt struck. The president of this prominent club told me that there would be an attendance of about 150 members, all women and civic leaders. Needless to say, I spent a long, sleepless night trying to put my thoughts together. After a few brief announcements, I was introduced as the speaker of the day. The president, Hilda Richardson, noticed my nervousness and quietly whispered to me, "Mr. Brucato, you know your subject. Don't try to make a speech. Just talk to them about what you are trying to do." At any rate, I stood up and viewed the audience (it seemed like there was a million people out there), and looked at the chairperson who immediately smiled and said something like "Let them have it, John."

I remember funbling a line or two. (I spoke from notes, but

didn't dare look at them.) I suddenly found myself saying things that came clearly to me. By the time I finished my 40-minute talk, I began to feel like a veteran. Evidently, whatever I said was well-received, and I was invited to speak to four other groups.

We immediately set up goals. Harry Nelson trained a large number of City College instructors to go out into the neighborhoods to teach and advise homeowners on the same idea as the 12 Apostles spreading the faith. They concentrated on vacant lots. There were many during that period before San Francisco became a wall-to-wall community. We eventually had family gardens in Golden Gate Park, Laguna Honda, and at the Civic Center.

The first big project was Golden Gate Park where Julius Girod was the superintendent. With his advice and assistance, we developed 400 plots of 20' x 20' gardens. One section was on Ninth Avenue and South Drive; the other at the entrance of Fourteenth Avenue and Main Drive. San Franciscans became excited. The 400 plots were assigned in three days to 400 families.

The Park Commission, thanks to Commissioner Harry Budde, Sr., provided the amateur gardeners with free water, fertilizers, insecticides, utensils, seeds, and many plants. It was a fun project which brought people together. They had common problems, vegetables that is, and many a long relationship resulted.

The American Women's Voluntary Service (AWVS), a group of volunteer women in uniforms involved in great depth with providing many wartime services, jumped into the program in a big way. We arranged with the city's Public Utilities Commission to turn over to the AWVS the vast 30-acre future reservoir site on O'Shaughnessy Boulevard and Portola Drive below Twin Peaks known as the Glen Park Reservoir Site.

Over 350 gardens blossomed in this area overlooking the city. It was rather a windy site; nevertheless, the vegetables flourished. As the food shortage became acute, more people turned to the land. They called it the "Backyard Revolution."

Our program became a model and was copied on a nationwide basis. The Department of Agriculture told us that we were the best organized county in the western states, and perhaps in the country. It was no time to rest on our laurels. On the contrary, we redoubled our efforts to do something bigger, better and unusual.

The Laguna Honda Project became the largest community-sponsored project in the state, according to the U.S. Department of Agriculture. Laguna Honda was a county-operated hospital and contained a vast area of grassy, gentle slopes. The council secured from the city their approval to farm the two sides of this hospital complex on the Seventh Avenue slope and the Portola Avenue side. It was a gigantic undertaking and was successful because everyone helped. The city's park department plowed the land and agricultural experts set out the garden plots. Each plot contained 900 square feet, a rather sizable garden.

Lots were drawn and the first 400 families to qualify received a parcel of land, free and clean. We also provided picnic tables so that families, particularly on weekends, could farm their plots and enjoy a picnic lunch as though they had traveled many miles. It was one of the joyful aspects in our grim war for survival that seemed to be getting worse with each passing day.

The honorable judge, William O'Brien, was our philosopher who added color to his project. As one of the gardeners put it, "He who has his fingers in the soil, is close to God."

Victory Gardeners exchanged their crops so that those who had too much of one vegetable traded with others who were short of that item and heavy in another. They also shared in the exchange of seeds, tools, and also, help.

One day, one of our Laguna Honda gardeners noted a white gopher or albino gopher enjoying one of his choice carrots. (Today, white gophers are a rarity.) I was advised by experts from the University of California that an albino gopher represents one in ten million gophers.

Art Caylor, a writer for the *San Francisco News*, and other columnists had a field day with the "Albino Gophers of Laguna Honda." Caylor visited the project to get a first-hand idea of what was going on. As a coincidence, one of the gardeners had just trapped a second albino gopher. Much to his delight, other gardeners told him that a total of four albino gophers had been caught. Taking the University of California's figures of one albino to ten million, Caylor wrote the following in his column in the *San Francisco News*: "According to the learned projections of the university experts, there should be a total population of 48 million gophers." We sure had a lot of gophers to contend with and hoped that the remainder of the 48 million were very far away, like in Texas.

The Victory Gardens on the slopes of where the Laguna Honda Home now stands in San Francisco — 1942.

One of our big triumphs was the California State Garden Club Conference in San Francisco. The main order of business was the Victory Garden. Lo and behold, I was selected to chair the meeting at the Fairmont Hotel. There were 32 garden clubs involved, meaning that each group was scheduled to make a report. How do you control a meeting where there would be 32 reports to be made? And all by women? I called my brain trust together to discuss a possible solution.

The notice of this important conference received widespread publicity, particularly in the garden pages of all the local newspapers. Norvelle Gillespie, well-known garden editor of the *San Francisco Chronicle*, noted, "John Brucato is prepared to chair this meeting and is planning to see it through the weekend. John has stated that everyone will be given an opportunity to speak. Good luck, John."

The clubs' representatives were informed that each report would be limited to three minutes, which was to be controlled by a large-size hourglass. It was referred to as a three-minute egg timer. No one objected. It was to be quite an experiment. Some doubted the possibility of limiting a woman down to just three minutes. Well, everything turned out fine. No one lasted the full three minutes since many were able to complete their reports in just two minutes. Everyone was quite pleased and I received a standing ovation for my efforts. Although I was prepared to leave town in a hurry, I was sure relieved with the outcome.

The next project was to get special, reduced water rates for the Victory Gardeners. We had to go before the city's Public Utilities Commission, which was now headed by a tough general manager named Ed Cahill. He practically threw me out of his office when I proposed the special rates for the gardeners. I urged him to consider the important need for this assistance, but to no avail. I also curtly informed him that he would soon be able to get a bird's eye view of a thriving Victory Garden in the Civic Center just by looking out his window.

I went to see Henry Budde, who at that time was president of the Park Commission and had jurisdiction of the Civic Center Park. He lost no time in the planting of a model garden. As a matter of fact, it was fully planted in three weeks. I was quite sure that Cahill must have seen this masterpiece each time he came to the window.

Several weeks went by and the best I got from Ed Cahill was that "he had the proposal under study." Having had some experience in city procedures, I figured that perhaps the decision would be made in six months, one year, or more. It seemed that we always came up with solutions when we hit a stone wall or a hardplace. The newspapers and radio stations were the answer. Editorials appeared in all the four dailies, the *San Francisco Progress*, neighborhood papers, and practically all of the radio stations. They all urged the need for reduced water rates in order to grow food for the war effort. This all happened in late November of 1942. As a typical politician susceptible to the spotlight, Ed Cahill and the Public Utilities Commission shined.

I was expecting a call from the city hall. Cahill invited me to his office, remarked how very much impressed he was with the success of the Victory Garden program, and offered his help. The following week, he presented a resolution to the PUC recommending their approval of the reduced rates for the Victory Gardens. After many flowery speeches by the commissioners, the water department was motivated to come up with a reduced rate that would be acceptable for all parties concerned.

The interesting part of this story was that I had taken a civil service examination and passed in the top position for superintendent of the water department's agricultural and land division. In other words, I had some apprehension as to my future status, whereas I was at this time actually engaged in a battle for the Victory Gardens. Cahill was to be my boss when I assumed my new position. (As it turned out, he and I became good friends.)

Our original goal of 60,000 Victory Gardens was almost an accomplishment. We were out to plant every square foot available. The program was now going full blast.

Experts from the colleges, farm advisors and farmers assisted in conducting neighborhood clinics, not only in the care and growing of vegetables, but in canning and preserving the surplus grown. Like "Schnozzle" Durante would have said, "Everyone was getting into the act."

The State Department of Agriculture issued a bulletin stating that the value of the vegetable crops grown in the San Francisco Victory Gardens was over $1,750,000. (There was no inflation in those days. That was real hard cash.) The city provided patrols to guard against sabotage or pilfering. The Board of Supervisors passed an ordinance containing heavy penalties to protect the city farmers from those who stole their produce.

Pest control teams were formed to assist gardeners with the ever-increasing problem of insect and plant disease control. The more we planted, the more the problem. The biggest of all seemed to be the garden snail.

The snail has an interesting history. Sometime in 1890, there was a French importer of snails in North Beach who supplied the many flourishing French and Italian restaurants with edible snails. The French called them *escargot* while the Italians referred to them as *crastune*. It seemed that one day, the good *monsieur* importer forgot to cover his six cases of snails, which just arrived from France. There was no doubt that there were hundreds of these luscious creatures in those crates. Seeing the light, they crawled out and disappeared into the sunset. Since that auspicious moment of freedom, the snails just spread out in every direction; first to the truck farms of the Bay Area, and eventually into every corner of our heavy-producing agricultural state of California.

All kinds of controls were used. You might say that the controls were temporary with little success as to extermination. A snail lays a minimum of 300 eggs, which hatch and spread. They are quite prolific. Again, we called the brain trust together. What was the solution? There were no new answers.

Being of Italian origin, a bolt of lightning struck me with such a suddenness that I wondered why we did not think of it before. I was sure that the California garden snail, being of French origin as previously stated, was edible. Many oldtimers in North Beach's Italian and French colonies assured me that the snails were just as good, if not better (because they were fresh), than the imports from the mediterranean countries.

I talked to my father who was a retired importer from New York. He gave me the name of a reputable snail importer for the New York market and other areas where people of Latin backgrounds were his customers. We wrote a letter to the Anthony Puca Company, importers of snails and *cipollini* in New York City. Puca replied by stating that he certainly was interested inasmuch as there was a scarcity of *crastune*, because of the ongoing war which cut off his mediterranean suppliers. He gave us packaging and shipping instructions.

There was widespread publicity as to this turn of events. The local press headlined, "Snails in Your Garden? Don't Worry . . . Eat 'Em!" People reacted by saying, " Oh, the slimy things." It had to be explained that the snail was a clean morsel of food. It only ate vegetation, unlike the crabs, lobsters, or other crustacean, which were actually "low down scavengers."

In conjunction with the Chamber of Commerce, we issued a bulletin with instructions on how to prepare the snails. This is how it appeared in our dailies:

> "How to gather, cook and serve the common brown snail for human consumption," was the subject of a fine point list of instructions issued by the Chamber of Commerce yesterday.
>
> 'Snails are a delicacy that have been enjoyed by Orientals and people of mediterranean extraction for centuries,' the Chamber said in offering this list of suggestions.
>
> 1. Gather only live snails.
>
> 2. Place snails in covered containers allowing air. Put in either corn meal, bran or grated stale bread for the snails to eat. The 'feeding' or curing period requires fifteen days and then they are ready to boil alive.
>
> 3. Boil in water for ten minutes.
>
> 4. Change the water and boil another ten minutes, season and serve.

Thus, we added a new source of food, a plentiful source.

We never went into the snail business. The demand would have been to supply 5,000 pounds per week. The war came to an end and Antonio Puca resumed the importing of snails from France, Italy, Spain, Algeria, and other mediterranean sources. We gradually expanded from food production to food conservation. The army was taking more and more food from every possible source in order to maintain a well-fed force. All of a sudden, another crisis hit the farmlands — a shortage of harvest labor.

A serious situation developed in the Colma, San Bruno, Daly City, and Half Moon Bay coastside areas. There were 4,600 acres of heavy intensive truck crops growing in this important vegetable area. (This took place before Henry Doelger and other developers pushed the growers out and raised houses and people instead.)

Vegetables were quickly maturing and decaying on the ground. Many farmers, unable to harvest their lettuce, cauliflower, artichokes, cabbage and other perishable crops, began to plow them under to at least get some fertilizer out of their efforts.

Max Leonard, agricultural commissioner of San Mateo County, called the matter to my attention. We publicized what was going on in hopes of getting volunteer harvest labor. Not everyone could work in the fields, especially doing stoop labor and under sometimes-unfavorable conditions. We were able to strike a good source of labor when we asked our Board of Supervisors to make it possible to release 200 prisoners at the San Bruno Prison, which was owned by San Francisco. The suggestion worked out exceedingly well. Under supervision and "on their honor," the prisoners went to work, were paid for their labor, and helped out in a big way. Since the army wanted the vegetables, they were asked and supplied some manpower as well.

The spirit of cooperation was everywhere. The vegetable crops were instantly saved, the farmers were happy, and the Victory Garden Council added one more notch to its long list of achievements. We had passed our goal of 60,000 Victory Gardens. Dr. Archie Cloud, using the facilities of the City College of San Francisco, conducted an intensive survey. His official figures documented that San Francisco had over 70,000 Victory Gardens.

Those closest to me in our program were active civic leaders and people who devoted a lot of their time and effort. This group remained with me and eventually became the executive committee when we founded the Farmers' Market the following year. The members of the original executive committee of the Victory Garden Council were:

John G. Brucato, chairman (retired; manager, agricultural and land division, San Francisco Water Department)

*Edgar Brownstone (past president, Polk-Van Ness-Larkin Merchants Association)

*Charles "Scotty" Butterworth (San Francisco Juvenile Court)

*Dr. Archie Cloud (past president, City College of San Francisco)

*Herbert Dalton (California Farm Bureau)

*Philip Dindia (past president, Bernal Heights Association)

*Ann Dippel, Jr. (past president, City and County
Federation of Women's Clubs)

*Frank Helbing, vice chairman (past president,
San Francisco Apartment House Association)

*Evelyn La Place (past president, Central Council of
Civic Clubs)

*Carroll Newburgh (past president, County Grand
Jurors Association)

*Russell Powell (past president, Parkside
Improvement Club)

(*deceased)

When we practically reached the saturation point in the successful Victory Garden program, we were asked by the War Services Committee to see what could be done in the food conservation section. Thus, ended an interesting era that brought many people together in a common cause they called the "Backyard Revolution."

Chapter 18

San Francisco's Famous Farmers' Market

Something happened that was to change our direction into one of the biggest civic enterprises ever attempted by a group of amateurs. It all began when I received a telephone call from Tom Peryham, agricultural commissioner of Marin County.

The pear growers in northern Marin County were in trouble. They could not sell their pears, because the canneries, under wartime pressure, were jammed and couldn't handle Marin County's famous Bartlett pears. Pears in Marin County? Yes, there were 600 acres of choice Bartletts in what is now Novato, Ignacio, and up in the direction of Petaluma in Sonoma County.

For the benefit of the new generations coming on, this was 1943. Marin County, other than San Rafael, was a quiet, rural agricultural county. There was no highway traffic congestion or urban development. These headaches came later.

The pears were rotting on the ground. There were over 300 tons picked and boxed which could not be sold. Canneries were paying 4 cents a pound for choice pears, while pears in the retail markets in San Francisco were going from 17 to 22 cents a pound. We thought, why can't the consumer journey to the source and get the pears cut rate? This is just what we did. Again, with the help of the news media, we publicized the problem and showed people how to get to the Novato area. They were assisted by posted roads with directions on how to get to the various orchards. The price was 4 cents a pound if you brought your own containers.

The response from San Franciscans and the Bay Area was

so enthusiastic that the entire 300 tons of pears disappeared in one afternoon. This avalanche of customers encouraged the growers to pick the remaining 400 tons on the trees. As a result, San Francisco housewives saved their precious "Blue Points" (rationing coupons), and the little farmers up in Novato thought the whole thing was pretty nice on the part of the city folks.

It was surprising that the people of San Rafael and surrounding communities were not aware of the surplus pears. It wasn't until the rush of buyers from San Francisco and the accompanying publicity that Novato's neighbors arrived to participate in the fruit bargain.

This little lesson on primitive economics started San Franciscans thinking. It was an age-old question. Who's getting all the money between the producer and consumer? They reasoned that something must be wrong with our system of food distribution since they paid such high prices in the city while, within a radius of 35 miles, the farmers couldn't give their crops away.

The Novato experiment was watched very closely by neighboring Sonoma County pear growers as well as those in Santa Clara County. Through the agricultural commissioners and farm advisors, I was beseiged with requests for assistance. The growers there began to shout, "Hey, we, too, have lots of pears and Gravenstein apples. Help us." Our problem was that being wartime, we were on gas rations. The Office of Price Administration (OPA) informed me that no extra gas would be allowed for this purpose. What were we going to do? How were we going to satisfy that pent-up desire on the part of consumers to get fresh fruit? It seemed that all our problems, as big as they were, were always solved in simple ways. What was the solution to this urgent situation where fruit growers were facing bankruptcy because there was no outlet for their fruit? Well, "If the consumer can't go to the farmer, let the farmer come to town." This is how the San Francisco Farmers' Market was born.

Joe Sanchetti was up earlier than usual on the morning of August 12, 1943. He had a bumper crop of pears on his trees and quite a few had dropped to the ground. There was no market for his high-quality Sonoma County pears. While the fruit-starved people in San Francisco were paying 22 cents a pound for pears, Joe was lucky to get 4 cents a pound; that is, if there were any buyers. He was too far removed from the consumer. Joe and many other fruit growers in Sonoma, Napa, and Santa Clara Counties heard that farmers were welcomed in San Francisco and could sell their crops directly to the public. There was no middle man, no commission to be paid, no consignment sales; just farmer to consumer and pure, hard cash.

The event was highly publicized in the San Francisco news media. My little group of civic-minded citizens negotiated for a vacant lot owned by Gantner, Felder and Kenny, who happened to be morticians. With the help of some of our city officials and the generosity of the property owner, we were able to obtain the full use of the one-acre lot on Market and Duboce Streets in the heart of the city at no cost to us. The morticians even took out the necessary insurance coverage.

The farmers came in on the first day. There were only six truckloads, but they sold out in less than two hours. A box or lug weighing 25 pounds sold for a dollar as most of the farmers had from 40 to 100 lugs on their trucks.

We never realized that we would have the immediate opposition of the Wholesale Produce Merchants and the Retail Grocers Association, but we did. Joe Sanchetti, who drove in the first truck, followed by Paul Mancini from Santa Rosa, were the first two who dared to oppose the entrenched merchants who did everything possible to stop this "newborn infant," the Farmers' Market, from taking hold.

Thursday was a trickle of six trucks and Friday's total was only eight, but on Saturday, all hell broke loose. They came from the north, the east, and the south. First it was fruit and then, vegetables. No one really realized the plight of the farmers. They were desperate.

Here it was, wartime, and food was going to waste. My little group of the Victory Garden Advisory Board suddenly became the Farmers' Market Advisory Board. We didn't have a plan. We just tried to help a few farmers sell their crops and at the same time, give the fruit-starved consumer a chance to buy the fruit and vegetables at unheard-of prices. We opened a Pandora's box.

Who ever thought that this six-pronged spearhead would prick the monopoly of the Washington Street Wholesale Produce Commission district? Although fully anesthetized by the morphia of profits, the commission merchants scarcely noticed the first gentle insertion of the economic lance; that is, not until the first Saturday when over 135 farmers sold their fresh-picked produce to an all-day crowd of more than 50,000 people. They came on foot, in cars, and by public transportation.

Assuming the success of this unplanned venture, our next stop was to have the city take over. It required eleven months before our citizens' committee convinced the supervisors that this was to be the function of the city. We, as civic-minded citizens, with the backing of the news media and the general public, had no choice. We kept the market going by forming a combined farmers and citizens committee, which I headed. We insisted on tight inspection by the agricultural commissioner, Bill Carroll, who was to be a thorn in our side for years to come.

After much deliberation, the Board of Supervisors reluctantly accepted the Farmers' Market as a legitimate part of the city's food distribution system. In the eleven months of infighting, intrigue, and political opposition, six of the eleven supervisors fought us tooth and nail with the assistance and insistance of the powerful wholesale merchants and retailers officials. I must have appeared before the Board of Supervisors at least once a week during that period.

The Farmers' Market became a reality only because the news media and the public were on our side, and because we had to agree to various restrictions which, while detrimental, we managed to live with. The market proved its worth by using its facilities to save surplus crops that would have gone to waste. This was the salvation for many of our California family-size farmers. We did not need the big grower, because he didn't face the problem the little farmer did. His outlet was mainly on consignment, which meant that he never knew when he would be in the black. It was generally the other way around.

A public opinion poll was conducted which showed ten-to-one in favor of a permanent Farmers' Market. We knew that if we placed the question of a permanent Farmers' Market on the ballot, we would encounter strong opposition. Again, the most powerful opponents were the Wholesale Produce Merchants and the Retail Grocers Association. Strangely, it was mainly the retail association officials, along with the produce group, who were putting up a fight.

As a citizens' group, we had no funds. Our opponents had a half-million dollar war chest. The Farmers' Market matter was placed on the ballot. Without going into the many details involved, the citizens of San Francisco responded with a 145,000 to 25,000 victory. The seven-to-one verdict was the highest margin of votes ever to be garnered on a policy matter in San Francisco. Although we were quite elated, we were not so naive as to think that our troubles were over. As a matter of fact, they had just begun.

Our opponents didn't give up. They merely regrouped and formed a campaign committee against tax subsidization of the Farmers' Market. Chairman of the group was Frank Tissier, secretary of the Retail Grocers Association. William Hadeler, state secretary of the association, was the other front man. Their plan was to convince the retailers that the Farmers' Market would put them out of business. To this, I replied at a standing room only hearing before the Board of Supervisors that, "If the Farmers' Market was responsible for one retail clerk losing his job, I would take immediate steps to close the market." Strange as it may seem, I was never challenged. In fact, many smaller retail grocers were seen at the Farmers' Market early on Saturday morning buying their "shorts" or the very freshest from the fields.

The second campaign started four months before election day. I, as the farmers' leader, was singled out as a radical, Communist, and many other "affectionate" names. The more they attacked me, the more support we received from the many civic groups and the public. Then came our big break. Joseph L. Alioto, a former special assistant to the U.S. Attorney General, invited me to lunch. He was the prosecutor for the government against the Retail Grocers Association, which had violated the Sherman Anti-Trust Act and robbed an unsuspecting public during wartime for its personal profit.

Over a two-year period, the San Francisco consumer was saddled with an extra cost of almost $2 million in his grocery bill, which was a lot of money in those days. I learned from Alioto that on March 4, 1942, William Hadeler and Frank Tissier were indicted by a Federal Grand Jury in San Francisco as the principals in a conspiracy to fix prices of foods, groceries and allied products at unreasonably high levels, within a territory extending from San Luis Obispo to the Oregon border. (Dean David Snodgrass of Hastings Law College was the foreman of the Grand Jury.)

These defendants and others went to trial before Judge Michael J. Roche and were found guilty as charged. They paid a heavy fine, lost their appeal, and went to the Supreme Court which refused to hear the appeal. These, then, were the men who had the gall to come out in this campaign to protect the assembly district in San Francisco — a district that had twice

The Farmers' Market at Market and Duboce Streets in San Francisco — 1943.

During the first year of operation at the permanent Farmers' Market on Alemany Blvd. — 1944.

John Brucato and farmers discussing plans to publicize potato surplus with Frank O'Connell, Farmers' Market manager — 1947.

voted for the Farmers' Market. He also noticed that many were sent within a few minutes of each other, so he wired some of the people whose names were signed to the telegrams. They denied that they had ever sent them. Maloney presented the phony telegrams to the Legislature. Needless to say, we won an overwhelming victory.

Leaving the assembly chamber, we ran into Hadeler. He was heard to say, "This is the last time I will be pulling their chestnuts out of the fire," referring to the Wholesale Produce Merchants. We never heard from him or Tissier again.

The new Farmers' Market, now owned and operated by the city on city-owned land at Alemany Boulevard and San Bruno Avenue, opened to the public on August 4, 1947. It started as an open-air market; the sheds came later.

The first week of operation attracted more than 80,000 people. They purchased more than 125 truckloads of fruits and vegetables on one Saturday alone. Consumers came from a radius of over 50 miles from San Francisco, while farmers came anywhere from the Coachella & Imperial Valleys in the south to the potato-growing Klamath Basin in the north.

Our die-hard opposition, in the meantime, began to mount. They worked through the agricultural commissioner's office in which the inspectors actually framed some unsuspecting grower, citing him for selling inferior fruit. Just to cite a classic example, Bill Carroll, our "beloved" commissioner, assigned two of his agricultural inspectors to get the goods on Chet Monez. Chet was a first-class farmer, who operated more than 200 acres of diversified fruit in Solano County. He was also one of my active members on the growers' committee who constantly worked for the good and welfare of the Farmers' Market. He was noted for his high-quality, fresh-picked fruits. Chet was a key target for Bill Carroll. Embarrassing Monez would definitely affect the market.

Of the 2,500 boxes of fruit brought in by Chet in the past three weeks, the inspectors found 14 boxes of so-called "inferior" or "below standard" fruit. The advisory board considered the market at stake in this issue. I asked an old friend, John Molinari, a former assistant district attorney, to defend Chet.

John Molinari was quite familiar with the goings on in Bill Carroll's office. All this fanfare seemed to surprise Carroll, who apparently thought that Chet would plead quilty to the charge, resulting in negative publicity about the market's so-called "low quality" produce. Molinari confused the inspector on the witness stand. He couldn't remember whether he had inspected a packed box or a loose box, as well as other incidents.

The case, after several postponements, was dismissed. There were other petty cases that met with the same fate. (Later, John Molinari went on to become Presiding Judge on the State Court of Appeals.)

As time went on, these farmers became my family. They discussed their problems with me as I listened and smiled, but I never gave them any advice. They seemed satisfied just to get the problems off their chests.

Farmers have a way of dealing with customers. One of the big problems was the squeezing of a tomato or peach by a consumer to determine whether it was ripe. This, of course, was rather annoying as no doubt, it was harmful to that tomato or peach.

Mike Cozzolino, a tomato grower from San Mateo County, had the perfect solution. Over one box of tomatoes, he placed a large sign which read: "Tomatoes for squeezing." The customers got the message. "Some of them would try to squeeze a coconut," confided Mike.

An incident worth mentioning involved Mrs. Mario Brasher, wife of a Filipino farmer from Mountain View. She always accompanied her husband on his trip to the market. Already a mother of six, she was on her way to adding a seventh as it became obvious to the other farmers. The day came when the condition of Mrs. Brasher caused real concern among the farmers and they referred the urgency of the matter to Mario. He looked anxiously at his wife and then at his partly-filled truck of produce. She understood, saying to her husband, "We will wait, Mario." Not until all the vegetables were sold when Mrs. Brasher added, "Now, let us hurry, Mario." An hour later, Mario, Jr. was born in a peninsula hospital.

A sprinkling of appreciative seasoning, it seems to me, is an appropriate garnish for a potpourri. Some three years after the opening of the Farmers' Market, Mrs. Emilio Giovanonni beckoned me from her stand. She said, "I just wanted to thank you for buying us our brand new Dodge truck." This puzzled me until I noted the twinkle in her husband's eyes. The artichoke grower from Half Moon Bay then told me that this was one of the many benefits the market had brought them.

The Farmers' Market was not the solution to the high cost of living. It was, however, one of the many steps that could be taken to decrease prices and supply quality, fresh-picked, vitamin-filled foods. It was never designed or created to eliminate the middleman. He has a definite place in our food distribution system, which needed a thorough clean-up.

Too much food is destroyed in order to maintain high prices. There is too much emphasis on high quality standards for our foods, and we neglect giving the public its choice of the good lower grades at low prices. But if we are to be a healthy, well-fed nation, we had better start doing this right now before we starve to death in this land of milk and honey. There was no shortage of food in this country. There was no overproduction and there was no surplus. The problem was with the distribution methods.

Something besides nature had gone wrong in these times of so-called overproduction. If the people were given the chance to absorb this overproduction at fair prices, there would have been enough food for all with some to spare.

Five years have passed since Joe Sanchetti arrived in San Francisco with his pears. You, who have read this far, will agree that those pears were indeed the fruit of controversy. During these years, we fought hard to make Joe's stay a happy and permanent one.

Now, after the fifth year, I can happily say that *The Farmer Came to Town* and like *The Man Who Came to Dinner,* he stayed.

The first five years was a period of establishment, controversy, and a struggle for survival. It all happened without a plan. One thing followed another and happily, we survived.

We established a civic enterprise that was a credit to the city of San Francisco and perhaps one of the greatest accomplishments in the history of urban-rural relations. The farmer felt at home, and likewise, the city consumer responded in ever-increasing numbers as judged by the Saturday crowds. They now came from a radius of 75 miles to meet, shop and chat with the farmers. At the same time, relationships were established that were mutually enjoyed, in many cases, on a first name basis.

During this period, the Farmers' Market enjoyed good management. The best and most beloved manager was Tom Christian, a former agriculture inspector under the regime of Bill Carroll, the likable but controversial agricultural commissioner. He was the third manager and reigned for many years. Tom was a fair man who made many friends. I don't believe he had any enemies.

We were fortunate that we had a mixture of old and young farmers who did things together. If there was a surplus of cauliflower, they informed me so I could then publicize a surplus sale of large, medium and small cauliflower at an attractive price. We emphasized small sizes, which were never available in the supermarkets, to apartment house dwellers who welcomed buying a small cauliflower. The same approach was applied to apples where small "school boy" apples were ideal for the little one's lunch.

Whenever we managed to get a few lines in the newspapers and an occasional plug on radio and television, this brought out the housewives, or we should say, the "shoppers." Then, we noted a new type of shopper — people seeking organic vegetables and fruits. The public was concerned that the supermarkets, handling the produce of the large-scale, mechanized, and chemically fertilized crops, could no way carry the organic produce.

What is an organic fruit or vegetable? The Department of Agriculture shied away from giving an official definition. The public became conscious of the small grower, the family-size farmer who, on a smaller scale, was still using manure and green cover crops that were ploughed under; thus, supplying the organic matter and humus necessary to produce a vitamin-filled fruit or vegetable.

Another most welcomed shopper, the "co-op" buyer, came to the Farmers' Market to buy for groups of families or neighbors. Gradually, the student co-op groups from the Bay Area colleges, fraternity houses, rest homes, small restaurants, and the increasing number of younger couples came looking for fresh-picked, vitamin-filled produce. It was a changing scene.

Perhaps the biggest change took place with the influx of Asians, Africans, and the many Arabic groups who shopped early, generally at daybreak and in the early morning. This augmented the old-time Europeans who also preferred to shop during the early hours of the morning.

Our struggles with our adversaries had come to an end. I constantly warned the growers not to be naive and let their guards down. We had to protect what we had gained. This was not an easy task to keep the farmers informed. I put out my semi-monthly newsletter which was distributed to all the stall holders, and we also had occasional meetings.

The problem we faced was the seasonal changes of farmers coming into the market. We did have a small number who were there the whole year-round. The citrus growers and various vegetable truck farmers, who made up half of the growers at the market, stayed from three to six months. The others were seasonal with one or two crops, usually peaches or apricots.

As time went on, we lost a few farmers and gained newcomers. It was a constantly changing situation where many growers, especially the seasonal ones, never knew what was going on. Some didn't care despite the handing out of information by word-of-mouth or newsletter. You might say, "There was nothing to fight about."

I called meetings at various times to update the growers with any information that would be pertinent to them. Sometimes we just got together to socialize or air out any problems they might have at the market. If you ever attended a farmers meeting, you will understand what I was up against. While all this was done in a friendly atmosphere, I always had to keep control.

A farmers meeting was held in the same manner of a committee meeting. It was usually short, but was filled with a lot of input. I felt that it was best to have the farmers express themselves and let out any steam they held inside. At the end, they would comment, "John, that was a good meeting." That was all I wanted to hear.

I was greatly impressed by a statement made by Lee Iacocca in his book, *Iacocca*, where he gave his impressions of dealing with committees. He said, "The most important decisions in corporate life are made by individuals, not committees. . .You need committees because that is where people share their knowledge and intentions. But when committees replace individuals, then the productivity begins to decline. Listen to the committees, the ideas, the suggestions and say, 'Okay, I have heard everybody. Now here's what we are going to do.'"

With the approach of the 25th anniversary since the founding of the Farmers' Market on August 12, 1943, we decided to celebrate this Silver Anniversary. I appointed Frank Helbing, president of the Apartment House Owners Association and a prominent member of my Farmer's Market Board, as chairman of this colorful civic event.

There was a gala celebration with more than 50,000 attending, causing a half-mile back-up on Alemany Boulevard. The crowds were efficiently handled by the police and special officers. It looked like a county fair. Prizes were given out for the most attractive decorations. Each farmer was permitted to decorate his stall based on what crops he produced. This was rather unique and developed into quite a challenge. A grape grower would decorate with grape vines, leaves and clusters of grapes. Some would add a wine press or a grape crusher. An artichoke grower would use plants with the artichokes attached to the vine. It was up to their own imagination. National attention was garnered for their displays of talent and originality.

It was a beautiful, warm San Francisco day as everyone enjoyed the music of the municipal band and the street-strolling musicians. Eleven boys' clubs entered a watermelon eating contest, with Mayor Joseph Alioto awarding the prizes. The highlight of the festivities was a luncheon held at the Sun Valley Dairy adjacent to the Farmers' Market. Vince Palmieri and his wife, Josephine, along with co-partners Ben and Doris Teshera, hosted this annual affair for our citizens' committee, farmers, and civic dignitaries.

That following Wednesday, a banquet was held in my honor at the San Francisco Press Club on Post Street. It was sponsored by the Municipal Executives Association of which I served as president from 1956 to 1957. There was a capacity crowd of 350 people. Joseph Allen was master of ceremonies as the Honorable John B. Molinari, Presiding Judge of the California Court of Appeals, made my introduction.

The mayor of San Francisco, Joseph Alioto, was the speaker of the evening. He played an important role in the formulative years of the Farmers' Market, especially during our continuous problems with the Wholesale Produce Merchants and the Retail Growers Association. Others in attendance included Thomas Mellon, the chief administrative officer, many city, state and federal officials, civic dignitaries, and those representing the Farm Bureau and other agricultural bodies. It was quite a memorable affair.

Occasionally, there were charges and accusations made by those who were opposed to the Farmers' Market, claiming that the fruits and vegetables sold there were substandard. Unfortunately, each time these statements were made, we had to be on the defensive by proving that they were only lies. Otherwise, the Farmers' Market would have died in its infancy a long time ago.

There was the case of a Porterville orange grower, Ray

Thompson, who was accused and charged (by our old, lovable but vengeful Bill Carroll, the agricultural commissioner) of selling unfit grapefruit. He was arrested and was to appear before Judge John J. Fahey in the Municipal Court. I publicly charged Carroll with instituting a reign of terror. The half crate of Thompson's spoiled grapefruit which he happened to inspect was set aside as garbage to be dumped. The balance of the load of 50 boxes was above standard. Judge Fahey found Thompson guilty and sentence was to be passed in a few days.

I asked Joseph Alioto to appear in court to protest on behalf of the growers who, by this time, were being terrorized by Carroll's agricultural inspectors. There were many minor violations found such as having no name on the containers or some other trivial-like matter. Alioto pleaded before Judge Fahey to review the case inasmuch as the Farmers' Market had become a local political issue and this was merely an example of the harassment going on. After re-examining the evidence, Judge Fahey decided that Thompson was the victim of an unjust and incomplete inspection made by Carroll and stated that, "I hereby reject this case on insufficient evidence."

The publicity generated from this case was to the market's benefit by bringing out record crowds. Several days after the court hearing, I met Bill Carroll at the market and said, "Thanks, Bill. You certainly gave us quite a boost." I couldn't hate the guy. We wound up having a cup of coffee in a nearby restaurant as if we had been lifelong friends.

Many years later at another one of our public celebrations, I had the pleasure of introducing Mayor Alioto and publicly thanked him since we never received a bill or statement from him for his many services. His immediate response was, "A dollar bill would settle the matter." One of the farmers handed him a crisp one dollar bill, which he immediately endorsed and gave to me. I now have this signed dollar in my treasured possessions.

The Farmers' Market helped the city in more ways than one. Its Civic Center had been plagued by pigeons since the days of political boss Abe Ruef. Back in 1949, Mayor Elmer Robinson inaugurated a campaign against the messy pigeons. Most everyone, particularly the tourists, enjoyed the hundreds of colorful birds that seemed to be everywhere looking for handouts. The San Francisco pigeons had the reputation of being the best-fed pigeons in the United States. This did not sit too well with Mayor Robinson. His main objection was that these well-fed birds made no effort in using the many public restrooms in the Civic Center. They did, however, favor the dome and the many window ledges adorning our beautiful city hall. The Board of Supervisors rather agreed with the mayor and urgently passed a city ordinance that made the feeding of pigeons a misdemeanor.

The pigeons themselves were quite organized. Realizing that their feeding grounds were in danger, they sent out scouts to look for greener pastures. Much to our surprise, we noticed one day about 20 to 30 pigeons in the central area of the Farmers' Market. With the abundant supply of food available there at that time, how could they resist staying away? There were large quantities of peas and cherries as well as other attractive tidbits. The next day, their number grew to 100 and by the end of the week, we must have been feeding at least 300 to 400 a day. So where do they roost at night? It didn't take too long to figure out that the pigeons were actually commuting between the city hall and the Farmers' Market.

It turned out to be a bed and board situation. We fed them at the Farmers' Market and Mayor Elmer Robinson and the Board of Supervisors boarded them at the city hall. The market enjoyed this new attraction and so did the many children who with great glee made sure the pigeons would not go hungry.

The new ordinance was not enforced, because too many senior citizens defied the city and resumed feeding the birds. After all these years, the problem still remains. I had lunch with Mayor Robinson one day and convinced him that since Venice was noted for its pigeons, why shouldn't San Francisco?

Time and again, the Farmers' Market saved a farmer's crop from financial loss. Sebastopol is known as the Gravenstein apple capitol of the country. The Gravenstein is an early maturing apple and one of the most flavorful. It also makes outstanding apple pie and cider.

The *Santa Rosa Press Democrat* printed a headline story stating that "Gravenstein growers must find a market for a million boxes of apples, or they would be lost." The problem was that the export market had collapsed. Again, the Farmers' Market came to the rescue. There was no way we could sell a million boxes. The best we could do was probably sell 30,000 to 50,000 boxes with a citywide newspaper publicity campaign. Well, it turned out that we did better than that. We became the catalyst for a nationwide promotional campaign that swelled from a hill to a mountain. A parade up Market Street with truckloads of apples developed into an avalanche of community cooperation that spread to the Bay Area and eventually all over the state. They literally disappeared as many of the communities declared it "Apple Week."

The Farmers' Market also came to the aid of potato growers. In early 1950, a news story out of Washington stated that the government was holding more than 50 million bushels of surplus potatoes and didn't know what to do with them. This huge amount had accumulated because of the Department of Agriculture's "price support program" in which certain quantities of potatoes were bought in order to maintain prices. We learned that they were beginning to go bad in the Tule Lake area near Klamath Falls, one of the biggest potato-growing areas in California. We also found out that a movement began in government circles to divert large quantities of potatoes for hog feeding and converting potatoes into alcohol and fertilizer. No one gave any thought to the many hungry people there were as a result of increasing nationwide unemployment. Judging from high prices in the retail market, you would think that there would be a scarcity of potatoes rather than a huge surplus.

Once again, the brain factory at the Farmers' Market went to work. The idea began to jell that since we helped solve a huge peach surplus and more recently, the successful Sebastopol Gravenstein apple surplus, why not follow a similar program using the market as the catalyst and hopefully spreading the movement nationwide?

A story appeared in the *San Francisco Chronicle* which stated:

> "A plan to distribute surplus potatoes to needy persons has been proposed by John G. Brucato, chairman of the Farmers' Market Advisory Board. Brucato wrote Charles F. Brannan, Secretary of the Department of Agriculture in Washington, that America's surplus potatoes (50,000,000 bushels) could be put to good use by feeding the increasing number of people who are in great need by reason of unemployment and other difficulties.
>
> Brucato's plan is for civic, labor and other groups throughout the country to set up central distributing points for disposal of the potatoes. Needy persons would be designated by proper agencies of welfare and relief.

'Utilization of the surplus potatoes to help relieve human suffering would meet with public approval and justify the Department of Agriculture's price support program,' Brucato said."

Evidently, we hit the proverbial jackpot. My letter and subsequent telegram to Charles Brannan made the Associated Press and all the national news wires. With that underway, we concentrated on California, particularly the Bay Area. The Farmers' Market was the central focus point. The *San Francisco Chronicle* carried a headline, "Surplus Potatoes for San Francisco Needy on the Way Soon."

The first carload of surplus potatoes from Tule Lake arrived. Calling for volunteers, the 36,000 pounds of potatoes were sacked in 10, 20, and 30 pound bags. They were trucked to the public welfare office on Bush Street as the result of arrangements made with Ronald Born, head of the city's welfare department. The tremendous publicity received by this first shipment and its orderly distribution was unbelievable. The local newspapers were wonderfully generous with their coverage.

It seemed that the community woke up with a bang. "This was no publicity promotion," as one columnist pointed out. "It was the real thing." We took care of every recognized agency as truckload after truckload of potatoes continued to arrive in ever-increasing numbers. Then, it was Turlock's turn. Situated in the productive San Joaquin Valley, their surplus potatoes began arriving.

Everyone was rooting for us. One of my first moves was to make sure the St. Anthony's Dining Room and the many agencies set up to feed the poor and hungry received all the potatoes they needed. The results were exhilarating. The *San Francisco Progress* reported that several thousand San Francisco families had already received a month's supply of potatoes. "In one case, the freight charges on one carload received totaling $160 were paid by Daly City's automobile row." The Union Square Optimist Club paid the freight charges on another carload, the St. Vincent De Paul Society became heavily involved, and churches jumped into the program.

We were swamped with inquiries from all over the country. Our plan was simple and it worked. The potato surplus disappeared and it seemed that there were more potatoes than originally reported. Nevertheless, the retail outlets throughout the country offered special potato sales and used every gimmick possible to prevent these much-wanted potatoes from becoming fertilizer, hog feed, or alcohol.

It seemed that the Farmers' Market thrived on surpluses. California was blessed with the soil, the climate, and its outstanding farmers. It was nature, however, that ignored the rules and regulations. Shortly after we disposed of the potatoes, we were faced with a spring overproduction of strawberries. A few berry growers met with me one Saturday morning. I told them to bring the strawberries in and they would be sold. I was never questioned. Huge quantities of strawberries were brought in and with the help of the news media, we publicized a "Strawberry Shortcake Week." The *San Francisco Chronicle* came out with a headline that thousands of baskets of strawberries would be available on Saturday in honor of "Strawberry Shortcake Day." That did it. The surplus soon disappeared and things went back to normal in about two weeks, for strawberries that is.

Referring back to nature, and this was truly a year of surpluses, we did the same for the cherry and apricot growers right through the fall season.

A committee of farmers asked that I meet with them because they wanted to do something to show their appreciation for all the times I have come to their rescue. Money was out of the question. After all, this was my labor of love and their expressed appreciation was enough for me. But they were not satisfied, and if you know farmers, they are an obstinate breed. They decided that the market needed a flagpole and wanted the tallest one in San Francisco to be dedicated to me with an appropriate plaque affixed at the base of the pole. It was estimated to cost $3,000 (1950 prices). My condition was that no farmer was to contribute more than $5 each and they agreed. I said, "All right, now present your plan to Thomas Brooks, the chief administrator, and if he approves, we can proceed."

The funds were raised in a week and turned over to the city for proper disposal and management. The city, of course, donated the land, and Stu Greenberg, one of the city's public utilities commissioners and owner of a foundry that made most of the Bay Area's fire hydrants, donated the large bronze plaque dedicated to me as "Father of the Farmers' Market." The immense flagpole was 83 feet high and proclaimed the tallest in San Francisco. In later years, the flagpole developed dry rot and was condemned in 1975. I was led to believe by Ray Bozzini, the agricultural commissioner who had jurisdiction over the city's Farmers' Market, that the city would replace the flagpole with a smaller one.

Bill Berner was market manager at the time and he, too, agreed with an incensed farmers' committee that the city, because of its neglect to periodically painting the flagpole, should replace it. Time dragged on as Bozzini never had the intention of replacing "my" flagpole. It meant so much to me because it was the farmers' way of saying "thank you."

A series of debates over a three-year period suddenly came up out of a clear horizon. The San Francisco Chamber of Commerce, which tolerated the Farmers' Market only because their agricultural committee was always pro-market, initiated some roundtable discussions. In October of 1961, the subject of "Shall the Farmers' Market be Abolished" was the topic that was to be aired on radio station KNBC. I, of course, was the proponent while Ralph Moyse, the perennial secretary-manager of the Wholesale Fruit Produce Association (the commission merchants) was the opposition.

Ralph Moyse was the principal spokesman for the merchants since the beginning of our controversy in 1943. He was a likable person and we both had a great deal of respect for one another. However, when he was sitting on the other side of the table in discussion or debate, you never saw a more vicious and relentless opponent.

The debate received widespread publicity. All this, of course, helped to publicize the Farmers' Market and keep the city-operated institution in the public eye. The consensus of opinion was that I gave Moyse a real thrashing besides a lesson in basic economics. Sometimes I had two or three others on my panel, but Moyse was always alone. In this respect, I asked him where his buddies were to which he always replied, "You know, John, I am getting a little tired of fronting for these unappreciative bastards." Then, I asked, "Why do you continue?" Moyse's response was, "How else could I get all this exposure?" With that, we wound up having our usual cup of coffee.

Joseph Alioto served as mayor of San Francisco for eight years, the "Alioto Years." He was the Farmers' Market's staunchest proponent during our formulative years and saved us during the vicious attacks by the Retail Grocers Association, exposed their two leaders, Tissier and Hadeler, who had been convicted of raising prices during wartime, and aided us on various other occasions when we needed legal help. Alioto appeared at our annual festivities for eight years in a row. At one time, he was attending a labor convention in Miami where he was the main speaker and flew in about a half-hour late just to attend our ceremonies.

During Mayor Alioto's terms of office, we used the facilities of the Sun Valley Dairy, our neighbor to the west of the market, for the luncheon that always followed the festivities. The spacious meeting hall on the second floor was artistically decorated for the occasions and accommodated 225 people. These were primarily members of the citizens' committee, farmers, politicians, and friends of the market. The hall was made available by Vince Palmieri, who co-owned the dairy with Ben Teshera. Vince was my right-hand man and Ben was always there when I needed him. Their wives, Josephine Palmieri and Doris Teshera, were hosts of the banquet.

One year, I mentioned to Mayor Alioto that my wife, Joan, and I were going to Sicily in September and planned to visit St. Elia near Palermo, the birthplace of his parents. St. Elia was primarily a fishing village when the Aliotos migrated to San Francisco. As everyone knows, the Alioto name stands high in the fishing industry along the California Coast as does their restaurant on Fisherman's Wharf. On this note, Joe Tarantino, a cousin of the Aliotos who was a member of my group, was also a giant in the fish and restaurant business. His family also migrated from St. Elia.

A year later at the Farmers' Market's annual festivities, I made my report to the Mayor. "Your Honor, the village of St. Elia is no longer a small fishing hamlet, but a thriving city of over 100,000 people. . .We had a small problem as we entered the *Via Alioto*, which was under reconstruction. We got mired down and called for help. The construction crew graciously assisted us out of *Via Alioto* and we landed on the adjacent *Via Tarantino*, which was also under reconstruction so we were mired down again. Anyway, we were once again assisted and hauled into what was known as *Piazza Alioto* (Alioto Square). At this point, your Honor, we felt like we had enough of *Via Alioto*, *Via Tarantino*, and *Piazza Alioto*, so we decided to return to Palermo where, no doubt, life was a little easier."

The Mayor turned, looked me straight in the eye and said, "John, I am very much disappointed with your so-called report. You missed the biggest attraction in St. Elia." "What was that, your Honor?'' awaiting the bombshell. He continued, ''You missed seeing the biggest organ in all of Sicily, which I donated and is featured inside the church in St. Elia.'' No wonder he is one of the biggest trust-busting lawyers in the country. How can you beat this guy?

An incident that should not be overlooked occurred when my book, *The Farmer Goes to Town,* was published in 1948. Receiving statewide publicity, we ran into a snag in Fresno. It seemed that our persistent opponents, the Wholesale Produce Merchants, came up with another one of their strange moves.

The local media carried such stories as ''Fresno Stops Sale of Brucato Book,'' ''Pressure in Fresno Halts Sale of *The Farmer Goes to Town*'' and so on. Evidently, local produce merchants in Fresno did put pressure on the various bookstores. For a while, it was impossible to buy this book anywhere in the Fresno area. As the story was filtered down to us, we were told that ''unless the distributor in the Fresno area pulled *The Farmer Goes to Town* out of the bookstores, he would find it difficult to sell his other lines.'' We immediately got in touch with the local district attorney, James Thuesen, and threatened with a Restraint of Trade suit. While Mr. Thuesen was most cooperative, his conclusion was that he could find no law to cover such a case.

We did, however, fight back with the best tools at our disposal. The local farmers, together with the Farm Bureau members, put pressure on the various bookstores. Eventually, all was back to normal and Fresno, the ''raisin capitol of the world,'' went about its business as usual.

Somebody stole the garlic wreath. Now who would stoop so low as to steal our coveted garlic wreath just two days before our 1954 celebration? It was to be used in our coronation ceremony honoring Jesse Nunziati, one of our outstanding artichoke growers from Pescadero near Half Moon Bay. The wreath was on the backseat of my unlocked car while I was at the Farmers' Market meeting with some of my committee. Our local newspapers had a field day with this story, especially with how they described the 54 selected cloves strung one-by-one with the most meticulous patience and of course, the most outstanding characteristic of the garlic itself — its enticing and overwhelming aroma.

Jackie McAbata went right to work as soon as she heard the news. She worked far into the night and the next day. Outdoing herself, she produced one of the most beautiful wreaths in the history of the Farmers' Market.

Continuing in the annual selection of outstanding farmers and honoring them for their contributions, we selected Rose Acosta and Bertha Benzler for the 1976 celebration. Both Rose, who raised vegetables, and Bertha, whose specialty was table grapes, were from the San Joaquin Valley. With the emphasis on recognition of rights and equality for women, the double selection was well-received. (We were probably a little ahead of our time.)

Two directors from the First National Bank of Daly City were selected to perform the honors. Elton McGraw placed the garlic wreath around the shoulders of Rose Acosta, while Roe Ariani, chairman of the board of the bank, did likewise with Bertha Benzler.

On the Farmers' Market's 28th birthday, we did something different by featuring a Farmers' Market Public Auction. It was not the usual kind of auction where you bid the highest price, but more of a "reverse auction." The farmers had an unusual, heavy supply of just about everything at that time. The idea was to line up as many lugs of both fruits and vegetables and put them on the auction block. We managed to have over five thousand lugs of surplus produce pledged and made available in the central market area. The heavy publicity from the news media brought out the shoppers.

The *San Francisco Examiner* headlined the story, "Farmers' Market Reverse Auction." It read:

"A mock public auction, where the bidder bids down instead of up, will highlight the Farmers' Market 28th Anniversary Celebration on Saturday, August 7th. In this reverse auction, prices start at a higher level and are gradually bid down."

How in heaven's name did this work? By pre-arrangement, the farmer stated his cost, plus a markup of ten percent which totaled his selling price. It was all controlled by the auctioneer, who had the price before him when the particular commodity was to be sold. In simple terms, assume that a farmer had a lug of tomatoes containing 25 pounds in the box. He fixed his cost at $3.00 a lug and added ten percent, making his selling price $3.30. The auctioneer, knowing the price on this particular box of tomatoes, would start the bidding with "I have $6.00. Do I hear $5.50?" He got $5.50. He continued with "Do I have

$5.00?'' and so on until the price got to $3.30. With a loud bang of the hammer, he then shouted, "Sold!"

Mayor Joseph Alioto officially started the auction at 11 a.m. After conducting a few initial sales, he was relieved by one of our professional auctioneers. In three hours, the 5,000 lugs disappeared. We not only had a helluva lot of fun as one committee member put it, but we moved a lot of fruits and vegetables in record time. Sales of 10 to 50 lugs were sold to the many group buyers who bought for the various student co-ops from all over the Bay Area, and the block groups who bought for a number of families and neighbors.

Very little effort was needed from the farmers to keep the market growing. Each mayor in office strongly supported the Farmers' Market. I remember with great fondness on our 35th anniversary when Mayor Dianne Feinstein performed the honors. The event took place on August 14, 1979. Carla Molinari was crowned queen, an honor given to the prettiest farmer's daughter. She was the 18 year-old daughter of Vic and Carol Molinari, vegetable growers from Mountain View. We had honored her grandfather in the early years as "Farmer of the Year." Here was an attractive, personable and all-around young lady who could go places in Hollywood. George Elmer Friend, an 80 year-old citrus grower from Ojai was also honored for being the oldest active farmer selling at the Farmers' Market.

I have had many fond memories of the "farmers who came to town." There was Paul Mancini who, for over 45 years, regularly brought his apples, pears and prunes to the Farmers' Market. He was the second farmer to come in on August 12, 1943. He had 140 lugs of Bartlett pears weighing 25 pounds each and sold them at one dollar a lug. I can remember Paul standing on the back of his truck collecting one dollar bills as his eager customers grabbed lugs of pears and headed for their cars.

Paul Mancini still comes in every Saturday with a small pick-up truck containing no more than six boxes of fruit, which wasn't enough to pay his expenses. Recently, one Saturday morning after our usual greetings, I asked him why he keeps coming to the market. He said, "John, I am lonely. . .lonely for my many friends." I must say that his friends number in the thousands. To know him is to love him. One of my oldtime committee members, Isabel D'Aloisio, who purchased the first box of pears on the opening day, still comes down to shop regularly, but mainly to chat with Paul Mancini.

The Molinari family has been the mainstay of the Farmers'

Market since its inception. Two generations were represented. They farmed nine acres in Mountain View surrounded by Silicon Valley industrial giants. The family had owned many more acres at one time, but progress forced them to sell profitable vegetable-growing land at astronomical prices. The remaining nine acres was their homestead and the rich, black soil produced the most flavorful vegetables ever brought into the Farmers' Market. Every Saturday morning at the market, the Molinaris have no problem selling out by mid-day. In addition to their nine acres, the family farms a spread down at Morgan Hill in the Santa Clara Valley, one of the few remaining farms resisting the avalanche of industrial progress.

Angelo Molinari and his wife, Yolanda, were one of the first farmers in 1943. Their son, Victor, became the second generation farmer. Together with his wife, Carol, and their four lovely daughters, Carla, Yolanda, Julie and Diana, they sold their produce every Saturday to their many friends and customers. We had honored Angelo and Victor in a double ceremony on August 12, 1972. It was billed as a father and son combination.

A year later, Angelo passed away. He was 74. The family farm was passed on from father to son. To this day, mechanization and conglomerate farming has not yet been able to overtake the Molinari farm.

Another member of the Molinari family is Vickie Martinelli, who farms in Morgan Hill and operates independently from her brother, Vic. Her specialties are corn, onions, and some of the best garlic grown in California.

Victor Martino is another young second generation farmer who raises fruit in the Stockton area of the San Joaquin Valley. Now 26, he succeeded his father, Nick, who passed away five years ago at the age of 74. Vic assumed management of the family orchard, married a beautiful girl who recently gave birth to a son. Could this be the future third generation? Vivian, Vic's mother, no longer comes to the Farmers' Market to help sell. She now takes care of the family roadside stand close to home.

One of my special farming families are the Ramireze's, who farm their own 25 acres, plus another 10 acres which they lease. They are vegetable growers specializing in oriental vegetables. I call them the wonderful family of "giants," although John Ramirez is only five feet tall and his talented wife, Terry, is just a shade below that. They are the cream of the Filipino farmers.

John Ramirez came from the Phillipines where he farmed

in the rich agricultural area of Narvacan, and Terry was from the neighboring valley of Caba La-Onion. As leaders of the increasing numbers of Filipino farmers coming into the Farmers' Market, we honored them during our anniversary celebration in 1982.

From the fields of Half Moon Bay adjacent to the Pacific Ocean come the Andreotti family to sell their artichokes, sprouts and pumpkins. Dino Andreotti, Sr. was one of the first vegetable growers to come to the Farmers' Market. He gave way to Dino, Jr., who continued to farm the rich, black soil that made coastside vegetables so tasty and nutritious. The famous Half Moon Bay fog, of course, contributed greatly to the high-quality of crops grown.

Dino Andreotti, Jr. married a wonderful girl, Terri, who is the businesswoman. She sells mostly at their roadside stand on Kelly Avenue in Half Moon Bay. On Saturdays, she assists her husband in selling their choice crops at the Farmers' Market. Although they sell some of their produce at the South San Francisco Wholesale Produce Market, the Farmers' Market is their "insurance" inasmuch as whatever they sell is for cash, which is not always the case when selling through the wholesale commission brokers.

Dino and Terri worked hard with the growers committee and did much to promote the market, particularly in the fall when they brought in huge quantities of pumpkins. They had such unusual displays that San Francisco school children were taken in busloads to view their stand, especially during the Halloween season.

One of the highly respected farmers is Garland Eggman, a citrus grower from the San Joaquin Valley. He is seen every Saturday working like a Trojan and at the same time, trying to convert whoever he can to the Mormon religion. I guess I must have been singled out as a good prospect, for Garland has been working on me for over 15 years.

One day, one of Garland's fellow bishops was visiting with him and collecting the ten percent tithe for the Mormon Church. He introduced me in a way that I felt somewhat embarrassed by pointing out that as the founder of the Farmers' Market whose labor of love has continued for over 40 years, I helped at least 100 small farmers save their farms from going into bankruptcy. The two bishops really ganged up on me after hearing that. They strongly implied that I was needed and would make an outstanding Mormon, and promised that I would sit at their right hand when we entered the "pearly gates." I was offered the title of "bishop" if I agreed to be one of them. They brushed aside the fact that I was a practicing Roman Catholic, a former officer of the Knights of Columbus, a member of the prestigious Serra Club, and a prominent member of the Knights of Malta (perhaps the highest lay organization in the Roman Catholic Church). "This is why we want you, John. You have excellent qualifications." At any rate, they did not succeed, but Garland hasn't given up yet.

When I sat down to dinner that evening with my wife, Joan, I mentioned the happenings concerning Garland Eggman and his fellow bishops. I said, "You know, Joan, all these years of my deep relationship involving my church and faith, I have never received any kind of offer from my archbishop or anyone else who could hardly scratch the surface of what was proposed by Eggman's bishops." "John," she replied, "I have a feeling that our lives will continue along the same religious lines until the very end. Now eat your dinner before the ravioli get cold." Joan, after all, is always my so-called "balance wheel." She has a way of bringing me back to earth, especially when my thoughts stray into strange areas.

The Ferrari family from Linden in the San Joaquin Valley holds a unique distinction. Not only do they contribute much to the success of this city-operated institution, but they are the only family involving a third generation farmer. Wayne Ferrari is the 40 year-old son of George. He was educated at Delta College in Stockton and chose to continue in his father's and grandfather's footsteps. He represents the future of family farming in America.

The first generation Ferrari was Constantino, who raised vegetables near San Jose. In time, he sold the farm and moved to Linden where he planted a diversified orchard. There were nine children in the family. One of them was George, who took over the more than 200 acres of peaches, apricots, cherries, apples, almonds, walnuts, and some 25 acres of vegetable land. George and Wayne became the Farmers' Market's strongest supporters. They were the backbone of the successful growers promotion committee. Although three generations of Ferraris have been selling at the market, there is now a fourth generation — Wayne's oldest son, who is preparing to attend Stanford University. He assists his father every Saturday at the market. Recently, I asked him if he was going to continue in the operation of the Ferrari orchards in due time. His immediate response was a broad smile to which he added, "No way."

There were many other giants who were part of the passing parade of farmers. Some were here for a few years; others came and stayed on a little longer. They all left their mark in some form. To me, they were my family. I got to know them and they got to know me — a former farmer, a "city slicker," but one who had their welfare always close to my heart as long as they played by the rules. The beauty of the Farmers' Market is compared to a League of Nations, where there are so many ethnic groups and a mishmash of almost every religion.

There was a headline in the August 14, 1978 issue of the *San Francisco Examiner* that read, "City Snubs Celebrated Farmers' Market." Since the market's beginning, the city always assisted us financially in publicizing and promoting our annual celebration. While under the control of the county agricultural commissioner, the market came under the overall supervision of the chief administrative officer (CAO). Expenses of the annual celebration were submitted to the CAO and he paid them. We never asked for more than a thousand dollars. I kept the expenses at a minimum inasmuch as most of the performers and participants donated their services. I loathed taking up a collection or asking for money.

Thomas Brooks, the original chief administrative officer, gave us no problems. He went out of his way to help us as did his successors, Sherman Duckel and Thomas Mellon. As a matter of fact, these able officials conducted the city's business with a minimum of help. There were only three administrative assistants in a relatively small office. With the retirement of Tom Mellon came a change that was not only disastrous, but rather final as far as we were concerned.

Roger Boas, a wealthy automobile dealer who had served on the Board of Supervisors, was now the new chief administrative officer for the City and County of San Francisco. While he was a supervisor, I cannot recall any outstanding legislation which he authorized, but now he was the CAO — an appointment many wondered how he got.

Boas' first appearance was before the Municipal Executive Association, the only organization of its kind in the United States which consisted of department heads and top city officials. A dinner was held at the Press Club and as always for this event, it was a packed house. I will never forget his opening remarks: "I am just a green pea and have lots to learn. I promise you, however, that I will surround myself with the best brains that money will buy."

Roger Boas made good on his boast. Today, I believe there are about twelve administrative assistants and possibly another ten or more in minor posts, all carrying out the duties that were so ably conducted by Thomas Brooks, Sherman Duckel and Thomas Mellon. His office space on the second floor of the city hall was unbelievable compared to his predecessors.

Having a good personal relationship with Roger Boas over the years, I never realized that I was in for a shock. Our problems began when I received a letter on June 29, 1978. I had applied for the usual partial funding just prior to our annual festivities. My request was only for $500. The letter read:

> "Dear Mr. Brucato:
> I wish to advise you that your organization will not be receiving funds from the publicity and advertising fund for the fiscal year 1978-79."
>
> Roger Boas

It went on to state the many reasons why we were to be denied the funds. When you consider that the publicity and advertising fund was primarily used to publicize and promote San Francisco with monies coming from the hotel tax fund, we were at a loss as to why we were eliminated. If we were not receiving such favorable local, state and national publicity for our activities, particularly during our annual civic celebration which attracted thousands from all over California and out of the state, I might have accepted his letter. Of all the city activities, the Farmers' Market was the most publicized. What's a measly $500?

I will not go into the unbelievable stacks of papers that had to be filled out — the mass of spaghetti-like red tape. We, all prominent San Franciscans on the citizens' committee, felt like we were treated like outsiders and "nin com poops." "To hell with it," we said.

The headline in the *San Francisco Examiner* of July 10, 1979 stated that "Roger Boas will Hand Out $4 Million from the Hotel Tax Fund to 92 City Groups." Of course, the Farmers' Market was not included. The recipients included many organizations which most had never even heard of. I believe the Farmers' Market did more to publicize San Francisco than at least 80 of the 92 groups benefitting from the $4 million appropriation. We carried on despite the city's snub.

It should be noted that later in this narrative, we eventually had to take up a weekly collection from the farmers and vendors in order to carry on the promotional campaign. Nothing came easy as we had to fight to get anything done . . . that is, anything from the city. We were like the proverbial duck, letting the water run conveniently off its back, but nevertheless kept going. We fought to get our area cleaned and painted, and miniscule odds and ends repaired, but only after much persistence and extreme patience. The city was never easy to deal with. What really kept me going was that no matter how difficult things were, I had only to be reminded of Garibaldi's famous motto, *"Sempre Avanti"* or "Always go forward."

Over the years, my activity with the Farmers' Market brought me many new friends. One of the individuals who I recall with great fondness was the late George Burger. I first met him long before he assumed the title of "Potato and Onion King" of the San Francisco Wholesale Produce Market.

After I graduated from college in New York and before going into the champagne business in California, I worked as a seasonal agricultural inspector for the California State Department of Agriculture in the early 1930s. I was assigned to an agricultural inspection station on the top of Pacheco Pass for the purpose of inspecting trucks carrying produce from the San Joaquin Valley to the San Francisco, Oakland and Bay Area markets. These inspection stations were located at many key points throughout the state for the purpose of inspecting and upholding the high standards of California fruits and vegetables, and to protect the consumer from inferior and substandard produce.

Signs were posted on the highway ordering drivers of trucks carrying produce to stop for inspection. We always knew when George Burger was coming. His broken-down Ford truck carrying a few sacks of potatoes would chug-chug and finally make it to the inspection area, with the radiator steaming like Mt. Vesuvius. We all felt sorry for poor George. He had patches on his pants and gnarled hands which clearly indicated that he had to work hard to make a living. In spite of this, I took a liking to him.

I lost track of George Burger until 1943 when the Farmers' Market was born. Unwittingly and unplanned, I found myself facing him on the other side of the table. He was one of my biggest and perhaps most bitter opponents, together with Ralph

Moyse, Jacobs, Malcolm, Burtt, and a score of others from the Wholesale Produce Market.

Between the period of my inspection duties and 1943, George Burger cornered the potato and onion market. Evidently, as it turned out, there was a severe shortage of potatoes. The spuds sold like they were diamonds and were nowhere to be found until he turned up one day with a truckload of potatoes. He came in with another truckload the next day, and the next, and the next. Burger knew a few potato growers in the San Joaquin Valley who had potatoes to sell, lots of potatoes, and he made a killing.

George Burger was not an educated man, but a "diamond in the rough." He was a businessman, following up his success by signing up one potato grower after another. They nicknamed him "the potato king." He also did the same with onions, now making him "the potato and onion king" of the Wholesale Produce Market. He bought property and land. Burger was now a big operator and everyone wanted his potatoes — restaurants, hotels, supermarkets, and other institutions.

Our early friendship was a thing of the past. Burger attacked me with vigor and bitterness. He hated the Farmers' Market, and accused me privately and publicly of being a Communist, a radical, and just a no good guy. You had to know him to be on the receiving end. He had become a very important political figure in San Francisco. He was strong with labor, and if you were seeking public office, you went to see Burger.

Things occur in life that in no way could ever have been planned. It happened at El Retiro, the well-known Jesuit Retreat House in Los Altos. For years, I headed a group of my Dante Council Knights of Columbus members on an annual three-day spiritual retreat there. Although El Retiro is conducted by the Jesuits, anyone of any denomination is welcome. In fact, many Protestant ministers, rabbis, and many other faiths attend. The Jesuits are great teachers.

George Burger was also a steady retreatant. His group was eventually combined with my group. One of the requirements at El Retiro was silence. There were periods during the three-day retreat known as "free" periods where silence can be broken and one could speak to his heart's content. The first year, Burger and I didn't speak to each other. However, during one of the free periods the following year, he approached me and with his arm around my shoulder, we walked through the attractive, landscaped paths as if we were long-lost friends. He told me that he misjudged me and I told him that I was happy to be his friend again.

George Burger, to the day he went to his eternal reward, became one of my best friends. We met often at the Franciscan Restaurant at Fisherman's Wharf which he owned and counseled me on the activities at the Wholesale Produce Market. Eventually, he became a strong proponent for the Farmers' Market. Strange as it may seem, I always thanked the Good Lord for making it possible to have a sincere friend in Burger. Every year, when we held our annual celebration luncheon at Vince Palmieri's Sun Valley hall, I would repeat the George Burger story in a rather low key. This is the way he wanted it and seemed to enjoy it.

Most every convent, rest home, and many other institutions in the Bay Area received free potatoes from George Burger. Huge quantities of spuds were disposed of in this manner every week. This was his way of remembering the time when he had little more than that "chug-chug" Model-T Ford truck that barely made it over Pacheco Pass. I often introduced him as the man I knew when he had patches on his pants.

Once again, a former enemy became a good close friend. What few people knew was that George Burger's charities became legend.

I might say that up to this point, the San Francisco Farmers' Market, the "granddaddy" of all the farmers' markets in California, had survived 31 years of a most interesting and unusual era. I have been asked by people time-to-time, "How is the market doing?" Rather than give a standard reply, I found that the only true and honest response has been, "Any institution that has survived all these years must indeed have a great deal of merit."

During the period of 1976 through 1984, the Farmers' Market continued to enjoy increasing favor and patronage from shoppers coming in from the entire Bay Area.

The handling of the market's promotion and publicity was always left for me to do instead of the market manager. Had it not been close to my heart, I would never have taken on such a responsibility, especially since there was no compensation for me. I only agreed to do it because I had a strong belief in the concept of the Farmers' Market and a commitment to the struggling, hardworking farmers.

In this effort, I had no plan. All that I knew was if I didn't inform the news media of what was available at the market, no one else would. Because of my close relationship with the journalists since my involvement in the Victory Garden campaign, I had the knowledge of how to go about securing the necessary publicity. This enabled the farmers to get a fair price for their produce as well as aided them in selling out early. It was a wonderful sight to see farmers going home with their trucks full of empty crates and their pockets stuffed with hard cash.

I had no problems calling the city desk or sending out news releases. At times, I would say, ''We have a little problem at the Farmers' Market. We're expecting a flood of apricots and peaches this Saturday and I would appreciate your help.'' The response from the city editor was, ''All right, John, I will give you a reporter who will take your story. Good luck.'' Sometimes we would get a big story and the farmers would be happy. I followed this procedure for the past 33 years.

With the advent of Bill Berner, the new manager, I decided that the responsibility of publicizing the market should be his. I told him that I would be happy to assist him. He did send out an occasional press release to the news media, but to no avail. They were not familiar with him at the city desk and Bill's efforts generally wound up in the trash basket. Without timely and proper promotion, the market's revenues began to drop. Shoppers became fewer while the farmers brought in smaller loads.

The loss became noticeable at the city hall. The market was supposed to pay its own way, but at this point, it wasn't. We were in the red. There were those unfriendly to the Farmers' Market, who were patiently waiting for an opportunity to snipe or attack us. It surfaced with the 1976 Grand Jury Report.

The County Grand Jury, as part of their duties in reviewing the operations of all city departments, took a sharp look at the city-operated Farmers' Market. They noted the falling receipts and recommended that perhaps the market site of approximately four acres could be put to a higher use. I didn't like that report and smelled trouble. The Grand Jury Report was well-publicized and noted that 84 percent of the Farmers' Market's budget went towards the salaries of the market manager, clerk, janitor, and Ray Bozzini, the agricultural commissioner. It was generally known that downtown investors, developers, speculators and others long had their eyes on this desirable four-acre site situated at the junction of Alemany Boulevard and the Bayshore Freeway.

The first bombshell was dropped in the form of a letter written by William O'Keefe to Quentin Kopp, then president of the Board of Supervisors. O'Keefe was a former member of the San Francisco Public Utilities Commission who generally got himself a few headlines involving the use of small aircraft at the San Francisco International Airport. Because he was a PUC commissioner, various references involving a conflict of interest made breezy reading. At that time, the airport was under the jurisdiction of the Public Utilities Commission. Presently, it operates with a separate airport commission.

I had known William O'Keefe since my days as manager of the water department's land division. He was a member of the Public Utilities Commission whose jurisdiction the water department came under. We became quite friendly because of the weekly meetings I had attended at the city hall.

The letter to Quentin Kopp was a lengthy one listing many irregularities which decreased the income to the city, and many charges which were definitely not true. O'Keefe pointed out that the day of the small farmer was over and the city was involved in a "socialistic handout." There were many offensive and unqualified statements. Supervisor Kopp called me and asked me for my reply, which I was very happy to give. In a four-page response, I not only answered all the charges and ridiculous statements that were made, but I really believed that this would satisfy O'Keefe and end the matter.

Lo' and behold, another long letter was received by Supervisor Kopp, who thanked me for my previous reply and again asked me to address this new "epistle." I mentioned to him that perhaps O'Keefe must be preparing himself for next year's supervisorial election and probably felt that a public hearing would provide him with some much-needed exposure. At any rate, I felt that my reply would finally put the ridiculous and unfounded charges to rest.

I was wrong, again. This time, O'Keefe called and invited me to meet with him in San Francisco. In this respect, I informed him that if he wanted to meet with me, it would have to be at my home in Millbrae where I maintained my office. On October 5, 1976, a three-hour meeting took place. When he found out that Joan was Irish and raised in the Mission District of San Francisco, the atmosphere changed and discussion moved from the Farmers' Market to growing up in that heavily Irish-populated area. I chuckled as I listened to the two reminisce of their younger days. O'Keefe thoroughly enjoyed his visit as the business at hand was temporarily put aside.

Another meeting was held on January 10, 1977. After a spirited discussion on the Farmers' Market, Joan decided to serve some of her homemade Sicilian *biscotti* and a bit of *frittata*. The meeting came to a close and O'Keefe agreed to drop his attack. However, his parting words that afternoon were in a rather friendly tone and with a smile, he said, "We shall meet again, John. I am not through."

I called Supervisor Kopp, who jokingly requested a sampling of Joan's *biscotti* and *frittata*. He said, "Keep in touch anytime this matter comes up again. I will be happy to assist the citizens' committee." While we put the O'Keefe matter to bed, something else happened, a very serious something else.

Mother Nature decided to play havoc on the farmers and the Farmers' Market. She brought upon a drought — one that lasted almost three years. The entire state of California suffered one of its worst dry periods of the century. Many small farmers were facing ruination. The lack of water for irrigation, dry wells, and unusually hot weather drastically curtailed the planting and growing of vegetables and crops. Fruit trees were especially hit hard, resulting in short crops, small sizes, and sick and drying trees.

On my usual Saturday morning visit, the farmers sought me out to discuss the situation. They brought their grief and despair. These were my friends, my family, and they were in serious trouble, but I couldn't help them. The number of farmers' trucks coming into the market had reduced considerably. The stalls were only one-third full. It was indeed a sad picture. It became so bleak that the future of the Farmers' Market was at stake. Perhaps, I thought, that the time had come when drastic measures had to take place.

Larry Schriber was part-owner and operator of the adjacent Farmers' Market Arcade. This was a huge complex which included a canned goods discount outlet, dairy, meat market, and an out-of-season produce market. He submitted a fantastic proposal to me in which the entire Farmers' Market land of four acres could be converted into a complete large-scale food center. It would include nine restaurants of various nationalities, fish vendors *a la* Fisherman's Wharf, and colorful shops featuring many types of food products. The city would continue to operate a limited Farmers' Market with about 50 stalls and reduced fees. In other words, the market would be used as a come-on to attract shoppers. It would be a glorified

Hollywood-type Farmers' Market (a misnomer if there ever was one).

The famous Hollywood Farmers' Market was started by the local farm bureau as a genuine Farmers' Market several years before we began in 1943. It was quite successful in a sense that it was a true farmers' market, allowing only genuine farmers to sell direct to the public. However, someone in charge got a little greedy and allowed a few vendors to come in making it difficult for a farmer to compete. Eventually, the vendors increased to the point where the farmers were being squeezed out one-by-one. How could a farmer compete with a vendor who had access to the Wholesale Produce Market where he could buy unsold produce at rock-bottom prices, especially on Fridays when everything had to go to avoid wilt and decay? Eventually, there were no farmers left at the famous Hollywood Farmers' Market. They did, however, retain the misleading misnomer of "Farmers' Market." I am surprised that no one has ever filed suit against this great rip-off. What has happened to the Farm Bureau, the Grange, and other farm organizations?

Larry Schriber went to great length to put together his proposal. He invested a sizeable sum in an architectural plan that looked rather exciting. It called for the city to grant the developer a 40 year lease. The lessee would construct the entire project at his own expense, setting a minimal capital investment of $1,500,000. This would also include ample parking and an attractive, landscaped shopping complex. Meetings were held with Roger Boas, the chief administrative officer, who had the overall jurisdiction of the Farmers' Market, as well as with his administrative assistants. Much time was consumed in going through the tangle of bureaucratic procedures. It was so exasperating and discouraging that Schriber "gave up the ghost" and publicly stated, "I am convinced that you can't do business with the city."

The unexpected happened. The drought was over. The land responded to the rains and the farmers rushed to plant their crops. It was like a glorious spring after a harsh winter. Slowly, the farmers returned. Then, they came in increasing numbers. Like the swallows, the farmers returned to their *Capistrano*.

We were not quite out of the woods. Something had to be done to get the consumers back into the Farmers' Market. After much soul searching triggered by this change of events, I discussed the situation with my citizens' committee, the farmers, and other interested groups. We all realized that we had indeed reached the crossroads again. I felt that the farmers, themselves, had to make the final choice. In this repsect, I called a meeting of all the farmers who were available. There were 27 on that particular morning. My first questions were, "Where do we go from here?" "Do you or don't you want to continue the Farmers' Market?"

The meeting took place in the office of Bill Berner, the market manager, in May of 1979. It was unanimously decided that the market should continue as a bonafide farmers' market. I asked for an ad hoc committee and appointed nine farmers who were willing to work for the benefit of the market — their market. They were very close to me. We rejoiced and suffered over the years as the market had its ups and downs. The members included Vic Molinari from Morgan Hill in the Santa Clara Valley; George Ferrari from Linden in the San Joaquin Valley; Dino Andreotti from Half Moon Bay in San Mateo County; Jackie McAbata, our Filipino representative who also came from Half Moon Bay; Vic Martino from the San Joaquin Valley; Ruby Osburn from Ojai in Ventura County; Tim Hurst from Sebastopol in Sonoma County; Jim Quinn from Fresno; and Frank Daniels from Modesto.

It was agreed that we should hire a professional public relations firm to promote the Farmers' Market. A plan was adopted and approved by Ray Bozzini, the agricultural commissioner, and Bill Berner. Berner gave his enthusiastic support. He and Bozzini really had no choice. It was either this or close down the market in which event, Berner would have no job and Bozzini would suffer a loss in pay. He was never friendly to the Farmers' Market. He could care less.

It is unbelievable how fate somehow helps solve a problem. By coincidence, I ran into an old family friend at a bank opening in San Mateo whom I hadn't seen in many years — Alessandro Baccari — a nationally recognized technician in media communications. I asked him if he would assist us in promoting the Farmers' Market and proceeded to explain the situation, pointing out that the market was at a low point and it would be an uphill battle to re-establish its popularity. I also mentioned that we had no funds and that it would have to be raised from voluntary fees. Because of our longtime friendship, Baccari agreed to work for us as a challenge without compensation. I accepted this only on a temporary basis. We would pay him an acceptable fee as soon as we could get organized.

It was May, just in time to promote the spring crops like cherries, strawberries, apricots, and the early vegetables which were beginning to arrive in increasing volumes. The committee decided that each stallholder would be asked to contribute various sums every Saturday in order to cover expenses. I immediately put together a newsletter and distributed it to each of the growers at the market. I followed up every two weeks to keep the farmers informed of what was going on. This is a difficult task when it must be realized that most farmers are seasonal. Depending on their crops, some only stay a few weeks out of the year. It was a constant, changeable flow. We did, however, have a good backbone of farmers who remained as long as six months each year.

Alessandro Baccari's promotional efforts brought back the crowds of shoppers. The parking area was always full, especially on Saturdays with long lines of cars waiting to enter the market. Growers brought in bigger loads of produce and sold out by early afternoon. They returned home with empty crates and cash in their pockets. It was incredible the change that took place. Feature writers from the newspapers and magazines were generous with their columns. Local television stations constantly featured crowd scenes and seasonal displays that became a photographer's paradise. The radio coverage was unbelievable.

Weekdays at the Farmers' Market were never good. It became a "Saturday" market where early morning shoppers appeared at daybreak. The farmers never had it so good. By midday, the market looked like it was hit by a cyclone, judging from all the empty crates and boxes. Those who had the freshest and best produce with the lowest prices sold out and went home early.

Attracted by this new publicity, more growers came in from every corner of the state. The spotlight was on Alemany Boulevard and Bayshore in San Francisco. In the meantime, probably due to the success of this "granddaddy of them all," the State Department of Agriculture created a special department to promote and encourage farmers' markets throughout California. This development was quite gratifying to me. The rules and regulations of the San Francisco Farmers' Market were then copied and modified according to local conditions. In 1982, there were 60 certified farmers' markets in the state. Two years later, there were over 80 such markets.

We enjoyed the all-out cooperation of Bill Berner. There

seemed to be a feeling of good fellowship, and the farmers' spirits were high. No wonder. . . they never had it so good, thanks to Al Baccari and the ad hoc committee. However, a honeymoon does not last forever. Like a bolt of lightning, Berner announced that having reached the retirement age of 65, he decided to retire as manager of the San Francisco Farmers' Market as of December 31st. Thus, it could be said that the last two years under his management were indeed outstanding.

The drought years had not been forgotten and we were now heading for a rosy future.

Mary Vienot was the market's civil service clerk serving under Bill Berner for eight years. She was very efficient and had ambitions to succeed him as market manager. Mary placed number one on the civil service list and became manager. It was a good choice. The market flourished during her regime.

The time was getting near to celebrate our 40th anniversary. The celebration turned out to be the biggest ever, thanks to Alessandro Baccari's promotion. Ben Teshera started the festivities, a chore he had done for the past 39 years. Hank Sciaroni, farm advisor for San Mateo County, and his agricultural extension service group conducted cooking demonstrations featuring international cuisine with sample portions for hundreds of viewers. The market was decorated with the growers' very own fruits. So colorful were the displays and the farmers' costumes. It was jammed with people everywhere and cars were lined-up along Alemany Boulevard for a half-mile. One of the oldtime farmers remarked, "It was a glorious confusion," but no one complained. Mayor Dianne Feinstein put on a superb performance with her wit and charm, and I had the honor of placing a garlic wreath around her shoulders. After the ceremony, she asked me how she could keep the seven pounds of garlic from spoiling. In response, Hank Sciaroni promised to send her a list of 29 recipes in which garlic, the "king of vegetables," could be used.

The origin of the garlic wreath ceremony best describes why the Farmers' Market honors its outstanding farmers and citizens each year.

GARLIC WREATH FARMERS' MARKET TRADITION
Ancient Order of the Garlic Wreath
(Adopted by Farmers' Market in 1943)

The highlight of the Anniversary celebration is the presentation of the Ancient Order of the Garlic Wreath to the Farmer-of-the-Year. The Garlic Wreath symbolizes the highest honor given by the Market to outstanding growers and farmers.

The Ceremony dates back to the reign of King Hammurabi, Emperor of Babylonia, 2000 years B.C. At the time, garlic was considered the king of vegetables and was used to honor its foremost citizens. Rome used the olive branch, the Greeks honored its outstanding citizens with the palm wreath. Among other things, this wise Babylonian king was responsible for setting up 285 laws and codes which are still in use today, beginning with the "written contract," "let the buyer beware," "sharecropping of land," etc.

Jackie McAbata, one of our original Filipino farmers from Half Moon Bay, had been making the priceless wreaths for the past 38 years. Since her untimely death, Doming, who was associated with the Ramirez family of farmers, continued where Jackie left off. The wreath weighs seven pounds and consists of 100 cloves, each carefully selected, strung, and interspersed with dried red peppers and other material.

The highlight of the 40th anniversary celebration was the honoring of 30 farmers who had been patronizing the Farmers' Market for the past ten years. Mayor Dianne Feinstein presented each of them with a Certificate of Honor from the City of San Francisco. These were the small family farmers who managed to survive despite the extreme competition from the large-scale, mechanized corporate farmers.

So the 40th anniversary came to a close with a champagne reception, two huge birthday cakes, finger food, and a large assortment of Filipino, Mexican, and Italian dishes.

I was 37 years of age when my little band of dedicated citizens, all civic leaders, joined me in creating this great enterprise. They suffered with me during our many battles, political and otherwise, and we rejoiced together when we won a little skirmish here and there. As time went on, I lost one friend after another until they were all gone. May they rest in peace. I was the only survivor and I made note of this every year when I published our annual anniversary circular.

Now in my octogenarian years, I find myself quite alone without their help and advice. It was time for some reminiscing. I sit back in the quiet of my study, close my eyes and think about the past and what the future could bring. In the meantime, I can't help but notice the great ethnic change that has suddenly taken place. The Italian, Portuguese, and Native Americans were conspicuous by their diminishing numbers.

The farmer came to town on August 12, 1943. Joe Sanchetti drove the first truckload of apples and pears into the vacant lot on Market and Duboce Street in the heart of San Francisco. He was followed by Paul Mancini from Santa Rosa, who came in with the second truckload of apples and pears. They both made history.

Today there are over 180 certified farmers' markets in California. We proved our point that there was a pent-up desire on the part of the San Francisco consumer to buy fresh fruits and vegetables at reasonable prices. Because of the success of the Farmers' Markets in the state of California, hundreds of family-operated farms will remain on the land. These are the farmers who are the "backbone" of American agriculture.

Chapter 19

An Island For Sale -
The Forgotten Story of Angel Island

If I have a fault, it has been that throughout my life I have constantly gotten involved in one project after another, most of which were civic and without renumeration of any kind. Some have told me that if I were to apply all my energies and talents solely to business ventures, I would be a very rich man. But then, if I followed their recommendation, my curiosity would never have been satisfied and I never would have had all the fun in my life. This brings up another cameo of my adventure with Angel Island.

The story of Angel Island is a fascinating one. It is also a story of political blundering and indecision. If it were not for an ad hoc citizens' committee, the one-square mile island sitting in San Francisco Bay off Marin County would have been sold to a private group for their sole use with the exclusion of the public.

In 1948, a story appeared in all the Bay Area newspapers stating that the War Assets Administration (WAA) had declared Angel Island ''surplus'' and would entertain bids for its sale. The appraised value of the island and all its facilities was $700,000. Several private groups were suddenly motivated. One of them included a private airport for their private use. There seemed to be no public interest in the future use as a park or recreational development for the people of the San Francisco Bay Area. Not even the news media showed the slightest interest. No one cared.

By coincidence, several of my Farmers' Market committee members were enroute to have lunch with me at the Alta Mira

Restaurant in Sausalito. Included in this group were Frank Helbing, head of the Apartment House Association; Russell Powell, president of the Parkside Improvement Club; and Evelyn La Place, president of the Central Council of Civic Clubs. We had read about the proposed sale of this beautiful island and were quite aware that private groups were already moving in the direction of acquisition by purchase. During the course of lunch, we couldn't help discussing Angel Island and were in agreement that something should be done to save it from private developers. We also agreed that perhaps we could interest San Francisco in the acquisition of the island for public recreational use. If San Francisco was interested, the War Assets Administration would sell the island at half the price, $350,000.

Here was a public-spirited group that served as members of the Victory Garden Council and later, on the Farmers' Market advisory board. Why not interest them in wearing another hat? So, we declared ourselves the Citizens' Committee for the Acquisition of Angel Island. We envisioned a recreation or vacation area for the people of the Bay Area and for tourists. It would mean the restoration of the ferryboat ride on the bay. It had a lot of possibilities. All in all, it would be a place in the country at San Francisco's front doorstep where no bucking the highway traffic would be necessary to reach the picnic grounds or vacation spot areas.

A few days passed and we sent out a press release to all the newspapers and radio stations. It had its results as we were successful in arousing public interest. Stories began to appear in our local newspapers. Our committee gathered background information starting with the historic value of this beautiful gem in the bay.

In 1775, Lieutenant Juan Manuel de Ayala discovered the island and named it *Nuestra Senora de Los Angeles* (Our Lady of the Angels). By an executive order of the federal government issued on November 5, 1850, the island was set aside as a military reservation. In 1900, the military garrison on Angel Island was officially named Fort McDowell. It also served as an immigration center. While immigrants from across the Atlantic poured into the United States through Ellis Island, the Pacific entry became more painful.

Between 1910 and 1940, over one million Chinese immigrants were imprisoned on Angel Island for periods ranging from weeks to years. Because of the Chinese Exclusion

Act which allowed only diplomats, merchants, teachers, and their relatives to enter the United States, life for a Chinese immigrant involved separation from his spouse and family, and months of loneliness and utter despair. This law was repealed in 1943 after the United States forged an alliance with China during World War II. Not only was Angel Island an immigration center, the German, Japanese, and Italian prisoners of war were stationed there during World War II.

In the fall of 1946, the war department declared Angel Island surplus and turned it over to the War Assets Administration (WAA) to be sold to the highest bidder.

The next effort of our committee was to get the San Francisco Board of Supervisors interested. Although over two-thirds of the island came under the boundaries of Marin County (the remainder in San Francisco County), we could not arouse the necessary interest. We sent a letter to Thomas Brooks, San Francisco's chief administrative officer, who submitted the proposal to Chester MacPhee, then-president of the Board of Supervisors. A series of meetings took place. They didn't say no, but they showed enough interest to pursue the matter.

The big problem whenever you are dealing with a public body is money. Although the city was offered a bargain price, it was still reluctant to come to a decision. We offered to take the eleven supervisors to Angel Island. The WAA provided a boat and made certain that there would be a thorough inspection of the island and all its facilities. The news media was also invited, so that for the first time photographs would be shown to their readers in order to create a tremendous, favorable public reaction. Angel Island became the subject of discussion wherever groups gathered.

Our citizens' committee suggested that the city sell 200 of its 318 acres in McLaren Park for housing development inasmuch as that portion was never used. The proceeds would go to buy Angel Island with an option of either operating the island under the parks department or leasing it to an acceptable group that would provide the recreational facilities.

On our tour of Angel Island, we found a 200-bed hospital. Herb Caen, columnist for the *San Francisco Chronicle*, suggested that it be turned over to the Shriners Hospital so that the children would have a place in the country. Many of the buildings were in good condition. There were several boat harbors available, particularly at Ayala Cove on the Raccoon Straits facing Marin County. The recreational possibilities were unbelievable. There were two sandy beaches and the best fishing in San Francisco Bay, riding and hiking trails, and picnic areas that could accommodate thousands, all in a natural setting away from the hustle and bustle of the city.

A group of prominent San Franciscans put together a lease proposal that should have been acceptable to the city. This group came together as Holiday Island, Inc. and was headed by Frank D. George, who operated a successful travel bureau in San Rafael. The principals in the corporation were well-qualified representatives: Harry Fialer, president of Golden Gate Sightseeing Company; Carl Sunberg, general traffic manager of Pacific Greyhound; Al Elledge, president of Harbor Tug & Barge; L.F. Thompson, president of Convention Services Association; Gelston Judah, owner of Gelston Judah Travel Agency; and Sam Gazzano, president of Mediterranean Trading Company. They offered the city an attractive lease proposal with a minimum guarantee, plus a percentage of the gross. The city would be protected by a Faithful Performance Bond, and the necessary public liability and property damage insurance.

My committee of civic leaders met with the Holiday Island directors, who were no strangers to San Francisco. They represented businesses that brought in millions of dollars to the city. Their proposal would have made Angel Island the "Catalina of Northern California." The financing, knowledge and ability were all there.

Ideas began to develop on how we could promote Angel Island to the public and to our officials. We set the date of April 24, 1949 as "Salute to Angel Island Day" and executed one of the most exciting events ever staged on San Francisco Bay. All the yacht clubs in the San Francisco Bay Area were brought together, along with the California Marine Parks and Harbors Association. This represented more than 500 yachtsmen from all over the Pacific coast. The event corresponded to the opening day of the annual yacht season.

The support and participation was unbelievable. Al Elledge, president of Harbor Tug & Barge which operated the Bay Area Cruise and Sightseeing Boats from Fisherman's Wharf, guaranteed enough boats to transport at least 10,000 people to Angel Island at fifty cents roundtrip. The 500 yachts were a sight to behold as were the city's fireboats, which put on a spectacular water display. The Marines staged a landing with 200 fully equipped servicemen and City College of San Francisco provided a 40-piece band. A Lloyds of London insurance policy for $1 million was secured and the Red Cross was invited to set up first-aid stations in various locations. Picnic tables were made available and food was sold at nominal costs.

The expected attendance at this event was 10,000 people. Over 16,000 were transported to Angel Island beginning at 8 a.m. from Fisherman's Wharf. By 7 p.m., everyone was brought back safely to the wharf and only a few minor scratches were the casualties of the day. My committee was the last to leave the island. Frank Helbing and I sat at the rear of the motorboat completely relaxed on cloud nine. Never had we seen the waters of the bay so calm. What a perfect ending to a perfect day. Angel Island was finally discovered and enjoyed by all. It became front-page news with many pages describing the activities that took place.

Judge John Molinari, who later became Presiding Justice of the State Court of Appeals, went out of his way to praise the successful event as did many other prominent officials. Some came to criticize, but left with nothing but favorable comments and offers to assist the committee. The next step was, ''Where do we go from here?''

Despite the tremendous public interest demonstrated on our first Angel Island Day, the wheels of bureaucratic government began to grind. Frustration caused by procrastination weighed heavily on members of my committee. We all agreed on one thing: ''What do we have to do to convince our representatives in local government that this was a great opportunity to acquire a bargain that could not and should not be refused?'' Eventually, the city turned us down stating that the hidden costs would be too much. We hit a stone wall and were left with a choice of either giving up or retreating. We decided to retreat and suggested to the Holiday Island group that they withdraw their proposal to the city and request the return of their $1,000 deposit. The Citizens' Committee for the Acquisition of Angel Island was no more.

We gave up on San Francisco and decided to try a new approach towards Marin County or the state. In this respect, we completely reorganized our committee and became the Angel Island Foundation. In 1950, we formally completed our membership in this new organization. In addition to my original group, we added as trustees: Fred Bagshaw of the Marin County Board of Supervisors, M.E. Cremer, Aubrey Drury, Mrs. Norman B. Livermore, Charles Winslow, Dr. Aubrey Neacham, Thomas

Plant, Jr., A.O. Tomlinson, and A.A. Moran. Fred Bagshaw was named chairman, and Mrs. Norman Livermore and I were chosen as vice-chairmen. Mrs. Livermore was president of the Marine Conservation League. It was quite a formidable and influential group.

Our first objective was to have Marin County take over Angel Island. It adopted a serious interest and agreed on an intention to purchase. Again, the bureaucratic wheels of county government came to a grinding halt. They couldn't agree, so we then decided that the best hope for everyone concerned was for the State of California to acquire the 626 acres.

Since the first Angel Island Day proved to be so successful, we came to the conclusion that again, we had to prove the island was worthwhile. We named Mayor Elmer Robinson of San Francisco and Mayor Clifford Rishell of Oakland as honorary chairmen. The mayors of all the other Bay Area cities were included as well. We wanted to make sure everyone was involved. Seven co-chairmen were chosen: Harold Dobbs, Thor B. Graven, Frank Helbing, Mrs. Norman Livermore, Commander Elmer Towle, Charles A. Winslow, and myself. The general committee consisted of over 100 Bay Area people representing all walks of life including political, business, labor, and civic. The Angel Island Foundation went to work immediately. The date of September 21, 1952 was chosen as Angel Island Day. The foundation raised funds in various ways to cover costs. A souvenir program was even published and sold for 35 cents.

Angel Island Day proved to be a tremendous success, far exceeding our expectations. Newspaper headlines stated in bold print, "20,000 Flock to Angel Island." The *San Francisco Chronicle* and the *San Francisco Examiner* wrote: "By noontime, 20,000 people were checked in. They came with cameras, they went wading and some swam on the sandy beaches. They picnicked, they hiked, and there were several Golden Gate Park 'elephant trains' that toured the well-paved roads around the island at all times jammed with passengers."

The weather that day was sunny and warm, inducing many to sunbathe or dip into the cold waters. The yachts performed in their festive attire. Holman Lenhart, who served as the committee's operations manager, called it "the most orderly crowd I have ever seen. Just think of it, hundreds of people stood in line over three hours patiently waiting for boats without any complaints." We had to stop at 20,000 for fear of not being able to get them back to the city by dark. We did not count the several excursion boats and private crafts which landed several hundred more.

They say that success brings envy and problems. We sure faced a big one from an unexpected source, the Sixth Army of the Presidio. Perhaps they were envious of the Marines when they set out from Treasure Island with a force of 200 in a mock invasion of Angel Island during our first Angel Island Day in 1949. Evidently, the Sixth Army kept their purpose for taking over the island a military secret.

We were quite upset over this turn of events. With all the time and effort that was already put in, we were not about to give in to the Sixth Army. I sent a telegram to General Swing, the Army Chief of Staff in Washington, asking for a clarification of the Army's intentions toward the island. We never heard from him, but finally received a reply from a spokesman for the Sixth Army. "The headquarters of the Sixth Army is fully aware. . .and will make studies for the use of Angel Island. The headquarters of the Sixth Army directed that those studies be considered classified." The spokesman also informed us that other Army agencies involved could not be named because this information was also classified. Later, it leaked out that the classified information involved the installation of a Nike base on the island. As it turned out, the Army did install a Nike base on Angel Island, but they became quite generous and cooperative on the usage of the land.

On October 23, 1953, the California State Park Commission announced the acquisition of 35 acres of the land surrounding Hospital Cove. This, at least for the time being, would provide a small boat harbor and recreation area. Newton Drury, chief of the State Division of Beaches and Parks, made the application, and the General Services Administration of the United States Government drew up the deed. Drury also applied for an additional 140 acres adjoining Hospital Cove, which was under the jurisdiction of the Department of the Interior. The area included a portion that had great historical value.

The Army eventually reduced its holding to several defensive areas. They did help to partly solve the water and sewage problem, the improvement of some of the roads, and other minor items.

With tremendous assistance from Congressman William Maillard, Congressman Jack Shelley (who later became mayor of San Francisco), Governor Edmund G. Brown, State Senator Eugene McAteer, and scores of city and county officials, the park was now a reality. A limited area of Angel Island was open to the public under the supervision of John Biggio, park superintendent. Much work was required and shortly after, the park was closed.

On October 1, 1959, the park was reopened. Improvements included ten finger piers to accommodate small boats. There was a new sewage disposal plant installed, more comfort stations, and picnic areas containing 50 redwood tables, 20 barbecue fireplaces, and drinking fountains. When the park opened, there were 36 acres; later, another 183 were added. Two wells now produce 40,000 gallons of water per day. Angel Island features a variety of vegetation, much of it not otherwise found in California. There are many wild deer and other natural wildlife.

Before concluding the story of the "Forgotten Island in San Francisco Bay," it must be mentioned that there is a gold mine on Angel Island. We had heard rumors about this alleged gold mine and decided to do some investigating. If there was a gold mine with gold, wouldn't it be an added attraction for people, particularly students? How many persons have ever seen a gold mine? Wouldn't it be fitting to have an operating gold mine right here on the bay? After all, wasn't San Francisco the center of the famous Forty Niner Goldrush? The more we thought about it, the more eager we were to solve this mystery.

I received a call from Harry O'Connor, who was a member of a fraternal organization in which I was still active. He met with me and revealed the fact that he spent many years on Angel Island. Being an engineer, he had the opportunity of becoming familiarized with the island thoroughly. O'Connor told me about the gold mine and produced a diagram of its layout. He also gave me an original, slightly soiled letter dated May 12, 1893. It was addressed to a "Sandy" and read: "As requested, I mail you in another package an ore sample taken from a barge shipment of ore to the Selby Smelter Mine at Ft. McDowell, Angel Island (you know where). If we had a slim chance, would like to work over there...P.S. Have sample assayed just for fun." The letter was signed by a Jack Dillon.

As the story goes, this mine was openly worked by some members of the Army stationed on Angel Island. In the note containing a drawing of the mine, a notation by Henry O'Connor appeared at the bottom: "Ore barges taken to Selby

Smelter, Hercules, Army major operated mine, 1893. He was courtmartialed and about that time it was filled in. Back files in *Chronicle & Examiner.*"

In 1948, Henry O'Connor submitted the sample of ore to Abbot A. Hanks Inc., assayers, chemists, engineers, at 624 Sacramento Street in San Francisco. He payed two dollars for the assay. The report showed that it represented 576.20 troy ounces of gold valued at $35.00 per ounce or $20,167. (Today, gold is worth $400 an ounce.)

Frank Helbing, Russ Powell and I decided to keep this discovery a secret as far as the information I had was concerned. The fact that there was gold on Angel Island was not really a secret. Others may have heard about it.

Back in 1953, a group of ten people in Marin County including several writers, historians, lawyers, and engineers filed a placer mining claim under the name of Hardrock Mining Association concerning 160 acres on the island. News of the claim caused consternation in official circles. It seemed that the Army got there as a military reservation before Hardrock Mining. However, the claim was ruled illegal, and the hopes and aspirations of the Hardrock Mining Association disappeared into the sunset. Thus, we bring to a close the fascinating story about the "Forgotten Island in the San Francisco Bay."

How far the State Division of Parks will go towards fully developing Angel Island for much greater use, we do not know. Perhaps the time has come for a more intensive recreational use, especially in this day of bumper-to-bumper traffic trying to reach the distant vacation spots.

I strongly believe that we still have an undiscovered island sitting in what is one of the most beautiful bays in the world — San Francisco Bay. We dreamed of a "second Catalina Island" where thousands of Californians and tourists from all over the world could visit in a leisurely way right here in our own backyard, without having to battle through our congested highways. The State of California is not doing enough to develop and attract more people to this gem so close to home. We did our part when we "discovered" Angel Island. We were successful in blocking commercial development with all our civic might and helped to preserve it for posterity by our own stubbornness and persistence. Now, it is up to others to follow through.

Chapter 20

A Palace for the Cows -
The World Famous Cow Palace

Governor Edmund "Pat" Brown was on his way to San Francisco when Robert McCarthy met him at the airport. They were longtime friends - McCarthy being a substantial "checkbook contributor" to the Governor's many campaigns since he held his first state office as attorney general.

Robert McCarthy was a prominent builder and developer in San Francisco and Marin County, and was very active in the Democratic Party in California. What was rather unusual was that his two sons were both state senators; one a Republican from Marin County, the other a Democrat from San Francisco.

Governor Brown was going to a political meeting in San Francisco. McCarthy's primary interest as president of the Cow Palace Board of Directors was to urge the Governor to fill a vacancy on the board replacing Jack Mailliard III, longtime director, cattle breeder, and socialite whose term had expired. During the ride from the airport, the Governor noticed the unusually heavy traffic when they approached the intersection of Bayshore and Alemany Boulevard. He turned to McCarthy and said, "Bob, what is going on here? It's a Saturday and only 8:30 in the morning." "Pat, my friend, John Brucato, is responsible for the Farmers' Market and its activities. This morning, I heard on the radio that the market was publicizing a big sale of peaches and other fruit, and this line of cars is trying to get into the market. You should go see it one day. It's a wonderful experience which not only helps the farmers, but benefits the citizens of the Bay Area. It's like this every Saturday morning."

While McCarthy's Cadillac was stopped in traffic with a good view of the long line of cars inching into the Farmers' Market, he was suddenly struck with a thought. "I've got it, Pat. There is our man. He is just the one who can help build up the Cow Palace. I've known John for many years. He's not only creative, but has the ability to get things done. I think you should call him as soon as possible." It did not take Governor Brown long to agree. He had known me in the past and was somewhat familiar with the Farmers' Market. It made headlines for many years.

The following day was a Sunday. My wife and I had sat down for a quiet breakfast. I was half-way through my shredded wheat when the telephone rang. We both had the same thought in mind. "Now who would be calling us so early on a Sunday morning?" Reluctantly, I answered the call and the voice on the other end was unfamiliar. "Hello, John. This is me, Pat." For a moment, I hesitated and replied, "Pat who?" "This is me, John, Pat Brown, your Governor." I thought, "Wow, Governor Brown was calling me on a Sunday morning!" He asked me if I would be willing to serve on the Cow Palace Board of Directors. After a few seconds of disbelief, I regained my composure and agreed to serve. (I don't believe I ever finished my shredded wheat.)

I received a letter a few days later in which Governor Brown strongly emphasized that I should do everything possible to build up the faltering Cow Palace revenues. He strongly stressed that the Cow Palace had been operating in the red too long, and that the State of California could no longer subsidize the popular Grand National Livestock Show for which the Cow Palace was receiving $250,000 each year. The problem at the Cow Palace had been the lack of use of this monstrous pavilion during the year. There were few money-making events and this was what the Governor wanted me to do: "Put it on a paying basis." *Mama mia*, I thought. What a challenge this is going to be for this poor, little Sicilian boy.

The Cow Palace, officially known as Agricultural District 1A, is owned and operated by the State of California, which also owns 35 other districts primarily used as county fairgrounds throughout the state. The Cow Palace is different, however, because it operates on a year-round basis. It is one of the largest institutions of its kind in the country, and is administered by nine directors appointed by the Governor and a general manager. The directors serve at no salary and generally represent high society — business leaders and important political checkbook contributors.

✓ The Cow Palace complex was completed and opened in 1940. It was a gigantic undertaking during the WPA (Works Progress Administration) days involving the State of California, San Francisco, and San Mateo County. It was also one of the major projects during the depression years to provide jobs. The primary purpose was to sponsor and promote the Grand National Rodeo, Livestock and Horse Show, one of the biggest of its kind. This show attracted agriculturists from all over the country, but a very few were from San Francisco and the surrounding areas. The original law specifying this purpose only was changed in 1947, so that the facilities could handle other large-scale events.

Bob McCarthy, president of the board of directors, appointed me as chairman of the newly formed rentals committee at my first meeting. He also appointed Steve Zolezzi to serve with me. This was a splendid choice as Zolezzi was an outstanding and successful businessman who owned and operated a famous San Francisco institution, O'Brien, Spotorno and Mitchell, one of the country's top poultry establishments. He made his killing when he began to supply several of the major airlines with their inflight meals. We hit it off immediately as we spoke the same language: "Let's bring in some permanent activities that would pay the Cow Palace a substantial revenue."

We started off with the Beatles and followed with other popular musical and stage events. Although wrestling was held on an on-and-off basis, we decided to make it a Saturday night feature. An agreement was entered into with the Shire brothers, who controlled wrestling in northern California. It now became an important sizable source of income to the Cow Palace.

Tom Rooney was approached to enlarge his boat show and make it really big-time. He was at a disadvantage, because he could not get his larger boats through the big doors of the facility. The huge cruisers and large-size boats were essential in making it the biggest sport and boat show in America. The problem was brought to the board of directors and it was agreed that the front doors be enlarged with the expense to be shared between the lessor and the lessee. Today, Tom Rooney's Sports and Boat Show is just about the largest event of its kind in the world, and the Cow Palace's income reflected this in a big way.

My role on the board, particularly as head of the rentals committee, was exciting and most encouraging. We sought out new fields, new sources of attractions, and we always had the green light to go ahead.

One of our first and unusual accomplishments was to get a major ice hockey team to use the Cow Palace. We were approached by Al Leader, president of the Western Ice Hockey League, on the possibility of San Francisco having a team and using the Cow Palace as its home base. As it turned out, a group from Vancouver headed by Coleman Hall formed an ice hockey club, the San Francisco Seals, and became part of the Western Ice Hockey League. The contract was signed during a luncheon held at Tarantino's Restaurant at Fisherman's Wharf. The formal signing included Coley Hall, Al Leader, Robert McCarthy, and myself.

We pushed a hard bargain. The league wanted the Cow Palace in a big way with its 14,000-seat capacity. We also wanted them, but we didn't have an ice rink. How can you play ice hockey when there is no ice rink? During my long experience in leasing city lands, I always made the lessee pay for the improvements in return for a reasonable longtime lease. In order to be fair, we also had to give the organization something for their investment. The cost at that time to build a complete ice hockey complex was over $273,000 (pre-inflation). The agreement was that they put up the money, and we would supervise the construction and give them a substantial reduction in the rental with an agreed minimum based on a percentage. This is how the Cow Palace got its ice rink at no cost.

The ice hockey season started with a new manager, Joe Allen, a well-known city official who eventually became manager of the War Memorial Opera House. On November 12, 1961, the Western Ice Hockey League made its debut. It required five weeks of intensive, round-the-clock work in order to start the first game on November 17th. Mel Swig of the Fairmont Hotel family became head of the San Francisco Seals with Joe Allen remaining as manager.

With the acquisition of an ice rink, we went after some of the big "Spectacular on Ice" productions in order to get full and profitable use of this new facility. The problem we were facing, however, was the general condition of the huge structure itself. It was becoming outmoded and outdated, and needed a complete facelift. Where else could we turn to for funding but Sacramento, the State Capitol?

In 1967, I was elected president of the Cow Palace Board of Directors and decided that we should head for Sacramento. Bob McCarthy, Howard Gilmore, and I made the trip together with Ed Diran, manager of the Cow Palace. We met with Governor Pat Brown, his financial advisors, and those familiar with the operation of the Cow Palace. After five hours of discussion, we got what we wanted — $1,850,000. In subsequent presentations before the State Legislature, we had to promise to repay the money. The important thing was that now we could proceed to transform the so-called "old barn" into an attractive and comfortable pavilion that would entice outstanding shows and exhibits.

A meeting was held with Franklin Mieuli, owner of the San Francisco Warriors basketball team, who was anxious to play in the city. As president of the Cow Palace, I affixed my signature with Robert J. Feerick, general manager of the team, on a five-year contract that included 21 home games for the first year. Things were now looking up in a big way.

The $1,800,000 modernization uplift included 7,500 plush theatre seats in the arena. The capacity now ran to 17,000 and up depending on the event. The Republican National Convention packed more than 22,000 people. The Beatles and the many rock-and-roll attractions were all at capacity.

We eventually lost both basketball and ice hockey events to our competitor, the new Oakland Coliseum. It offered a better deal with more seating than the Cow Palace had. The Warriors did from time-to-time play a few games during the season at the Cow Palace as they were not doing as well as expected in Oakland, and the Seals folded because of the lukewarm interest by fans in the East Bay.

Our next step was to build-up the Junior Livestock Show, which we felt needed special attention. This show was generally held during the Easter vacation season in the spring. We developed it into one of the greatest youth achievement events ever attempted. Each year, approximately 1,700 youths were housed and fed on the Cow Palace premises. They came from the various agricultural colleges and high schools, 4-H Clubs, and the many farm groups all over the state. Art Caylor, a columnist for the *San Francisco News,* wrote: "You never had to be concerned with juvenile delinquency with this group of boys and girls. They were too busy to get into trouble." These same sentiments were expressed by other writers and observers as well.

The purpose of the Junior Livestock Show was for the youngsters to exhibit their cows, steers, calves, horses, lambs, sheep, and every other kind of domestic animal, and sell them at a public auction. This was a community event that involved local businessmen, chambers of commerce, restaurants, and any group interested in this worthy extravaganza. The auction sales brought out unusually high prices by the bidders and a sizable sum for the young sellers. It did, however, bring many tears to youngsters when they had to let go of the animals they raised for an entire year.

The show lasted one full week, terminating with a huge, privately funded barbecue banquet held on the floor of the Cow Palace arena. I had the happy privilege during the two years that I served as president in handing out trophies and awards to the most gifted youngsters. When you have the opportunity of seeing these young people in action as I did for eight years, it makes you feel that all is not lost. The future of our country is in the hands of our youth.

Attracting the city folks to the Grand National was a task. In 1967, we decided to go Hollywood and opened the first night with Eva Gabor and Pat Buttram of television's popular show, "Green Acres." I had the duty and pleasure of greeting Eva Gabor at the airport. After presenting her with a bouquet of red roses, we headed a long line of decorated autos to the Cow Palace. The next two days, all attendance records were broken by the appearance of Jim Nabors, the longtime star of "Gomer Pyle." The following days featured Eddie Albert, also of "Green Acres," and entertainer Wayne Newton, whose crowds surpassed Jim Nabors'. In addition to his hit songs, Newton showed his versatility by skillfully riding one of his choice Arabian horses several times around the arena to a stand-up audience. He later confessed to me that he owned and operated an Arabian horse ranch in Nevada, and riding horses was his relaxation activity.

Our next Grand National featured one celebrity only, Lorne Greene, who was riding high with his popular series, "Bonanza." As president of the Cow Palace, I was able to become quite friendly with him. We lunched several times and discussed the great opportunities for western-style, outdoor recreation. This, of course, was because of his television program. He was told about my jurisdiction over the more than 64,000 acres of watershed lands of which 30,000 were in grazing. Mr. Greene was anxious to see the properties, which were located in Alameda, Santa Clara, and San Mateo Counties. One day, I had the chance of showing him some choice grazing land near Sunol in Alameda County.

Lorne Greene indicated that he was interested in a large-scale operation such as a dude ranch. In addition to the vast open space, the dude ranch would concentrate on a horse and livestock arena, a restaurant, overnight facilities, riding stables, equipment, a store, and a bar. He kept hammering heavily on the bar as he stated, "This is where we make the money." After further discussion, his agent decided that rather than lease land from the city, it would be better for him to buy and own the facility outright. I learned that he later purchased a 400- acre spread in Sonoma County and was to enlarge his present facility in Nevada, the Ponderosa Ranch.

We had many outstanding events at the Cow Palace. One of the popular shows was the Mexican rodeo, which performed there several times. Tony Aguilar, Mexico's singing cowboy-actor, and his talented wife, Flor Sylvestre, put on a south-of-the-border version of the American rodeo. His horses included Lippizzaners from Austria, Andalusians from Spain, Pasas from Peru, and some well-trained Portuguese horses. His performances attracted standing room only audiences, particularly from the Latin Americans.

During my stewardship, we hosted the Republican National Convention in 1964. Barry Goldwater was the top Republican candidate. The convention was sold out, especially to the San Francisco Republican delegates. The Republican leaders in the city did not receive any seating, so they were not on speaking terms with Goldwater. The group was headed by Tom Mellon, the city's chief administrative officer, and Al Derre. They asked if I could accommodate them in some way. Because the Cow Palace Board of Directors had reserved seats for all events (this is part of the "goodies" we received for our unpaid services), we were able to take care of our San Francisco Republicans. Incidently, Barry Goldwater was not elected president.

It is always a good idea never to wave your arms during a livestock auction. During one of these events, I had invited some of my wealthy cattlemen friends from the Sunol area to attend the livestock auction. Carl Swizig was a mean guzzler of some of the better brands of beer. He was having a discussion with one of his friends. Feeling rather high, he raised his hand high in the air to make a point. At that exact moment, the auctioneeer had reached a nine dollar high per pound for the Grand National champion steer. "Do I hear ten dollars?" he cried. He noted Swizig's hand and quickly shouted, "Sold to that gentleman for ten dollars." Carl didn't know what hit him. He was immediately surrounded by photographers, reporters, and the Cow Palace beauty queen. I nudged him and said, "Congratulations, you have just purchased the Grand National champion steer." With all this sudden attention on this 69 year-old bachelor, he came out of his stupor and said, "Gosh, this is wonderful!"

For the next six years, Carl Swizig became one of the most popular attractions at the annual livestock auction. He was not only a wealthy man, but he also had a big heart. Whatever Carl purchased, he donated to the 4-H Club in Pleasanton and other worthy youth-oriented farm groups which he sponsored.

One of the big problems facing the Cow Palace was the conflict of dates with our rival Oakland Coliseum. It seemed that no one thought of how this could be resolved; that is, until I became president. Actually, it was just a coincidence. Robert Nahas, a wealthy developer from the East Bay and one of the prime movers in making the Oakland Coliseum possible, became president of the Coliseum complex. Our paths had crossed several years ago when he and a few of his fellow developers became interested in leasing 500 acres of choice water department property in Pleasanton owned by the San Francisco Water Department and under my jurisdiction as manager of the water department land division. He was also a director of the East Bay Municipal Water District (known as East Bay MUD). This was their equivalent to our Hetch Hetchy water supply system in the Sierra.

I called Bob Nehas one day and suggested that we have lunch, so we could discuss our mutual problem. It turned out to be profitable for both sides. On the basis of this breakthrough, he took the initiative by inviting the Cow Palace Board of Directors and their wives to the Oakland Coliseum for an Oakland Raiders football game followed by dinner and cocktails. It is surprising what can be accomplished over a few cocktails. The end result was that Bill Cunningham, manager of the Coliseum and Ed Diran, manager of the Cow Palace, were instructed to get together to work out a mutual arrangement so that there would be no further conflict of dates when events were held at either place. This worked out beautifully when you realize the type of executives on each board, especially people like Edgar Kaiser and Senator William Knowland, publisher of the *Oakland Tribune*, both responsible for the development of Oakland's downtown, Jack Maltester, and Judge Joseph Schenone.

We extended an invitation to our East Bay friends and their wives to attend the Grand National as a return gesture. It was not possible for them to attend this event, but they came in force as our guests during the Sports and Boat Show on January 19, 1968. They were our guests for dinner and cocktails in our attractive Arena Sky Club. All directors from both organizations were present. (It should not be forgotten that this group strongly opposed the state's grant of $1,850,000 to refurbish the Cow Palace.) Perhaps the best way to summarize the latest achievement is an article that appeared in the *San Francisco Chronicle* entitled, "Peace." It stated, "There won't be any major conflict in sports dates between the Cow Palace and the Oakland Coliseum arena. Whatever differences they had in policy (and they did, dating back to the Cow Palace's request for, and Oakland's objections to, State funds for repairing the Cow Palace) have been resolved. President John G. Brucato and the Cow Palace's Board of Directors played host to the Coliseum's board recently and a love pact was sealed in steaks and fine wine."

I was blessed with a wonderful board of directors that worked well together and accomplished much. We all enjoyed our work and became good friends. Ed Diran was an outstanding manager. He was followed by George Strathearn and John Root. Edith McDonald was the first woman ever to serve on the board. She was a rancher and sports enthusiast. Fred Parr Cox was a well-known horseman, polo player and Hereford cattle breeder. Robert McCarthy was a leading contractor, civic leader, and political supporter of governors and public officials. Howard Gilmore, of Gilmore Envelope Company, was a banker and president of the Peninsula Racing Association. He was deeply involved in Democratic politics. John R. Metcalf was head of a national insurance company, a director of the San Francisco Museum of Art and the San Francisco Opera Association. Joseph G. Moore was a cattle rancher, breeder of horses, civic leader, and owner of a national heavy equipment business. Walter Rodman was a cattle rancher and breeder of horses who also managed the California Beef Council. L.C. Smith was a wealthy contractor known as the biggest road builder in San Mateo County. He served two terms as president and did much to enhance the Cow Palace's growth. Larry Lane, Sr. was owner and publisher of the prestigious *Sunset Magazine*. He hosted many of our directors' luncheons on his attractive and beautiful grounds in Menlo Park. We lost a good friend when he passed away in 1967. These were the members of the board of directors who saw fit to elect me as their president for two years.

Daly City wanted the San Francisco Cow Palace to change its name to the "Daly City Cow Palace." They had good reason since the Cow Palace was 99 percent in Daly City's city limits or what would have been after annexation. A small portion — less than two percent — of the parking lot was in San Francisco's city limits. The Cow Palace was known all over the world as "San Francisco's Cow Palace." Thus, began a battle of words between the officials of Daly City and the Cow Palace Board of Directors.

L.C. Smith was president of our board at that time. He was rather cold to the pleas of Daly City officials to sit down and resolve this growing political and controversial problem. If Smith was cold, all the other directors were frigid — all of them, that is, except me. I felt that the least we could do was to sit down, break bread, and perhaps have a cocktail or two. It was a serious problem, I thought, and I tried to reason with my board that we were not in San Francisco, but under the jurisdiction of our neighbor, Daly City.

Increasing pressure was coming from San Mateo County, particularly from their board of supervisors, the various communities, and Daly City. The board reluctantly decided that the time had finally come to swallow our pride and start talking to them. Smith appointed me as a committee of one to start discussions with Daly City. No one else on the board volunteered to join me. It so happened that because of my Farmers' Market activities, I was not a stranger to them. Long before Henry Doelger blitzed the north peninsula, especially Daly City, with his gigantic housing development, it was famous for its truck farms whose growers found their principal outlet at the San Francisco Farmers' Market.

I met several times with Mayor Frank Pacelli, Frank Verducci, De Bernardi, and Ed Frank, all Daly City officials. I suggested that perhaps we had reached the point in time when both sides should sit down and face the facts. They told me that if I could convince my board that this would be the only way to go, they would be very happy to participate. By this time, my fellow directors began to feel that they could no longer swim against the tide. The meeting was held in the Sky Room Lounge at the Cow Palace. Again, I was to prove that the only way to have a friendly meeting was via the cocktail route.

The meeting lasted three hours. We all parted as friends and were in agreement that the Cow Palace would be annexed to Daly City. One thorny point was resolved with very little discussion. Daly City would not impose any kind of tax on the Cow Palace's gross receipts. Eventually, the Cow Palace was annexed to Daly City and it assumed all police, fire and health responsibilities.

There were many repercussions as time went on at the Daly City public level. "Is the Cow Palace a blessing or a blight?" Everything, however, worked out favorably for both sides. The main benefit to Daly City was that it was no longer the San Francisco Cow Palace. It was now the Daly City Cow Palace. What's in a name? It all depends on where you sit. No doubt, it brought a lot of business to Daly City. The Cow Palace was now operating in the black, and there are no problems when everybody is making money.

Many events will long be remembered. During my presidency, we hosted one of the most popular of all attractions, the Canadian Northwest Mounted Police. Whether one likes horses or not, this had to be one of the most interesting shows. I will never forget the opening night. As president of the board, it was my duty to stand on an outstretched platform and greet the mounties. In a thrilling display of horsemanship in their colorful uniforms, the mounties lined up in front of where I was standing, presented arms, and stood at attention for the Canadian and our national anthems. I then saluted the Canadian Northwest Mounted Police. They returned the salute and proceeded with the show. I had a severe attack of goose pimples, but what glorious goose pimples they were.

One of my last duties as president was to appoint George Strathearn as manager of the Cow Palace. He replaced the longtime interim manager, Ed Diran, who contributed so much during the multi-million dollar expansion program. I always rated him as one of the best. He returned to his civil service position as the Cow Palace's chief administrative officer.

As my term of president was expiring, we elected John R. Metcalf. This was an excellent choice and I felt sure that this noble institution would be in good hands. Ronald Reagan had been elected Governor of California and he appointed George

Keyston, Jr. to fill a vacancy on the board. I made a full report to Governor Reagan as to the condition of the Cow Palace (a sort of "State of the Union" report). It was a good report which recited many of our major achievements. I gave full credit to the board of directors.

My resignation was submitted effective December 31, 1968, because I felt that I had to go on to other pastures since I was involved in many, many civic enterprises. I was also to retire from my city job in May of 1970. Governor Pat Brown appointed me to help put a failing public institution in the black. The closing paragraph in my letter of resignation stated that "I succeeded in what I had set out to do." I received a beautiful letter from Ronald Reagan in appreciation for my services. Thus, ends my stewardship with the Cow Palace; otherwise known as "Agricultural District 1A."

Chapter 21

My Love Affair With Millbrae

I was never one to enjoy living in a big city. Coming from New York and Brooklyn in particular, I always thought that someday I would like to eventually settle down in a small community not too far away from a big city with all its hustle and bustle.

When I came to California, my wife and I settled on a ranch in Sonoma County. Necessity made us move to San Francisco to participate in the operation of the family-bonded winery with my two brothers. It wasn't until many years later that I was able to settle down in the small community of Millbrae, 15 miles south of San Francisco, with a population of 21,000 people. The city was an ideal suburban place to live.

My love affair with Millbrae began in 1947, the year I became superintendent of the agriculture and land division of the San Francisco Water Department. My jurisdiction covered the department's vast holdings in four counties. My main office was on Mason Street in San Francisco, but I also had field offices in Millbrae where the peninsula headquarters was located and in Sunol in Alameda County. It was my job to lease every available parcel of land for whatever suitable use as long as it did not interfere with the primary purpose of water production.

The water department owned various parcels of land in Millbrae, including the corporation yards and the peninsula headquarters. This was known as the operating division of the San Francisco Water Department. Out of the large parcels was the so-called Silva tract, which consisted of 100 acres in the heart of Millbrae. This city-owned parcel actually cut Millbrae in two. There were really two Millbraes. The first part was north of the Silva tract while the other was south of it. The only way you could travel from one end of the city to the other (exclusive of El Camino Real) was through what is now Broadway, the main street. San Francisco owned that part of Broadway. Millbrae's usage was by suffrance, that is, there was a revocable permit issued by San Francisco to the city of Millbrae for the purpose of going from the south part of Millbrae to the north part or vice versa. This permit was in existence for many years. San Francisco remained adamant in not giving this up to Millbrae in any way, shape or form.

Millbrae was kind of rural at that time. As a matter of fact, the entire 100-acre Silva tract was leased primarily for agricultural purposes by the water department. The tract ran from El Camino Real west to Skyline Boulevard and separated Meadow Glen from Millbrae Highlands. The reason for the water department's ownership was that the 44-inch pipeline originating from the San Andreas Reservoir (a part of the Crystal Springs Reservoir Complex in San Mateo County) through the Silva tract and across El Camino Real was part of the water distribution system.

Between Skyline Boulevard going east, one-third of the land was leased for grazing because of its nature. The balance of the land was highly productive and leased to three flower growers. Along El Camino, the frontage was leased to a lumber yard and a pigeon farm.

The flower growers were all Italians. The Berni family farmed 12 acres, the Curotto family farmed 15 acres, and the Massolos cultivated 10-acres. They raised a large variety of flowers year-round and the area was a beauty of all colors. Being oldtime Italians, they preferred to pay the monthly rent in cash. Somehow, they didn't trust the mail and seldom wrote a check. I enjoyed visiting these colorful characters as the usual ritual was to enjoy one or two glasses of their homemade wines and engage in some pleasant conversations. Their wines were not what I considered premium. They were a bit on the heavy side with a high touch of acidity, but who cared? We drank in the spirit of friendship and good feeling.

The routine was always the same - two glasses of wine at the Curottos', two at the Bernis', and the final two at the Massolos'. Incidently, Mel Massolo, one of the founding fathers of Millbrae who was later a councilman and four-time mayor, was born on the Silva tract. By the time I left the Massolo farm, I was beginning to feel no pain. Fortunately, I was not too far from my Millbrae office where there was always some hot coffee available in the building.

Life went on in this fashion until Millbrae began to feel growing pains. Since the city was incorporated in 1948, its growth was rather slow at the start. San Bruno was on the northern border while Burlingame was on the south. San Francisco Bay and the San Francisco International Airport blocked any eastern expansion while the same could be said about the western border because of the watershed lands. In the meantime, San Francisco owned the heart of Millbrae, the 100-acre Silva tract. At that time, I was living in San Francisco and in the course of my visits to Millbrae, I felt sorry for this little community that wanted to grow.

I had become acquainted with Earl Wilms, who was also a founding father of Millbrae and served as longtime councilman and mayor. Along with Mel Massolo and several other localities, we discussed the city's problems with San Francisco. It seemed to them that San Francisco could not care less about its southern neighbor. They pleaded, "If only San Francisco would assist us in solving this problem of a unified city that we so dearly want."

As early as 1953, I began my urgings with the San Francisco Public Utilities Commission to declare the Silva tract as surplus, so that it could be sold and Millbrae would have political jurisdiction of the property, making it possible to have a unified city instead of the present divided community. This was timely since the 44-inch pipeline was no longer in use and the land could now be sold. I deeply respected these people for their sincere desire to preserve their city and the more I became involved, the more I began to push in Millbrae's favor.

My persistence did not sit too well with two of the commissioners, Ed Baron and Donald Cameron. There were many heated discussions on the matter in the chambers of the Public Utilities Commission at San Francisco's city hall. I had a great deal of respect for these two obstinate and controversial commissioners and they had the same for me. However, they decided they were not going to be pushed around by little Millbrae.

Baron and Cameron wanted Millbrae to grant San Francisco immediate rezoning of the property from agriculture to a higher use, so that the city could get more money (a natural and necessary requirement). I tried to explain to them that Millbrae would grant the city a rezoning, but not immediately. The procedure as they well knew would require some time in going through the various bureaucratic steps before the property could be sold. This, of course, was not acceptable to them. The dispute broke out into the newspapers. Both sides became emotional and irritating to one another. One of the city newspapers wrote: "It was Millbrae that first drew the wrath of PUC Commissioner Edward Baron. We're letting little Millbrae push us around," he complained. "Here, they want us to extend a street over water department property, and for two years, they have refused to grant us a rezoning on our property. . .I'll be deaf, dumb and blind to any request Millbrae makes until we get our rezoning."

I convinced Oliver Rousseau, president of the Public Utilities Commission, that Millbrae's request to extend Center Street westward on a water department right-of-way should be granted. He carried his point and won 3 to 2 (the dissenters were Ed Baron and Donald Cameron).

The ill feelings went on for some time. Then, things began to break. James Turner, manager of public utilities, instructed me to begin unofficial negotiations with the city of Millbrae. I had gone so far in an unofficial capacity that I strongly insisted that the only way these two warring communities could resolve their problems was to have both sides sit down at a neutral location and attempt to work out this vexing situation.

It was not until 1956 that the first official meeting between the two cities took place. Millbrae was represented by Mel Massolo, then mayor; Lee Ham, the city engineer; and Robert Thompson, the city attorney. The San Francisco representatives were George Burr, assistant manager of the water department; Thomas O'Connor, the city attorney; and myself. This committee met often and worked diligently to come up with a solution that was acceptable. However, there was another problem. We had not fully convinced Ed Baron and Don Cameron. I then suggested that all parties concerned meet at the San Francisco International Airport, a neutral location, for lunch and cocktails. It was a delightful meeting, and there was much toasting and mutual praising. They came to the conclusion that "our neighbors in Millbrae were not bad fellows" and that "our friends in San Francisco were really great guys." The proposal was adopted by both sides. We devoted one year to bring this about.

There is nothing like diplomacy via the cocktail route. We received the proposed zoning with delight. The portion from

El Camino to Broadway would be zoned commercial, about 60 acres rezoned to professional and administrative, and the balance was to be residential.

The Silva tract was finally sold on January 15, 1960. Today, Millbrae's main shopping center is centered on what was once that parcel of land. The civic center developed from a portion of the tract while Broadway was now free and clear. It now belonged to Millbrae and there was no more usage by suffrance. The city was now a united, respectable community. Thus, began my love affair with Millbrae.

I lived in San Francisco's Sunset District fog belt for 22 years. In April of 1961, we moved to the Mills estate section of Millbrae because I truly fell in love with the town and the many beautiful people I met there. Once a resident, I soon became actively involved in the community. I remember Mayor Earl Wilms saying, ''John, I would like you to accept my appointment on the newly created Beautification Commission. It won't take too much of your time.'' How naive I was. Mayor Wilm's term had expired. I received a call from the new mayor, Lewis Grasberger. This was the beginning of yet another stormy, but successful and interesting period of my life.

Mayor Lewis Grasberger informed me on September 17, 1969 that the council unanimously voted to appoint me to the city's newly created Beautification Commission. My other colleagues were some of Millbrae's outstanding civic leaders. Earle Call was president of the Lions Club and involved in many civic activities. Helen Habeeb devoted much of her volunteer time serving the Peninsula Hospital. Her husband, George, was also a top Lions Club official. Valli Slate operated a gift shop and was quite active locally. Robert Osberg was a teacher and another active civic leader.

At our first meeting on October 7, 1969, I was unanimously elected chairman. We were told that although we were a commission, we would serve only as an advisory board. There was no objection to serving in an advisory capacity so long as we were not just a ''rubber stamp'' group. Whatever we recommended should be seriously considered, not just acknowledged and lost in a bureaucratic file. We were ambitious in doing an outstanding job, but were somewhat naive as we would soon find out. Our term of office was to be three years.

Millbrae is a beautiful city, a community primarily of homeowners. It is also a place where the citizens took a deep interest in protecting themselves from becoming an asphalt jungle. The Beautification Commission embarked immediately on a Beautification Week. It was to be a clean up, spruce up and fix up program. The *Millbrae Sun, San Mateo Times*, and all the local newspapers gave us front-page publicity. We never realized that we would get tremendous favorable response from the merchants and homeowners. Fifteen hundred trees were given away to be planted along El Camino Real and along Broadway. Fifty boyscouts were enlisted to plant them on bare slopes during the Easter holidays.

Our next step was to induce the city to install new trash receptacles for the downtown area. Parking lot owners cooperated by cleaning up and planting trees and shrubbery. Just as we thought we were accomplishing much and had strong community support, we ran into trouble; that is, trouble with the city's council members. It seemed that we were getting too much publicity and they accused us of being overly ambitious. We were asked to slow down. The principal objector was James O'Connor, who went out of his way to put the reigns on us. The new mayor, William Glang, was urged by O'Connor to appoint one of his councilmen, Harold Purpus, to sit in at our meetings. We did not believe that we were being overly ambitious as we only felt that we had a job to do. For the first time, I got a good look at local politics.

We then took on the Southern Pacific Railroad and requested that the depot be painted. It was considered a historical landmark and the last paint job was done over 40 years ago. A big issue was also made over the fact that the depot facing Millbrae Avenue was the gateway to Millbrae and was a disgrace to the city and to the railroad. Not getting any response from Ben Biaggini, president of Southern Pacific, we took to the news media. The publicity was unbelievable and my name was prominently displayed in every story. After two weeks of this bombardment by the news media, we broke the ice.

I received a telephone call from Carl Olson, manager of the public relations bureau of Southern Pacific. He and I had a three-hour lunch at the El Rancho and it turned out that we knew quite a few mutual friends. The depot was going to be painted. In the meantime, the commission was feeling the heat from Jim O'Connor. We were reminded that we were only an advisory commission and told that we were not doing our job, because we did not go through the proper channels. Our efforts, once again, were criticized by jealous politicians. Anything a politician dislikes is to see a group of laymen basking in the sunshine of news media publicity when by his rights, he should be getting the attention.

I began to realize that all this unnecessary hindrance and opposition was starting to wear me down. I didn't need all the flack, and was already too busy with my own business and many other social and civic affairs. To bring matters to a head, I submitted a letter of resignation to Mayor William Glang outlining my frustrations and the lack of support given to the commission by the council. On September 9, 1970, the *Millbrae Sun* outlined our grievances and frustrations in a front-page news story. My fellow commissioners joined in their protests to the city council. Earle Call, president of the Lions Club, said that the council would be making a serious mistake in accepting my resignation. They refused to honor it.

On September 16, 1970, I was informed by Mayor Glang that the council voted not to accept my resignation and he promised that the commission would receive full support. I went back to work with my commissioners while we were getting ready to reopen our negotiations with Carl Olson regarding the painting of the Southern Pacific depot. Then, something happened that aroused the people of Millbrae.

A news story broke out in the dailies that the famous Sixteen Mile House, Millbrae's oldest landmark, was to be torn down in favor of a paint store. There was no historical society at that time, but a group of Millbrae citizens banded together to try and save this famous landmark. At one time, it was the stopping place for the horse-drawn carriages which were a means of transportation to the peninsula, and served as a bordello. It was decided that a public meeting of protest be held. Valli Slate and Bob Osberg, two of my fellow commissioners, chaired the meeting. It was unfortunate that neither had ever chaired a meeting of this nature, so the meeting got out of hand. Valli Slate called me up to the rostrum, handed me the gavel and said, "John, you take charge."

The meeting finally came to order. Opposition developed to the point that we decided to put the issue on the ballot and ask the voters of Millbrae if they wanted to save the Sixteen Mile House. However, our problem was that we had no money. Because of the tremendous publicity generated, the city council, avoiding involvement, directed the Beautification Commission to do everything possible to save the landmark.

Again, they gave us a job to do, but denied us the necessary funds needed for a successful campaign.

The voting took place and the issue of saving the Sixteen Mile House lost by a narrow margin. We tried to get the city council interested, but to no avail. Slowly, this small band of diehards began to grow. The feeling was that something should be done to protest and save the few remaining historical landmarks in Millbrae. We decided that the thing to do was to organize a Millbrae Historical Society. I was elected its first president and our first active function was to hold a "wake" for the Sixteen Mile House before the bulldozer went to work.

The wake was held on March 16, 1970. While it was a sad event, it developed into one of the most memorable in the city of Millbrae. The committee put together a most attractive brochure with a photograph of the Sixteen Mile House with a horse-drawn carriage in front of it. The proprietors set a very attractive menu. It featured filet mignon with all the trimmings. Almost all of Millbrae turned out dressed in "gay nineties" style.

The bulldozers went to work the next day. While the city of Millbrae lost its Sixteen Mile House, it gained much more — the Millbrae Historical Society. We vowed to preserve everything in Millbrae that had a historical value.

Negotiations were reopened with Carl Olson to have the historic Southern Pacific depot painted. There was some delay because of the announcement by the Division of Highways that Millbrae Avenue was to be widened.

Jim O'Connor became mayor of Millbrae and that was when our problems really got started. His plan was to dissolve the five-member Beautification Commission and change it to a beautification committee of 25 members. This was the old Parkinson's law where if you wanted to accomplish something a small committee would do it, and when you wanted to do little or nothing, appoint a large committee.

The storm clouds broke when a story appeared on the front page of the July 28, 1971 issue of the *Millbrae Sun*. It was an article entitled, "Lionesses Show Their Claws," referring to Helen Habeeb and Valli Slate, the two women of my commission. Another headline in the same issue read, "Lions Bulletin Irks Mayor." The mayor publicly stated that he would be "the first to grab the resignation of any commissioner." Then, he lashed out at me. His attack was a classic as stated: "Frankly, we don't need big time politics in Millbrae, and that's what we seem to have. Mr. Brucato seems to forget that we're a small community, not San Francisco." "It is now my intent to broaden the commission by making it into a committee of 25 people," he continued.

I don't believe the mayor was a drinking man, but his next uncalled-for remark led many of us to have some doubts. "I am tired of people running around with Gold Seals saying they are commissioners, trying to pass themselves off as something other than someone who is interested in serving the community." When my fellow commissioners and I read this in the papers, we felt that the city had cheated us when we were appointed. If we were to receive a Gold Seal, they either forgot about it or gave it to another group.

The city council met and by a 3 to 1 vote, the Beautification Commission was dissolved. They gave us 30 days to pack up and get out. We respectfully requested a stay of 120 days, because we needed this additional time to complete our negotiations with Southern Pacific to paint and landscape the depot area. We also informed the city council that when this matter was completed, we would then submit a complete report on just what the commission accomplished for the city of Millbrae.

The Southern Pacific depot was painted. It was moved several hundred feet south due to the widening of Millbrae Avenue. The eyesore at one of the main gateways to Millbrae was gone. In its place, we had a beautiful historical structure that we could be proud of. At a later date, the Millbrae Historical Society was able to dedicate the depot as a historical monument. A plaque was placed on the building following a huge city-wide celebration.

The final meeting of the first and last Beautification Commission was held on October 11, 1971. We adjourned to Earle Call's home to join our spouses in a most glorious celebration. . .or was it another wake? Before the new committee was appointed, we were asked individually by the mayor if we were interested in serving. Each of us rejected the invitation with grace and dignity.

As the first president of the newly formed Millbrae Historical Society, I felt a sense of relief associating myself with a fine group of dedicated people. In 1970, we established as our main objective a historical museum for the city of Millbrae. Our first problem was that we had to educate the community that people belonging to a historical society were not all "old fogies." As a matter of procedure, we interested families in membership and held a successful drive to get young people involved. We concentrated on our local high schools (Mills and Capuchino) and the various elementary schools, and were pleasantly surprised at the favorable response. By the end of the first year, we had a membership of 180.

Various fundraising activities were programmed. I had no problem securing Pilarcitos for our first historical society picnic. The water department maintained a picnic area in the most beautiful portion of the Crystal Springs watershed situated approximately seven miles from the San Andreas reservoir gate, directly west of Millbrae. The scenery and beauty of this untouched watershed is actually the forest primeval. Pilarcitos Reservoir was the original water supply for San Francisco. As the population grew, so did the Crystal Springs watershed, which consisted of the upper and lower Crystal Springs lakes and the San Andreas Lake. The property is not open to the general public and to protect the watershed lands, the city gave jurisdiction to the State Fish and Game Division as a game preserve. Permission to enter the property was limited to equestrians, hikers, bird watchers, and various groups.

The Pilarcitos picnic grounds have been in existence for many years. It is an attractive area completely furnished with a barbecue pit, tables, and restrooms. San Francisco officials use the premises for public relations purposes. Various governmental groups are invited to meet with city officials, chambers of commerce, civic groups, the press, the county grand jury, and many others in this mutual get-together. Many local problems are resolved at these gatherings and more important, it brings city officials together with their counterparts in the Bay Area on a first-name basis.

During my years of stewardship with San Francisco, I was able to meet many officials and others I had to do business with at the Pilarcitos get-togethers, making my job a lot easier. In this fashion, there would be no difficulty in resolving whatever problems existed. With this prologue, I will return to our historical society's annual barbecue picnics.

We raised a few dollars amongst ourselves for the future museum and had the opportunity of enjoying Pilarcitos for 15 of the past 17 years. (One year of drought and one year of road construction closed it to everyone except water department personnel.) The meeting hall of the public library was used to exhibit our growing number of historical artifacts. As a director of the First National Bank of Daly City, I received the approval of my fellow directors to use the mezzanine area of the bank's Millbrae branch for storage or whatever we could not display.

After serving as the society's first president in 1970, I was asked to serve another term during 1975 and 1976. I also took on the job of chairman of special events in which I was to produce a special spectacular once a year at our November meetings. For these productions, we had the use of the city council chambers in order to handle the expected large attendance.

Reflecting back to the days when the Beautification Commission and I were under the vicious and personal attacks of then-mayor James O'Connor, perhaps he was right when he accused me of bringing "big city politics into this small community." Although I did not bring big city politics or politicians, I did something better. I brought some of the most outstanding leaders in their various fields to the little city of Millbrae. Here we were just starting a historical society, and who do we get for our first speaker but the top historian in the State of California, Dr. Albert Shumate, past president of the California Historical Society. He spoke to a standing room only audience at the council chambers on September 27, 1970.

The following year, the second leading historian in the state, Dr. Peter Conmy, also addressed an overflow crowd. He was a noted writer on early California history, author of numerous books, and served many years as chief librarian for the city of Oakland. Perhaps one of the most outstanding programs was when John B. Molinari, Presiding Justice of the California Court of Appeals, spoke on "Law and Order in Early San Mateo County."

The annual spectaculars became more and more popular. We hit the proverbial jackpot when we staged the "Past Mayors Night" on November 19, 1975. All the living past mayors were present and very appreciative of this salute. As one of the old-timers said, "It's nice to be remembered." On November 17, 1976, I staged a "Salute to the Civic Clubs of Millbrae" where every civic club was represented for this unusual gala program. The following year was a "Salute to the Millbrae City Government" involving every city department, and I did not overlook the importance of the San Francisco Water Department and their Millbrae headquarters.

We then decided to do something a little different. I suddenly realized that Millbrae was the home of many artists of national and local repute, so we staged a "Salute to the

Artists of Millbrae." The program was headed by our own internationally acclaimed Alex Nepote. An important outcome of this performance was the display of paintings by local artists in every bank, hall, or wherever they could be exposed to the public. The various schools even began to take more interest in painting and art.

The most interesting program, although it was of an ethnic nature, was given by Alessandro Baccari, famed historian, lecturer, and widely known publicist. It was about "The Migration of Italians in San Mateo County." Of course, it could be said that the most famous to migrate to San Mateo County was A.P. Giannini, founder of the Bank of Italy, which later became the Bank of America. He became a resident of San Mateo.

My last spectacular involved the story of the Hetch Hetchy water project in the High Sierras, a major source of San Francisco's water supply. It was then time to take a breather and step down to let someone else take over.

The steps leading up to the Millbrae Historical Museum was the culmination of 17 years of effort on my part and that of the many dedicated members of the society. This story could be applied to any city in the nation. People want to know how their communities began. If anyone has a spark of civic pride, he should ask that question primarily because we live in a great country — the only country where freedom and rights belong to all the people. The first step in finding the answer to the question is to get involved no matter how small or large a community may be.

I cannot bring this narrative to a close without telling the unbelievable story of how the Green Hills subdivision came about. I had made it possible for the Silva tract to become part of Millbrae, and played a large part in the city acquiring the two parcels of land that became a future park and the site of a senior citizens housing project. I also made it possible for Millbrae to finally acquire a museum in which others brought to reality years later.

There was a 22-acre parcel of choice land west of St. Dunstans Church, east of the Green Hills Country Club, and bounded by Ludeman Lane on the north and Helen Drive on the south. This land did not belong to the San Francisco Water Department, but the Catholic Archdiocese of San Francisco. The Archdiocese purchased the property many years ago for a possible high school site. As time went on, the proposed school, Serra High School, was built in San Mateo instead. In the meantime, the Archdiocese leased the land to several nurserymen. For the past 28 years, Joseph Figone of San Bruno leased ten acres. The Cozzolino family and others farmed the balance of the property. A minimal rental of only $450 was charged a year for the ten acres. The chancery office, however, required that the property be kept clean. It was a showplace of color and beauty.

I retired from my water department job on Friday, May 31, 1970. The next morning, I received a telephone call from Don Fazackerly, a banker and former supervisor of San Francisco, who was a high official on the staff of the *Catholic Monitor*. He had a previous meeting with Bert Soher, a former finance editor of the *San Francisco Chronicle*, and Robert McCullough, who were both financial advisors to Archbishop Joseph T. McGucken. Evidently, the Archdiocese, which covered the four counties of San Francisco, Marin, San Mateo, and Santa Clara, was experiencing a financial squeeze. They were land rich and dollar poor, owning many parcels of land that had no future use for the church's expansion. The 22-acre parcel in Millbrae was a classic example.

These gentlemen were well aware of my handling of the water department properties. They were also knowledgeable of the fact that during my tenure, I made millions of dollars for San Francisco in the management of their properties. As a result of several meetings held prior to my retirement, they recommended me as the proper person to handle the surplus Archdiocese properties. I informed them that I needed a vacation and would be happy to discuss the matter with the Archbishop later on. It seemed that they overlooked my plea for some rest and relaxation since they had already booked me for a meeting with Archbishop McGucken that following Monday morning.

The meeting with His Excellency just three days after my retirement developed into a most enjoyable relationship that lasted over seven years. My only conditions for accepting the assignment as his personal real estate consultant were that I was not to be involved with any parish group and that I would retain my office at my home. He graciously replied that I would be involved only with him and the then-Chancellor of the Archdiocese, Monsignor Donnell Walsh. (After the third year, Donnell Walsh was replaced by Father Daniel Walsh, who became a Monsignor and eventually Bishop of Nevada.)

My first assignment was the 22-acre parcel in Millbrae. It was a good thing for the Archdiocese that I became involved in many successful conclusions on their other properties over the next four years while waiting for the Millbrae acreage to be sold. On July 2, 1970, I was instructed to proceed on its sale. A chain of unbelievable events took place for the next five-and-a-half years involving public protests, and city moratoriums on the sale of the property for open space, which fortunately was defeated by the voters on a proposed bond issue to buy the property.

As with all land matters, the development of land requires many long procedures, public meetings, various required permits, environmental approvals, and many other delays, so that by the time the developer is ready to proceed, approximately one year will have gone by.

I adopted a policy for the protection of the Archdiocese against fly-by-nighters, speculators, and window shoppers by insisting on a substantial non-refundable deposit, plus having the holder of the option pay for all taxes and assessments against the property during the period it required to get all final approvals.

Levitt and Sons of California, a nationally known developer, submitted a proposal to purchase the 22 acres. However, their plan was to build a 400-unit apartment complex. The Millbrae city council acted favorably towards this proposal, but a group of environmentalists who were mostly residents of the nearby area did not. They were up in arms and began to protest violently. Their numbers grew to the point that on November 19, 1970, a public meeting was held in the auditorium of the Green Hills School. Some 193 people were in attendance.

I sat in at the meeting, but confined my remarks to the fact that I was representing the Archdiocese. At that time, I was on the Beautification Commission and was fairly well-known to most of the people in attendance. I stated to the group that it was up to the developer to satisfy the city and the public. I remained neutral on the matter.

JoAnne McMahon chaired the meeting with Harold Purpus, Jim O'Connor, and Bernard Esser representing the city council. Neil Davidson, from Levitt and Son, remained cool and dignified as he outlined the plan for a beautifully landscaped and attractive addition to the residential surrounding neighborhood. Whatever he said seemed to fall on deaf ears. Quite a few opponents spoke, and all they wanted to do was save the eucalyptus trees and preserve the 22 acres as open space. Natalie Gelhart was quite adamant in saying that "We will kick and scream, and fight this thing all the way." The property was zoned for single residential use and would have to be rezoned to a higher use.

Another protest meeting was held on May 5, 1971 with over 200 attending. An opponent rose to his feet showing a poster drawn by a schoolboy stating, "Please don't take away our field." At this point, Mayor Jim O'Connor closed the meeting with a final statement: "I think we have the feeling of the people." Many of the opponents were of the opinion that Millbrae should buy the property for open space. The inevitable reply was, "Where will we get the money?"

Roger Flores, one of the most progressive land brokers in the area who was representing Levitt, was also on the receiving end of the violent blasts coming from the supercharged audience. My feeling was that the developers were through as the opponents were never going to permit an "R-3" zoning complex. I told him that the only way this property could be sold was for the purpose of building single family homes. We already had the "R-1" zoning, so why proceed with the impossible? Flores agreed with me.

In my report to Archbishop McGucken, I specifically noted that the strange thing about this opposition was that it came primarily from members of St. Dunstans Parish. To quote Father Saulis, one of its priests who had previously attended a well-mannered meeting of the parish men's club on the same subject, he said, "I am astonished at the unsophisticated reaction of the people." My closing remarks to the Archbishop was that we would continue to meet with representatives of neighborhood groups rather than large crowds.

Roger Flores and Neil Davidson met at my suggestion. There was a possibility that Cal Prop. Corporation of Los Angeles, which had a small interest with Levitt on the property, might take over Levitt's option. Cal Prop. specialized in single family homes. In the final analysis, Cal Prop. took over Levitt's option and it was now a new ballgame.

Neil Davidson became Cal Prop.'s representative while Roger Flores remained as the broker. Cal Prop. had to start the cycle all over again, going through the procedures to build 104 single family homes. It was not going to be an easy path to follow as the storm was about to begin once again. The open space proponents organized into a strong opposition group and were determined to force the city of Millbrae to buy the property for open space. Their plan was to ask the voters to pass a bond issue to buy 22 acres of land. The question was, "How much should the bond issue be?"

Bill Baxter became chairman of the bond committee. He and I were close friends and worked diligently on the historical society. We both served as presidents of the society and were dedicated to establishing a historical museum for Millbrae. Many other close friends became my opponents on this crucial issue. In this respect, Mary Griffin, who later became councilperson and mayor, led the drive as petition chairman.

I was approached by a committee of the opposition and inquired as to how much the Archdiocese wanted for the 22-acre parcel. The price was already established — the value of the property being what a willing buyer would pay to a willing seller. To clarify the statement for them, I put it in dollar figures. Cal Prop.'s option called for a cash payment of $1,143,000 (1972 pre-inflation price). That is what we want for the property. I knew they were stunned, because Harold Purpus of the city council didn't agree with my numbers. He was employed by the county assessor's office and was somewhat an expert on property values, but so was I.

A meeting was held at the city hall to work out a reasonable price for the purchase of the property from the Archdiocese. Harold Purpus, Frank Gillio, city attorney, Roger Flores, and I partook in a hot cup of coffee and then opened the discussion, which lasted nearly four hours. Purpus set the value for the open space property at $440,000 as my established price was $1,143,000. To illustrate my point, I presented a file concerning a similar parcel of land owned by the Archdiocese in Kentfield in Marin County. That group wanted the 20 acres for open space while a developer offered us four times the price they quoted for a condominium development. In my conclusion, I repeated my previous statement that the value of a parcel is what a willing buyer would pay to a willing seller.

City Attorney Frank Gillio made the final decision and agreed with me that we had the legal right to get the full value of the property. To this, I added that it was only fair that if they wanted the property so badly, they should be willing to pay the fair price of $1,143,000, which was not excessive.

A vigorous campaign was underway and Mary Griffin was successful in getting more than the required amount of signatures. The bond issue for $1,143,000 went on the

November 7th ballot as Proposition I. Polls taken in various parts of Millbrae indicated that the open space bond issue would win by a 3 to 1 vote. Many of Millbrae's organizations joined the "yes" vote for Proposition I. Bill Baxter announced that a house-to-house campaign was underway. The local press was generous in the publicity given. Then, the bomb burst.

The *Millbrae Sun* came out with an editorial entitled, "Vote No on Proposition I," just five days before the election. It was an explosive factual piece specifying in no uncertain terms that the actual cost to the taxpayers was being unfairly minimized by the proponents, who were "under the magic appeal of open space." It emphasized in black and white that the purchase price was $1,143,000 with interest of $1,000,000, bringing the actual total price tag to over $2,000,000. The city engineer added a cost of $10,000 per acre for initial landscaping, $27,000 for personnel, and another $25,000 per year for maintenance equipment. "This brings the foreseeable costs to around $3,000,000 for this acreage," the editorial stated. Going into many detailed and unforeseen expenses, the editorial closed with a strong "We urge a NO vote on Proposition I."

The bond issue was defeated. It was an unbelievable decision as the proponents were stung. The best explanation given was that when the true costs were revealed, the Millbrae taxpayer still felt the sting of their annual tax bills which they received in mid-October. It didn't require too much thinking when the voter entered the booth to pull the right lever. The diehard proponents refused to give up and meetings were held to decide for another try.

The holiday season of 1973 slipped into the new year. Then, an unforeseen event happened. The Childrens Home Society was holding its dinner dance at Stanford University. My wife, Joan, was chairperson of this annual fundraiser. There were many representatives from Millbrae attending this gala affair. Amongst them were Mary Griffin and her husband, Don. My acquaintance with her began when she was one of the leaders against the Green Hills development. She approached me that evening and suggested that we have a friendly chat. (It should be noted at this point that Millbrae had imposed a moratorium on this property.) After some discussion, Mary said that her group would be willing to talk about a compromise. It was even suggested that a cluster-type townhouse might be acceptable provided that the developer would dedicate one or two acres for a park or open space. If I agreed to this, she would ask her group to end the opposition and we could jointly express our agreement to the city council. When we announced the agreed compromise to the city council, it seemed that they were glad to get off the hook.

The following year, Mary Griffin ran and was elected to a seat on the city council. I served as her treasurer during this election and her re-election. During her incumbency, she served as mayor on two occasions. She was a dedicated councilperson and an outstanding mayor. Two years later, I served as her treasurer for the third time when she was elected county supervisor by a huge plurality and again when she was re-elected.

Things were beginning to hum. Cal Prop. proposed a subdivision of 104 single family homes and also agreed to dedicate one-and-a-third acres as a public park. The council lifted the moratorium on the property, rescinded their decision, and later, definitely lifted the moratorium. The many time-consuming procedures were completed one-by-one, and the environmental impact report was finally approved. The planning commission, the fire department, the city engineer, and practically every city department got involved. As the late Jimmy Durante would have said, "Everybody wants to get into the act." Eventually, the city council approved the final map at the end of June in 1974.

The date of August 10, 1974 was set for the issuing of the building permits and final closing. It was not until the end of 1975 that construction began. The first phase of 40 homes was slated for completion in early 1976. I completed my assignment for the Archdiocese on the Millbrae property. Cal Prop. paid their option in full. It required over five years from the date of Archbishop McGucken's letter to me in completing the task of disposing of their property. During this period, I was instrumental in giving the Archdiocese of San Francisco much-needed financial relief by also disposing of much of their many surplus properties in Marin, San Francisco, San Mateo, and Santa Clara Counties.

My wife suggested that we sell our home on Sequoia Avenue in Millbrae and buy one of the new homes in Green Hills Estates. Fortunately, there were three lots unsold in the first phase. We selected one of them and watched our new home grow into the finished product. We were the second homeowners to move in. The streets remained to be paved and there were many finishing touches needed to complete the house. Trucks and tractors were going up and down all day long and the workmen were going in and out. Joan, being the public-spirited and friendly person she was, kept them supplied with hot coffee, homemade cookies, Sicilian *frittata*, and on occasions, a glass of wine.

There was to be no end to my many involvements. The homeowners got together and formed an association. I was asked to serve as its president and for once, I respectfully refused. I did, however, become the treasurer. Shortly after incorporation, the association, led by the president, Dr. Joseph Izzo, took on the city of Millbrae in a rather lengthy and heated series of encounters. We were fighting for 1.6 acres of park land that the city inherited from Cal Prop., the developer. Millbrae wanted to sell the acreage because of the high cost of converting this vacant plot to a park. They would, in return, develop the adjacent 1.8 acres for this purpose. I agreed with the city inasmuch as this parcel contained a grove of eucalyptus trees and was a perfect setting for a park. (The trees along Ludeman Lane would later be removed, being a menace to the homes and pedestrians.)

It took some persuasion to finally convince the homeowners that they were getting a better deal. The city of Millbrae agreed that the proceeds from the sale of the original Green Hills Park parcel would be used to develop the adjacent 1.8 acre parcel with the trees into a park. The timetable on the completion of this development was for late 1985 or early 1986. In 1987, the park became a reality and was opened in 1988.

When we had a cause to fight for, a good many of the 104 homeowners showed up at the meetings. They were supporting something that interested them personally. As time went on, the association was reorganized with Ted Newby as president. The meetings were sparsely attended and there was nothing to fight for. I told the group at a directors meeting of how I helped solve Lou Soucie's problem.

Lou Soucie was head of a committee of the Chamber of Commerce, which was trying to develop a face-lifting program for the merchants along Millbrae's main street, Broadway. I suggested that he send out a notice for a special meeting in which the topic to be discussed was a possible one-way street for Broadway. You never saw the merchants travel so fast to attend a meeting. In fact, Lou had a full house. There was self-interest involved and now something to fight for. We tried a similar tactic to get the homeowners out to a meeting by telling them that the future of their park was at stake. There was great improvement in the attendance thereafter.

The city of Millbrae loaned the historical society $12,000 to help relocate the O'Marie cottage from the water department property that was to house the senior citizens housing project. The society put up another $5,000 so that the future museum could be moved. The $17,000 was to be used to build the foundation at the new site in the civic center. The city council was most cooperative and donated approximately one acre of choice grassy plot adjacent to the public library.

I was fortunate in helping to get the first civic donation for the museum. Through the efforts of a close friend of the family, Eleanore Nettle, we obtained our first gift from the California Jockey Club Foundation. That broke the ice. The historical society, through the museum committee, now had its work cut out for them in raising the required funds and finalizing the museum. I had never seen so many dedicated people working together for a common cause. When people work together for a common cause, they not only enrich themselves in the services performed, but the entire community benefits.

I have always preached to my friends and family to get involved in something that would benefit the community they live in. This is how democracy really works. It starts from the grass roots and eventually you have a community that makes you proud to be a part of. This is the story of my love affair with the city of Millbrae.

Chapter 22

Personal Consultant to the Archbishop

I retired from my position as manager of the agricultural and land division of the San Francisco Water Department on May 31, 1970. During my 21 year tenure, my accomplishments were widely publicized in the local news media including editorials, news stories, and various columns by the specialty writers.

If there was pride in my work, commitment to my duties, and joy in my achievements, perhaps it could best be summed up by Dick Nolan in the *San Francisco Examiner*: "The taxpayers of San Francisco got more than their money's worth during John's tenure." The emphasis in his column dealt with my making millions of dollars for the city.

When I was asked to work with Archbishop Joseph T. McGucken and the Archdiocese to help them in developing a program to bring some relief to their financial problems, I hesitated in accepting. I had just completed a long chapter in my life which dealt with a lot of frustration, procrastination, and bureaucratic red tape, and my health was at stake. However, after meeting His Excellency for the first time in my life, I knew I couldn't turn him down. As I looked and listened to this man and sensed his greatness and despair, I suddenly realized that no one had ever approached me in such a warm and sincere manner. That day marked the beginning of a long and strong friendship.

The Archdiocese was land rich and dollar poor, and had a serious cash flow problem with a crushing debt, particularly to the Bank of America. The interest payments due each month were simply staggering. After a meeting with the financial advisors to the Archbishop, they stressed that I would be given a free hand in utilizing all the facilities needed to do my job. The agreement was that I would operate out of my own office at home and meet with the Archbishop every Tuesday morning.

I had my first meeting with Jim Durney, the chancery office manager, a no-nonsense oldtimer who kept the records and books. To my great surprise, no one seemed to know exactly what properties were owned or where they were. There were indeed many parcels of land ranging from part of an acre to the vast holdings at St. Vincent School for Boys in Marin County and St. Joseph's in Santa Clara, both covering more than 1,000 acres. Most of the surplus parcels were between 5 to 100 acres of raw land. I decided that I needed a complete inventory of each parcel and every holding in the four counties.

One of the major title companies which I dealt with while working for the city did an unbelievable job in supplying me with a complete list of all the Church holdings, including descriptions, maps, and the latest tax assessments. I also received a thorough map of each county showing all the Archdiocesan properties. What the title company did for me would have cost at least $15,000, but we got it for free. When I presented this material to the Archbishop, his eyes literally bulged. He said, "Do we really own all these properties?" He then called Monsignor Donnell Walsh and Jim Durney to his office. In his quiet way, Durney remarked, "No wonder we were paying all those taxes, especially on properties that I did not know existed." There was a total of more than 80 properties that were surplus to the Archdiocesan needs.

As it turned out, some pastors received deeds to property from well-to-do parishioners, acknowledged the gifts, said a few masses for the benefactors, and filed the deeds somewhere with no records in the chancery office. These priests were no doubt wonderful and outstanding pastors, but they were not good businessmen. On the other hand, there were members of the clergy who had keen business minds and planned well for the future, and later went on to become bishops.

The Church, particularly the San Francisco Archdiocese, was growing with the population and expanding out into the rural areas. While San Francisco was limited, Marin, San Mateo and Santa Clara Counties experienced an unbelievable growth. It was during the era of Archbishop Mitty, predecessor to Archbishop McGucken, that land was purchased at incredibly low prices. It was primarily used for grazing and agriculture, especially in Santa Clara County where tracts from ten acres to several hundred acres were purchased. Properties were purchased not for speculation, but for future new parish sites. However, they were all subject to real estate taxes and this is where the Church's finances were being strained. The only tax exemptions were on established churches, convents, and various religious institutions.

The sale of raw land falls under an altogether different category than the sale of a house, building, or any other type of real estate. Under normal conditions, the sale of undeveloped land would take at least a year or longer to consummate. The usual objections came from open space advocates and those who didn't want to see any kind of development near their homes that would destroy their use of someone else's property. Then, there were the governmental agencies who all had a say in what could or could not be done with your property. Because of the long period of time involved in closing a land sale, I suggested that when a bonafide proposal was received, the option holder must also put down a substantial non-refundable deposit, and pay all taxes and assessments during the option period.

I will always remember Bishop Norman McFarland, who was head of the Archdiocesan finances at that time. He always waited for me when I arrived for my weekly Tuesday meetings and said, "John, when is the next money coming in? We need it to meet our obligations."

As time went on, I truly enjoyed my meetings with the Archbishop. We would always discuss business matters and then drift onto other subjects. Sometimes after the business part was completed, I would look at my watch and say, "Your Excellency, I believe I have overstayed my time. I know that there are people waiting to see you." His reply was, "Oh, let them wait awhile." He was always looking for material for his many meetings with the many groups he had to meet. His schedule was unusually heavy, but he seemed to enjoy our visits.

Archbishop McGucken was an entertaining speaker. His talks could be serious or light-hearted. He told me that he was quite fond of the I.C.F. (Italian Catholic Federation) and really enjoyed its family-oriented organization. It was also the most active of all the Catholic organizations. Because of my Sicilian origin, he also told me of the time that he hiked all over Sicily during his seminary years while in Italy. The Archbishop was particularly interested in archaeology and Sicily had more preserved Greek ruins than in Greece. Sicily, at one time, was known as *Magna-Grecia*.

On another occasion, the Archbishop related to me that he had a Sicilian niece living in Los Angeles and that "Perhaps now you know that whenever I need a rest, I usually go to Los Angeles." Not waiting for my reaction, he continued, "She really knew how to prepare a good dish of ravioli." That was the human side of him; otherwise, he carried a tremendous burden of responsibility in administrating his far-flung four-county empire.

Since the revenue from the sale of some of the surplus properties negated some of the financial problems of the Archdiocese, Archbishop McGucken proudly published his "Second Annual Statement of Financial Accountability to the People of the Archdiocese of San Francisco." He started his report for the fiscal year 1971 to 1972 with an acknowledgement of the work of Bishop Norman T. McFarland, chairman of the finance committee. In the fourth paragraph, he stated, "We are happy to announce that we were able to reduce the external debt of the Archdiocese by two-and-one-quarter million dollars ($2,250,000). This was made possible to a significant extent by the advantageous sale of some surplus property." This no doubt, made me feel good. It also encouraged me to redouble my efforts.

My policy was to put only one or two parcels on the market at a time unless there was some urgency to sell a particular piece, especially if it was planned to establish a new parish in a specific location. The other policy was not to sell the "Church's patrimony." As an example, a 42-acre parcel on White Road in Santa Clara County, a rural area, involved the sale of only 36 acres. Six acres were held out as a future parish site. This policy proved advantageous in that after the 36 acres were developed for residential purposes, the remaining six acres were worth more than the acreage sold as raw, undeveloped land.

Another parcel involved 12 acres with eight acres for sale. The remaining four, which were being held for the future, would actually triple in price after the property sold was developed. Thus, the Church would receive the highest possible price for the bulk raw land and still retain a high value on the remaining four acres. This procedure was followed whenever possible.

Father Daniel Walsh had been ordained by Archbishop McGucken in 1963. He served as assistant pastor at St. Pius Church in Redwood City and was a member of the faculty of Serra High School for five years before he was assigned to the chancery office. I met Father Walsh in 1970 when I first started my assignment. I liked him from the beginning. He had a sharp, observing mind and besides being a devoted priest, he had a good business outlook. He became Monsignor Donnell Walsh's "understudy" in real estate matters.

Monsignor Donnell Walsh resigned as chancellor of the Archdiocese and became pastor of St. Brenden's Church in the affluent Forest Hills section of San Francisco. Monsignor Cornelius Burns became the new chancellor while Father Daniel Walsh assumed his new duties as secretary to Archbishop McGucken. The position of chancellor corresponded to that of a chief administrative officer, while the secretary is the closest to the Archbishop.

I enjoyed working with Father Dan. Many times while sitting in his office and chatting away, I jokingly predicted that someday soon, he would become a monsignor. When he did become a monsignor, I called it to his attention that he still had the "Father Walsh" sign on his desk. In his humble way, he said, "Just call me Father." In a later conversation, I said, "Someday Father, you will be a bishop and I want to be the first one to kiss your ring." (Monsignor Walsh was ordained as Auxiliary Bishop of San Francisco on September 24, 1981, three-and-a-half years after I retired from my Archdiocesan assignment.)

Prior to my appointment as consultant to Archbishop McGucken, there was a self-appointed group of prominent Catholics who got together in San Mateo County for the purpose of assisting the Archdiocese in selling some of the surplus properties in order to remove the Church's debt. I don't believe the Archbishop was happy with this ad hoc committee of well-meaning people. They took the name of "Padriax" and somehow managed to secure office space and equipment at St. Patrick's Seminary in Menlo Park. Shortly after my appointment, the Archbishop confided in me in a letter stating that he did not want to start a "wholesale selling of properties." After some discussion, we decided to give them a chance and submitted a list of six properties which were subject to all terms and conditions having our approval prior to any final action. This didn't work out too well as we felt that the Church was not getting a good deal on some of the properties offered for sale. In the final analysis, Padriax was dissolved and we continued to move along in a more systematic way.

Bishop McFarland was a strong, tall and handsome man with a kind Irish face, who was brought up in the tough Irish-populated Mission District in San Francisco. He could have easily qualified as a linebacker for the Forty Niner football team. One day, he told me how he had just come from a luncheon meeting where he was discussing church finances, emphasizing that the Church's wealth was in its churches, schools, and the various religious institutions. He further stated, "Did you ever hear of anybody buying a church?" When he noticed my smiling face, he said, "John, what did I say that is so amusing to you?" To this, I replied, "I am sorry to say, or I should say, I am glad to inform you that we just sold a church." I don't believe the good bishop heard what I said, so I repeated, "Yes, Your Excellency, that little church in Sausalito, Star of the Sea, was sold yesterday." (Star of the Sea was not in use since another church was built closeby.)

One of the most interesting properties to be sold was a 22-acre parcel on Bon Aire Road, adjacent to Marin Catholic High School in Marin County. This property was partially swampland, but it was buildable. We received some very attractive offers for a condominium complex development and there was an immediate objection from a group of conservationalists who wanted to retain the property as open space. They had access to county funds and seemed quite anxious in spending the money. We had no objections to selling this property to them provided they could come up with the price offered by the developer, which was four times more than what they were willing to pay.

There was a series of public hearings before finally reaching the county planning commission. We thought we would get instant approval until a little, gray-haired old lady rose to her feet and signaled to the chairman that she wanted to be heard. It was so quiet you could hear a pin drop. In a very soft, sweet voice, she stated that "This was the habitat of the red-bellied harvest mouse, an endangered species." After a pause of puzzling silence, the chairman banged his gavel and said, "This matter will be postponed for two weeks."

Several months later through extensive scientific research, we proved that the existence of the red-bellied harvest mouse was well-established on the swampy shores of St. Vincent's School for Boys, along the San Francisco Bay shoreline that was part of the school property. It seemed that this rodent lived a rather prolific existence and did not appear to be in any way endangered. We got our approval from the planning commission and Goodwin Steinberg was able to build his condominiums.

One of the major properties owned by the Church included the St. Vincent School for Boys in Marin County, which consisted of 1,000 acres of choice land east of Highway 101 and extending to San Francisco Bay. This acreage contained the school buildings, and a vast agricultural hay and livestock operation. About half of the land was used for grazing, and milking cows and steers for beef. This area had tremendous possibilities for a light industrial and residential development. The problem was the county's "no growth" policy, which limited this type of development. Approximately 350 acres along the bay front had great possibilities for an "American Venice" type of residential and recreational development.

Much time and effort was devoted in trying to develop St. Vincent's, but bureaucratic county and environmentalist roadblocks became unsurmountable. We then received an interesting and most unusual proposal from a group of wealthy Iranians living in Marin County. They wanted to purchase the 530-acre parcel of wild, hilly land west of the highway, which was not fit for grazing or even raising nanny goats. The purpose was to build a huge mosque on top of one of the hills. The idea of a Moslem mosque didn't receive any objections from the chancery office. I believe that the reasoning in this case was that in Jerusalem, the Catholics had the Church of the Holy Sepulchre and the Jews had their sacred Wailing Wall, while closeby is the Dome of the Rock, a beautiful golden dome where Mohammed was believed to have ascended into Heaven.

The proposal involved cash for over four times the value of the property. The Iranians had put up a substantial deposit and there was no objection from the county due to the large number of influential Iranians residing there. Lo and behold, the Shah of Iran was deposed and the wealthy Iranians packed up their belongings and flew back to Tehran in a big hurry. We never heard from them again and often wondered if they joined the Ayatollah Khomeini or just disappeared to Switzerland with all their assets.

St. Patrick's Seminary in Menlo Park had 62 acres of surplus land. We had developed a program to lease the surplus property long-term for condominiums and particularly, for a senior citizens retirement facility. (I ran out of time when I resigned after the Archbishop's retirement, but I'm sure that this type of a timely development will someday be possible.)

The St. Joseph Seminary property in Santa Clara County was a very interesting project. There were 735 surplus acres of beautiful rolling hills of which 340 acres were not suitable for anything but open space. (The seminary was not included in this acreage.) We had several lucrative proposals for 155 acres on the flat portions that were ideal for a 620-unit condominium development or deluxe townhouse complex.

Negotiations went on for four years, because of the opposition from the open space proponents. There must have been at least thirty meetings with the Cupertino city officials, who definitely wanted to see this type of development take place inasmuch as the new area would be annexed to the city of Cupertino, assuring all utilities and benefits. We had the strong backing of many prominent people in that area, especially Paul Mariani, a very influential man whose family was famous for its prunes and apricots. He was considered the apricot and prune tycoon of the Santa Clara Valley, operating a vast acreage of these luscious fruits. He later developed 20,000-acres of orchard land in Australia and met an untimely death while on one of his frequent flights to the land down under. Mariani was a spark plug for this development, and was a close and long-time friend of Archbishop McGucken.

Maryknoll, a religious community and part of the Jesuit Order, owned approximately 28 acres adjacent to the area that was to be developed. They, of course, had no objections. The Maryknoll buildings are now a historical monument and well-established landmark with its beautiful Spanish architectural characteristics. The property is now used as a retirement home for the Jesuits.

It didn't take long for me to realize we were beating a dead horse. The environmentalists were too strong and discouraged the developer. With the approval of the Archbishop, I asked the developer not to withdraw his proposal, because we needed this to establish a value on the land. Out of the clear blue sky, we received an offer from the county of Santa Clara. They were interested in purchasing 340 acres of the beautiful rolling hills for an open space and park facility. Here, again, we were faced with a situation involving two values, open space and a development complex value. Fortunately, there was an established offer from a willing buyer, and we were the willing seller.

At our many meetings with the county officials, we maintained that the value of this land had already been established, although the proposal to develop the property fell through because of the opposition. We also stated that we had a precedent in establishing the value of a property, citing the Kentfield and Millbrae properties that were under similar circumstances. Of the total 735 acres of the St. Joseph Seminary property (not including the seminary), the county wanted 340 acres. In our dealings with the county representatives, Monsignor Dan Walsh showed his keen business sense. At first, both sides were far apart, but after several meetings the county offered $2,954,000. Our price remained at $3,230,000. Evidently, they wanted the property so badly that they finally agreed on $3,200,000. Thus, we received a substantial amount for our land. The county was happy and so were we.

In the case of Millbrae, again, we were up against a tough-skinned group of open space-minded people. As one local businessman said to me, "If you turned them upside down, nothing would fall out of their pockets."

There were many properties, each one a different and individual case. I met many pastors and priests during my seven-and-a-half year tenure. When you get to know the clergy as close as I was able to, you develop an admirable sense of praise and dedication in whatever they are involved in. Many of them had problems, mostly financial. A particular parish would be in debt and happened to have land that was not in use. I was instrumental in helping a good many of these pastors and felt like I was accomplishing something in seeing a number of new parishes established with the monies coming from the sale of the surplus lands.

The people I met at the chancery office, the headquarters of the Archdiocese, became my friends as time went by. I saw bishops, monsignors and priests with their sleeves rolled up working long hours in their particular assignments. My deepest admiration was for Archbishop Joseph T. McGucken and Monsignor Daniel Walsh. The end of my association as consultant to the Archbishop came upon the retirement of Archbishop McGucken at the age of 75. I wound up my affairs and unfinished business with Monsignor Walsh.

Several years later, Archbishop McGucken passed on to his heavenly reward. He was living in retirement at St. Brenden's parish where his former chancellor, Monsignor Donnell Walsh, was pastor. I lost a good friend, a loveable humanitarian with a strict sense of business and management, and a wonderful sense of humor.

Archbishop John R. Quinn succeeded McGucken as the new spiritual leader of the four-county Archdiocese. Monsignor Daniel Walsh became his secretary and on September 24, 1981, he was ordained Auxiliary Bishop. Bishop Pierre DuMaine was appointed as the new bishop of the Diocese of San Jose. Shortly after Archbishop Quinn took over, he proceeded to split the Archdiocese with the approval of the Vatican by creating the new Diocese of San Jose, which consisted of the entire county of Santa Clara. Thus, the Archdiocese of San Francisco retained jurisdiction over the counties of San Francisco, Marin, and San Mateo.

I now look back and can say with a great deal of pride that this assignment was one of the happiest periods of my life.

Chapter 23

A Bishop is Installed

For seven-and-a-half years, I served as personal consultant on property matters to Archbishop Joseph T. McGucken. One of the joys of that assignment was working with young Father Daniel Walsh, a very capable and most likable person. Since then, it has been my privilege to watch this good priest rise to the rank of Bishop.

Monsignor Walsh and I became good friends over the years. On a number of occasions, we entertained him at our home in Millbrae. At times, we jokingly discussed the Irish and Italians, but inasmuch as he always sided with Joan, my Irish wife, I was outnumbered 2 to 1. However, I made it a rule that she should only prepare Italian food and spaghetti with a Sicilian tomato sauce, which he seemed to enjoy.

It was only a few years later that Monsignor Walsh's hard work and dedication was rewarded when he was made Auxiliary Bishop of San Francisco. I shall never forget the date of August 6, 1987. It was a happy day for my wife and I when we traveled to Las Vegas to witness his installation as the fifth bishop of the Nevada Diocese. The ceremony took place in the Guardian Angel Church, the Cathedral of the Diocese of Nevada. This magnificent church was completely surrounded by the high-rise gambling casinos and hotels with their glittering neon signs. One might ask, "Why a cathedral in this location?" As it happens, gambling is legal in Nevada and regarded as a business just like any other. He was installed by Archbishop John R. Quinn. When Monsignor Walsh and I met again, I couldn't resist the temptation of telling him, "I told you that someday soon you would be made Bishop." With his warm smile, he replied, "John, when will you stop teasing me?"

There were more than 800 people who packed the church. Over 300 priests and bishops took part in the ceremonies. The priests all wore white cassocks, while the bishops and the heads of the many religious orders in attendance were attired in their most colorful garments. They came from all over the western states, particularly California and Nevada. It was an unbelievable sight to behold, and as a member of the Knights of Columbus, I was thrilled to see the Honor Guard of the Fourth Degree Knights of Columbus leading the procession into the cathedral. As the procession passed where Joan and I were seated, we received smiles from the principal celebrants and the many we knew, including Bishop McFarland.

Following the procession, the mass took place with all its beauty and splendor. Assisting Bishop Walsh were Bishop McFarland and Archbishop Roger Mahony of Los Angeles. It was difficult sitting in the pew without having one's eyes filled with tears of joy. I was touched when Joan reached over, squeezed my hand, and whispered how fortunate we were to be present on this special occasion for such a holy and dear friend. As Bishop Walsh concluded his sermon, he paused for a moment and carefully gazed out to those assembled in the church. Then with a firm voice, he announced, "I am now one of your fellow Nevadans. I am one of you." At the conclusion of that statement, the entire congregation rose and gave him a thundering ovation. The recognition Bishop Daniel Walsh received sent goose pimples through my body. As all those around me continued to applaud, I had a flashback of him on the first day we met. He said to me, "John, the most important title I will ever have will always be 'Father.' "

The banquet which followed was also a major event. Over a thousand attended and many were turned away. Again, it was a tribute to Bishop Walsh's popularity. What pleased me more were the hundreds of people who journeyed from California to show their affection. The Terrace Room of the Desert Inn Hotel never looked so impressive and beautiful. Everywhere we turned were bishops to greet, including Bishop Francis Quinn of Sacramento, a great humanitarian and scholar (formerly a priest at Holy Name, my parish in San Francisco). With respect and affection, many called him the "poet laureate of the secular priests of the West Coast."

Most of those from San Francisco stayed at the Desert Inn. As we exited from the hotel following the banquet, my curiosity led me to ask the question, "Who were the other four bishops before Bishop Walsh?" I had done some research on Nevada's history, so the next morning I told Joan, "We will do some more research." Following breakfast, we walked to the cathedral and found someone in the bookstore who was knowledgeable on the subject.

The Diocese of Reno was created by Pope Pius XI in 1931. At that time, Las Vegas was just a gasoline station roadstop. The first bishop to be appointed to the Diocese, a thriving western community famed for its silver and "quickie" divorces, was Bishop Thomas J. Gorman from Fort Worth, Texas. After 21 years of dedicated service, he was succeeded by Bishop Robert J. Dwyer. With commitment and dedication, Bishop Robert Dwyer accomplished much, including the renovation of the magnificent St. Thomas Aquinas Cathedral in Reno.

The third bishop was Bishop Joseph Green, a noble individual who, unfortunately through poor advice, ran into financial difficulties in the administration of the Diocese. While he had the ability to overcome the obstacle, he was struck by a series of major illnesses, which forced this worthy and dedicated man to retire.

From San Francisco came Bishop McFarland, who served as Auxiliary Bishop under Archbishop Joseph T. McGucken. For seven years, he was head of the finance committee. I had worked closely with him when I was the Archbishop's property consultant. If there was one thing I could say about Bishop McFarland at that time without hesitation, it was that he would have made one hell of a bank president if he was not serving God as a priest.

In February of 1976, Pope John Paul II appointed Bishop McFarland as the fourth bishop of Reno. It was he who petitioned the Pope to redesignate the Diocese of Reno to the Diocese of Reno-Las Vegas with the Guardian Angel Church to serve as the new cathedral. When Bishop McFarland departed on February 24, 1987 to his new assignment as Bishop of Orange County in southern Calilfornia, he left the Diocese in a sound and healthy condition. As I put it to a friend, "Nevada will greatly benefit from the energy, intelligence and personality of Bishop Dan Walsh." At the age of 49, he was the youngest bishop to serve the Silver State.

It had been 20 years since the last time we were in Las Vegas, so what did we do for the rest of our stay? We did what the majority of people do when they go to Las Vegas; we tried our luck at gambling. First, we hit the slot machines and the poker machines. Lady Luck was not with us and before we knew it, we were moving from one casino to another in the 110-degree heat. When we returned to the Desert Inn, I turned to Joan and said, "Father Dan will need our prayers." No sooner had I finished that sentence when I turned my eyes to where the "Jumbo Dollar" slot machine was and saw a nun playing the monster machine. To my surprise, an unholy miracle happened. She hit the highest jackpot possible, three blue "7's." Her reward was 1,000 silver dollars that came tumbling out of the machine. The clinking of the coins attracted a large crowd to witness the phenomena of this nun, who was too excited to respond to the well-wishers around her. I tried like hell to find out which order of nuns she belonged to, but I was not successful. For the remainder of the afternoon, Joan and I laughed as we thought about what had happened.

Later on that evening, we heard a scream coming from the direction of that same slot machine. It was from a dwarf who must have been all of four feet in height, assisted by his wife. They, too, had hit the jackpot with the avalanche of silver dollars going into their bucket and onto the floor. Would you believe a few minutes later he did it again?

As we sat in our seats on the plane awaiting departure for San Francisco, I looked out the window and repeated my remarks from the previous day, "Joan, remember that in a place like this, Father Dan will need our prayers; not because of the temptations that will confront him, but that he will have the ability to help the congregation of this community that lives under neon lights 24 hours a day." Completely relaxed in my comfortable seat as we headed home, I was struck with another pleasant occurrence which to me was the real highlight of the evening at the end of the banquet. Bishop Walsh spotted me and came over to greet me in his very warm manner. He asked, "Where is Joan?" I replied by pointing to our table. With this, he left the company of Archbishop John Quinn and the Apostolic Delegate Archbishop Pio Laghi and went over to greet Joan with a hug and kiss. I will never forget that moment. What a guy.

Chapter 24

La Mia Bella Sicilia

The average American tourist traveling to Italy seldom gets down to visit the beautiful and extremely interesting island of Sicily. He usually goes to Venice, Florence, Rome, Milan, and the Bay of Naples. It seems that the only time he visits Sicily is when he has relatives there. Those who do get to see it are impressed in the richness of its history and famed archaeological finds. The waters surrounding the island are a sparkling clear blue and with the turn of the head, there is a panoramic vista more beautiful than the next. The pure beauty of Sicily are its people and the dialects that are still heard in the different communities of the island. The many attractive resorts are populated by the English, German, and Scandinavians the year-around.

During the reign of the monarchy from the *Risorgimento* of 1860 to the end of World War II, the south of Italy from Naples on down received the ''crumbs'' from the Italian government. The wealth of Italy was preserved for the manufacturing and financial centers in the north, particularly Rome, Milan, Piemonte, Bologna, Genoa, and Venice. At the end of World War II with the establishment of the Italian Republic, the powers that be realized that a united Italy must include the south and Sicily. Here were the ''sleeping giants'' and here was where help was needed.

The *Cassa per il Mezzogiorno* was a fund established by the new republic. In 15 years, $3 billion was spent in improving agriculture, communications, roads, utilities, water supply, reforestation, elimination of ghettos, and everything else that spelled progress.

When Rome ruled the world, Sicily was its breadbasket. Before the Romans were the Greeks. There are more and better preserved Greek ruins in Sicily than in Greece. Sicily was known as *Magna Grecia* (Greater Greece).

The history of Sicily goes back to the Sicans, Elymians, Sicels, Greeks, Carthaginians, Romans, Saracens, and Normans, followed by the hated French, the welcomed Spaniards, the *Risorgimento*, the kingdom, and the present republic. Sicily was the crossroads of the ancient and the new world.

It was under the Arab rule from 831 to 1072 that Palermo began her real splendor and greatness. She was the jewel of the Arab world, and here it was during the Dark Ages and long before the Renaissance that Palermo and Sicily were the centers of learning and science. Then came the Normans, who wisely permitted the Arab culture to remain. This intermingling of their architecture and knowledge developed some of the world's greatest masterpieces.

I am not trying to render a history of Sicily, but only dwelling on bits and pieces that have been lost in the annals of time, and of people who have helped develop the Sicilian character. The importance of Sicily to Italy is well-described by the famous German poet and writer, Johann Goethe, writing from the Hotel De Les Palmes in Palermo in April of 1787. He wrote: "Italy without Sicily cannot be conceived. Here is the key to everything."

Sicily had been a subject colony over the centuries with no improvement under the monarchy from 1860 to the advent of Benito Mussolini in the 1920s. He gave Sicily a mild renaissance in the elimination of the infamous Mafia that had strangled the island for so long. With one sweep, most all the *Capo Mafiosi* wound up in the island jails only to be liberated after the conquest of Sicily by the Allies. Dictator or not, Mussolini did much to restore the island's prosperity in many ways, including beautiful *autostrade* (freeways), public buildings, irrigation dams, and work for the downtrodden.

Despite the past, the Sicilians have withstood the ravages of time and conquest, but they have never been absorbed nor have they lost their hope for the future. Perhaps all this can best be described from *The Leopard* by Giuseppe Di Lampedusa, the famous Sicilian author. He wrote:

"We are old, very old. For over twenty-five centuries, we have withstood the weight of the superb and heterogeneous civilizations, all from the outside; none that we could call our own. We have been a colony for 2,500 years. It's been our fault. But even so, we are worn out and exhausted.

The violence of landscape, this cruelty of climate, this continued cruelty in everything, and even these monuments of the past. A lot of these things we could not understand, but taxes we understood, too well, and which they spent elsewhere.

They took our forests and our agriculture, and left us our blood and our tears. All these things have formed our character. Now we turn to Rome. We must do it ourselves.''

Little is known about the English influence in Sicily and the importance these transplanted Englishmen played in the history of the island. Raleigh Trevelyan vividly described this contribution in *Princes Under the Volcano*. It is the true story of the British dynasty's 180 years in Sicily, which began circa 1800.

We all know the Englishman's love for Port wine (Origin, Oporto in Portugal), his Madeira wine from the Island of Madeira, and the Marsala wine from the region of western Sicily. History tells us that Lord Nelson had a great deal to do with early Marsala beginnings. However, it was here that the Florio family, Vincenzo and Ignazio, established the world-famous vineyards that produced the Marsala wines. The Florios were responsible for the industrialization of Sicily, the Banco di Circolazione, the development of the tuna fisheries at Favignama near Palermo, and the control of over one hundred ships.

The English came in the person of Benjamin Ingham, England's greatest tycoon. He made a fortune in Marsala wine, which he primarily shipped to England. This fortune, along with a knowledge of Sicilian culture and a Sicilian duchess, gave him entry into Sicilian aristocracy and international society. The other tycoon, Joseph Whitaker, became involved in Sicilian politics, the revolution against the Neopolitan Bourbons, and eventually, the campaigns of Garibaldi. Here, it must be said that Italy's liberator, Giuseppe Garibaldi, may not have succeeded in the conquest of Sicily which later resulted in the liberation of Italy, had it not been for the assistance given to him by the English colony in Marsala.

Giuseppe Garibaldi left Genoa with his famous *mille* (one thousand) volunteers, which consisted of ill-equipped, underfed and unpaid "rabble in arms" (reminiscent of George Washington's similar group). They headed towards Marsala when he was almost intercepted by the Bourbon Navy. Had it not been for several British warships in the vicinity that succeeded in diverting the Bourbons, the expedition would have ended and so would Garibaldi. The red-shirted liberators landed in Marsala and were enthusiastically greeted by the Sicilians and the British colony. It was here that Giuseppe Garibaldi was re-equipped with guns and ammunition, food, supplies, and money to pay his rabble in arms and got a fresh start. Here, again, was where the *picciotti* (Sicilian teenage youths) formed the Garibaldini, and thus, began the conquest of Sicily starting at Calatafimi and onto Palermo. Italy was eventually liberated when Garibaldi handed the keys to the kingdom to Victor Emanuele in Rome.

Englishman Benjamin Ingham had become a part of Sicilian aristocracy. The famous Palazzo Ingham in Palermo eventually became the famous Hotel De Le Palme. My great grandfather built the first condominium in Sicily on the Villa Ingham property, one block from the Hotel De Le Palme on Via Roma. (In 1983, it was demolished for a commercial highrise.) In World War II, the Hotel De Le Palme was the headquarters of General Mark Clark during the American invasion. And here, it can be said in passing that the Mafia was reborn, thanks to the generosity of the American command.

One of Mussolini's greatest accomplishments was that he put all of the *Mafiosi* behind bars. They were completely annihilated and spent their remaining days in the jails of the various islands surrounding Sicily. They were finished.

We dropped the atomic bombs on Hiroshima and Nagasaki, saving the lives of thousands of Americans prepared to invade Japan. In Sicily, we used the Mafia to pave the way for the American invasion. The Mafia, with their knowledge of the island and their sabotaging of the Germans in every possible way, resulted in a clean-cut American invasion with the loss of very few lives. In contrast, the British who landed on the eastern end and advanced toward Messina, lost heavily due to the German resistance. (Eventually, the American advancement from Palermo arrived at Messina before the embattled British.)

As a reward for their "services," the Mafia was released from their island jails and took over the various towns and cities of Sicily as mayors and local officials. What a resurrection for this infamous society, which subjected the population to a life of misery and exploitation. Perhaps there was a need for such a society in the past. They were the "Robin Hoods" who originally robbed from the rich and gave to the poor.

The origin of this infamous organization came during the cruel French occupation in the 13th Century at vesper time (Easter 1282) in retaliation of the rape and death of a Sicilian girl by a French soldier. In a spontaneous eruption of the Sicilian temper, the people upon hearing the news dashed out of the churches during vespers and shouted, "Death to the French!" It was a death cry, a pent-up outburst of exhausted patience. This is where the word "Mafia" was coined: _Morte _Alla _Francia _Italia _Anela (Death to the French is Italy's Cry).

We come to the story of Danilo Dolci, who was known as the "Gandhi of Sicily." Since 1952, Dolci had been conducting a non-violent crusade against the misery and violence of western Sicily where the Mafia had its deepest roots — Montelepre, Carini, Partinico, Borgetto, Castellamare, Balestrate, Alcamo, Roccamena, Corleone, Piana Dei Greci, and Portella, with Palermo as its center. He had been risking his life daily to alleviate the shocking conditions in this fabulously beautiful land still gripped by the fetters of its feudal past. He became a striking symbol of hope in a world that was rapidly darkening for lack of spiritual values. Dolci was called the "St. Francis with a degree."

With the help of a small band of collaborators, Dolci provided a direct example of what can be done where the people were subject to hunger, poverty and degradation. He aroused the poverty-stricken people who lived in fear, despite the *omerta*, to the point where with the increasing force of the trade unions, he gradually began to make progress. Most of his support came from English groups. Although Dolci was born Catholic, he fought the Church in western Sicily for not alleviating the misery of the people. He took on Cardinal Ruffino of Palermo and attacked the government of Rome for their many plans but little action in resolving the problems of Sicily. He especially took on the Mafia. They didn't harm him, because he was widely known, received high honors for his work, and earned the Nobel Peace Prize. Everything he did was well-publicized, so they dared not harm him under the circumstances.

Dolci's headquarters were in Partenico. He fought for the dam on the Jato River. Sicily was without water, so the dams (on other rivers) provided water, jobs, and irrigation for the farms.

Several ghettos in Palermo were eventually eliminated, especially the *Cortile Scallila* and the *Cortile Cascino*. Sicily still has a long way to go. How successful the region of Sicily will be remains to be seen.

Danilo Dolci did much for Sicily by giving the people hope. Then came the Marshall Plan and the Trade Union Movement, and the Sicilians were able to take advantage of these new developments. Today, Sicily is just as modern as the Italian mainland. There is just as much traffic congestion in Palermo as in most of Italy. This, of course, is a sign of progress — that is, as we see it today.

Many Sicilians are actively engaged in the elimination of the Mafia. The efforts of the Sicilian officials in conjunction with the Italian government have achieved definite results. In recent trials in Palermo, over 300 *Capo Mafiosi* have been convicted and are serving time, many for life, in Palermo's Ucciardone Prison. These conclusive results have brought much pride to Sicilians like myself and for those who lost their lives as martyrs in the elimination of these infamous bastards. Perhaps it is just the real beginning. Time will tell.

As a boy growing up in Brooklyn, one of my greatest heroes was Joe Petrosino. He was a New York police officer and the first Italian to become a lieutenant. Most of the city's police were of Irish descent. Because of the odds he faced, he left an imprint in my mind that made me so very proud of this son of a Sicilian immigrant.

The Mafia was predominantly a provincial and an agricultural phenomenon. At the turn-of-the-century in 1900, New York was the second largest Italian city after Naples. One-fourth of its population was Italian. Cheap labor was needed in the New World. The people came from Ireland, Poland, southern Europe, and particularly, southern Italy. They were poor, mostly illiterate, and looking for work. Language barriers and poverty created a ghetto existence. Poor sanitation, misery and crime caused by poverty all added to a human ant heap.

Joe Petrosino's devotion was to rid his countrymen of crime and poverty. The origins of the Mafia, which he hated with a passion, were in his native Sicily. Actually, the rise of the Mafia in Sicily could have been blamed on the government in Rome.

When Giolitti became Italy's premier, the Mafia's golden age began. He knew little of the Mafia's character as they infiltrated politicians, industry, and big cities. The peasant did not have criminal tendencies, but was dominated by the Mafia because he was not protected by the law. If he had proper protection, he would have turned against them.

Emanuele Notarbartolo, a noted Sicilian banker, attempted to expose conditions in Sicily placing the finger on Raffaele Palizzolo, a Sicilian deputy in Parliament who was known as "Don Raffaele." It ended when Notarbartolo was murdered on a train as it passed Trabia near Palermo. Don Raffaele was arrested on December 8, 1899. Every merchant in Palermo closed his business out of civic mourning for the popular Notarbartolo. After ten years and during many trials, many witnesses died or lost their memories. The "Don" was finally acquitted.

Don Vito Cascio Ferro, the new *Capo di Capi*, became part of the New York crime scene. He was accused of many murders, but was never convicted. With Joe Petrosino in hot pursuit of this master criminal, Don Vito retreated to his headquarters in Sicily and lived a life of leisure while conducting his New York operations from Palermo. Petrosino undertook a secret mission in Palermo where he was shot down and killed in the Piazza Marina on March 12, 1909. He had refused the protection of the Italian police, because he was so convinced that his mission was of the utmost secrecy.

The real culprit of this story was Theodore Bingham, the New York police commissioner. It was he who leaked the secret to the *New York Herald* and put Joe Petrosino on the spot. The Mafia knew every move he made. The New York Board of Aldermen finally fired Bingham as the speaker of the board said, "From what I can find out, the real killer of Joe Petrosino is you, Commissioner Bingham."

Petrosino's murder enraged the whole world, particularly Italy and the United States. The Italian police were strongly criticized. His body was returned to New York and services were held in St. Patrick's Cathedral. The day was declared a public holiday. Over 1,000 mounted police took part as 200,000 people lined Fifth Avenue. The procession lasted over five hours. No prominent American had ever received so great a tribute as the homage paid by the people of New York to this Italian-American police lieutenant.

In time, Don Vito was arrested after Mussolini wiped out

the Mafia, thanks to the tireless efforts of Prefect (Mayor) Mori of Palermo. Don Vito died at the age of 81 in Palermo's Ucciardone Prison. Before his death, he confessed that he personally killed Joe Petrosino, because he didn't trust anyone of lower rank. He, as the *capo*, had to do it himself.

Joe Petrosino did not die in vain. While the Mafia's cancer is still with us, the Sicilian population is finally stirring to action. Huge parades of women have marched the Via Maqueda, Palermo's fashionable boulevard, shouting, *"Basta! Basta!* (Enough! Enough!). The *omerta* has been broken and the big "Dons" have been caught. Some of them have begun to sing. There will be new "Dons" with many on the younger side. They will be daring, but they will be caught. It's a new ballgame.

Sicily is now undergoing a major change. New hotels are going up, attractive resorts are sprouting along its many beautiful beaches, and *autostrade* (garden-type freeways) now make it possible to circle and cross the island in a short span of time. Perhaps the American tourist, like the European and Asian tourist, will find reason to travel and discover this paradise island and the picturesque islands that surround her like Ustica, which is north of Palermo; the *isole* Egadi west of Trapani; the many islands north of Messina containing the famous volcano, Stromboli; Pantelleria, a beautiful vacation island between Sicily and Tunis; and nearby Lampedusa, a famous naval base when the Americans invaded Sicily from Africa. All these islands are situated in the blue Mediterranean with its warm waters.

Every visitor to Palermo will eventually go to Monreale, a town situated on top of a mountain overlooking the beautiful postcard city of Palermo, with Monte Pellegrino and its picturesque bay. However, the big attraction at Monreale is its great cathedral built by the Norman monarchs with its Latin and Byzantine flavor. The famous mosaics make this one of the most beautiful and unusual creations of man in the world.

Inasmuch as I was born on the Via Francesco Crispi in Palermo, I should mention in passing that Francesco Crispi, a Palermitano, was the prime minister of Italy in 1887 and amongst other things, Giuseppe Garibaldi's right-hand man. He gave Italian politics a new impetus and was responsible for the Italian colonies of Libya, Eritrea, and Somaliland in Africa. He strengthened the government in many ways and created the Italian banking system.

The Sicilian table is the meeting place of the family,

whether you are wealthy or born poor, *a tavola non s'invecchia* (you don't grow old at the table). I challenged my northern Italian friends to make a better tomato sauce than the Sicilian. I could say the same about my many other Sicilian dishes. There is much more to be said, so as they say on a television commercial, "Go to the frig, help yourself to a beer, relax in a comfortable chair, and I will continue with this 'Island in the Sun.'"

Chapter 25

An Island in the Sun

I could be slightly prejudiced if I said that the jewel of the Mediterranean, Sicily, has to be one of the greatest beauty spots of the world. It is a spell-binding island with its history, romance, and beauty. This is the place of my birth.

Don't be swayed by this rhetoric or by my seemingly enthusiastic description of this most unusual region of the Italian Republic. The summers are hot with nine months of rainless weather, while the winters bring heavy, seasonal rains. It is an articulated land where the abstractions of a contour map come to life. The mountain ridges contain the umbrella pines, while the oleanders, cedars and palms are not only found here, but throughout Italy. It is the Sicilian palm, however, that is especially healthy, thriving in a semi-tropical climate. Azaleas and jasmine are everywhere.

Sicily, the land of the lemon and the orange, is a joy to behold when these fragrant blossoms are in full bloom. Then, there are the olive trees, so plentiful, productive and flavorful. Sicilian olive oil, although not well-known like the olive oil of Tuscany, is now coming into its own. Most of the Sicilian olive oil goes to Lucca and the olive center of Tuscany. The Sicilian olive oil is blended, loses its origins, and is sold worldwide as the "best olive oil of northern Italy."

The most famous of the cactus, *fichi d'india* (prickly pear), grows profusely in all parts of Sicily. It is relished by all those of Mediterranean extraction, because it is juicy, sweet and very rich in Vitamin C.

Palermo, once known as the jewel of the Arab world during their occupation in the tenth century, is one of the most thriving and bustling cities in all of Italy, with a population of over one million. If traffic congestion means progress, then it must be said that Palermo must be one of the world's most progressive cities. Here, you will find wealth, beauty, poverty, and the most unusual and best cuisine on the European continent.

With my Sicilian roots, I have long withstood those who assail the Sicilian as being *Mafiosi*. We have to live with all that and we make no excuses. We know what Sicily has suffered during the long occupancy by foreign powers and recognize the neglect of the south by the government in Rome. So be it. Where in this troubled world of ours do we find people that live in glass houses? Am I speaking of northern Ireland where Catholics and Protestants slaughter each other? Am I speaking of the violence in Lebanon, Israel, the streets of New York and the Bronx, San Francisco's Tenderloin, Angola, Central America, South Africa, or the Soviets with their many suffering and subdued former satellites like Poland, Lithuania, and Hungary? *Basta*, I will stop here.

As an Italo-American, I take great pride in being identified as a Sicilian. They are my people and I love them. I deeply resent and hate those of my own race who disgrace the good name of Sicily. I am not preaching paradise on this enchanted island. Again, I refer to the famous German poet, Goethe, who wrote most of his works from Palermo. He spoke of the world-famous luxury hotel, Villa Igea, situated on a secluded cape which dated back to the Edwardian era. He could not help but notice that adjacent to this temple of luxury were some of Palermo's worst slums. He complained about Palermo's garbage in the late eighteenth century when trash was conveniently thrown out the window onto the dirt street to be picked up by the street sweeper the next day.

Although the splendors of Sicily far outweigh the miseries, there is much to see and do on this island in the sun. The tourist is just as safe in Palermo as he would be in most American cities. The great attractions throughout Sicily are the monuments and the temples of the past, which are better preserved than in Greece or other parts of the ancient world. To see the attractions of Palermo, including the island of Ustica which is 30 miles by hydrofoil, would require at least three weeks.

The Norman cathedrals of Monreale and Cefalú are spectacular. Both cathedrals are famous for their interior mosaics. The Palace of the Normans, the *Cappella Palatina*, the *Sala of Re Ruggero*, and so many unusual gems of art and architecture are musts to be seen. There is also a startling pleasure palace found in the park, the *Palazzina Cinese* (Chinese pavilion). This was built by King Ferdinand I for his consort, Maria Carolina, who was Marie Antoinette's sister, during their Sicilian exile.

Agrigento, near Palermo, holds its internationally famous Almond Blossom Festival in February. I can still remember a similar festival held in Santa Clara Valley before Silicon Valley and the surge of population destroyed this most colorful spectacle. Oh well, progress has its price.

The beauty of the Sicilian countryside now fast disappearing was enhanced by the ever-popular Sicilian donkey cart, painstakingly painted in so many colors depicting the knights of old and the battle scenes in which the hated Saracens were defeated. What a colorful sight to see the Sicilian two-wheel donkey cart with the plumed and dressed-up donkey, and the *contadini* (occupants of the cart) in their peasant costumes.

On one of our visits to Palermo, Joan and I were invited to a factory where the *carrettini* (donkey carts) were produced in all sizes and colors. Giuseppe Di Vita, probably one of the oldest in the business, showed us the many processes handed down from generation to generation in the production of these famous carts.

Perhaps one of the greatest boosters of Sicily is Mary Taylor Simeti, a graduate of Radcliffe College who lived most of her life in New York, married a Sicilian, and has now lived in Sicily for twenty years. Her life is spent between Palermo, which she loves with a passion, and her husband's farm in Bosco. She claims that the best *cannoli* are made by the Benedictine nuns in Palermo's Piazza Venezia. Simeti wrote an interesting book on Sicily, *Persephone's Island*, a Mediterranean paradise in the Shadow of Mt. Etna. I would love to meet her and exchange anecdotes.

There are many expressions I have long since forgotten, but they are so colorful and expressive, especially with the accompanying arm and hand movements typical of Sicilian speech. Here are some of the common phrases heard:

When two oldtimers greet each other:
Bacciamo le mani. (We kiss our hands.)
E i piedi cuando sono cotti. (And the feet when they are

cooked.)

When looking for a parking space in traffic-congested Palermo:
Sant' Antoninú vestutú di velutú fammi trovare un posto fotutú.
(Little St. Anthony all dressed in velvet, help me to find some damned parking spot.)

When guests arrive expecting to eat pasta, they say:
Cala la pasta or *Butta la pasta.* (Throw the pasta into the boiling water.)

When things in particular go wrong, it is blamed on:
Maladetta terra (this Godforsaken land.)
Malocchio (the evil eye.)

A frequent question asked of American tourists (a joke):
Como canta il gallo in America? (How does the rooster crow in America?)
The American's reply would be "Cock-a-doodle do."
The Sicilian jokester's reply:
In Italia il gallo canta chi-chi-re-chi. (In Italy, the rooster crows chi-chi-re-chi.)

What the *contadino* wine lover would say:
U vinú ti fa sangú. (Wine will make blood.)

Some Sicilian names and expressions used include:
Cassateddi di San Giuseppe. (A sweet roll with ricotta cheese and filled with chicken meshed together with sugar, cinnamon and chocolate.)
Cortigghiano. (A gossiper.)
Consatala come vuoi, e sempre cucuzza. (Explain it as you will, it is still a squash.)
E chiu cornuto di un panare di babalucci. (He has more horns than a basket full of snails.)
Cornuto. (One who is married and suspected or caught "playing around.")
Acqua dAgusto, ogghiú, meli e musto. (The rains of August bring olives, apples, grapes, and must for the wine.)
Uno superbo. (A snob.)
Fissa. (A stupid person.)
Sbirro. (A policeman.)

Porca miseria. (Describes one's poverty.)

Strafalaria. (One who flaunts her sex; a whore.)

Strunzo. (An insult meaning "turd"; can be used as a term of endearment if said with a smile.)

Compare. (A godfather.)

Strunzicello. (A beautiful child; a cute boy or girl.)

Casino. (A gambling joint if the accent is on the "o"; otherwise, it means whorehouse.)

Panelli. (A Sicilian specialty made of either corn meal or chick pea flour, boiled to a paste, sliced, and fried in olive oil.)

Guasteddi. (A large, soft roll containing thinly sliced beef which is boiled and then sauteed in olive oil, sprinkled with a sharp cheese, and fried in olive oil.)

Let me say a few words about Sicilian pastry. Visitors to Sicily and Palermo are amazed at the great variety of pastries and gelatos. It is said that the beginning of the Sicilian sweet tooth was discovered during the occupation of the island by the Saracens in the ninth century. They introduced the famous *cannoli*, which are cylinders of pastry filled with sweetened ricotta cheese, candied fruits, and chocolate. Later, the Sicilians improved on the Saracen sweets and followed up with the *cassata*, a layer of sponge cake with practically the same ingredients of a *cannoli* and it was used mainly for weddings, feast days, Christmas and Easter. On All Soul's Day, the *ossi di morti* (bones of the dead), a most delicious *biscotto* is the dessert following the main meal.

The Neopolitan pizza is supposed to be the best pizza in the world, but for me, the Sicilian pizza is rated number one. Of course, I will not attempt to argue this with a Neopolitan as surely he will outshout and outgesture me. The Sicilian pizza has a simple thin crust filled with a tasty cheese covering pure wholesome tomato sauce with fresh tomatoes. There's no garbage or I should say, all the mixture on pizzas that resemble all the leftover vegetables found at the Wholesale Produce Market on a Friday afternoon.

The same can be said about Sicilian pasta with a simple tomato sauce and plenty of sauteed onions that give the sauce that delicious sweet taste. Another famous dish is *pasta con sarde*, a pasta with sardines cooked Palermo-style.

The Sicilians eat little beef, but lots of veal. Fish, however, is a main staple. The Mediterranean has the best tuna and swordfish, and everything else that swims or crawls is fresh and appealing. One of my favorites is *caponata*, a dish that is generally served with fish or just as an appetizer. *Caponata* is sliced eggplant cooked in a tomato sauce with a mixture of peppers, tomatoes, onions and celery. Added to this is wine vinegar, capers, small ripe olives, a little tomato sauce, and a bit of anchovy sauce. As one famous gourmet chef said, "It is one of the subtlest dishes I have ever tasted in all of Italy."

The Sicilian table always contains the fruits and nuts in season. The early cherries and the wild tiny strawberries generally make their appearance in late April, followed by the apricots, peaches, and *nespoli* (loquats).

This is not meant to be a cookbook. I am merely an amateur who happens to like good food, especially good Sicilian food. I will not overlook another of my favorite delicacies, especially when the weather is hot. *Caffé granita* (ice coffee) reminds me of the many times Joan and I have sat in a sidewalk cafe on the fashionable Via Maqueda in Palermo, watching the world go by while sipping our refreshing drink. The finale to this anecdote is to sip some of the delicate Marsala wine and of course, the wines from Alcamo and Mt. Etna, red or white, as a part of your Sicilian experience.

In order to understand and appreciate Sicily, its people and its history, I recommend reading *The Leopard* by Giuseppe di Lampedusa. This great historical novel was written by a Sicilian prince who died in 1957 thinking his work would never be published. He was born in Palermo in 1896, a cosmopolitan prince who married a Baltic noblewoman. He knew several languages fluently and in his palace in Palermo, he met with the literaté of his day. For 25 years, di Lampedusa meditated on a novel based on the figure of his paternal great grandfather and set in Sicily during the Garibaldian era. It was not until he was 60 before he began to write the story, and he completed it only a few months prior to his death. He was told by an Italian editor that his novel would never be published. Many months later, his manuscript was reviewed by an enthusiastic editor whose prompt inquiries brought to light the story behind the prince, who never wrote anything in his lifetime, but left a masterpiece after his death.

Today, his story, *The Leopard*, has already been acknowledged as a fine piece of work that will certainly take its place amongst the classics of world literature.

Many magnificent *palazzos* remain in Sicily today.

Gioacchino Lanza Tomasi di Lampedusa, the Duke of Palma, is the adopted son of Don Fabrizio, the Prince of Lampedusa. He is a professor of music and history, and lives in the palace while restoring this historic masterpiece to its original charm. Donna Stefanella di San Vincenzo resides in the famous Palazzo Gangi in Palermo, which at one time was the focal point of Sicilian Belle Epoque society. This eighteenth century *palazzo* has been compared with Versailles.

Donna Faimonda Lanza di Trabia, a descendant of King Ferdinand II of Sicily, spends a good deal of her time at the Castello di Trabia restoring this historic fifteenth century castle. Then, there is the famous Belmonte Castle where the descendants of the Prince of Belmonte are also in the process of restoration. Other famous *palazzos* bear the names of Butera, Paterno, Miscemi, Villa Spedalotto, Camporeale, Villa Urretia, and many more.

The essence of Sicily changes with every attempt to grasp it. This crown of the Mediterranean has gradually assimilated the influences of its countless invaders and colonizers since its ancient times. It is an intricate mosaic of sights, flavors and characteristics — Arabic, Greek, and Spanish, but especially Italian and Mediterranean.

Christopher Hemphill, writing for *Town and Country*, carefully describes Sicily as "ancient and contemporary, brash and meek, ugly and beautiful." He further states that it is "infinitely untouchable, never straight forward, always complicated, often chaotic. A graceful adaptability is the trademark of this culture forever affected by the shifting sands of civilization."

As a result of this history, the nobles of Sicily have ancient and meandering roots. Through their bloodlines, some are Spanish, others Norman, Roman or Greek, but as a group, they are purely Sicilian. This is very important to me as my bloodlines have been traced to the early Norman and Arabic period. What few years I have remaining in my golden years will be devoted to some extent in ferreting out my past.

As an Italo-American having emigrated from Sicily at the age of four, I feel proud, very proud of my Sicilian roots. That is why I write in depth in various parts of this book about Sicily. Palermo and Sicily have been around for countless ages. This enchanting island in the sun awaits you, but don't take too long to deprive yourself of perhaps one of the greatest experiences of your life.

Chapter 26

Sardinia, Another Island in the Sun

I had always wanted to go to Sardinia. This 'enchanted island, one of the 20 regions of modern Italy, sits at the bottom of the ''Mezzogiorno'' program initiated by the Italian government shortly after the end of World War II, with the establishment of the Italian Republic. The purpose of this program was to assist the impoverished south, which meant everything south of Rome.

The regions comprising this neglected part of Italy are Campania, Basilicata, Puglia, Calabria, Sicily and Sardinia.

The average American tourist who visits Italy, by the millions, seldom goes below Naples and Capri. They go to Rome, Venice, Florence, Genoa, Milan, Turin, and the other parts of the industrial north. That is where the wealth of Italy is at the present time. The real wealth of Italy, however, the undiscovered and undeveloped wealth of Italy is in the south, Sicily and Sardinia.

This chapter is a story of Sardinia, the neglected Sardinia, and my main reason, after nine previous trips to Italy to see for myself what this island in the sun is all about. The three largest islands in the Mediterranean Sea are Sicily, Sardinia and Corsica. Corsica, at one time Italian, is now French, although the Italian language prevails and the inhabitants are more Italian than French. Corsica of course, is the birth place of Napoleon Bonaparte, while Sardinia is where Italy's liberator and one of the world's greatest generals, Giuseppe Garibaldi, lived and was buried on the tiny island of Caprera off the north coast of Sardinia. This little island, now preserved as ''Garibaldi's island,'' is a must whenever you set foot on

Sardinian soil. Little Caprera is situated in the straits of Bonifacio. From its rocky soil and sparkling granite comes the pungent perfume of the myrtle and the thorny acacia to blend with the smell of the sea. But it is from the red geranium, which grows profusely on Caprera, that Garibaldi adopted the red that made up his famous "red shirt" his followers wore when going into battle.

On the terrace of his island home, which served as his refuge, the old General still in his flaming red shirt is now at rest. His spirit, however, stares out over the indigo blue of the Mediterranean towards the Italian mainland, and if his lips could move they would say, "There is the Italy we fought for." He also would say that Plato at one time remarked, "Only the dead have seen the end of war."

In this day and age we refer to trench warfare as a stalemate, while the blitz is lightning mobile warfare. Garibaldi, however, fought a guerilla war, never facing a stronger enemy. He, like General George Washington, would hit and run until the enemy was worn out. They won what they fought for, independence; one for Italy, one for the United States. They fought Indian style. The blitz came later. In the American war college at West Point, future army officers are taught about guerilla warfare and what made Garibaldi not only a national hero, but the exponent of deception, courage and the will to win against any and all odds.

So when you think of Sardinia, think of Giuseppe Garibaldi, a true Sardinian.

A turning point in the history of Sardinia occurred in 1950 when for the first time there was not one single case of malaria reported during the past year. This confirmed the success of the Italian government's program to rid the island forever of this scourge that afflicted this gem of the Mediterranean.

This then attracted the attention of Prince Karim Aga Kahn, who long understood the future possibilities of the island as a tourist attraction. He fell in love with the northeast coast and created the Costa Smeralda (Emerald Coast). What was previously a wilderness of unbelievable beauty suddenly became an attractive tourist center with luxury hotels, restaurants, marinas with miles of sandy beaches, nightclubs, shopping centers and other attractions. Sardinia was launched as a holiday resort. This brought the cooperation of the Italian government who realized that there were thousands who wanted to visit this enchanted, undiscovered island paradise.

The government spent huge sums under the M*ezzogiorno* program resulting in modern highways, transportation and up-to-date facilities of every nature. It was like a resurrection. More steamer and airline services, airports and what was once an isolated agricultural and pastoral community, gradually, and then rather swiftly was brought into the 20th century. Cagliari, the capital seat, is a bustling city of over 350,000, modern in every way, beautiful, attractive, historic and with traffic jams the equal of any modern city. Such is progress. The standard of living rose and things were inproving for everybody.

In addition to this phenomenal change, the fascinating history of the island was uncovered with its wild mountains, its ancient ruins, and its prehistoric monuments. At last Sardinia is now a part of Europe. In the period 500 B. C., the Greeks who controlled Sardinia lost the island to the Carthaginians who in turn were succeeded by the Romans. Then came the Vandals followed by the Byzantines (Eastern Roman Empire). The Moors attempting to invade the islands were driven off by the Maritime Republics of Genoa and Pisa. In this era, Sardinia began to export minerals, grains, cattle, cheeses, skins, salt, honey and coral.

The Sardinian language has retained much of the Latin, is very much Italian, but has a strong dialect similar in some aspects to the Sicilian. Dining in Sardinia is a pleasure. Ravioli filled with fresh sheep's milk cheese is an experience. I will not go into the gastronomic delights and the variety of menus found in this surprising island. No one will leave Sardinia hungry.

The climate of Sardinia is typically Mediterranean. The summers are dry and hot, while the rains come in the autumn and into April. There are almost 1,750,000 inhabitants. It is an autonomous region of Italy (one of the 20 regions). Cagliari is the capital while Nuoro, Aristano and Sassari, all thriving modern cities are the three provincial capitals.

La Costa Smeralda is about 25 years since its creation by Aga Khan, a group of international financiers and the Italian government. They had a lot of guts to create this 25 miles of enchanting coastline from Olbia north, along its picturesque coastline to Santa Teresa Gallura. They were successful because they kept to certain high standards. The buildings had to be in the Sardinian manner and in other Mediterranean styles. They wanted the elements of first class tourist resorts and an attraction for the luxury jet set elements which now crowd the many harbors with fashionable hotels, marinas and everything that makes the Costa Smeralda one of the world's most picturesque and highly desirable attractions in this troubled world of ours.

So Joan and I decided, what the hell, let's go to Sardinia. Now in our octogenerian years we decided to put wheels on our baggage with straps to pull, rather than carry our three pieces of luggage, and another "to hell" attitude with the cost of a trip to Aga Khan's paradise on earth. We figured that we had no idea how much longer we would be inhabitants on this trouble-plagued planet. Why not get a sample of this "Heaven on Earth" before we finally settle down in some God forsaken retirement home where every day and every night, we would be saying in our prayers, "How much longer, dear God?"

At this point I called my favorite travel agent, Grace Duhagon, who masterminded and outlined our previous 10 trips to Europe and said, "Grace, we want to spend three days in Rome, one week in Sardinia and one week in Mondello where we wanted to do some research on my family roots, with the able assistance of my Palermo relatives, who would, as usual, receive us with open arms and the familiar red carpet treatment that would be available to us in a true warm Palermitano manner." I also told Grace that instead of the flight from Olbia to Cagliari to catch the flight to Palermo, I wanted to avoid the headaches of inter-regional flight connections and inasmuch as I wanted to meet and talk to the many faces of Sardinia, the man in the donkey cart, the pastoral herder of his sheep, for which Sardinia is noted, the *contadino* taking care of his vineyard, the cork oak orchards and the olive groves. I wanted to meet the true people, the "Sardo." We wanted to taste the life of the jet set that made up the Costa Smeralda. We reasoned "Why should they have all the fun?" So we were booked at a four-star resort "Luci Di La Muntagna" located at Porto Cervo.

Pisa and Genoa vied for control of Sardinia in the 11th and 12th centuries. These warring city-state republics ended their rivalry when the Pope awarded Sardinia to Pisa as a reward for assisting in the defeat of the Saracens in the Balearic Islands in 1113-1115.

The Genovese influence spread from Sardinia to Corsica and between these two christian countries, they christianized both Corsica and Sardinia. They also married into the Sardinian families.

Aragon, from Spain, became Sardinia's rulers after the Pisan, Genovese era. The Spanish feudal lords bled the island and it was not until 1720 when the Treaty of London awarded Sardinia to Victor Amadeus of the House of Savoy. It became the kingdom of Piedmont and Sardinia.

After the long mismanagement by the Spaniards, the mines were reopened, agriculture flourished and the country returned to normal. Following Amadeus, King Victor Emanuel became King of Italy. The Italian government had little money to spend on the island and it was not until the reign of Mussolini that Sardinia developed a system of roads and super highways. He also developed the island's rivers furnishing electric power, irrigation and most of all, eliminated the swamps and the dreaded malaria that afflicted the inhabitants.

While all this meant progress, the lack of employment and investment to develop the island's economy resulted in a period of lawlessness and banditry.

World War II inflicted considerable damage to Caglieri and the maritime cities. The return of the war veterans caused a new spur to the economic development and at last, there was money to be invested principally by outsiders who saw the great tourist possibilities.

The mines with coal and metal deposits consisting of lead, silver, zinc, resulted in about 200 mines, and many oil refineries, giving the people much needed employment. The latest statistics indicated that last year over 20 million tons of crude oil brought in from the oil producing countries were refined at Porto Torres and vicinity in northwestern Sardinia.

The fisheries, however, are dominated by Sicilian and Napolitano fishermen. Some of the world's most prolific habitats of tuna, swordfish and shellfish of all kinds give the island an *abondanza* of fish of many kinds.

There is much more to be said about Sardinia, another island in the sun.

Chapter 27

Back into Memory Lane

My life story covering 87 years would not be complete without the spotlight shining on the Roaring Twenties. These were the early years of my youth, the years when I breathed the fresh air that came in through Gravesend Bay and the Jersey Meadows. The Jersey mosquitoes were our public enemy number one. I don't remember how much citronella we applied to our itchy bodies in self-defense or how well we screened our porch, windows and doors. It was a constant losing fight.

It was the period covering the Bootleg Era, the Flapper Era, the Charleston Era, Tin Pan Alley, vaudeville in all its glory, the days of the Stutz, Studebaker, and the Model-T Ford.

We lived in what was known as Brooklyn, the greatest city's greatest borough. Manhattan was the center of everything from Wall Street and Times Square to the pushcarts of the lower east side. "Little Italy" vied with the Jewish east side. Somehow, the Jews, Italians, Irish, Poles, and all the other immigrants seemed to get along, for were we not all minorities?

Thanks to "Honest" John Hylan, mayor of New York City, the subway fare always remained at five cents. You could travel from the Bronx to Coney Island, cross the platform and ride back to the Bronx for the same nickel. Hot dogs and corn-on-the-cob were also a nickel. A kosher pickle was a bargain at two cents and if you had two cents leftover, that would have bought you three large pretzels or some halevah (Jewish candy).

In the evenings, the family sat on their well-screened front porch with a slow-moving hand-held fan to create a breeze. There was no television to pass the time away. The crystal set radio was just coming in as the forerunner to the improved radio that brought us the "Perils of Pauline" serials, the "Voice on the Wire" (a humdinger of a whodunit mystery), and the beginnings of the likes of Jack Benny, Eddie Cantor, "Schnozzle" Jimmy Durante, and a score of the outstanding Tin Pan Alley greats.

There was the ding-a-ling of the ice cream vendor on the street to help us weather the hot, sultry atmosphere that was part of the Brooklyn summer. For about five cents, we could purchase a large ice cream cone. Generally, we took turns to go to the corner *gelateria* and bring back a pitcher full of lemon ice or ice coffee. A little later, my father would go inside and play a few of our favorite opera records on the family victrola. I believe I knew practically every Italian opera by heart. My father frequently took the family to the opera during the opera season at the Metropolitan Opera House. We always sat in the front balcony. The real opera lovers sat in the rear balcony, while society would occupy the orchestra and the many boxes. Those in the rear were the real critics. In opera, the stars had to be perfect. If you did well, you came out for a few encores, but God help the tenor or soprano who missed a few notes.

I will always remember one evening while watching "Cavaleria Rusticana," a popular opera that was usually twin-billed with "Pagliacci." It so happened that the tenor who was to sing the leading part was indisposed. There was always a stand-in ready to go on stage. It was not to be a good performance by the stand-in. He missed quite a few notes and judging from the murmuring in the upper balcony, we realized something was beginning to develop. It was towards the end of this popular opera when Turiddú was coming to the most exciting conclusion when the husband, whose wife was having an affair with him, caught up with Turiddú and sent him into eternity. At the conclusion of this tragedy, a voice is heard backstage announcing, *"E morto cumpare Turiddú"* ("Cumpare Turiddú has been killed"). Breaking the silence of this moment, a voice from the gallery was clearly heard throughout the opera house from one of the disgusted patrons, *"Era l'ora"* (It's about time").

Then, there was the Saturday night movie, the silent movie. The talkies were yet to come. Pop would take the family to the Park Theater on Cropsey Avenue in Bath Beach. There was the lone piano player who supplied the action on an outworn, upright piano for the silent movie. Before the show started, one of the attendants would go up and down the aisles with a perfumed blower-sprayer to purify the stagnant air (there was no air conditioning yet). This would be repeated during intermission or at times when body, garlic, and kosher pickle odors would permeate the theater. We paid ten cents to see the movie. The prices kept going up. When it reached twenty cents, my father cut out some of the Saturday night shows.

With this brief introduction, I will get into the politics of the day, the people who ran the city, the Roaring Twenties, bootlegging, and the melting pot atmosphere of the greatest city in the world - that is, if you were a New Yorker.

We lived in the era of Tammany Hall, probably the most corrupt political organization that ever lived. In a thumbnail description, I will relate the highlights in the reign of "Gentleman" Jimmy Walker. During the decade of the Twenties, the era of flappers, speakeasies, the stock market crash, and a time when civic corruption had a curiously innocent quality, Jimmy Walker ruled New York from 1926 to 1932. Although responsible for some of the most flagrant scandals, Walker could do no wrong and was returned to office time and time again. Eventually, the day of reckoning arrived when the Seabury Investigation revealed the many acts of corruption that forced Walker's resignation.

Jimmy Walker's relationship with Betty Compton, the actress, was a well-known scandal. He later divorced his first wife and married Betty. This also ended in divorce.

Walker was New York City's most colorful mayor and he lived the period of the times, the Jazz Age. He made millions of dollars in bribes, graft, and had all kinds of illegal income. His estate at his death was less than $38,000. He was a *bon vivant*. He eventually made his peace — spiritually.

Tammany Hall was originally a Protestant organization headed by Boss Wood and Boss Tweed, both Protestants. Later, it was the way of life of the Irish Catholic Church, which controlled and ruled this political organization. It was the most corrupt organization of the century. By the time Boss Tweed was exposed, they had looted the city of New York of over $200 million. . The first Irish Catholic mayor, William R. Grace, was a saloon singer. Then came the inevitable change. Someone had to destroy Tammany Hall. The man who would eventually accomplish this was a young congressman who represented the Bronx, one of the city's five boroughs. At this time, the Bronx was mostly Italian and Jewish. Harlem was part of the Bronx and was famous for its nightclubs. The most exciting nightclubs were Black.

The Bronx at that time was not the Bronx of today. In those days, it was a safe place to go and enjoy the restaurants and nightclubs without the fear of being mugged. The Blacks were orderly and the Harlem area even had a Black police department. They were tough.

Fiorello La Guardia was a man of medium height, intelligent, and had a fiery spirit. He was also a fighter, and was colorful in many ways. What brought him into the national spotlight was during Prohibition when he demonstrated on the floor of Congress how easy it was to make bootleg booze at home by actually setting up a small distillery. He and Alfred E. Smith, who later became governor and was almost elected president, led the drive to repeal the Prohibition Amendment that was so unpopular with the average American citizen. The breaking of the Prohibition law was considered patriotic and the thing to do in defiance of the "Drys." Charles Garrett tells it best in his book, *The La Guardia Years*, which gives an idea of how great a giant of the times Fiorello ("Little Flower" as he was affectionately known) was.

La Guardia was mayor of New York City for twelve years from 1934 to 1945, the "La Guardia Years." He defeated the machine politicians — Boss Tweed, Richard Crocker, the "Forty Thieves," "Honest" John Kelly, and Charlie Murphy. He was the best mayor in the history of the city and was also the first mayor from the ranks of Italian immigrants. His father and mother were born in Italy; she was an Italian Jewess. Fiorello was born on Varick Street in Manhattan, baptized a Catholic, and became an Episcopalian. He was the enemy of Tammany Hall, machine politics, and gangsters, particularly the Mafia. He gave New York City honest and good government. Parks, markets, buildings, welfare, and civil service were placed on a higher level.

La Guardia was one of New York City's most colorful products. He was constantly pictured leading police raids into gambling establishments, breaking up slot machines, roulette and other gambling devices. By his raids, he accumulated the biggest collection of guns and ammunition from the city's hoods, after which they were ceremoniously dumped into the ocean with much fanfare. He died of cancer shortly after the end of his term.

It was the heyday of mob executions. While Al Capone ruled

the Chicago territory, Frankie Yale ruled Brooklyn. The mobsters killed each other in their struggle for territorial rights. Gangland killings were so common that the general public went about their business in a normal way. It was a way of life.

I was in my doctor's office one day in Borough Park undergoing a physical by my favorite doctor, Doctor Ceravolo. Suddenly, we heard four shots and a crash. Interrupting my visit, we both went out into the street to see Brooklyn's most notorious gangster lying face up in a pool of blood. He was evidently eliminated by a rival who was anxious to take over the bootleg empire that was ruled by Frankie Yale. Our curiosity complete, we returned to the doctor's office to wind up my physical with the news that I was in good shape.

When I think of the '20s, it brings back the memories of when Peter, my brother, and I were choir boys at St. Finbar's Church in Bensonhurst. The church, almost cathedral-like, was located in a heavily populated Irish, Italian, and Polish residential neighborhood. The pastor was Father William Gardiner, a tough Irish priest of the old school who preached hell and damnation. He was a disciplinarian on one hand and a most lovable person on the other. He was tough on the Italians, because of their somewhat lackadaisical religious habits, but he also had a great love for them.

Father Gardiner's greatest affection was for his choir boys, all sixty of them, of which Peter and I were a part. We sang at the eleven o'clock high mass every Sunday and on special holidays like Christmas, Easter, St. Patrick's Day, and numerous other occasions. We were actually altar boys and choir boys. About fifty percent of the group were Italians, thirty percent were Irish, and the remainder were Poles, Germans, and other minorities. Once a week, rehearsals were held in the parish house. Father Gardiner wanted us to be perfect and insisted that "You can't sing through your teeth. You have to open your mouth wide." If we didn't follow this rule, we'd be reminded with a whack.

One day, Peter evidently did not open his mouth wide enough. "Open your mouth, Peter, wider, wider." The good padre was not satisfied, so he inserted his fingers into Peter's mouth. "Wider, wider," insisted Father Gardiner. Well, at this point, Peter, who was not a rebellious person, brought his teeth down on Father Gardiner's fingers with such force that we thought surely his fingers were bitten off. After this most unusual development, Peter was serving the six o'clock (in the morning) mass for the next three weeks.

"Dinty" Moore, who was the sexton of the parish, was the tenor and sang solos. He was the star performer in all the shows, minstrels, and other activities in which St. Finbar's excelled. Moore was a great lyrical tenor and was considered the John McCormack of his day. Because of him, I learned practically all the Irish ballads of the time, which I still remember and cherish today along with my Neopolitan, Sicilian and Mexican ballads. He had one outstanding characteristic, an Adam's apple that went up on his throat when he struck a high note and down on a low note. Sometimes it jumped up and down like a yo-yo when he reached the climax of one of his most passionate and exciting endings.

One of the wealthy parishioners left Father Gardiner a beautiful estate and lodge on the shores of Glen Lake in his will. Glen Lake is near the city of Glen Falls in the Adirondack Mountains of New York, close to Lake George and Lake Champlain near the Canadian border. This area is loaded with history from the Revolution, and is the most scenic and ideal vacation paradise in this part of the state. The lake is about one mile long and a half-mile wide with lots of fish and plenty of space for swimming, boating and sailing. What did this tough little disciplinarian and oldtime Irish priest do with this lovely lodge on this most beautiful of all lakes? "Primarily," he announced one day from his pulpit, "It will be for my boys, my choir boys."

Over the years, Father Gardiner's sixty choir boys, including "Dinty" Moore, our tenor, and Maggie O'Hoolihan, our Irish cook, would spend three weeks in August at Glen Lake with all expenses paid . . . but by whom? About two months before the annual retreat, Father took up a collection after several announcements from the pulpit. He told the parishioners that when the time came for the special collection for his boys, he wanted a "silent" collection. If you knew Father Gardiner, every time he asked for something he got it.

It was a lot of fun going on these trips year after year. All we had to bring were our own clothes, a bathing suit, and a toothbrush. Blankets, sheets, pillow cases and towels were supplied through the generosity of the parishioners. At ten o'clock each night, it was lights out which signaled the beginning of our pillow fights. However, these didn't last long when we would hear Father Gardiner's footsteps coming down the hall. In checking up on us, he saw nothing but sixty angelic faces and gave his nightly blessing. Walking to the door, he looked around once again and in a low-key voice said, "Okay, boys. Now you can go to sleep. It's going to be a long day tomorrow." (How could you not like this man?)

When you get sixty boys together, there is always bound to be some mischief. Some of us wanted to surprise and teach one of the boys, who was a bully, a lesson. We knew that he was going to pass through the hallway, so we waited for him. I had three luscious eggs in my hand and was elected by the committee to drop these on Tony's head on the right cue. We saw him coming, but didn't see Maggie O'Hoolihan step in front of him just about where the target was. Lo and behold, the three eggs left my hand and by a swift, gravitational downward pull, they landed on top of her head. It was one of the most perfect *frittatas* that ever landed on anyone's head. Poor Maggie O'Hoolihan. We all loved her very much. She was like our second mother and was one of the best Irish cooks this side of Galway Bay. She also made a mean plate of pasta that delighted many of the Italian boys.

Father Gardiner called everyone together in the library. "Well," he said in that inquisitional voice of his, "Who did it?" We all had stone faces and gave no reply. "Did you all hear what I said? Who did it?" Again, silence. Father Gardiner knew his boys and none of them squealed. Out of curiosity, he wanted to seek out the culprit. Being a Roman Catholic priest, he had the perfect solution. "All right, boys, we are all going to Confession, and we will start right now." A priest cannot reveal the secrets of the Confessional and Father Gardiner was not about to do that. As a result, my penance was to join him at six o'clock each morning for the next ten days and take a dip into the cold waters of our beautiful Glen Lake. No wonder everyone loved this tough little Irishman. I know I did.

Let me pass on another anecdote relating to my early life. As I mentioned in one of the earlier chapters, we all had big backyards and gardens where we raised a lot of vegetables and fruit. One of the reasons we had such bountiful and tasteful crops was because of our access to organic fertilizers, real old-fashioned horse manure. Peter, my brother, worked for Pat Lee, the neighborhood grocer. He worked after school and on Saturdays as a delivery boy and received three dollars a week, which was very good pay in those days for a young boy. He filled out the grocery orders and when Pat was ready, he loaded them on the wagon for delivery. The power to pull the wagon was supplied by Shamrock, a lovely, well-fed gentle horse resembling one of the Burgermeister's Percherons. While he stopped at each delivery, there was always a well-meaning horse lover who offered Shamrock a carrot, lump of sugar, cookie, clump of grass, or anything that was classified as food. Shamrock, the smart horse that he was, never turned anyone down. He was sociable and lovable, and always had a healthy appetite.

This brings me to the reason for the anecdote. Besides Peter's weekly pay, he was also the recipient of a barrel of manure every two weeks. To all of us organic vegetable gardeners, this was a very important necessity. Because it was too fresh to use immediately, we dumped the manure into our compost, adding leaves, trimmings, clippings, leftover leafy food from the kitchen, and some lime. When it was fully mature or decomposed, it was ready for the soil. The manure compost was applied to the ground in the autumn, spaded under, and by spring we had a heavy production of the most flavorful and highly vitamized food.

One of our neighbors, Angelo Franco, also had a high-producing vegetable garden. His problem was that he didn't need all the manure that he had access to. There was one horse and wagon on each corner, meaning there were two horses. In both corners were peddlers selling their wares for a four-hour period. During this long span of time, there was bound to be quite an accumulation from the horses. In those days, there were no public restrooms for horses nor did they wear diapers. Horse manure meant fertilizer, so there were never any chemicals added to our gardens.

The Francos, Angelo and Angelina, spent a great deal of time relaxing on their front porch. They were in their early seventies and retired. All they did was take care of their home and garden. When it was time for the peddlers to leave, Angelina would call to her husband, "Angelo, the shovel." Out came the shovel and wheelbarrow to collect the manure from each corner. The Francos, being good neighbors, always gave us some of their surplus. After all, what are friends for? My mother canned and dried a lot of tomatoes primarily for tomato sauce during the winter months. Thanks to Shamrock, Pat Lee, and the Francos, the Brucatos put up the best tomato sauce in Bensonhurst.

There were no frozen vegetables in those days and very little was imported from foreign countries. Florida and

California supplied the limited out-of-season produce. However, the big event every spring were the wild dandelions, which grew abundantly in the many vacant lots around the neighborhood. Following a winter without fresh, green vegetables, the dandelion was like the spinach of its day. Families went out into the vacant lots to gather this tasty green for their salads and cooking "a la spinach." Dandelions also had another use. We gathered and sold them to the many *paisanos* who, besides making their own grape wine, paid us ten cents a quart for the dandelion blossoms, which made excellent dandelion wine. This was done by adding sugar, raisins or prunes. A fermentation took place that brought the alcoholic content to fifty percent or more, much more.

We had all kinds of ways to make spending money. The winter, with its abundant and frequent snowfall, was a profitable season. The boys in the neighborhood who were my age got together and divided up the territory. That way, there were no jurisdictional disputes. Inasmuch as each house sat on a large lot, we set the going price at fifty cents for the frontage and seventy-five cents for a corner house. Many times, we cleared the snow after a heavy fall only to be followed by another in the afternoon. Of course, it was a bonanza to us as we were happy to have a doubleheader of this nature.

The summers brought more opportunities to earn money as we mowed lawns, raked leaves, and did whatever else that was necessary in suburban life. Actually, we had little time to become delinquent. We smoked a few cigarettes, and there seemed to be no problems with drugs and very little with alcohol.

Most Italian families drank very little milk. We were weaned from milk at the age of two or three. What we drank at the table was wine diluted with water. Perhaps that is why the average Italian can hold his liquor or wine. In this respect, wine became our way of life, enjoying it as a food and part of our meals.

My favorite studies were history and geography. I relished and enjoyed maps of every kind, learning about countries, islands and continents all over the world. I became an expert in geography. During World War I, I had maps all over the walls of my playroom. I followed every detail, every advance, and every retreat with wall pins, covering the Western Front in France and Belgium, the Eastern Front (Russia), the Italian Front in the Italian-Austrian Alps, the Dardenelles, the Turkish, and everywhere else the war was fought. The same was done when World War II came. I was too young for the first war and too old for the second as was my brother, Peter. Frank, my eldest brother, served in World War I in naval aviation.

We did not have playgrounds because we didn't need them. There were no automobiles to speak of, so we did not have the traffic of today. Everyone played in the streets and vacant lots unless they were physically handicapped.

When I look back into "Memory Lane," I suddenly realize that we have come a long way. What is happening today is called progress. In my youth, we were participants in almost all of the sports. We came up from the sandlots. Today, most of the youth are watchers, watching television.

No story is complete without love and romance. My first romance was with an attractive fifteen year-old, Margaret Newman. I was sixteen. I always met her in the neighborhood public library; that is, I was attracted to her, but quite some time passed before I had enough courage to start up a conversation. I purposely dropped a book at her feet while she was examining some books on an upper shelf. From that time on, we met daily to talk and I carried her books while walking her home. One thing led to another and the time came when I invited her to a local dance. When I rang the doorbell, her mother answered. Mrs. Newman was really a lovable person. However, at this point in time, she seemed to just have arrived from the frigid North Pole. "John," she said, "You are a nice boy and I know you come from a fine family. However, Margaret is only fifteen and we have an understanding that she is not to go dating until she is sixteen." That was the first disappointment in my early lovelife. What was I to do? We were both very fond of each other. Well, I just couldn't wait it out for a whole year, so after a few days I began to play the field.

The teenage hangout during my early years was Semkens Pier in the summertime. This is where we would dive about eight feet off the pier into the cool waters of Gravesend Bay. You could meet everybody here. There was an attractive, green-eyed Irish-Italian beauty, Loretta Baldwin, who was the most beautiful and sought-after girl in Bensonhurst. I didn't believe I was in her league or even in her thoughts. Well, one day while enjoying the goings-on at Semkens Pier, I heard a cry for help. It was Loretta Baldwin, who was suffering from a cramp in the water. She had already gone down once and her swimming companions were too far away, so they couldn't hear her. Not waiting for anyone else to do something, I kicked off my shoes, stripped myself of my jacket, jumped into the water (forgetting to remove my brand new Panama straw hat), and swam towards her. She grabbed me and almost choked me in her wild attempt to save herself. Suddenly, I remembered what to do in this situation. I must have slapped the poor girl several times until she lost consciousness. Somehow, I managed to reach the pier where a rope was lowered and with the help of several friends, we brought Loretta back into the reality of life. When she came to after a few swallows of brandy, she hugged and kissed me like I was never kissed before. "You saved my life! You saved my life!"

After this episode, I took Loretta home and again, she repeated the words, "You saved my life." With this, we were in an embrace I never expected. "I belong to you. I want to marry you." That was great I thought later on in the quiet of my home while pondering the happenings of the day. How can I marry this girl. I'm planning to enter college in the fall and I don't even have a job. The romance lasted about two months. I enrolled in college and we saw less and less of each other as time went on. Six months later, I was told that Loretta eloped with a wealthy rug salesman and disappeared.

When you are young, a romance comes and goes. In my case, I believe Loretta Baldwin probably did the right thing and I felt quite relieved. There were a few others which didn't add up to much in my early romantic life. My problem was I was not ready. All of them wanted to get married and I still had to think of my education and career. Perhaps it would be appropriate to wind up these early romances with a note from one of my flames, who announced that she was getting married. She told me how much she cared for me and left me with this note: "John, be like a piano — grand, square and upright." Not to be outdone, I hand-delivered my reply, leaving it in her mailbox. "Maggie, love is like an onion. You taste it with delight and when it's gone, you wonder, whatever made us bite?" I never heard from Maggie again.

Chapter 28

The Irish vs. The Italians — or Vice Versa

Holy Name of Jesus was my parish church for the many years that I lived in the Sunset District of San Francisco. Father Richard Ryan was my pastor. He founded the parish in 1925 and went on to his heavenly reward in 1956. He trained many promising priests who later became monsignors and bishops. Many of his trainees became pastors in other parishes of the Archdiocese.

In the mid-1920s to the 1950s, Holy Name School was one of the most advanced elementary schools in the entire area. It was also very proficient in all the various athletic activities producing champions. The parishioners were average middle-class people. There were few who were wealthy and few who were poor. The ethnic groups were primarily Irish and Italian, followed by German, Hispanic, and a miscellaneous sprinkling of other nationalities. (During the 1970s and 80s, a complete change took place. The majority were Asians, primarily Chinese and Filipinos, and the minorities were the Irish and Italians.)

Father Ryan was a forward-thinking man and enjoyed working close to his parishioners. Because of my Farmers' Market and Victory Garden activities, I was well-known to the parishioners and Father Ryan took a personal pride in my many civic accomplishments.

There were no Fathers' Clubs in the entire San Francisco Diocese. Father Ryan kept talking about starting a Fathers' Club to support and encourage the parish's athletic program. He received much professional advice from some of the private schools in the Bay Area where these clubs were somewhat successful. With some ideas in mind and a strong desire to start this much-needed program, he invited all the men in the parish to attend a public meeting in the school cafeteria. (The cafeteria was to serve as an all-purpose hall for the next 22 years.) Responding to the enthusiasm of the more than 250 men in attendance, Father Ryan decided that if we were ever to have a Fathers' Club, we should start now. He announced that he was going to call for a nomination of officers, and asked everyone to kneel and offer a special prayer to the Holy Ghost for guidance in order to select the right individuals, particularly the president. Refreshed by this spiritual interlude, he asked for nominations for president. There was a momentary silence broken by the voice of Louis Maffei who stood up and loudly said, "I nominate John Brucato." There was an immediate second followed by a close of nominations.

I became the first president of the first Fathers' Club in the San Francisco Diocese. Matt Carberry was vice president with Manny Hipps as secretary. I never saw such an enthusiastic group of men. Everybody present had a personal interest, because they had a son or daughter attending Holy Name School. (My son, Peter, was a student there at the time). My problem was that with every committee, there was an overabundance of volunteers.

We planned a parish picnic as our first fundraiser. Over 3,500 people attended this event held at Fairfax in Marin County. Because of the Irish-Italian influence, it was decided to hold a big Columbus Day feed in October and a rival one on St. Patrick's Day.

Before I begin the story on our first Columbus Day celebration, I must point out that one of the reasons we had outstanding football, baseball and basketball teams was because of the influence of Sister Francesca. She was young, attractive and full of life. She was not the coach, but taught in the parish school and lived in the adjacent parish convent. Sister Francesca was an expert in all phases of sports, and demonstrated the proper way of throwing a forward pass and hitting the receiver with a spiral pass that was unbelievably accurate. In those days, the nuns still wore the lengthy habits that reached to their shoe tops, but it didn't make any difference to her. She just raised her skirts and kicked the ball so far and so accurate that onlookers shook their heads in disbelief. In baseball, she was a home-run hitter; in basketball, she demonstrated how to ring the basket and seldom missed.

With some of the best coaching by members of the new Fathers' Club and the assistance of Sister Francesca, it was no wonder that Holy Name was the team to beat in whatever athletic activity was involved.

We began planning for our first big Columbus Day feed for our club members. Anticipating two hundred people, we decided to serve pasta. I was the spaghetti and meatball chef assisted by a kitchen crew of nine. (All Italians, no Irish.) Lou Maffei and I rolled meatballs for two hours at my home the night before. I used one of my mother's famous Sicilian tomato sauce recipes, which was to be the big surprise. Generally speaking, the average spaghetti eater thought that all sauce had to be Bolognese or Neopolitan. They didn't realize that the Sicilians, too, were noted for their outstanding tomato sauce.

The cafeteria was decorated in such a fashion that it looked like Joe DiMaggio's hometown at Isola delle Femme on the outskirts of Palermo in Sicily. Six gigantic pots with boiling water were ready to receive more pasta as the crowd came in. We estimated 250 people as we didn't go with reservations. We ended up feeding 350 with pasta and meatballs, tossed salad, Italian garlic bread, lots of Chianti, dessert, and seconds. I made it a policy that whenever we had any kind of an event like this, we made sure that there was plenty for the Sisters in the convent, especially Sister Francesca.

The Irish had their turn on March 17th. Matt Carberry, who later became a city supervisor and then sheriff, was in charge. Their first problem was that they were short of good chefs and kitchen help. It didn't embarrass the Irish to seek the help of some of the more experienced cooks who just happened to be Italian. Another tremendous crowd showed up for corned beef and cabbage. However, no one told the Irish that corned beef shrinks. Consequently, they ran short. Charlie's Market came to the rescue and rushed in a huge supply of bologna and salami. That saved the day for the Irish; that is, for that year.

Two things happened on St. Patrick's Day the following year. The Irish made the same mistake. The corned beef shrunk and in came the bologna and salami to save the day again. (The Italians had a field day. Will the Irish ever learn?)

The second incident involved a piece of the Blarney Stone. Matt Carberry had visited Ireland a few months earlier and jubilantly displayed a piece of the Blarney Stone prior and during the St. Patrick's Day dinner. Before the evening was over, someone discovered that it was missing. There was a sign of panic, but fortunately, cooler heads prevailed. It was a low blow and some of the leading Irish patriots declared, "Revenge will be ours." One week later, the Blarney Stone showed up in an unmarked package delivered to the Carberry residence. The announcement was made at a Fathers' Club meeting and there was a show of jubilation and relief. However, the spirit of vengeance prevailed. "We will find the culprit and take care of him in our own way."

I knew that I was suspect. The Irish showed unusual patience. Matt Carberry succeeded me as president. The night of his installation involved six Irish bagpipers. Have you ever been close to an Irish bagpiper group whooping up oldtime Irish music? Have you ever been as close as three feet away from the deafening noise of the bagpipes blowing away in that ear-piercing fashion? Evidently, Carberry had set up his tribunal. They decided to find me guilty in absentia. (Where was the American Civil Liberties Union in those days?) The verdict was kept secret until that night. I knew something was radically wrong and being of Sicilian ancestry, I expected the finger any minute. Carberry announced that John Brucato, our beloved past president, was to occupy the seat of honor. (At this point, I felt the blade slowly being twisted in my back.) The seat was in the first row just three feet in front of the six bagpipers. There was no escape inasmuch as I had a bodyguard on each side. They were two of the huskiest policemen on the San Francisco police force. Both were very congenial and were so Irish that you could actually see the map of Ireland on their faces. I didn't notice that their ears were stuffed with cotton. Mine were not, and I dared not show my weakness. Was not the honor of all my Italo-Americans at stake that night? It was a great show and I was actually deaf for the next three days. The Irish got their vengeance, but the Italians retained their honor.

This great rivalry between the Irish and Italians was all in the name of fun. They always joke with each other almost in the same vein as the Sicilians and the Genovese. I am not anti-Irish in any way. As a matter of fact, I was brought up in an Irish-Italian neighborhood, my best friends were Irish, and most of all, I have the most wonderful Irish wife. My oldest son, Frank, is married to an Irish girl and they have beautiful children, my grandchildren.

A silver jubilee committee was formed to celebrate two important anniversaries, the 25th birthday of the parish and the 40th anniversary of the ordination of Reverend Richard Ryan. I was the general chairman of both jubilees. The main event was a civic banquet held at the Fairmont Hotel on May 29, 1950. Bishops, monsignors, the archbishop, mayors, judges, and just about every top local and state official was in attendance. I was thrilled to chair this banquet for my beloved pastor.

Holy Name was getting too small to hold the ever-increasing number of parishioners, so it was decided that a fundraiser be held for a new church. We needed $300,000 — a lot of money in the middle 1950s. Father Ryan wanted me to head up the building fund drive. As in all building fund campaigns, it pays to hire a professional. It is a necessary evil. You can't depend on volunteer help.

We were soon well organized with one hundred percent support from the parish. During my meeting with the hired professional, I immediately objected to the methods suggested in soliciting the affluent parish families. They were to be tagged for a specific amount. He didn't agree with me. I tried to convince him that this was a well-knit parish and was sure that those who would be requested to subscribe to a certain amount (generally a substantial sum) would show some resentment. I didn't get anywhere, so I resolved that perhaps someone should take my place. Father Ryan came over to see me after my meeting. He listened to my reasoning and asked just one question, "John, is this the way you want to do it?" I said, "Yes."

The drive was a huge success as we raised close to $400,000. No one was asked to contribute any specific amount. The slogan was "Give what you can reasonably afford." It worked.

Father Ryan was once called the "Padre of the Sand Dunes," for that was where he built his church — in the middle of the sand dunes at what became Fortieth Avenue and Lawton Street in April of 1941. His new church was his life's ambition, but he never got to see it. He developed cancer and it became noticeable when he couldn't genuflect during the course of saying mass. His condition advanced rapidly and he called me to his bedside and proudly presented me with his personal breviary (a prayer book from which a priest must recite several pages daily during his lifetime). What a gift. I couldn't speak, because I choked every time I opened my mouth.

I lost a good friend and so did Father Ryan's parishioners. I loved that man. He was a great inspiration to me. He was so human and understanding. Now you can understand how much I love the Irish. Father Ryan was one of them.

About this time, my wife and I had decided to move out of the parish after having lived on Thirtieth Avenue for nineteen years. We purchased a new home on top of Twin Peaks where we lived for three years before finally settling down in Millbrae.

Monsignor William J. Flanagan succeeded Father Ryan. I was well acquainted with him and was very happy to see him installed as pastor of Holy Name of Jesus Church. When he heard that I was moving away, he grabbed my arm and said, "John, you can't do that to me." I replied by saying that I felt quite sure he was going to build a new church, Father Ryan's church. I also told him that with the kind of parishioners at Holy Name, he wouldn't have any problems.

On May 24, 1984, I was invited to participate in an Oldtimer's Night and addressed the group as their first president. I couldn't help noticing the change. I said to myself, "Where have all the Irish and Italians gone?"

Chapter 29

Boulder Creek Days

San Lorenzo Park is six miles north of the community of Boulder Creek. The San Lorenzo River flowed along the eastern border of my property situated amongst the giant redwoods, some of them dating back thousands of years. The two-lane Skyline Boulevard follows the river practically into the city and resort area of Santa Cruz.

The town of Boulder Creek is the gateway to some of the most scenic and historic country in America. Here are the famous big trees, giant sequoias that have been preserved for posterity, particularly in Big Basin Park which holds some of the largest and oldest redwoods in the world.

In 1944, I purchased a one-acre parcel from one of our neighbors in San Francisco, a recent widow who no longer wanted the country property. The entire estate was covered with giant redwood trees. In the clearing was a two-bedroom cottage with almost all modern facilities. The heating and cooking were by means of butane gas. There was a family orchard of apples, pears, peaches and plums totaling about twelve mature bearing trees. In this most interesting and unusual setting, we could communicate with nature whenever we felt like relaxing. When you live amongst these redwood giants, you can forget the outside world. You find peace from the silence of the forest and purity in the air. All you hear is the chirping of the birds and the movement of the water in the San Lorenzo River.

The property became our playground for sixteen years. The river was reached by descending twenty steps to the flow of the stream. It was icy cold. With my sons, Peter and Jack, we built a dam so that we had a man-made lake that was shared with the Marsac family, our neighbors across the river. The dam was built so that the center portion could be removed in the fall to permit the river to flow during the heavy rainy season in the winter, without damaging our permanent rock and concrete base. We also provided a waterfall effect, so that the constant flow during the summer allowed the river to flow naturally.

We belonged to our own water district that supplied the purest water for eighty families in the immediate area. There was complete privacy living in the forest primeval. Frequent visits were made by friendly deer, raccoons, rabbits, and numerous species of birds, giving us a fresh outlook on the beauties of nature.

To get to our place, it was necessary to cross a homemade bridge that was built by the lumber companies which, until a few years prior, carried on intensive lumbering activities. There was a narrow dirt road that passed our western boundary, climbing a hill that eventually terminated at a former sawmill site. It was named McGaffigan Hill Road after the owner of the lumber mill. There were at least a dozen summer homes scattered in all directions in this most picturesque portion of the redwood forest. The lumbering operations ceased when a rising protest of open space-minded people forced the lumbering to go elsewhere.

There was an old gentleman in his seventies who visited with us each year. His permanent home was in Oakland and every year during the Memorial Day weekend, he hibernated to his summer home, which was a one room shack way up on top of McGaffigan Hill Road. I don't remember his name except that we called him "Uncle Joe." He was a kind, bearded man with two eyes that sparkled like Tiffany diamonds. He lived a back-to-nature life communing with the animals and birds. Once a week, Uncle Joe came down from the hill with his cane and knapsack to place his order for the following week's groceries at Dick Dillon's store before coming to our "reservation." His knapsack was then filled with the previous week's order.

Dick Dillon was something else. The grocery store that he operated was not too well stocked. He never cared whether he sold anything or not. He was an old Alaskan "sourdough" who, we all thought, made a killing during the Yukon Gold Rush. No one knew what he was worth, but he did own the grocery store and a gasoline station on the highway. Dillon kept three Irish wolfhounds, the most beautiful dogs this side of Killarney. The smell of the wolfhounds, while occupying their winter quarters, permeated the store. The smell never left even in the summer. Those of us who knew him seldom entered the store. Whatever income he had came from the gas pumps and here again, he didn't care if he sold any gas or not.

Everyone liked Dick Dillon. He was a reservoir of knowledge, a strong supporter of Harry Truman and the Democratic Party. He sort of looked out for everyone's property. When there were strangers about, he inquired as to their business. If there was something wrong like a burst waterpipe or a fallen tree, he notified us. His greatest love was cribbage. It seemed that everyone in that summer community was a cribbage player. I was good, but Dillon was tops. On weekends when people came down to their summer cabins, there was an ongoing cribbage tournament played at Dillon's — outside that is. He seemed to enjoy playing with me as we were close competitors. If someone pulled up to buy gasoline, he waved them on and shouted, "Sorry, out of gas." Nothing interrupted his cribbage game except on one occasion.

In the midst of a very close game seated near the highway, a car suddenly pulled up and slowed down. Out came a large bundle of garbage that was carefully wrapped up. Dillon halted his game, walked over to the garbage bag, and slowly sifted through the debris. He found what he was looking for — identification with the name and address of the culprit. What did Dillon do? He asked Mr. Donati to take his place at the cribbage table. He then took the bundle of garbage, rewrapped it, wrote the name and address that he found, hopped into his car, drove six miles to the Boulder Creek post office, and mailed the package registered with a return receipt. Can you imagine the surprise when the recipient opened the package? (Yes, Dillon received the signed return receipt.)

I wanted to build a rock wall against the hillside and around the barbecue pit. Having never been brought up as a carpenter, electrician or plumber, I liked fooling around with concrete and cement. Rocks were plentiful, so we had no problems building a rock wall and later a rock barbecue pit and rock steps down to the river. I was halfway through with my rock wall and was unhappy with it because it wasn't straight. Some of my neighbors and visitors remarked that the wall was so beautifully natural and rustic. This not only encouraged me to finish it, but to expand the project. I was so heaped with praise that I began thinking about my future occupation as a rustic wall builder. At home, I had built rock steps and walls in my garden that also drew many comments. However, this was the extent of my future career.

There was the annual incident of the green apples. As we all remember when we were young, we always liked to eat green apples straight from the tree whether we got a bellyache or not. My Gravenstein apples had an unusual Gravenstein/redwood flavor. Every year, some of the neighboring children raided my two trees to eat the green apples. I always had fresh Gravensteins from the Farmers' Market available to offer them, but to no avail. They wanted to pick their own. Whenever one of the apple snatchers developed a tummyache, we joked, "Eight-one-two green," referring to a fictitious telephone number.

While on the subject of apples and my family orchard, I must say that I had heavy-producing fruit trees with rather flavorful fruit. I attributed this to the procedure I followed over the years in that all vegetable and kitchen trimmings, leftovers, together with leaves and plant trimmings were spaded into the orchard soil, thus, producing the best organic fertilizer. This, of course, not only produced flavorful fruit, but bountiful crops.

I purchased an adjacent one-acre redwood grove with giant redwoods, giving me a lot of privacy. There was an old, unused dirt road that ran along the river from my cabin to Redwood Grove about two miles away. This was one of the most beautiful pathways in this idyllic paradise with the San Lorenzo River on one side and the majestic redwoods on the other. We made good use of this road, particularly during our evening strolls. There were so many wonderful neighbors including the Atterburys, who lived there year-round; the Gallis (he was a San Francisco deputy fire chief); the Wrights; the Sannaconas; Martin Cummings, who was our water district manager; and so many others.

Every year shortly after the first of June, the State Division of Fish and Game stocked the San Lorenzo River with trout. Because of our manmade lake, it was a natural spot for trout. My son, Peter, always smelled the trout truck approaching. When they dumped the trout into the water, he waited until they departed and immediately got his limit. Peter did this every day. For a while, we enjoyed this delightful fish until we just couldn't look at a trout straight in the gills.

Another delectable prize we obtained from the river was

the delicious crawfish. If you like lobster you'll enjoy crawfish, which is nothing more than a fresh-water lobster. We harvested the crawfish in buckets and together with the Marsacs and some of our other neighbors, we held a crawfish feed. Most of the time, the crawfish was part of a *cioppino* which included the trout and a tasty Sicilian tomato sauce that only the Brucatos made.

These were carefree days, although we worked hard on the weekends. We had a lot of friends, many who were passers-by or stop-ins during lunch or dinner time. While we were considered unusually hospitable, the pace began to tell and it was getting to be too much. My children, Jack and Peter, had grown up and as time went on, they sought their place first in their growing up world and later, in the world we all lived in.

In the meantime, Josephine, my first wife and the mother of my children, developed a serious problem which became terminal. It was best to sell our beloved paradise and we did, reluctantly. Eventually, after much suffering, I lost Jo. The memories, however, will always remain.

Chapter 30

What Happened to Our Patron Saint?

The city of San Francisco was named after St. Francis of Assisi. From time to time, someone thinks about the good saint and something is done in his honor and remembrance. With the passing of time, he is quickly forgotten.

Perhaps we can go back to 1928 when the publication, *San Francisco Water*, a monthly pamphlet published by the Spring Valley Water Company, (predecessors to the San Francisco Water Department) came out with a front-page headline, "A Plea for a Statue of St. Francis." It was pointed out that October 4th would be the Feast Day of our city, San Francisco. Although he is known throughout the world as everybody's saint, he is in a special sense our St. Francis.

Bishop William Ford Nichols, an Episcopalian, was president of the Province of the Pacific from 1915 to 1921. He was also an author of distinction who resided in San Francisco where he died in 1924. Bishop Nichols was the prime mover for a statue of St. Francis. He envisioned a statue of heroic size patterned after the beautiful statue of St. Francis in the Umbrian town of Assisi in Italy. His conception, however, was of a civic nature. He imagined St. Francis holding aloft a beacon to symbolize "character enlightening the world." He also said, "We have great sculptors here and someday, someone will create the appropriate statue." We did have a local sculptor, the world-famous Beniamino Bufano or better known as Benny Bufano. He was a prolific sculptor who had various statues of just about everything strewn in many parts of the world. He also had a statue that was left to gather dust in a warehouse outside of Paris for twenty-seven years.

For quite some time, I never understood why the Feast of St. Francis was not observed in the city nor did I know if an appropriate statue of the good saint existed. The Catholic Church did observe October 4th in honor of St. Francis, but this was a religious observance, not a civic or civic-religious celebration. Was he not everybody's saint?

With the Knights of Columbus as a spearhead, I started a non-denominational citizens committee for the observance of St. Francis of Assisi Day. It seemed that people of all faiths were interested in St. Francis. At this point, I must confess that I may have been a little prejudiced for the good saint inasmuch as there were many in my family with the name of Frank. There was my grandfather, my father, my older brother (Francesco), my sister (Frances), and my oldest son, all named after St. Francis.

I teamed up with Father Alvin Wagner, pastor of St. Francis of Assisi Church in North Beach. The church is located on Vallejo Street near Grant and Columbus Avenues. It was the first church built in California after the missions. Father Wagner learned about the Bufano statue in Paris. The next question was, "How do we get it to San Francisco?" He visualized the statue on the front steps of the church. The problem, of course, was money.

Bufano's compelling 18-foot statue made from black Swedish granite weighed 12 tons. As it turned out, we had no problem raising the funds required for the project. There was a storage charge of a thousand dollars that was paid by one of our benefactors. The story of Bufano's statue received a lot of good publicity. This, of course, helped tremendously as the statue was considered by a leading world art critic as "the most significant piece of sculpture done within the last five hundred years." A crew of workmen from Farnsworth and Ruggles carefully packed the statue and shipped it without cost aboard the French line steamship, "Washington," which arrived in San Francisco in June. That gave us time to prepare and set the statue at the entrance to the church much before the saint's birthday on October 4th.

In the meantime, I learned the identity of the mystery benefactor. Mrs. Annunziata Sanguinetti, who had recently passed away and left a trust fund for the care of San Francisco's physically handicapped children, bequeathed $3000 for the statue of St. Francis. This took care of most of the cost. When the statue was first put in place in 1955, it bore a plaque with the wording, "Gift of Mrs. A. Sanguinetti."

One dark night at two o'clock in the morning, Benny Bufano tiptoed to the church with his hammer and chisel and removed Sanguinetti's name. He readily admitted doing this and said that there were ten others who helped him. His explanation was that if her name was to be on the statue, then "everybody's should be on it."

It was a tremendous civic affair in addition to the religious ceremony in which four bishops, eight monsignors and about forty priests took part in the mass and benediction held in the church of St. Francis. Practically every civic leader, city, and state politician was in attendance. Traffic was tied up on Columbus Avenue for several blocks. Twenty policemen, along with Tom Cahill, the chief of police, were in charge of handling the crowd. It was an orderly and respectful tribute to San Francisco's patron saint.

Father Wagner got his statue and the city of San Francisco finally had a landmark worthy enough to honor the patron saint for whom the city was named. While I served as chairman of the committee for this event, full credit for making it a reality with strong city support had to be given to Mayor Elmer Robinson. Additional support also came from the president of the Board of Supervisors, Clarissa McMahon, who served on the committee. Through their combined efforts, a St. Francis of Assisi Day was staged in Golden Gate Park and for awhile, it was an annual musical event.

The first park concert was held on October 2, 1955 and the last was on October 4, 1959. Mayor George Christopher, who succeeded Elmer Robinson, enthusiastically supported this annual event. All went well until Father Wagner was transferred to another parish in Oakland. The new pastor was Father John Curtin, a kindly man who lacked the administrative skills and charisma of Father Wagner. Right from the beginning, his leadership abilities failed in maintaining St. Francis Day at the Park as an annual event. The growing division amongst his parishioners regarding the location of the statue and its future was of great concern to those who devoted much time and effort in putting together this civic, religious celebration.

In passing, I must relate a conflict that occurred during one of the years of the annual celebration. It seemed that the Lief Erickson Day committee wanted the use of the Golden Gate Park bandstand for their observance. Their celebration date was also October 4th. Both committees met with little success, because we wanted the same date. Dick Nolan of the *San Francisco Examiner* wrote:

"The St. Francis Day people meeting with chairman John Brucato had about given up in despair when a lady committee member came up with the answer. 'I shall offer a prayer to St. Francis, she declared.' 'He will find a solution.' " "Brucato had no sooner returned to his office when a Lief Erickson spokesman was on the phone. 'We have decided on Sunday, October 11th,' " he said. Brucato adds, 'St. Francis sure works fast. Now who is going to speak for Columbus since the Columbus Day celebration is also on October 11th?' "

Father Curtin couldn't resolve the controversy over the statue amongst his parishioners. Father Wagner's skills were no longer available and after serving five years as chairman of the St. Francis of Assisi annual celebration, I, too was gone. The result of this predicament was unfortunate. The decision was made to move the statue from the steps of St. Francis of Assisi Church to the entrance of a restaurant in Oakland. Someone said that moving St. Francis to Oakland was like sending him to purgatory. Strangely, no one in the city hall was interested. Those who were his proponents were now gone. It was only through the efforts of Harry Bridges, leader of the San Francisco Longshoremen's Union, that the statue of St. Francis was brought back a few years later to San Francisco where today, it rests on a beautifully landscaped setting at the Longshoremen's Memorial property in San Francisco's Fisherman's Wharf.

The diminutive sculptor, Benny Bufano, is now gone, but the statue stands as a tribute to his artistic greatness, and respect for his philosophy and lifestyle. In his own words, he eloquently expressed his commitment to peace. He wrote:

"Lord, make me an instrument of your peace,
Where there is hate, let there be love."

My wife, Joan, and I have traveled to many lands. Wherever we go, the fame of Bufano is known, but in San Francisco, he was just another sculptor, a "prophet without honor in his own country." Shame on you, San Francisco! It is a disgrace that the city I love so much which has been acknowledged as "the city that knows how" never made an effort to showcase the amazing works of its own artist. Today, some of his most beautiful creations are housed in the patio location of the Hillsdale Shopping Center, San Francisco International Airport, and other scattered areas in San Mateo County. Again, shame on you San Francisco!

One of the most cherished honors I received during my lifetime which occurred in January of 1973 was from Mayor Joseph L. Alioto. Only seven people have received this award for their contribution and services to benefit the city of San Francisco.

I was the sixth recipient of a miniature bronze replica of Bufano's statue of St. Francis of Assisi. I am proud to say that all the recipients were close friends of mine. Amongst them were Father Albert Boeddeker, a Franciscan priest and a Nobel Prize winner for his work for the poor; Bishop Mark Hurley; the late Benjamin Swig, owner of the Fairmont Hotel and noted philanthropist; Cyril Tobin; and Maestro Kurt Adler, late director of the San Francisco Opera.

Chapter 31

Everyone is a Gambler

The person who says he is not a gambler, I would treat with suspicion. When you cross the street or drive your car, you are gambling with your life each day. The farmer is the world's greatest gambler. He is constantly gambling with nature, the price he will get for his production, and his ability to harvest his crop.

This is not an essay on gambling or gamblers. It relates to my involvement and personal liking to gambling on a small scale. My feelings have been to gamble for fun, not for profit.

For the past 21 years, a group of my longtime friends would gather at a different home each month on a Saturday evening to play poker. There are four couples including Dr. John and Rosina Zolezzi, John and Ann Monteverde, Lou and Melba Maffei, and the Brucatos. (We lost Lou a year ago from a heart seizure while playing golf. He was one of my oldest and closest friends. Melba still continues in our tradition.) The Maffeis live in the Sunset District of San Francisco, the Monteverdes in the Marina District, the Zolezzis in Atherton on the Peninsula, while we, the Brucatos, reside in Millbrae.

The usual routine was to dress up in our best finery, meet at the host's home at five o'clock for cocktails and hors d'oeuvres, engage in some interesting conversation, head on to a high-class restaurant for a seven o'clock dinner, and return home to play poker. What kind of poker would a group of affluent people engage in? I mentioned earlier that we were not gamblers. All these years, we've played "penny ante" with only three three-cent raises allowed. At midnight, there is a showdown or last play, which involves 25 cents each for the pot and ten cents each on the high spade, high club, low heart and low diamond. Each player goes home either winning or losing a few dollars. I think we prove a point here in that everything is relative. We find that despite the fact that we are playing for pennies, they have the same value (relatively speaking) as though we play for quarters or dollars. The important thing is that we have a fun time and enjoy each other's company.

As a contrast, I will relate to the poker habits of one of my sons, Peter, who also enjoys friendly poker games. He gets together frequently with some of his friends to play. The difference is that they play for dimes, quarters and dollars. We wonder if they have as much fun as we do playing penny ante.

Occasionally, we spend a few days at one of the hotel casinos in Lake Tahoe. People and people habits have always intrigued me. I would sit for hours playing Keno and watch the parade of people go by in a great variety of dress or in some cases, undress. I never realized how many people are overweight. We really are a well-fed nation, judging from the fat asses as compared to the skinny fannies. Some overweight women wear tight-fitting pants and tops that emphasize their bosoms. Sometimes, I would speak to some of the overweight fatties and they seem to revel in their superfluous *avoir dupois.* "Don't you know that fat is beautiful?" I don't think I ever tried to answer that question. Well, as long as they are happy, what the heck.

There are many chartered buses that come from every part of the state. Most of the Bay Area charters involve an overnight stay, giving the gamblers one night and two days to play. The majority of these people arriving on the buses are senior citizens. What a wonderful way to spend their declining years. Occasionally, the average senior citizen goes up to the lake or Reno. In some of my conversations, it seems that there are quite a few who are lonely or just alone. Nothing to worry about as they enjoy their ride through some of the most beautiful country on the face of the earth. The buses usually stop for a coffee break in the broad Sacramento Valley and then continue through the foothills, over the summit, through the breathtaking Sierras, and down to the stateline (I am referring only to South Lake Tahoe) to the casino of their choice. Upon arrival, the passengers are greeted by a casino representative and guided to the reception booth where each receives some gambling money ($15 to $25 in coins), discounts on food, and free drink coupons. In other words, they get a free trip.

Joan and I visit South Lake Tahoe about five times a year. It is a five-hour drive from Millbrae with a stop at the Coffee Tree in Vacaville for a rest. After a light breakfast, Joan would take her turn at the wheel of our Chrysler New Yorker to a location past Pollock Pines where I would take over and proceed through the 7,230-foot Echo Summit to the stateline. We either stay at the High Sierra or Harvey's and always have a room with a beautiful view of Lake Tahoe and the Sierras. The bellhop shows us to our room and departs with a cheery, ''Good luck!''

It is strange how everyone connected with the casinos always say the same thing, ''Good luck!'' In this strange world, money assumes a new value. I will always remember a scene in Las Vegas some time ago. I was in a supermarket check-out in back of two housewives who were relating to each other the many savings on the grocery items they purchased. After leaving the counter, they cheerfully took their savings and inserted the money into the slot machines located by the exit doors. In less than three minutes, their savings were gone. No jackpot . . . not even two cherries. It didn't bother them as they went about their business.

We follow a routine where upon arrival in our hotel room, we would freshen up, put away our clothes, and head on to where the action takes place. Joan and I would set our watches and meet at a specific location at a certain time. My advice to any couple or group is not to play together. Go your separate ways and do your own thing. There is nothing more annoying and irritating than to have someone next to you who keeps mumbling, ''Oh, look what I got,'' or ''Gosh, you hit a good one.'' A gambler wants to be alone to concentrate on what he is doing.

My favorite game is Keno followed by roulette. Of course, there is always the slot machines. I never play craps or blackjack, because I never had the confidence for either game. My Keno winnings vary. I always play a four-spot and an eight-spot. Occasionally, I hit the four-spot for $180 (I always play the same numbers: 7, 9, 13, 29, and for a $1 special). My eight-spot is my hope for a killing, playing the $1 special which would give me $25,000 if I win. In this respect, I never got past six spots for $80. Over the years, I realized that I was not ahead of the game, but who cares? Some day, my ship will come in.

Let me tell you a story about my former brother-in-law, Anthony, who was an ardent craps player and an expert on blackjack. He was the type to look down on my kind of gambling, because he was a high roller. He always reminded me of the odds on winning at Keno and said, "You know, John, you have one chance in thirty-three million to win the $25,000. You are wasting your time." My reply was always, "What the hell, to each his own." At any rate, fate performed the unusual. One day, we were having lunch at the High Sierra. One of the Keno runners left us some blank forms for the next game. Anthony, after his second glass of wine, decided to mark three Keno $1 specials. He tore up two of them and handed the runner one ticket with his bet. Watching the Keno board on the wall, he suddenly realized that he had six of the numbers and decided to advance to the Keno counter. While on his way, he saw a seventh number come up. Jubilantly, Anthony presented his ticket saying, "It looks like I have seven numbers." The Keno writer behind the counter looked at his ticket and calmly remarked, "Sir, you have all eight numbers for $20,000." I don't remember who picked Anthony up from the floor, but it took several minutes and a shot of straight brandy before he realized that he wasn't dreaming. When he returned to the dining room and calmed down, I looked at him straight in the eye with a smile and said, "Well, Anthony, it looks like you were the one in thirty-three million." That unusual incident transformed Anthony into a believer, a Keno believer. Being the high roller that he was, he began a series of frequent visits to the casinos. He forsook his craps and blackjack and went knee-deep into Keno.

Anthony has since passed onto his reward. I use the word "reward" because it involves money, and I do hope that wherever my former brother-in-law is, that his heaven would at least have a Keno game to pass the time after checking in with St. Peter.

Luck is the name of the game. If you try to force your luck, you lose. If you are not lucky at a slot machine, Keno, craps, roulette, or whatever game of chance, move on. Like they say in football, "When in doubt, punt." In other words, take a walk, go back to your room for a nap or shower, and come back feeling full of "vim and vinegar." If this doesn't work, be smart and go home. I am not an expert. To me, an expert is one whose confusion is well organized. I follow my own hunches and try to enjoy the people watching, the many free cocktails, and an occasional lucky streak.

I recall an incident which took place a year ago while

playing a certain quarter slot machine and hit for one thousand quarters. Have you ever seen a thousand quarters coming out of a slot machine? The bowl was overflowing and I had to keep filling empty cups until it stopped. I thought I was through until an attendant informed me that I had more coming. Evidently, I cleaned the machine out of seven hundred quarters. It was not a huge sum of money, only $250, but to see the coins coming out in a seemingly unending flow is a thrill to behold.

On another occasion while having just entered the casino at High Sierra, Joan immediately started playing the first quarter machine she saw. "These machines near the entrance never pay off" was my advice. Lo and behold, on her third play (using three quarters at a time), out came the three bars with a winning of $500. What was quite funny here was that Joan actually froze. She didn't know what happened. The machine suddenly lit up indicating that she had hit the big one. The first attendant showed up saying, "Congratulations, you hit it." There was no reaction from Joan. Three other officials came and she remained motionless. Well, the fifth official arrived and after congratulating her, he started to peel off five one hundred dollar bills. Only at this point did the color return to Joan's pale face, along with a smile of victory.

When you ask people, especially your friends, after their return from Reno or the stateline whether they had won, the general reply was, "Well, we just about broke even." or "We made our expenses." No one likes to admit that they lost money. In gambling, particularly casino gambling, if you go once, you go back again and again and again. The average person charges their losses to a brief vacation or holiday. Again, I say "Aren't we all gamblers?" Don't we all have a bit of gambling blood in our veins? The important thing is don't be a gambler unless you can afford it. We follow a simple system. Put aside a certain amount of money for gambling and when it is gone, quit and go home. On the other hand, if you are a winner, set aside most of the winnings and allot yourself a few dollars to follow up on your winning streak. When you lose this portion, it means your luck has run out.

Over the years, I believe we have come out close to being even. Again I say, we are simple "penny ante" gamblers. We enjoy our period visits to the casinos and have never been put into a position where we have had to eat pork and beans. This has never happened, although I do admit that we enjoy a good plate of pork and beans now and then.

I will bring this gambling story to a happy conclusion, that is for us, inasmuch as the events that follow prove that luck will strike you like a thief in the night when you least expect it.

Every Thanksgiving, the Brucato clan takes a five-day holiday to Lake Tahoe. For the past 19 years, we rent a four-bedroom, four-bath house for all 18 of us. It is always a gala affair in that everyone makes it a point to be there no matter where we had to drive or fly from. On Thanksgiving Day, we would have turkey with all the trimmings. Any leftovers are cleaned up the next day. Saturday night is my night. Everyone looks forward to Grandpa's pasta with his famous Sicilian-style tomato sauce. Sunday was get-away day when the youngsters would go skiing, the wives and gals go antique shopping, and some of the boys try their luck at the casinos.

Thanksgiving of 1985 was a memorable one. Joan and I drove to Incline Village (North Shore Lake Tahoe) five days prior to the holiday to inspect and determine what was needed. After this pleasant little chore, we drove down the Nevada side to the stateline where we had a reservation at Harvey's Casino Hotel. Losing no time during the check-in process, we decided to try our luck at Caesar's.

During the past two years, poker machines came into their glory. The draw poker machines played one to five quarters at a time and were better than the slot machines. Naturally, we played five quarters inasmuch as each poker machine was tied into the progressive group of machines where if I hit a royal flush, I could win the progressive, which was anywhere from $1,000 to $10,000. After inserting the quarters, my hand showed up on the screen. If I thought I had a winning hand, I held. Three-of-a-kind paid 15 quarters, a pair paid 5 quarters, two pairs paid 10 quarters, a straight paid 20 quarters, a flush paid 25 quarters, a full house paid 45 quarters, and four-of-a-kind paid 125 quarters.

After my fourth play, I drew and held an ace and a queen of spades. I had no reason to go for a royal flush with this nondescript hand, figuring that perhaps a pair or two would get my money back. It was time to press the play button. Lo and behold, out came a royal flush and I was in a daze. Joan, who was sitting next to me, shouted, "You hit the big one!" Slowly coming to my senses, I looked up to the progressive signboard and realized that the pot was $1,340. (The house puts in $1,000 and each play on the machines in that particular group keeps increasing by one cent per play.) All of a sudden, a flock of people gathered to see who the lucky winner was and how much he had won. After five attendants and casino officials came down to congratulate me, I realized that my silent partner, the Internal Revenue Service, was very happy to have me as a partner. My gambling winnings were reported to the IRS to make sure they will be remembered when filing my income taxes. I always wanted to join the "$1,000 Club." Actually, I didn't care about winning $25,000 or $50,000. I just wanted to get the feel of ten $100 bills in my hands. Now I know.

The name of the game, any game, is luck. It comes and goes. If you try to get lucky, it just doesn't happen. Don't go back the next day and feel that you can push your luck. You can't. My former brother-in-law, Anthony, is a classic example. He never hit it again regardless of how much he tried.

During that same Thanksgiving holiday in 1985, my sons, Jack, Peter, and I decided to play at the South Shore while most of the family went skiing. Peter walked into Harrah's, sat down at the first poker machine near the entrance, inserted five quarters, and drew a jack of clubs, an ace of clubs, and a ten of clubs. He punched the draw button and the most beautiful club royal flush appeared with the lights flashing, "Royal Flush. Royal Flush." He actually trumped me by hitting $2,500, which meant twenty-five $100 bills. We planned to have him surprise Joyce, his wife, upon returning to our rented vacation home at Incline Village. The family was waiting for us for dinner and in we came with our sad faces. Peter took Joyce aside and entered one of the bedrooms. He started to peel off the hundred dollar bills one after another until he went through all twenty-five of them. Joyce, being an emotional girl, screamed and then yelled, finally collapsing to the floor. After hearing the commotion, the others rushed to see what had happened. They saw her on the floor coming to and realized that this was not a time to faint with all those bills laying around. I don't know how many bottles of wine disappeared that evening at dinner, but after the many toasts to Peter and Joyce, everyone in the Brucato clan felt no pain.

It sounds nice to talk about luck, especially when Lady Luck continues to wave her magic wand. Unbelievably, three months later, Joan and I decided to celebrate our nineteenth wedding anniversary. Where was a good place to go for our anniversary? Europe? No, too dangerous. Mexico? No, we had been there before. Carmel? No, we didn't want to get involved in Clint Eastwood's mayoral campaign.

It didn't take much encouragement to decide to go to Lake Tahoe. We stayed at the High Sierra for two nights and three days. Arriving early Monday afternoon, we started off for Harrah's. I tried my few rounds at Keno where an old Filipino friend, Bonifacio, greeted me and wrote my two tickets, a four-spot and an eight-spot. I have known his family since 1943 when they drove one of the first truckloads of vegetables from their San Joaquin Valley farm to the Farmers' Market. His welcome greeting always included two free drink coupons and a little chit chat about his family.

Joan went her way and I went mine. My way took me to my favorite poker machine corner that always gave me peace and relaxation. I was doing quite well and my machine was paying off. I had a bucket full of quarters (over $100) and figured, "Well, I better move. I don't believe there can be much money left in this machine." I always believed that when you win a lot from a machine, it would be prudent to quit. The monsters have a habit of reversing themselves. In other words, if you keep playing the same machine, they will get it all back and then some. My decision was made. I was going to play one more hand, quit, and then pay a visit to Bonifacio at Keno. I drew an ace, king, queen, and a ten of diamonds and needed a jack of diamonds for a royal. I thought, "Golly, this was silly. Who ever drew an inside royal flush. The progressive royal flush lit up the board and told me that I hit $1,430.37. It was incredible. The same payoff procedure followed. I met Joan at our usual rendezvous spot, the Orange Keno. She wanted to know why I looked so sad. After I explained my shock to her, she came up with the most unusual remark, "What a wonderful gift for our nineteenth anniversary."

Does luck continue? Sometimes it does, but most of the time it doesn't. The following day, everything we did or played turned sour. That was it. Joan was right. It was an anniversary present, so we stopped, enjoyed dinner, and went home the next morning. The following Saturday, we played penny ante with our poker group. I played all night and didn't win a hand, not one hand.

Chapter 32

My First Failure

I was fired from my first job. It so happened that I was greedy and irresponsible. I took charge of a candy store and lasted exactly four hours. It was a neighborhood candy store owned by Wolfgang Gertzenheimer. The kids called him "Gertzy." He offered me a job to work part-time in his store. It was my first working job and I was twelve years old.

In those days, the big sellers were the penny candies like tootsie rolls, all kinds of chocolates, jaw breakers, suckers, and so many other indescribable sweets in all shapes and sizes.

It was a Saturday and I started my job at nine o'clock in the morning. Gertzy showed me everything I needed to know to make a successful candy salesman. He had a few chores to do, so he left me in charge of the store until his return. What he didn't know was that I had an uncontrollable sweet tooth. What was I to do? Here I was, a twelve year-old boy surrounded by the most tempting morsels of choice candies, which led me to sample them one-by-one. I was like a bull in a china closet. In between my samplings, I managed to make a few sales. Suddenly, Gertzy returned and caught me with my face bulging with candy. He looked at me with his eyes wide open and shouted at the top of his lungs in German, "Raus mitt you, oudt, oudt, gett oudt!"

I went directly home and wasn't feeling too good. My mother was shocked to see me as I came in holding my stomach. It was the beginning of a bellyache which became so bad that Mom, knowing what to do in situations like this, forced me to drink some castor oil. How I hated castor oil. I went to bed and was really sick. The next morning, I recovered sufficiently to tell my unfortunate story to my parents. I was not reprimanded, but I felt some remorse and started to shake my head. What was I to do? Well, mothers always come up with the proper words at the proper time. "John," my mother said, "You are not a failure. You just made a mistake, an important mistake. I don't believe you will make a similar mistake in your lifetime, because you can always think back on how you were given a responsibility and you blew it. Now get up and come down to breakfast. I don't believe you will want to eat anything sweet for a while." Mother was right. I have always remembered her words of wisdom.

Chapter 33

My Philosophy of Life

Some time ago, I was asked to speak to a senior citizens group in Millbrae. I was to tell them about the latest development, the new historical museum.

Ann d'Aloisio, the chairperson of the Senior Citizens Club, gave me a flowery introduction to the more than 150 members present. My first thoughts were, "How do I make an impression in my opening remarks so as to capture their immediate interest, or in other words, a proper receptive mood?" The historical museum was not a blockbuster topic. I then realized as I gazed out at this vast audience of gray-haired, wrinkled senior citizens, that I, too, was one of them. With this in mind, I embarked on my philosophy of life. This was what I said:

> "When I was 30, I thought 40 was old. I also dreaded the day when I would join the over-forty club, which, of course, automatically made me an old man. Then I passed forty, and again, I would feel that 50 was old. The change in my philosophical thinking came when I was approaching 65. At this point, I then thought that 65 was the old age of youth. Sixty-five meant retirement, which also spelled the end of the first part of my life."

I then told them that I was now entering into a new period, the youth of old age, and that middle age would begin at 85, and old age at 95. I never saw such an enthusiastic audience that relished what I said to them. They stood up and gave me a noisy ovation. I concluded my speech with these words:

"I have never been as old as I am now.
I have never known as much as I know now.
And I have never had less time as I have now."

I joked about our senior citizen status, and the many discounts and goodies offered to us. Looking at my watch, I realized that I had gone over the thirty minutes allotted to me. I thanked everyone for their wonderful reception and walked out with the chairperson to the parking lot. Suddenly, I stopped cold with an expression of surprise on my face. Ann looked at me saying, "What is wrong? What's the matter?" I looked at her with a big smile and said, "You know, Ann, I forgot to mention the new Millbrae Historical Museum." We both laughed.

A further thought in my philosophy of life was how or what to do to slow down the passing of time. I believe I have discovered the solution. We can live our lives, our senior lives, like the last quarter of a professional football game. There are four quarters to a game and each is fifteen minutes or more.

Now the question is, how can we apply this formula to our aging process? Well, as I previously mentioned, I made the discovery. I am now working on the solution.

Chapter 34

The Turisti

Experience is the best teacher. We made up our minds that we did not want to be regimented by traveling in groups with early morning departures and exhausting schedules, and seeing too many places in a short period of time. Many of our friends who travel regularly do not remember where they have been or what they have seen.

We made our first and only mistake when we started our travels in February of 1969 to Hawaii. This was a regimented tour with a group of forty. Our hotels were mediocre, the food was secondary, the bus rides were too long, and the descriptions by the guide were boring and uninteresting. On the third day, we said, "To Hell with all this," so we immediately evacuated Honolulu, with its Coney Island style of congestion and atmosphere, and left Don Ho singing his "Tiny Bubbles in the Wine." We wondered if he sang anything else.

Our destination was Maui where we stayed at the interesting Pioneer Inn. (The present-day resorts that clutter Kaanapoli were under construction at the time.) The inn was quite colorful as was the area known as Lahaina. The hippies were beginning to take root there. Our biggest excitement was the renting of a dune buggy with a couple from Detroit. We adjusted ourselves to this unusual vehicle with me as the driver. Deciding on some fun with our caps on backwards and wearing oversized goggles, we tore down the main street of Lahaina at the speed of twelve miles per hour. We looked like something out of the Gay Nineties. Tourists even came up to us seeking our autographs when we stopped. They probably thought we were either Ralph De Palma or Barney Oldfield, former winners of the Indianapolis 500.

We rejoined our tour group for our return flight to San Francisco.

Our ideal travel agent is an old friend who went into the business and has become quite successful. Rather than having to deal with unknown clerks who treat you like just another client, she provides us with personal service. Grace Duhagon owns and operates her own travel agency in downtown San Francisco. Her husband, Ralph, is a retired Bank of America executive. She is well-known in the North Beach section of the city. For fifteen years, she wrote a well-read column in North Beach's *Little City News*, a popular local newspaper. When Joseph Alioto was elected mayor of San Francisco, he proudly proclaimed that the only newspaper that supported him was the *Little City News*.

We decided that Europe was our future goal, together with a cruise or two to the Caribbean. Our first intention was to get to Sicily, particularly Palermo where we would meet with some of my relatives for the first time. The first European trip was in May of 1972. We decided to stay at the better hotels, and to be picked up upon arrival and departure. This procedure avoided the usual hassles getting to and from the airports. It was worth the extra costs, because we seemed to be more relaxed. Wherever we stayed, we made arrangements with the concierge for local sightseeing and perhaps an all-day trip to an unusual point of interest.

After eighteen years of traveling, we can truthfully say that we thoroughly enjoyed our travels because we did what we wanted to do in our own way. While in Rome, we enjoyed sitting in the colorful sidewalk cafes along the famous Via Veneto where we could sip espressos for hours. We were never disturbed as we watched the passing parade where people from every corner of the world passed by in front of us.

Prior to going to Palermo, we stayed a few days in Rome. Archbishop Joseph T. McGucken arranged for Joan and I to have a special audience with the Pope. We arrived in Rome on a Tuesday morning, suffering from jetlag and lack of sleep. We should have gone to bed for a nap, but we didn't. This was our first visit to the Eternal City and we wanted to take in as much as possible. We had a long, full evening with a tour of Rome's nightlife and enjoyed it, but we were tired, dead tired. Our audience with the Pope was the following morning and we never made it.

Finally rising from our sound sleep, we felt rather hungry and ordered our breakfast. The waiter came in and I greeted him with a *"Buon Giorno."* He replied, *"Buona Sera* (Good evening)." I guess I was still asleep and didn't realize what he had said. Both of us felt something was very strange. Joan opened the blackout blinds and remarked, "It's still night. The lights are on." We didn't reach the panic stage yet. I said, "Something is wrong." I phoned the desk for the time. The clerk said that it was seven o'clock in the evening. I was shocked. "Joan," I shrieked, "Do you realize that we slept through our Vatican audience?" We couldn't do anything but laugh. Then, the thought came to me, "What am I going to say to Archbishop McGucken when we get home?" When I saw the Archbishop upon my return, I rather sheepishly related our sad experience. He never batted an eyelash and proceeded to discuss other matters.

The following year, 1983, Archbishop McGucken, again, made arrangements for an audience with His Holiness during our second trip to Italy. I didn't immediately grasp his meaning when he remarked, "I am quite sure this time that you will meet the Holy Father." We arrived in Rome after spending one week in the Emerald Isle where we enjoyed the Irish people and their countryside. This time, we went to bed early Tuesday night and made arrangements with the hotel desk for a wake-up call at 7 a.m. The Pope was at Castel Gandolfo, his summer retreat, twenty miles south of Rome in the cool Alban Hills. We planned to hire a taxi to take us there. After breakfast in our room, the desk clerk called to notify us that our limousine was ready. "What limousine?" I said. We hadn't even ordered a taxi yet. When we arrived in the lobby, we were met by a tall, liveried chauffeur who, in broken English, said, "Mr. Brucato, your limousine is ready." (There are five Vatican limousines in Rome, plus two limousines at the American Embassy.)

Getting over our very pleasant surprise, the chauffeur escorted us to the car, opened the door, and with a broad Italian smile said, *"Per piacere, entrate."* We enjoyed a leisurely ride along the famous Appian Way where many centuries ago, the Romans, famous for their architecture and road construction, traveled along this road in their two-horse chariots. Just as we were approaching the entrance to Castel Gandolfo, we recognized a group of people who looked rather familiar. Our chauffeur, being Italian, honked his horn not once, but three times in order to pass them. They were members of the Alioto and Tarantino families from San Francisco's famous North Beach area, so I ordered the chauffeur to stop the car. There were twenty of them who had just left their chartered bus and were walking the short distance from the parking lot to Castel Gandolfo. After an exchange of warm greetings, they told us that after leaving Rome, they were heading for St. Elia near Palermo in Sicily, the birthplace of both the Alioto and Tarantino clans. We enjoyed a few laughs and thought that the Aliotos should have been riding in the limousine while the Brucatos rode on the bus.

The private audience with the Pope, together with a few other people, was a joyous and memorable one. The feel and closeness to such a person, the direct descendant of St. Peter, was an unforgettable moment.

On the way out, another incident occurred. Our chauffeur, quite a character, playfully almost ran down the Aliotos and the Tarantinos. We stopped for a chat and decided to all meet in Palermo on a certain day for a typical North Beach-style *cioppino* at the Villa Igea. It never came off as there was a sudden change in their tour plan by their agent. It was too bad as we had also planned to visit the hometown of the Joe DiMaggio family outside of Palermo at the Isola delle Femme.

After a few days in Rome, we boarded the Alitalia plane to Palermo for the one-hour flight. What a pleasure it was to meet my Italian family for the first time. What a reception we received at the Palermo airport. My nephew, Filippo, drove us in his new Fiat to our hotel, the De le Palme, on the Via Roma. This grandiose hotel served as the American headquarters in World War II with General Mark Clark in command. Unfortunately, most of the beautiful original works of art and furnishings were gone — spoils of war.

The beauties of Palermo were indescribable. The unbelievable panorama as seen from the heights of Monte Pellegrino were breathtaking. We promised my cousins, nieces, nephews, and the many friends we met that we would be back soon. (It was sooner than we thought, because we returned the following year.)

We took the overnight steamer to Naples. It was an elegant ship serving the best pasta and *scallopini.* After visiting Vesuvius and the beautiful bay of Naples, we boarded the *Rapido*, a luxury train that took us across the lower Italian boot through the Appenines via many tunnels reaching the picturesque Adriatic Sea by way of Bari to our port of embarkation, Brindisi, where we took a ship to Patras, Greece.

We had an interesting incident while trainbound. Being a history and geography buff, I always travel with maps. I noted every station or town that we passed through on the *Rapido*. Involved in conversation with some people in our compartment, I sort of missed the town that we had just passed through. I called out to Joan, "What was the name of that town? Quick, look back!" Rather unperturbed, Joan calmly said, "Uscita." I couldn't find that name on my detailed map, so I passed it up. Twenty minutes later, the same thing happened. Again, I asked Joan what the name of the town was. she remarked, "Calmati (don't get excited), we just passed Uscita." "Uscita," I said, "How could that be. There can't be two Uscitas. Perhaps we have turned back or we may be going in circles." I kept repeating, "Uscita, Uscita" and then it suddenly dawned on me. *Uscita* means exit. No wonder we couldn't find *Uscita* on the maps. Finally, Joan made a suggestion that we start studying Italian when we got back home.

When we arrived in Brindisi, we boarded a taxi to our hotel. You never saw such a crazy driver, going in and out with near misses here and there. At one point, Joan had to scream at him to slow down. At any rate, we managed to arrive in one piece. I gave the driver an unusually large tip. He looked at me with a surprised face and in my best Italian, I said, "We died a thousand deaths and this tip is in thanksgiving for delivering us alive." I then added, "No wonder the best auto racers are Italian. They're not only crazy drivers, but they know no fear when they are behind the wheel."

We crossed over to Greece on a Greek ship for the one-and-a-half day trip to Patras. Upon our arrival, we were subject to customs. At that time, Greece was under a rigid dictatorship ruled by Pappadopoulos. There were five Greek officials who each took turns examining my passport. They kept passing it back and forth while giving me suspicious looks. Their superior was then called in, a pompous official with a half-dozen medals on his chest. He gave me a thorough going-over and finally let me by. The moral here is to make sure you have a good picture of yourself on your passport. When I looked at my gosh-awful photo, I said, "No wonder they were suspicious."

We cried for three days in Athens because the smog was so bad. Amidst the congestion, the old trucks, vans, buses, and cars seemed to outdo one another in emitting the most exhaust.

After enjoying a four-day cruise aboard the "Galaxy," we returned to Athens and back to Patras for our return trip to Brindisi on the Italian ship, *"Appia."* Prior to boarding, we were held up for three hours. The Greek secret service was looking for some student troublemakers as there had been a series of riots recently in Athens. They finally spotted a young couple and handcuffed them before we were able to board ship. We then took a long, but interesting train ride on the *Rapido* to Florence and eventually wound up in Rome.

Rome is our playground. We sit on the Spanish Steps, walk through the fashionable Via Condotti and patronize the family-style *trattorias* where the food is always good. On our first visit there, we were astounded by the unbelievable traffic jams. If you tried to cross the street, your life would be in danger. Traffic signals there are meaningless. A Roman behind the wheel is another person, not a human being. One day, we were attempting to cross from the Coliseum to the Forum and had to negotiate a traffic island. We were left stranded there for about fifteen minutes until we were approached by four little nuns. They had seen our predicament and one of them motioned to me, "*Viene con noi* (come with us)." Together, we walked fearlessly straight through the traffic. The Fiats came to a screeching halt and we safely made our way to the Roman Forum. (I don't believe the ancient Romans had any traffic problems with their chariots. Life must have been a bit more orderly then.) We soon learned how to cross a street in Rome:

1. Look for some nuns.
2. Look for a pregnant woman.
3. Look for a woman holding a child.
4. By following the first three steps, it is always well to say a few "Hail Marys" just for insurance.

Parking is another serious problem because there are few garages. If there is room on the sidewalk, a driver would ask for assistance from passersby (Italians are always obliging). Three or four men would pick up the Fiat and gently fit it into the small space.

When you pass a car with a young male driver on the many *autostradas* (freeways), you have challenged him. He will pass you and give you the "Roman salute," the upstanding thumb. You then had a choice of either passing him and giving him the thumb or laughing it off and going about your business.

While we at home have two traffic periods, the morning and evening rush hours, the Italians have their ''siesta'' time between 1 p.m. and 4 p.m. That makes four rush hours against our two. It's all a matter of adjustment.

Chapter 35

Shangri La

The island of Ustica is between Sicily and Sardinia in the Mediterranean. It is a beautiful island about thirty-six miles from Palermo and is reached in forty minutes by hydrofoil or two hours by steamer. There are numerous *grottos* — some of them would make Capri second rate. About two thousand people live there who raise lots of flavorful fruits and vegetables.

Ustica is one of the great fishing areas of the Mediterranean abounding primarily in tuna, swordfish, octopus, shellfish of all kinds, and an incredible variety of assorted fish. The clarity of the waters attract international underwater fishermen, biologists and archaeologists.

The picturesque houses are whitewashed. During the month of August, artists from all over Italy gather in competitive painting on the walls of these homes. The finished result is like an art gallery. They paint during the day and at night, it becomes a fiesta. Everything takes place in the *piazza* and everyone makes you feel at home. The children, dressed in their parochial uniforms, are a sight to behold.

There is no such thing as juvenile delinquency. The town jail is in an old Norman tower, which was built to defend the island from the Arabs circa 1100 A.D. The doors have no locks. Records show that the last prisoner who inhabited the jail was more than 20 years ago. We fell in love with this ancient tower and seriously thought of leasing or buying the three-room apartment at the very top with its sweeping view of Ustica and the Mediterranean. (A few years ago, the tower was converted to a museum.)

Caroline DiMauro and Joan were very close friends, having both been neighbors in the Mission District of San Francisco. She owned a beautiful villa on Ustica, which she leased during her long absence. Upon her retirement, she returned to her native Ustica, but could not have the use of her villa. (Under Italian Law, a landlord cannot evict a tenant.) There were many complications, so Caroline rented a three-room ground floor apartment on one of the picturesque sidestreets. On our first visit to Ustica, we stayed with her at her insistence. Everyone on the island called her "Zia Carolina" (Aunt Caroline). She was much loved by the natives and she, in turn, loved them.

One day, Caroline introduced us to the parish priest, Padre Carlino. My first impression was that I had met St. Francis himself. He was the same size, had the same face, and with his Franciscan robe, he surely resembled the good saint. Padre Carlino was up in years. He told us that he no doubt had baptized everyone on the island, given them their First Communion, wedded them, and of course, buried them when their time came. The day we met him was a holy day and there was to be a 5 p.m. mass. It was about 4:30 when we finished our conversation. We told Padre Carlino that we would attend mass, but we first wanted to visit a nearby home where a friend of Caroline's was expecting us. In his friendly way, he told us to take our time, but to hurry back. Time went by and we realized that it was past five o'clock. "Mamma mia," I said, "Let's get going!" We were about twenty minutes late. Would you believe what this pious Franciscan priest did for us? He actually held up the mass by having the congregation recite the rosary, which had five decades of ten "Hail Marys" each. We hesitated before we entered and could hear Padre Carlino dragging out the last two "Hail Marys." When he saw us, he quickly completed the rosary. The altar boys lit the candles and Padre Carlino, with a somewhat "victorious" smile, immediately raised his arms upward and blessed the congregation. Later, we left a sizable donation in the collection.

Zia Carolina had a nephew who managed the town's only bank. He and his wife took good care of her in her declining years.

On our second and third visits to Ustica, we stayed at one of the island's finer hotels. Inasmuch as it was before the regular season, we had the hotel to ourselves and were able to have our *prima colazione* (breakfast) with the owners who made us feel like we were part of the family.

The Usticiani are a proud people. They do everything possible to protect their island. There are two *carabinieri* (police) stationed on Ustica with little to do. A committee of six young men with college degrees from the University of Palermo are there to prevent trouble before it happens. We witnessed one such incident when one evening, the town square was alive with people, many of them tourists. There was music, dancing and singing. Everyone was having a good time when suddenly, three young men began to make nuisances of themselves. They were rowdy and getting out of hand when two from the committee approached them and suggested that they behave like gentlemen. It turned out that they were not gentlemen because a few minutes later, they became abusive. A second warning did not take effect, so the six-man committee escorted the ruffians down to the pier, put them on a hydrofoil, gave the boatman a handful of *lire* and told him to take them back to the mainland. "This is our home and our island. We welcome people as our friends as long as they behave themselves." No wonder we fell in love with Ustica.

We never ate such delicious assortments of fish as they prepared and served in the few restaurants in the village. When you speak of *calamari* (squid), *gamberetto di mare* (shrimp), *granchio* (crab), *ostrica* (oysters), *merluzzo* (cod), *aragosta* (lobster), and *sogliola* (sole) all on the same platter, you are talking about the Usticiani specialities. Add to the menu tuna, swordfish, some of the island's flavorful vegetables, homemade wine, a *cannoli, spumoni* or *gelato a la Palermitana*, and this will give you an idea of the good life in Ustica. There is an old Italian proverb, "*A tavola non s'invecchia*" (You never grow old at the table).

Our wonderful Caroline passed on to her heavenly reward. The entire population of Ustica attended her funeral. She was their Zia Carolina and she was also "our" Carolina.

A few years ago, the Italian government decided to pour some of the *mezzogiorno* money to help southern Italy. Some of this was used to develop a large-scale hotel and *pensione* complex. We don't know what effect this will have on Ustica's future. With more visitors, will they have to increase the size of their vigilance committee? Who knows?

This is our story of Ustica, our Shangri La.

Chapter 36

Ships of Happy Fools

If you are on a diet, you should not take a cruise. You will be subjected to the three regular meals of the day, plus a mid-morning snack, a mid-afternoon refreshment, and then a midnight getaway gourmet meal of meals. Don't forget the many liquid refreshments that are part of the deal. It becomes a glutton's paradise. Of course, if you have really overindulged, there is always the ship's doctor who will fix you up with a concoction short of castor oil that will relieve your suffering so that you'll be able to start again the following day.

A cruise lasting five days is bearable. If it is over seven days, don't complain about tight-fitting pants or shorts. What the hell? Look at all the fun you've had, all the dancing, the games, the promenades on deck, and all the friendly, silly people you've encountered. Today, the cruise is the "in" thing, so enjoy it, act like a fool, be happy, and remember that when you return to your homeport, your dull life will start all over again until the next time, the next cruise.

Sicilians are natural seamen. Perhaps that is why we went on so many cruises. We enjoyed the Caribbean where pirates once rode the waves in search of plunder, and the many islands showing the extreme wealth of some of the people. In the Mediterranean, we thought of the glorious days of Greece, the Turks who ravaged the seas, the Carthaginians who were finally destroyed by the Romans in the days of the Roman Empire, and of course, the heroic exploits of the Knights of Malta, who held off the barbarian Ottoman hordes during the days of the Crusades before defeating them, ending the threat of a Moorish-Arab Europe.

Cruising is fun. When I think of our forbears who immigrated to our fair land at the turn-of-the-century undergoing the inconveniences such as lack of sanitation, maggot-infested food, crawling and biting of vermin that infested the cabins, the beds, and clothing, we sure have come a long, long way.

I was born on the Via Francesco Crispi in Palermo overlooking the Mediterranean. My grandfather once told me that I would have a love for the sea and would travel on many ships. He also prophesized that someday, I would return to the Mediterranean and see it in its entirety. (This prophecy was eventually fulfilled.)

Our first experience at sea was a four-day cruise of the Greek Islands in May of 1972. We boarded the Greek ship, "S.S. Galaxy," at Piraeus, the port for Athens, and visited the islands of Rhodes, Kusadasi, Santorini, and several others. Most of the houses were whitewashed, which greatly added to the beauty of the surroundings. We met interesting and friendly people.

In May of 1974, we embarked on a Caribbean cruise aboard the "Nordic Prince," a new luxury cruise ship out of Miami. After arriving from Oakland, we had four hours before boarding time. A bus tour was arranged for us, giving us the opportunity to see Miami. The day was hot and muggy and we were quite relieved when we set sail at 3 p.m. We were introduced to Phil Sena and Tony Gyle, our tour directors. They were both from Brooklyn and this made our day. When Brooklynites get together, it's like a family reunion whether they come from Brownsville, Bay Ridge, Coney Island, or Bensonhurst. What a coincidence that the two men were from Bensonhurst, my former neighborhood. Brooklynites not only speak Brooklynese (now recognized as another language), but they go out of their way to help each other. We were given the royal treatment on our cruise and were the honored couple at the captain's table the first night. The ship's captain, Osten Andreassen, was a gracious host. Despite his Norwegian background, he did justice to a platter of the best Italian ravioli and spoke a most elegant Italian and Brooklynese. (He did a rather poor English.)

The ports of call included San Juan, Puerto Rico, the Virgin Islands, Martinique, Caracas, Aruba, Jamaica, and Port-au-Prince in Haiti. The poverty and misery in beautiful Haiti was unbelievable. We got away from the conducted tour that showed the mansions and estates of the wealthy. Rather, we wanted to see how the common, the poor and the downtrodden lived under the regime of Papa Doc Duvalier, the tyrant and "president for life" dictator of this little kingdom. It was no wonder that many years later, thousands of boat people fled the island in order to get to freedom and liberty in the United States. We rejoined the group just in time to stop in a certain area where it was possible to buy native artifacts from some of the poorest Haitians.

As a prelude to my little story, Joan and I always had a sweet tooth. We enjoyed our chocolate bars and everything else that's classified as dessert. It seemed that every day, we would find a basket of fresh fruit and four Hershey bars in our stateroom. We ate the fruit, but saved the chocolate for later.

While I was in the process of purchasing a beautiful handmade mahogany cane from one of the natives, I heard quite a commotion nearby. It turned out to be my wife, Joan, surrounded by at least fifteen Haitian boys screaming, "Me too! Me, too!" Upon approaching the scene, I saw her handing out chocolate bars, my chocolate bars, to the screaming, eager street urchins. I looked at her and laughed. What a sight she was with her broad-brimmed straw bonnet holding this basket full of Hershey bars and happy as a lark. I nicknamed her "Lady Bountiful." Actually, I, too, felt a little better seeing these children so happy with something we would consider so little.

In September of 1974, we returned to the Mediterranean for an unusual cruise on the "Buon Vivant." After a refueling stop in Bangor, Maine where we had time to sample some fresh, juicy lobsters, we set off for Palma on the island of Mallorca off the coast of Spain. It was an enjoyable and restful seven-day stay. The cruise ship arrived the next day for a seven-day tour of the Mediterranean. Tunis was our first stop. Having read a great deal of Roman history, I was anxious to see the ruins of Carthage. In the days of Hannibal, the Romans and the Carthaginians were engaged in the Three Punic Wars. Rome was becoming quite a bit weary of the Carthaginians and while Hannibal was holding the Romans at bay in Italy with his elephants, the Romans dispatched their entire fleet to the Carthaginian shores. Scipio Africanus was directed to not only destroy Carthage, but to leave no trace of this warlike nation. The ruins testify to what the Romans accomplished.

After our visit to Naples and Pompeii, we spent four hours in Capri. There were some beautiful shops and Joan needed a pair of slacks. We spotted a pair in a window priced at thirty-five dollars. As we entered the shop, we noticed two attractive clerks behind the counter. They spoke in Italian and I heard one of them say to the other, "*Queste qui sono Americani, doppio il prezzo*" (They are Americans, double the price). I remained silent until Joan selected the slacks. I then asked for the price and the clerk quickly responded by saying, "Seventy dollars." With my best Italian, I protested saying, "But aren't these the same slacks you have in the window marked at thirty-five dollars?" I never saw two girls blush the way they did. It was such a red blush that it caused a slight degree of perspiration on their eyebrows. "*Scusi, signore, abbiamo fatto un piccolo sbaglio.* (Pardon me sir, we have made a small mistake). They were so embarrassed that we finally got the slacks for less than the stated price. They were very happy to give me a receipt for twenty-five dollars. I said to Joan, "Sometimes it pays to know Italian."

We made several other ports, but the one we were looking forward to with great anticipation was Cannes. While it is a beautiful and interesting city, we were particularly interested in boarding a chartered bus that would take us to Monte Carlo. My lifetime ambition was to break the bank at Monte Carlo. I played 29, my favorite roulette number, with French francs. After a few whirls, the thrill was over. I was able to fulfill one of my dreams, although I didn't break the bank. But it wasn't entirely over. We got a big thrill when we rubbed elbows with six of the Arab sheiks who were making headlines by being $2.5 million ahead playing roulette. They were really out to break the bank. (We later learned there was a change in their luck. They eventually dropped a cool million before returning to their oil wells.)

As we were walking through the lush casino, I said, "Eureka! Look into that room. It's full of American slot machines." We very seldom won back home, but here in Monte Carlo, I came out winning $32 from the quarter machines. It felt like winning a million dollars. Both of us were elated, but the time was getting late so we decided to sit down at an elegant sidewalk cafe decorated with pretty unbrellas. We ordered two espressos and petit fours. Boy, were the petit fours tiny. We almost fainted when we received the bill. It was exactly $32.50. I looked at Joan and we broke up in laughter. I couldn't help saying to my lovely wife, "Joan, we just blew the profits." We then returned to Palma de Mallorca after a brief stop in Barcelona and boarded our World Airways chartered flight back to San Francisco.

Our next cruise was in January of 1976. It was a winter cruise to the Caribbean on the Norwegian liner, "S.S. Southward." While we stopped at many islands, the most noteworthy was the Cayman Islands, a part of the British West Indies. We were introduced to barbecued turtle at a beach party in Georgetown. While I would not recommend the turtle to my grandchildren, I would suggest to them that they continue with the McDonalds and Burger Kings. The most amazing discovery we made in this small city of Georgetown (population of 7,000) was the great number of international banks. There were more than 140 banks. Very few of them looked like banks inasmuch as they were housed in ordinary Victorian-style homes. We learned later that this is one of the offfshore banking centers which specialized in the washing of money. Here was where the underworld, big business, politicians, tax dodgers, and others do their business. What amazed us was the lack of traffic and activity in this banking capital of the Caribbean.

Our last major cruise was in May of 1978. We had flown from West Berlin to Venice to connect with the "Andrea C" of the Italian Costa line. In addition to the Greek Islands, we stopped at the Port of Ephesus in Turkey. This was where the Virgin Mary spent her remaining days before her Assumption, and where Pope Paul VI met with the head of the Greek Orthodox Church and celebrated mass the following year. We saw the most interesting places including Istanbul, Rhodes, Corfu, and the most unusual Yugloslav city of Dubrovnik.

The "Andrea C" was noted for its entertainment and Italian cuisine. It was impossible to lose weight on board ship with breakfast, a mid-morning snack, a huge lunch, a mid-afternoon snack, the evening super-duper dinner, and then a midnight snack each day. There was a simple formula that we followed on our European and particularly, our Italian gastronomic adventures. We learned from the *contadini* (peasants) in our travels to drink the young, unpasteurized local white wine and avoided labeled wines. We found ourselves polishing off a fifth of the local white wine for lunch and another fifth for dinner, and ate like food was going out of style. When we arrived home, my scale indicated that I lost five pounds. This was the story of my weight control throughout many of our traveling years.

There were other cruises which Joan and I participated in. If there was any way I could communicate with my beloved grandfather wherever he may be, I would say, "*Nonno* (grandpa), your prophecy has been fulfilled."

Chapter 37

Turisti in Israel

We started our visit to Israel in May of 1977. After spending five days in beautiful and historic Vienna, we booked passage on the Israeli airline, *El Al*, leaving for Tel Aviv at 9 a.m. It wasn't until noon that we were finally airborne. Our plane was at the furthermost part of the airfield and was surrounded by at least a dozen heavily armed Austrian soldiers. There had been a great deal of violence in Israel due to the forthcoming elections and there was a fear of terrorists at the Vienna Airport. (Menachim Begin was elected to the Knesset, Israel's legislature.)

Before we boarded the bus that would take us to the plane, we went through a two-hour security check conducted by attractive, but very firm Israeli women soldiers. They went through everything and after going through the "ninety-nine questions," the ordeal came to an end. I rather enjoyed it and felt that the precautions being taken were justified.

The Tel Aviv beachfront reminded me of Miami with its many towering hotels along the beach. It was a rather attractive skyline with beautiful, sandy beaches, but Tel Aviv was an armed camp. Heavily armed soldiers were at every corner with patrols going in and out of the streets.

Our first experience occurred the day of our arrival at the Sinai, one of Tel Aviv's newest hotels. After freshening up, Joan and I went down to the lobby. I wanted to cash a traveler's check and approached the desk clerk, who was oblivious of my presence. I made a few remarks to get his attention, but to no avail as he kept writing and didn't look up. I had reached the heights of frustration when I turned to Joan and said in my best

"Brooklyn Yiddish" that this guy was a "schlamiel" and "that a trolley car should grow in his belly" (translated from a typical Brooklyn Yiddish expression). With that, he jumped up and grabbed my hand in a welcome handshake that almost floored me. He remarked, "I hadn't heard that remark since I left Brooklyn fifteen years ago. What can I do for you?" I asked him to kindly cash my traveler's check. While so doing, I turned to Joan and in my best Sicilian slang said, *"Questo qui e un grandissimo strunzo"* (This guy is nothing but a big turd). Again, the desk clerk beamed with delight and told us that he was brought up amongst Sicilians in Brooklyn and was quite familiar with that phrase as it was generally used in a familiar way (whatever that meant).

During our stay at the Sinai, Sam went out of his way to be of service to us and we were treated like royalty. I even remarked to Joan, "You see, coming from Brooklyn had its rewards."

We had a problem with the Jewish food. It wasn't quite the gefulte fish and the matzo balls I enjoyed in my youth. The food in Tel Aviv was different. The only meal we enjoyed there was breakfast. Somehow, Joan and I were always amongst the first waiting to enter the dining room, but always wound up entering last. (If you have ever been on a New York subway during the rush hour, you would know what survival means. It's every man for himself and may the Good Lord help you if you don't push your way in with the mob.)

My problem was Joan. She was too much of a lady. If someone pushed, she'd just step aside. This happened whenever we boarded or left a bus and in areas where there were crowds of people. The time had come when I decided to teach Joan the basic tactics to use in push-and-shove situations. I trained her to raise her arm with her hand on her chest, and position her elbow against the person who was beginning to shove. A fast push using her other hand would deal a strong blow. We made great progress until I began hearing screams of pain. At this point, I remarked to Joan that she was doing quite well and we had no further problems in this respect. I must say, however, that Joan has two sharp elbows.

Everyone should go to Israel at least once in his lifetime. If you are a Christian, you must visit this Holy Land. I must say we were terribly disillusioned in many respects. We walked the *Via Dolorosa* (The Way of the Cross), but it was so commercialized I had no feel for the place. We did visit the river

Jordan where I dipped my foot in the river and Mary's Well, which had been kept the same since her time. However, the Wailing Wall did give me a feeling of sincerity and I saw why the Jews regarded this shrine as holy. It was difficult to realize the three great holy places all within sight of one another - the Wailing Wall for the Jews, the Church of the Holy Sepulchre for the Christians, and Dome of the Rock where it was believed that Mohammed ascended into Heaven.

We joined a small group on a three-day tour and spent the first night in a *kibbutzum* (a rural, jointly owned cooperative settlement). It was interesting to see the Jewish farmer driving his tractor while at all times keeping a rifle or an uzi submachine gun at a handy distance. The Israeli have done much to convert their dry desert land into a Garden of Eden. With scientific agricultural know-how, they have produced miracles. Their fruits and vegetables are shipped all over the world and they have turned this once-arid country into a highly industrial and productive land.

We spoke to many Palestinians who seemed to be rather content. As one of them told me, "Before the Israeli came, we were sheep herders. Now we work for Israeli wages and live comfortably." (Of course, this was before Yassir Arafat organized the Palestinians through fear to fight against the Israeli.)

Our tour took us all over the West Bank. This area assured the security of Israel and the Israeli would never give it up. The same could be said of the Golan Heights, which the Israeli captured in the 1967 Six-Day War. We visited the demilitarized zone separating Syria from the Golan Heights, but we didn't stay very long as it gave us an eerie feeling. Standing on the Golan Heights, the Syrian artillery constantly shelled the Israeli valley below.

Since 1948, Israel has fought four wars including the War of Independence (1948), the Sinai War (1956), the Six-Day War (1967), and the Yom Kippur War (1973). The fifth war (twenty years later) is still in progress. It is not a declared war, but it involves Lebanon, Syria, and the Palestinians under Arafat.

We believe the Israeli deserve to live as a peaceful nation. The Diaspora scattered the Jews all over world. Now they have a homeland. The question is, "Can a nation of 3.5 million people survive surrounded by 35 million Moslems?" They have learned how to defend their country and how to win despite all odds. Their motto today is, "It will never happen again."

The Haganah was the Jewish underground group (Stern Gang) that became the Israeli Army upon the independence of Israel. They were joined by Jews from all over the world and molded into a nation. Now, a new group is coming into its own, the Sabra (native-born Israeli).

It was time to leave Jerusalem and Tel Aviv. We went through the strictest security and finally boarded our flight to Rome. The flight was detained for five hours and the plane never left the ground. Fortunately, we were transferred to an Alitalia flight. What a wonderful feeling when we saw the Dome of St. Peter. That night, after checking in at the Ambasciatore Hotel on Via Veneto, we made a beeline for Giovanni's, a favorite *trattoria* nearby. Joan and I agreed that the ravioli, the veal piccata, and that good old bottle of Chianti was like heaven on earth.

Chapter 38

Behind the Iron Curtain

Our next trip took us to East and West Berlin in May of 1978. When our Pan Am flight arrived in Frankfurt, we had to wait two hours for our connecting flight to West Berlin, which was well into the territory of Communist East Germany. We stayed at the Kempinski Hotel, one of the newest and best in this fabulous reconstructed city. Despite the excellent service we received, there was a feeling of Germanic coldness in the hotel, perhaps because we were Americans. This frigidity was broken, however, when we met the night manager who happened to be a warm Neopolitan.

Berlin was completely destroyed by the Allied air raids during World War II. Today, West Berlin stands out as one of the most beautiful and well planned cities on the European continent. There is absolutely no trace of the havoc created by the war. It just never happened?

We arranged to visit East Berlin on a guided tour. There were two buses — one for tourists and the other for the West Germans. We didn't understand this separation until we reached Check Point Charlie, the entrance to East Berlin. While we waited on the West Berlin side, we had an opportunity to inspect the eighteen-foot high infamous Berlin Wall. The Soviet side of the wall contained a vast area of electrically charged, barbed wire. We later learned that the wall is protected by 10,000 Russian guards and 300 dogs. Very few have escaped through or over this heavily guarded wall. In fact, there was a bulletin board on the West Berlin side which listed the names of the many who didn't make it. After waiting a half-hour before clearance was given, the bus zig-zagged through the narrow passageway to the Soviet side of Check Point Charlie. Then, the fun began. The busload of visiting West Germans were ordered out of the bus and forced to stand for a most rigid inspection. We felt sorry for them. In the meantime, we had to give up our passports to a group of important-looking officials. They checked underneath the bus with electronic devices followed by a similar inspection in the interior of the bus. After being given a thorough going-over to make sure we were tourists and not foreign spies, we were introduced to our East Berlin tour director. She was an attractive blonde in a snappy military uniform who beamed with authority.

Our brain-washing education began as the tour director immediately began to tell us of the good life enjoyed by the East German people, how families participated in the cultural movement, and the happiness and joy of life behind the Iron Curtain. Always having a curious mind, I decided to ask her some constructive questions. I didn't get too far with our blonde tour guide as my first question was completely ignored. My next question was received with a stern rebuke. She proceeded to inform me that there was no need for anyone to ask questions as she would have all the answers without the necessity of asking questions. (I never figured that one out.)

We noted the difference between the highly developed, attractive and busy West Berlin with its heavy traffic and Soviet East Berlin, which was still under a slow reconstruction after the ravages of World War II. There, we saw the lack of pedestrian and vehicle traffic. The stores (state-run) had very limited stock. There was a definite difference between the two sectors like night and day.

Our lunch break was welcomed by all as we stopped at an unnamed cafeteria in an unnamed park. We were hungry and quite anxious to partake of some of the good food and good life as so well described by our propaganda-minded tour guide. The smell we encountered as we entered the cafeteria was unbelievable. As hungry as we were, we passed up the food. My visit to the little boys' room left much to be desired. I had to go and with the fastest relief, I got out of that restroom as fast as my feet carried me.

Some of our tour group gathered outside of the bus in a state of disbelief saying, "How can they brainwash us for three-and-a-half hours telling us of the good life and the benefits of the Soviet society when they take us to a place like this?" They wouldn't show us the government buildings or Hitler's Bunker.

We were kept at a distance and that was rather disappointing. At any rate, it was one of the most exciting tours we ever participated in.

On our return to Check Point Charlie, the bus was rechecked underneath and inside, and after a delay of fifteen minutes, we reclaimed our passports and returned to Western Civilization. We thought of Jackie Gleason's famous line when we passed through, ''How sweet it is!'' Leaving West Berlin, we flew back to Frankfurt where we boarded an Alitalia airliner for *"La Bella Venezia."* We were met by Nino, who transferred us by taxi from the airport to a beautiful speedboat (water taxi). It took us through the many canals to the Bauer Grimwald Hotel where we enjoyed a beautiful view of the Grand Canal from our room. Like all Americans, our first visit was to Harry's Bar for a *cinzano* and a typical Venetian dinner with all the trimmings. San Marco Square never looked so good.

Chapter 39

The Orient Express

On September 25, 1982, Joan and I boarded the Venice-Simplon Orient Express at the Santa Lucia Station in Venice for a voyage into the past. Our destination was Victoria Station in London.

The original Orient Express was the most celebrated train in history. It retired ignobly in May of 1977 at the age of 94 years. The luxurious furnishings featured in the most sumptuous railway carriages ever built were the work of artists. The marquetry, the Lalique crystal, the furniture, and the brasswork spelled extravagance governed by good taste. It was a romantic train carrying the famous, dangerous, brilliant, and the wealthy. It was the train of kings and the king of trains. You thought of the famous Agatha Christie's *Murder on the Orient Express*, and were reminded of the escapades of kings like Carol of Rumania and his Magda Lupescu; Sir Basil Zaharoff, the wily munitions tycoon; and Nubar Gulbenkian, the mysterious Armenian oil dealer who was smuggled out of Constantinople rolled up in a rug on the Orient Express.

How the new Orient Express came about is an interesting story in itself. When the original Orient Express made its final run in 1977, James Sherwood, president of Sea Containers, bought the first two 1920 sleeping cars that were to be the nucleus of the present train. He was a 49 year-old energetic Kentuckian who headed the London-based Sea Containers group which, in 1981, had earnings of over $35 million. It is this group that eventually acquired and refurbished 35 old Orient Express cars over a five-year period of time at a cost of $20 million.

This shrunken outcast of the hurry-up age rose again in all its pristine opulence as a regularly scheduled, year-round deluxe train plying between London and Venice via Folkestone, Boulogne, Paris, Lausanne, Milan and Venice. Each car was rebuilt in the exact replica of the original down to the cups and saucers. There are eleven Pullman cars, three restaurant cars, a bar car, and two cars for the crew of thirty. The train accommodates 194 passengers. The sleeping compartments are marvels of compact beauty with comfortable bench seats that convert into upper and lower berths, mahogany drop tables, and inlaid doors enclosing an ornate wash basin. In keeping with the original, there is no toilet. The magnificently paneled toilet is at the end of each car along with a wood stove. As Sherwood said, "After all, we are not selling transportation."

When we arrived at Santa Lucia Station in Venice from a water taxi, we looked upon the most beautiful train we had ever seen. Each Pullman car had its own individualistic name like Perseus, Cygnus, Ibis, and Zena, just to name a few. As we boarded the train, we saw spotless white tablecloths, Chinese vases, and fringed lamps. We felt like we had suddenly entered another era, another world.

We settled down in our tiny stateroom. One of the liveried porters suggested to us that while one was preparing for bed, the other should go to the club car for a drink. I occupied the upper berth and Joan had the lower. At 80 to 100 miles per hour, there was a lot of lurching, pitching and tossing. After the first half-hour of this, I finally fell into slumberland and experienced one of the most restful nights. God bless Mr. Sherwood for making this possible.

The most eventful part of the evening was the dining. It was the most perfect, elegant, tasty and exciting dinner . . . and the most expensive. Who cared? We were living in the lap of luxury and felt that for once in our interesting lives, the $140 dinner, including parsley, was well worth it. The dining guests were like a passing parade. They were friendly and generous, and with their jewels and fineries they made one forget about the miseries of the world. Rounding out the evening, we sat in the bar. Actually, we really couldn't sit because we were jammed like sardines. I held a cinzano in my hand and Joan had a compari in hers. We all sang whatever the piano player came up with in either English, Italian, French or German. The singing wasn't the greatest, but no one cared as we were all on the Orient Express streaming through the night passing the

Italian Alps, the lakes of Switzerland, and the wine country of France.

After continental breakfast in our room, we headed for the French port of Boulogne on the English Channel. We were to end the continental part of our trip and board the Sea Link Ferry to cross the channel to Folkstone, where we would board the final stage of our journey on the English-style Orient Express to Victoria Station in London. The cross-channel trip was scheduled for ninety minutes. When the English Channel gets rough, it gets rough. We were told that the channel was at its worst and in fact, the stormiest, roughest crossing in five years. Everyone on the Sea Link Ferry was seasick to the Nth degree. People were tossed around and knocked down to the point where we couldn't help each other. I managed to help two women on the floor until my insides churned and ached like I never experienced before in my life. Joan was out like a light on the bench. There was no relief and the ninety-minute trip became a three-hour crossing. Personnel from the Orient Express greeted us at the pier with plenty of hot coffee and other amenities in an effort to get us back to normal.

Folkstone looked mighty good to us. We were on English soil ready to embark on the last leg of our trip to Victoria Station. Instead of a Pullman, we now had a parlor car and were back in the lap of luxury. After freshening up, Joan and I sat in the most attractive dining car and enjoyed our ascot luncheon in the style of the lords and ladies of the 1920s and '30s. Because of our ordeal in the English Channel, we welcomed the many assorted sandwiches, the country scones, the English-style ham and eggs, and the most delicious coffee and Norfolk fruitcake. We were living again. The English countryside never looked better and we were soon heading into Victoria Station.

James B. Sherwood made an interesting and delightful contribution to the luxury of the past. The Orient Express is now making money. There is an old Italian saying, "See Naples and die." I say, "Ride the Orient Express and live."

Chapter 40

Don't Travel Unless You Can Smile

When we left Shannon Airport for Rome in May of 1973, we were told that we could take four bottles of Irish whiskey into Italy. Arriving in Fumicino Airport in Rome, we were whisked through customs by the wave of the customs inspector's hand. That was great until we spotted two other customs officers approaching us. Evidently, they noticed the four bottles of Irish whiskey sticking out of our shopping bags.

One of the inspectors had a typical Genovese face. He stopped us and inquired about the whiskey. I informed him that we were told in Ireland that we were permitted to bring four bottles of whiskey into Italy. He probably thought we were a couple of wise alecks and decided that we should open our baggage for a thorough inspection.While he was about to reach the bottom of the bag, he casually inquired as to where we were stopping. I replied in by best Italian that we were stopping at the *Ambasciatore* (the Ambassador Hotel, which was across the Via Veneto from the American Embassy in Rome). When he heard me say *"Ambasciatore,"* he stopped rather quickly, closed the luggage, and with a red face he excitedly began saying, *"Scusi, signore, molti scusi"* (They no doubt thought that I was with the American Embassy.)

On another occasion at the same airport in Rome, I was attempting to cash some traveler's checks. There was no one in attendance at the booth. I inquired at the information desk about where I could cash my checks. I figured that by the way the man moved his hands, he was a Neopolitan. (As a rule, Neopolitans are usually warm and helpful.) He directed me to another booth at the other end of the airport. Again, there was no attendant. Not minding the exercise, Joan and I walked back to the first booth where it was still empty. My next move was to go back to my Neopolitan friend and inquire as to when he thought someone might show up to take care of my currency exchange. He looked at me with a puzzled face, threw his two arms up in the air in a typical Neopolitan fashion, and said, *"Non so, forse e andato a fare la pippi."* (I don't know. Maybe he had to go make wee wee.) While we held back our smiles, the attendant at the Foreign Exchange booth returned to his post and we were able to convert our dollars into *lire*. We walked back to the information desk and said to our Neopolitan friend, *"Abbi una bella giornata."* (Have a good day.)

We have been traveling for many years. The thought often occurred to us about how terrible it would be if we ever lost our luggage. I guess we had reached a point where we were convinced that it could never happen to us. Well, the inevitable happened. We were flying from Lisbon to Rome. Inasmuch as we were to change planes in Rome for a connecting Alitalia flight to Palermo, we checked our baggage through to Palermo as this was the naturally accepted procedure. We arrived in Palermo, but our bags were not there. Fortunately, we were met by our relatives. Mario, president of the College of Physicists at the University of Palermo, provided me with shaving cream, a razor, bathrobe, and some tight-fitting pajamas. Rosanna, who was with the American Consulate in Palermo, took care of Joan's immediate needs. She helped us call TWA headquarters and finally was able to inform us that they authorized us to buy what we needed and to collect through our agent in San Francisco.

Four days later, a representative of TWA called our hotel and informed us that they found our three pieces of luggage . . . in Cairo, Egypt. We were happy and somewhat relieved. When we returned to San Francisco, our agent went right to work. A bill was submitted for what we purchased and in ten days, we received a check for the full amount.

We now felt like real, seasoned travelers. We reached the heights by losing our luggage and eventually recovering them. It pays to have a good travel agent.

Chapter 41

And The Band Played On

Irving Berlin and Melvin Alexander, my first cousin, were very close friends who both had humble beginnings. Berlin was a struggling Russian-Jewish immigrant who made his living singing and dancing in the Bowery and Chinatown saloons in the ghetto sections on the lower east side of Manhattan. Alexander, also a Russian-Jewish immigrant, started his life in the same ghetto. He, however, became a merchant and eventually established himself in business.

Irving Berlin was in his late teens when he wrote the tune that made him a nationally recognized composer, "Alexander's Ragtime Band." He wrote it for his pal, Melvin Alexander. They had much in common and enjoyed life despite their struggles for survival in the ghetto of ghettos.

Perhaps I should start from the beginning. My father's two brothers, Peter and Joseph, came to America shortly after we arrived in Bensonhurst. We sort of lost track of Uncle Joseph who lived in New Jersey for awhile. Uncle Peter was the oldest of three brothers. He and my father were in the lemon shipping business in Sicily. However, he did not follow through in this regard when he arrived in America. He was married to an Italian girl of German descent, who came into a sizable inheritance. With this bit of good fortune, Uncle Peter converted his assets into real estate and investments. He became quite successful, comfortable and well-to-do in Italian-American society. I used to call him my rich uncle.

Uncle Peter and his family settled in Bensonhurst and occupied a spacious three-story, colonial-style ten-room home on Bay 28th Street. It was a showplace which included two tennis courts. The grounds were a horticultural masterpiece. They had three daughters. Catherine was the oldest followed by Marie and Lillian. Catherine married Mel Alexander.

During my growing-up years, we were frequent visitors to Uncle Peter's house on Saturday nights. As children, we played games and sometimes the girls made fudge. We lost track of Lillian as the years went by, but kept corresponding with Catherine. And Marie also married another young Jewish man, Louis Kalfon, a well-to-do merchant.

Melvin Alexander had a very interesting hobby. He had a five-piece band that enjoyed playing ragtime. They played for fun at parties, weddings, and other social events. He and Irving Berlin developed a close friendship. At times, Berlin visited Mel at his Bensonhurst home, especially during rehearsals. He was fascinated with ragtime music. One day, he suggested that he wanted to write a score about Mel and his ragtime band. About a week later, Berlin came to see Mel with a sheet of music in his hand. He said, "Mel, see what you can do with this." Mel and his band looked over the notes and words. "Alexander's Ragtime Band" was born. Berlin, beaming with delight, said, "I wrote this score for my pal, Mel Alexander." The rest is history.

As the years went by, Catherine and Mel retired to Florida. They were soon joined by Marie and Louie, and resided most of the time in Fort Lauderdale. Both girls were soon widowed. Catherine left the scene shortly afterwards and in 1984, we lost Marie Kalfon who had corresponded with me every month for the past ten years. Now, they are gone and only pleasant memories remain.

Recently, Irving Berlin celebrated his 100th birthday. The news media had a field day commemorating this great man of music and what he meant to America. They also headlined the song that made him great, "Alexander's Ragtime Band," his first success. My memory brought back to me, perhaps with a tear or two, Cousin Mel Alexander. With that in mind, I can only say, "And the Band Played On." (Irving Berlin passed away at the age of 101.)

Chapter 42

Director of the First National Bank

I became a banker on November 12, 1972, the date I accepted to serve on the board of directors of the First National Bank of Daly City. There is no comparison between this financial institution and the Bank of America. We hope there never will be.

The First National Bank is a small bank that was started in Daly City, a community of over 80,000 people just south of the San Francisco city limits. There was a need for a home-owned community bank in the area. It was through the efforts of a tough old, farsighted, business-like Genovese, Ricco Lagomarsino, that this was made possible.

Ricco Lagomarsino was a gravedigger who rose to the heights in the operation of a real estate and insurance firm that bore his name. His business was mostly with Italian vegetable growers who, at that time, covered what is now known as Daly City and Colma with the most delicious artichoke, cauliflower, cabbage, and all the vegetables including the once-famous "Colma Red" potatoes. He was a wealthy man.

Ricco, as he was called, became the first chairman of the board of directors of the First National Bank of Daly City in 1963. In addition to those of Italian heritage, he was quite successful in attracting the leading citizens of the city, making his bank an immediate success. He followed the principles of another Genovese, A.P. Giannini, founder of the Bank of Italy (Bank of America), in that this would be the first bank of the little guy, the family bank. Ricco also followed the principle of performing community services, for which the bank received numerous awards.

The greatest achievement was when Ricco Lagomarsino became one of the activists and founding fathers of Mary's Help Hospital, now known as Seton Medical Center, which is situated on twenty-eight acres high on a hill overlooking the entire Bay Area. The hospital was opened in 1965. The importance of this move led to the bank's future policy to get involved in the communities of northern San Mateo County.

The bank was an immediate success. New branches sprouted in Pacifica, South San Francisco, Skyline Plaza, and San Bruno, with the original site at 6600 Mission Street in Daly City as the headquarters.

In 1972, Lagomarsino suddenly passed away. In addition to this tragedy, Dick Minucciani, another member of the board, resigned because of ill health. He was a prominent realtor and civic leader in South San Francisco and the Bay Area. This created two vacancies on the board of directors. In early November of that year, I was invited to become a director by the chairman of the board, Romolo Ariani. I knew very little about banking, but felt that with my broad experience in business, management, and agriculture, I could perhaps contribute much to the future of this bank. It was quite a challenge.

I became acquainted with a wonderful group of directors and eventually would serve with them on the board for the next 20 years. They were a cross-section of the community and each was a success in his business or occupation. Romolo Ariani is a prominent attorney in Daly City; Elton McGraw is a retired pharmacist who spent most of his life in Daly City; Thomas Atwood is former head of Cypress Abbey Cemetery in Colma and presently involved in investments and development; Nelio Vannucci is a cement and building material contractor in northern San Mateo County; and Peter Mazzanti is a prominent nurseryman known as the "Carnation King." The seventh director is Michael Wyman, president of the bank.

I have enjoyed my weekly meetings serving as chairman on the loan and discount committee where we review the applications for loans and anything that has to do with the bank's finances. In all the 20 years, I can't recall a single serious disagreement with my fellow directors. We operated on the principle that whatever the decision, it would have to be in the best interest of the bank.

One of my first duties shortly after my appointment was to help dedicate the opening of our sixth branch in Millbrae.

We subsequently opened three more branches in Buri Buri (South San Francisco), Half Moon Bay, and Linda Mar. The final opening, our tenth branch, was in Colma where we erected a beautiful Spanish-style building, which now serves as our headquarters. Our policy was to remain in San Mateo County. We had no desire to be a big bank.

When I joined the bank, we had $33 million in assets. Fourteen years later, we became a $100 million bank. At a meeting with our federal bank examiners in 1984, we were discussing our status as a bank under $100 million. In replying to a question of mine, one of the bank examiners said, "You are considered a small bank." I asked, "When do we reach the category of a big bank?" "When you pass the $100 million mark." At our second monthly meeting in 1985, it was officially determined that we were in the big league passing $100 million. However, it was the feeling of our board of directors that we really enjoy being considered a big bank, although big banks have troubles. Sometimes they can get too big, too careless, and eventually bite the bullet. We feel that we have a very successful operating bank.

The annual stockholders meetings are generally a bore, but they must be held. We follow a routine of stating the bank's progress, reciting a lot of boring statistics, praise the employees, and hear reaction from the stockholders. However, I will never forget our annual stockholders meeting of 1984. Certain bank employees play specific parts in making motions and moving the agenda along to its conclusion. There was a young lady who was given the part to say, "I move that the meeting be adjourned." Evidently, she lost her script and became nervous, she froze. When it was time for her to say her line, we awaited anxiously to conclude the meeting. She finally came to and in a loud voice, she exclaimed, "It's all over. Let's go eat."

The big social event of the year is our annual Christmas party held for the directors, bank officers, and of course, their spouses or companions. I must not forget to mention though that our Chirstmas party is held in March. Why in March? Well, December is a busy month with so many parties, many of them conflicting with one another. A March party develops into a more relaxing occasion.

Suffice to say, I am very happy serving as a director of a bank. I always thought one had to be quite wealthy to be on the board. They certainly didn't select me for my wealth. I will say, however, that I am not poor, just comfortable with no intention of breaking the Bank of Monte Carlo. Too much money brings too many problems. At my age, who needs problems?

How many people understand the mystery of money? We read the financial pages noticing the many categories in which money is the prime factor whether it be stocks, bonds, shares, or foreign exchange. Perhaps I can shed some light in this regard. If you borrow $1 million from a bank, you're in trouble. If you borrow $1 billion, the bank is in trouble. If you borrow $100 billion, the country is in trouble. Banks set foreign policy. The more they loan to other countries, the more the government gets involved. Apocalypse tomorrow is better than Apocalypse today. Time solves all problems. If banks stop lending to debt-ridden countries, they collapse and the world follows; i.e. the government loan to Chrysler. If Chrysler didn't repay, a chain reaction would have started a depression. However, Chrysler did repay and today, it is a leader in the automobile world.

When money is tight, few can spend it. When money is free and easy to borrow, the masses enjoy the goodies of life (inflation). Commercial banks handle or receive demand accounts (checking accounts). A demand loan is secured by marketable securities. One man's payment is another man's receipt; one man's deposit comes from another man's withdrawal. New money is created in response to credit expansion by commercial banks. A commercial bank replenishes its reserve by selling securities.

The productivity of the American economy is the ultimate barrier to runaway inflation in our country. American wheat can be paid by Russian gold. What concerns me, not because I am a bank director, but as one who has lived a full life through the worst depression in history, two world wars, prohibition, incompetent politicians, the premature creation of the Third World countries, the idealistic theories of the Chamberlins, the Woodrow Wilsons, the Jimmy Carters, and others, are those who believe that the world's problems can be settled without the military strength necessary for back up when you are dealing with an unreliable, but stronger opponent.

We were victors in World War I, but lost the peace because of Wilson's idealistic policies of disarmament in which idealistically, we were the only ones who disarmed. After our World War II victory, the Marshall Plan allowed Europe and Japan to rise out of the ashes and helped many Third World countries to industrialize. We permitted the ones we helped to play by a different set of rules. Because of this, we are now paying the price and can't afford to do it any longer. With our financial and technical help, they have now overtaken us.

America was once the arsenal of democracy, Detroit, the car capital and Pittsburgh, the steel capital. This has now radically changed thanks to our stupidity and the greed of our multi-national corporations. Where once we were producers, we have now become consumers. Our producers are now out of work. The trade deficit is a staggering joke. We have forgotten the basic law of economics — You have to sell things before you buy things or you will go broke.

Financing is primarily done through banks. There will be bank failures here and there. Thank God, we have the protection of the depositors that we didn't have in the crisis of '29. That can't happen unless our system of government collapses. Fortunately, we have much diversification in this great country of ours to be severely damaged by a problem here or there in this broad land. What we really need is a stricter control of the many new banks and savings and loans that seem to keep sprouting with regularity.

No one really has the answers. I look with a jaundiced eye on the predictions of the so-called experts who seem to have a crystal ball (worn-out ones) on the financial future. In my opinion, most of them are "apostles of doom." We are a great country and a great people. The world looks to America whether they like us or not. I have always been an optimist and have always refused to accept failure. If things go bad, it means that we have to work so much harder.

Chapter 43

Colma Comes to Life

The city of Colma is having a Resurrection. There has been a building boom in this "city of the dead," which numbers a population of over 1,500,000. It is not in this category inasmuch as these are "permanent residents" who will be residing underground for perhaps eternity. May they rest in peace.

The boom concerns the living population, which has risen from 580 to over 1,000 living human beings. There are now condominiums, shopping centers, a massive auto row, shops of all kinds, and of course, the new modern, Spanish-style First National Bank building.

Colma has had an interesting history. Before its incorporation into Daly City in 1911, the area which extended from the San Francisco county line to Half Moon Bay was known as Colma. A small remnant of the original section of old Colma refused to incorporate into Daly City. It had a post office while its neighbor, Lawnsdale, didn't. To solve their dilemma, a marriage was performed between the unincorporated area of Colma and Lawnsdale in which the latter took the name of Colma.

The Holy Cross Cemetery recently celebrated its 100th birthday. This was the first cemetery to locate in Colma and eventually grew to 409 acres. In the early days, the Calvary Cemetery at Geary and Turk Street in San Francisco was the original burial ground for San Francisco Catholics. When it became full, the property was considered too valuable to expand as a burial ground. In 1887, Archbishop Joseph Alemany dedicated the new cemetery in Colma. Bridget Martin, a native of Ireland, and Timothy Buckley were the first to be buried there. As other groups noted this new ideal location, 13 more cemeteries were established nearby giving Colma the distinction of being one of the few towns in the world to consist mostly of burial grounds.

While they joke about Colma's "silent majority," few remember that the area and what is now Daly City had a world-famous reputation for its Colma Red potatoes that grew in its rich soil. They were noted for their sweet taste and were usually eaten with skins and all. Hundreds of carloads found their way to the eastern markets, along with the artichokes, broccoli, cabbage, cauliflower, and many other nutritious vegetables. Most of the farmers were oldtime Italians who worked hard and still found time to entertain their friends. Then, along came Henry Doelger, who had built hundreds of homes in San Francisco in the '30s and '40s, and spilled over into San Mateo County. He became San Mateo's biggest developer. The artichokes and the farms gradually disappeared.

In 1893, it was possible to reach Colma when streetcar tracks were extended there to reduce travel time. The roundtrip fare was fifty cents. A funeral parlor car could be rented for fifty dollars. When the train arrived at Cemetery Station, the deceased was transferred by a horse-drawn hearse into the cemetery while the mourners followed on foot.

According to the Archdiocesan's official publication, *Catholic*, the original receiving area at the gate of the cemetery was damaged by the 1906 earthquake. A chapel was added in 1914 and a beautiful, comfortable and impressive receiving chapel was completed in 1963. In the meantime, burial space had become more expensive. Buildings housing mausoleums are now changing the burial patterns. Cremations have been on the rise even in the Catholic Church.

We now shift to the city of Colma. New shopping areas are coming into the city of the dead and more homes are being built and sold before they are even completed. As one observer was quoted as saying, "Colma is coming to life." Perhaps it can be said that it is Colma's resurrection.

A *San Mateo Times* columnist recently wrote that "Colma is an unusual community." "If you counted the dead, it would be the second largest city in the State." He further stated that while there are fourteen cemeteries, there is also one exclusively for pets. Man's love for pets is clearly demonstrated in this unusual cemetery holding over 25,000 beloved pets. Phillip de Baca, who owns the facility, believes that the pet graveyard has more visitors than all the neighboring human cemeteries combined. It was established in 1948 and everything from ocelots to hamsters and turtles have been laid to rest in its five acres; some in underground graves with others cremated and stored in niches. "Humans love their pets," de Baca said. Such is the concern of Pets Rest that the grounds include a chapel. Candles may be lit and if requested, de Baca will conduct a service.

Cypress Lawn is the largest and covers 141 acres. Olivet Memorial Park and Woodlawn Memorial Park are the other major cemeteries. In addition, there is a Serbian cemetery, a Russian cemetery, and several Jewish ones including Salem, Eternal Home, and Hills of Eternity. One of the most interesting is the Italian Cemetery, which covers twenty-six acres on beautifully landscaped grounds with its many Romanesque and European-styled tombs catching a Renaissance spirit of the entire burial grounds. Also of interest are the ethnic cemeteries including the Chinese and the Tung Sen. There are also the Greek Orthodox Memorial Park, the Japanese, and a Russian resting place.

One of the most unusual establishments in Colma is the historic Molloy's Bar, which was started as a hotel and bar back in 1883. To this day, Molloy's is still a popular place to relax after the physical and mental fatigue of a funeral.

After the 1906 earthquake, Colma became the prizefighting capital of the nation. Between 1906 and 1915, some of the most historic fist fights were staged there. One of the world's most famous was the heavyweight title fight between James Corbett and John Sullivan. Colma's favorite champion, Joe Millet, who had an enviable record as a boxer, ran the town's largest training facility. James Coffroth promoted the first big fight on September 9, 1905 involving Battling Nelson and James Britt. The gate was $43,311. While Britt was knocked out, he collected $12,500. The winner's purse was $18,840 (not much compared to today's millions).

Boxing brought thousands of people to Colma. James Coffroth was not popular in San Francisco. Michael Svanevik wrote in the *San Mateo Times* on October 2, 1987 and described Colma's claim to prizefighting fame. He pointed out that Coffroth was an unsavory figure in early San Francisco sports, so he skipped across the county line to Colma and built the Mission Street arena on Sickles Avenue near Mission Road. All the big purse fights in Northern California were staged here and for a time, it was the most famous pavilion in the world. The location was carefully chosen. It was fifty feet from the county line; thus, Coffroth not only got police protection from San Francisco, but was operating under the more liberal rules of San Mateo County — and San Mateo County was more than liberal.

It was a bustling, roaring era. Streetcars brought thousands to Colma. There were usually more fights among the operators than in the boxing ring. At that time, the city boasted of a number of hotels and by 1915, every fourth business was a saloon, gambling hall, or another more intimate form of entertainment. Bare knuckle brawls were out. Records in nearby San Bruno tell of a marathon bare knuckle fight in 1866 which went for 119 rounds. Both fighters were frightfully mauled, but neither won the stakes.

Boxing was a brutal sport and outlawed in most of the country. After the heavyweight title fight between James Corbett and John Sullivan in 1892, American fights were governed by the Marquis of Queensbery Rules designed to make such fights less brutal. Gloves were required from then on. Each round officially became three minutes (previously, they only ended with a knockdown).

Michael Svanevik well described the times of these early days of boxing in Colma. It was the closest thing San Francisco had to a county fair. Those who crossed the county line into Colma found a different world with entertainment of all kinds, including beggars lining the road and promising good luck in exchange for alms. Every bar featured gambling. Sailors from the many ships in San Francisco Bay were so numerous that the provost guard maintained an office in Colma. Kids peddled sandwiches while San Francisco's mounted police kept the crowds moving.

James Coffroth became known as "Sunny Jim," but it wasn't because of his personality. Every bout he staged was always in an open arena with invariable sunshine. It was never rained out. He was acclaimed as the premiere boxing promoter in the country.

Colma's most celebrated match was in October of 1909 when heavyweight champion Jack Johnson fought against Stanley Ketchel. Fans came from all over the country. It was Coffroth's largest crowd. Big money attracted big gamblers and big money was bet on this fight. Johnson, the black champion, flattened Ketchel with a lightning punch to the jaw in the 12th round. It was so swift that no one present claimed to have seen the punch delivered. Many shouted that it was a fix, but Johnson retained his title.

Colma's golden decade ended in 1915 when the State Legislature outlawed boxing. At a later date, boxing again was permitted, but only under the strictest supervision of a State Boxing Commission.

Today, at Colma's city hall, they jokingly call their unusual community "Storage City." No doubt there are many jokes about Colma, but they don't seem to mind. The city treasury is bursting at the seams and despite the jokes, the city officials and employees are a jolly group of dedicated people who will always top your remarks with better ones.

Frances Liston, presently the city manager, has lived in Colma for over twenty years. She has seen many changes including going from hand-digging to mechanical digging of graves. A machine can dig a grave in fifteen minutes, however, many are still done by hand which takes about three hours. Oldtime gravediggers will tell you that they now average about ten graves a month. The rest of the time, they do the gardening and maintenance of the grounds.

The next time you visit one of Colma's cemeteries, stop in at Molloy's. You will see two shillelaghs hanging behind the bar and owner Lanty Molloy will deadpan to his customers, "This is where the spirits get to you."

Chapter 44

What About Some Chocolate?

There I was scraping the bottom of the pot with my spoon and my fingers. My sister, Frances, had just finished making some chocolate fudge for which she was famous. This was usually a Saturday night activity that she indulged in with a few of her Bay Ridge High School girlfriends. I am speaking of the time when I was a growing boy of thirteen and had clean-up detail, which I so looked forward to.

In those days, we didn't have the many diversions of today such as television, radio, rock n' roll, the automobile, and the restlessness of youth. The girls passed the time away by making their chocolate fudge, cookies, and so many other goodies. I also learned the art of making fudge from watching my sister and her friends.

Sixty years later on a June day in 1985, I rescued my twenty year-old granddaughter, Karen, who had reached the heights of desperation. She was entertaining several of her college chums and was making a fudge frosting for a cake, but the fudge wouldn't harden. It was soft and runny. Not to fear, as Grandpa came to the rescue. Adding more cocoa, sugar, butter, and milk, I continuously stirred the contents as it came to a boil. I dropped some fudge into a glass of water and lo and behold, it was as hard as can possibly be. With a great deal of satisfaction, I saved Karen's day. The cake was a huge success and I was proclaimed a hero.

Chocolate was always my favorite whether it was in candy, cakes or just plain hot chocolate. I remember when I was in grammar school, especially during the cold Brooklyn winters when my brother and I returned from school shivering and hungry. We were greeted by my mother with a cupful of hot chocolate. We also had hot chocolate for breakfast.

Being a lover of chocolate, I wanted to know everything about it. Where does chocolate come from? It is derived from the cacao tree which originated in the Orinoco Basin in the Amazon area of Brazil. In 1502, Christopher Columbus was the first European to run across the bean on his fourth voyage to the New World. The trail of the cacao bean went from the jungles of Africa and Brazil to the sophisticated chocolate factories of Europe and the United States. Cortes, the Conquistador, spread the plantings of the bean to the Caribbean islands. The Aztecs shared the bitter, watery drink with Cortes and later introduced drinking chocolate to Spain in 1528. The Spanish then added water, cane sugar, and heated the brew. Soon, chocolate was the favored drink of nobility. The drinking of chocolate spread throughout Europe and competed with coffee houses. It eventually became the favorite drink of the New World.

In 1828, Van Houten, a Dutch chemist, learned to press out some of chocolate's fat, cocoa butter, and made cocoa powder. Twenty years later, when cocoa butter and sugar were added to a paste of ground beans, eating chocolate became popular.

The Swiss developed a way to make solid milk chocolate. Machines were made to stir the liquid chocolate to vastly improve its smoothness. In 1875, Daniel Peter and Henri Nestle blended chocolate with condensed milk, giving to the world the famous Nestle chocolate. Today, Switzerland has high and strict quality controls and is considered the best and most expensive chocolate in the world.

In the United States, Milton Hershey devised his own process using fresh milk. He made chocolate affordable through mass production. In 1903, the Hershey Chocolate Company was born in a Pennsylvania town later renamed Hershey. (In one day, Hershey makes about 25 million "kisses.")

Today, some candymakers substitute vegetable oils for cocoa butter, so it cannot be legally called chocolate, but confectionery coating. Always read the ingredients of your favorite chocolate bar wrapper. Chocolate is virtually free of salt and cholesterol. It is a high energy food and is one of the best pick-me-ups. Joan and I continue making fudge and chocolate chip cookies. Remember, it is only fattening when you eat too much.

Chapter 45

A Knight of Columbus

There I was sitting in the back row talking to my friend and fellow knight, Louis Maffei, when I suddenly heard my name called. "John," the voice said, "Would you be interested in accepting the highest post in this council, the Grand Knight of Dante Council 2563?" I was rather stunned and speechless. Again, my name was called. The voice came from James DeMartini, the Grand Knight of the council. It was during an intermission that this incident took place. Evidently, the newly elected Grand Knight, Harold Tosetti, had informed the council that he could not accept because of a serious health problem.

I was not a stranger to the Dante Council as I had previously belonged to the Knights back in Brooklyn ten years prior. I was also well-known because of my civic activities, i.e. the Farmers' Market, Victory Gardens, Angel Island, and a few others. They didn't give me a chance to reply and elected me by acclamation. I served two terms from 1945 through 1946.

Why did I become a Knight and why have I remained active in this prestigious Catholic organization? Perhaps it is because of the breaking down of all social barriers and the feeling of brotherhood.

Who are the Knights of Columbus and what do they represent? It all started in 1882 in New Haven, Connecticut as an inspiration of a young Catholic priest, Father Michael McGivney. He saw the problem facing the great influx of Catholics who came to the promised land in droves. They came by the thousands, mostly from Ireland, Italy, Poland, and the rest of Europe, which was undergoing economic problems, famine, and unemployment. While they settled mostly in the cities, they accepted work anywhere. There were plenty of jobs available; however, there was also plenty of prejudice against these low-class immigrants, many of whom were illiterate. It was common to see signs posted at the factory gates stating that jobs were available, with the additional wording: ''Micks and Dagos Need Not Apply.'' This indeed was the age of prejudice and discrimination. These people were the minorities of the time.

Father McGivney saw the problem and visualized a Catholic organization offering insurance to the families of Catholic workers and at the same time, offering a social and spiritual life in serving their country. In this, he succeeded. From this embryo beginning in New Haven, it incorporated as a fraternal society.

In 1982, the Knights of Columbus celebrated their first one hundred years. There were now over two million members in this most active fraternal society. There were five councils serving San Francisco and Dante Council was one of them. There was a reason for the creation of Dante due to a strong anti-Catholic prejudice in the North Beach section of the city. North Beach was an Italian community, so to speak, with the center of its spiritual life around Saints Peter and Paul Church. It was known as the Italian National Church.

In the early part of the century, most of the Italians who wanted to be in business or profession became masons. Their families, however, remained strictly Roman Catholic. There were several Italian masonic lodges in North Beach and many successful Italian mason-businessmen. This was the reason for the establishment of a Catholic fraternal order. In 1925, Dante Council was born. In the same move, an organization for the youth was also established, the Salesian Boys' Club. Angelo Fusco was its director. There were others that were created, but it was the Dante Council that led the way.

As the years went by, the old prejudice vanished. The age of ecumenism shattered these prejudices. Various masonic lodges and Knights of Columbus Councils now join forces where there is an opportunity for civic or cultural benefit for the community. (In this respect, I will say that some of my closest and dearest friends were 32nd-degree masons.)

Dante Council was a very active one. Its membership was over eighty percent of Italian origin. I became a Knight in my early youth in Brooklyn. There was a period of over ten years when I left the council because of my travels between the east and west coasts, Florida, and other points. I also drifted away from the Church, but never lost my faith. Let me say that during this period, I was a non-practicing Catholic.

It was during the early forties when I was operating the winery with my two brothers that I became acquainted with Ernie Granucci. He was the top salesman for Belli Chevrolet in Colma. Frank, Peter and I each had a Chevy. Every year, he picked up our Chevrolets and replaced them with the new model of that year. We always had a new car with little concern for maintenance and upkeep. Ernie was very active in Dante Council. He finally persuaded me to join as a transfer from Archbishop John Hughes' council in Brooklyn. I was given a warm welcome and immediately made a lot of friends, some who I still see today.

At a recent Past Grand Knights dinner, I was introduced as the oldest living Past Grand Knight. When you get an introduction like this, it gives you goose pimples. But I am getting ahead of myself. I joined Dante Council in 1943. One year later, I was elected Grand Knight of the council and was re-elected for the 1945-46 term. The following year, I was appointed district deputy for the San Francisco jurisdiction involving five councils.

The membership of the San Francisco Council covered the entire city. The other councils were Golden Gate, West of Twin Peaks, and Mission. During my stewardship as district deputy, I installed a sixth council, Old St. Mary's. I felt that there was a need for a council that catered to the many Chinese and other Asian Catholics. I was happy to see that this eventually became a very active part of the Knights of Columbus.

One of my problems when I became Grand Knight was the low attendance at the regular meetings. The members only turned out when we had a special program. Having had some experience in the various organizations I chaired, I developed a really good gimmick that turned out to be quite successful. I had three of my close Knights sitting in various parts of the meeting room. After going through the preliminary reports of the committees, I signaled one of my conspirators to proceed. He rose and asked to be recognized. He then presented a controversial subject which brought the second conspirator into the act. After the third person started in, there was a spirited discussion in progress. Others joined in, many of whom probably never would have spoken up in a general discussion. After the second meeting, we broke all attendance records. As one of the more quiet members remarked after one of the meetings, "John, I was always timid about getting up and expressing my feelings, but when someone gets up and presents such a controversial subject, I just had to get up and let him have it."

Inasmuch as most of the Dante members were of Italian extraction, it was not a problem to have periodic feeds. A number of the members were associated with the Italian restaurants at Fisherman's Wharf. Frank Alioto was one of them. We had *crab cioppinos*, Past Grand Knight dinners, benefits and fundraisers. We became a very popular council and our reputation for good food and fellowship was city wide.

The charitable, civic, and welfare programs of the Knights of Columbus benefitted many. Their activities are legend. I always felt that it was a privilege and great honor to belong to an organization of this nature, especially in this day and age where there are so many problems with family life, disregard for authority, immorality, drugs, and pornography in the world we live in. At last, here is an organization that has done much to keep the home together.

While I was active in the early years of my knighthood, I still retained my contacts. There are monthly luncheon meetings held at Dante Benedetti's New Pisa Restaurant in North Beach where many of the oldtimers came.

At this writing as I had previously stated, I am the oldest living Past Grand Knight of Dante Council, Knights of Columbus. What an honor.

Chapter 46

A Knight of Malta

One of the greatest honors ever to be bestowed upon me was when I was invited to become a Knight of Malta. I was recommended and sponsored by Richard "Dick" Minucciani, the Hospitaller of the Knights. (Coincidentally, I succeeded Dick on the board of directors of the First National Bank of Daly City.)

The Knights of Malta represents the elite of all Catholic societies and is considered one of the most prestigious. The membership is limited and only by invitation. A member must be of high standing in his community, particularly with regards to his Catholicism.

The Sovereign Military Hospitaller Order of St. John of Jerusalem, of Rhodes and of Malta is the full name of this unusual organization. It traces its origin to a group of men who maintained a Christian hospital in the Holy Land in the 11th Century and was approved as a religious order by Pope Paschal in 1113. The original order, while continuing its service to the poor principally in hospital work, assumed military duties in the following century. All the Knights were professed monks and took vows of poverty, chastity and obedience. They later established themselves on the island of Rhodes and became a military power like the Sea of Republics of Italy and the Hanseatic cities of Germany, flying its own flag, coining its own money, and maintaining diplomatic relations with many nations.

The order was forced to abandon Rhodes in 1522 after the third long siege of the island by the Turks under Sultan Suliman I. Eight years later, the Knights were given the island of Malta where they remained as a bastion of Christianity until the end of the 18th Century. Headquarters have been located in Rome since 1834. Religious aspects of the order are subject to regulation by the Holy See. At the same time, the sovereignty by the order, which is based on International Law, is recognized by the Holy See in Rome and by thirty-eight countries with which full diplomatic relations are maintained.

The order is presently devoted to hospital and charitable work of all kinds in some sixty countries. The present headquarters for this world wide, religious hospitaller group is on the Via Condotti in Rome. It runs its own hospitals and assists with others. The order also staffs leper colonies, nursing schools, research institutes, volunteer first-aid corps, and prenatal clinics in many countries.

The military aspect of the order fought the invading Turks, who had declared a holy war against the Christians. Great battles took place and thousands of Knights and foot soldiers were slain. The Turks led by Saladin finally captured Jerusalem and converted the Christian churches into mosques. When the Knights retreated to Cyprus, they laid a new foundation for a new phase in their history — naval warfare. The battle ground between Christiandom and Islam shifted from the Near East mainland to the Eastern Mediterranean.

The order prospered as new Knights came from all over Europe. They kept the Eastern Mediterranean free from Moslems and pirates by manning a large fleet of fighting galleys. Meanwhile, the Ottoman Turks captured Constantinople and the Knights retreated to their stronghold on the island of Rhodes. At that time, Europe was devastated by the bubonic plague and torn by civil and class wars. Then, in 1522, a tremendous Turkish armada of 250 ships and 200,000 men, under the leadership of Sultan Suleiman the Magnificent, set siege to the island of Rhodes. There were only 600 Knights and 6,000 soldiers who faced that insuperable force, yet they fought off the enemy for an epic six months. At last, the Grand Master of the Knights surrendered the island on Christmas Eve in 1522 in order to save the civilian population. The Sultan, impressed with the valor of the Knights, allowed them to leave the island with all their ships, arms and possessions. Both city and population were spared as the order departed in honor.

The Knights were given the barren island of Malta by Emperor Charles V of France. The order fortified the island and continued to harass the Turks. From this point on, the Knights

John Brucato was made a Knight of Malta, the Catholic Church's most prestigious organization — September 1977.

of Malta held the upper hand against the Turks and at one time almost lost the island until they were saved by the arrival of fresh troops from nearby Sicily. The order not only kept Malta, but the entire Western Mediterranean from control by the barbarous Turks.

In 1571, the Knights took part in the famous naval battle of Lepanto when the Turkish fleet was finally destroyed in the last victory of the Crusades. The French Revolution portended the end of the order's reign on Malta. The Treaty of Paris awarded the island of Malta to Great Britain in 1814. The Knights of Malta ceased to be an active military order and confined its activities as a hospitaller order, establishing hospitals and clinics all over the world. In addition to their many works of charity, the Knights and Dames of Malta hold annual pilgrimages to Lourdes in France and to Fatima in Portugal. They supply ambulances and personnel to assist the thousands of pilgrims who visit these holy Catholic shrines.

I have had the privilege of meeting many wonderful, devoted people since my investiture. Mrs. Ralph K. (Louise) Davies, a Dame of Malta, annually hosts the newly inducted members at a reception in her beautiful Woodside home. I enjoyed conversing with Louise Davies, who was a charming and very friendly hostess. On one of these occasions, after she was describing to me her recent cruise on a tramp steamer, I suggested that she write an appropriate book on her very interesting life. I also suggested that because of her many activities and busy schedule, she should take another cruise on a tramp steamer so that she could enjoy privacy without interruptions in order to concentrate on this book. This conversation went on for a period of years. I mentioned to her that some time ago, I authored a book on the trials and tribulations of the San Francisco Farmers' Market. We agreed to exchange books and on October 17, 1982, I received the book on Dr. Ralph K. Davies, her noted husband, who founded the well known Davies Medical Center.

One of the many hospitals operated by the order is in Tehran, Iran. For some time after the takeover of Iran by the Ayatollah Khomeini, we did not know the fate of this most recent Knights of Malta hospital. Fortunately, the sisters operating the hospital had been permitted to continue the operation without interference (a noble gesture).

I thought this brief description of this most admirable organization would help people to more fully understand why there is an order known as the Knights of Malta.

Chapter 47

Seton Medical Center

One of the most enjoyable boards I serve on is the Community Advisory Board, in particular the Health Services Committee, of the Seton Medical Center. Formerly Mary's Help Hospital on Guerrero Street in San Francisco, it later moved to a hilltop overlooking northern San Mateo County in Daly City. It is one of California's leading medical centers.

In 1983, the name was changed to Seton Medical Center after their founder, Saint Elizabeth Ann Seton, who is one of our few American saints. Mother Seton was the founder of the Daughters of Charity of St. Vincent de Paul. This organization spread to every corner of the world numbering 3,548 houses of which 167 are in the United States. Most of them, 3,122, are in Europe of which 644 are in Italy.

I had a personal pride in serving on this board primarily because of my distant relationship to the Mother Superior of the Sisters of Charity Hospital at Caserta near Naples in Italy. Francesca Gallo was the mother of my mother, Rosina Gallo. Unfortunately, she died at childbirth at the age of thirty-two. She was born *"La Mattina"* and married at nineteen to Francesco Gallo. She was also the sister of Mother Superior Marietta who, for over forty years, directed one of the most important hospitals in Italy. Serving under her was the Queen of Italy, who gave much of her time helping the wounded during World War I.

During our first visit to Italy just before joining the Allies in World War I, we visited *Zia* Marietta in Caserta. She knew about my sweet tooth and made sure that the good nuns, who made the best Italian cookies, took care of me. Along these lines,

I remember visiting the Daughters of Charity in Monreale near Palermo with my mother and brother when here again, the good nuns made sure that *Giovanuzzu* (little Johnny) received his fair share of their well-known cookies. "My," I said to my mother, "The news travels fast, thanks to *Zia* Marietta."

I was appointed to the illustrious board of Seton Medical Center in October of 1977. This was when I met Sister Florence Urbine, D.C., chairman of the board. She is one of the most remarkable women I have ever met in my long life. Sister Florence, as she was known, had complete control of the operation at Seton. She had a soft-spoken, warm and a most charming and approachable disposition that is very seldom seen in persons holding high, responsible positions. I served many years on the Facilities Development Committee and in March of 1986, Sister Florence appointed me to the Health Services Committee. This was a broad and challenging committee that is very involved with senior citizens and the troubled youth of the community.

With Joan deeply involved with the Children's Home Society and having been recently elected as president of the Coast Counties Council, there is no question of the involvement of the Brucato family in community activities.

Chapter 48

The M.E.A.

The Municipal Executive Association (M.E.A.) is the only organization of its kind in America as well as one of the most influential political groups in San Francisco. Consisting of non-elected executives of the City and County of San Francisco, its purpose is to promote and improve understanding between the city and county government and the business community, civic and other groups, and to protect the civil service system from abuse of any kind. Department heads in city government are brought together in this unusual organization. Elected officials like the mayor, the supervisors, the controller, etc. are not eligible for membership.

One of the main objectives is to promote higher standards of professional ethics and efficiency among city and county executives. As the manager of the agricultural land division of the San Francisco Water Department, I joined the organization in 1952. In 1956, I served as president for one term. (George Christopher was mayor at that time.) Halfway through my presidency, Virgil Elliott, a writer for the *City and County Record*, headlined a story about the M.E.A. in this fashion: "John Brucato Puts Zest in San Francisco's Municipal Executive Association."

How does one become president of such an auspicious organization, a group that makes the wheels of municipal government go around? Perhaps I should mention that shortly after joining this organization, I suggested that we should make our meetings more interesting and engage in more attractive programs in order to get the membership out to the meetings. I complained that while it was necessary to go through the usual business items and all the uninteresting discussions that are usually a part of the meeting, we should have more social activities. Joe Allen, who was presiding as president at the time, thought my remarks were well-taken. "And what do you have in mind, John?" Mentioning a number of possible activities, I wound up by saying, "You realize, Mr. President, that San Francisco is the wine capital of America. We should go to the wine country at least once a year for educational purposes."

Joe Allen, who served as executive secretary to two mayors and was presently manager of the War Memorial Opera House, was noted for his sharp, witty tongue and sense of humor. He said, "John, I think you have a brilliant idea. I believe if we can have an annual or semi-annual outing to the wineries, it will attract a lot of our membership to participate." The audience quickly responded by saying, "Hear, hear." Taking this as a sign of approval, he looked at me and stated, "John, I am appointing you as chairman of the First Annual Wine Excursion." Well, I had been chairman of the winery tours for 30 years, resigning in 1985.

The total membership of the M.E.A. was 130. No more could be added as this was the number of the top city executives eligible to belong. The wine seminars were limited to 80, which was the capacity of the two chartered buses. I made all the arrangements at the winery for lunch and the program. Joe Allen, my perennial co-chairman, arranged for the buses. We provided continental breakfast aboard each bus including coffee, sweet rolls, and plenty of brandy. There was also accordion music which made the trip all the more enjoyable. It was a day to have fun and forget the responsibilities of running the city government.

We always scheduled our seminars on Lincoln's Birthday, which came in February and was a city holiday. It can be said that we did not neglect the city's business. The excursions were planned at least six months in advance and we never had difficulty in closing reservations long before the day of the event.

Our first excursion was a memorable one. We had just gone through a drought that caused much concern amongst the farmers, particularly the vineyardists. Two days before our trip to the Napa Valley, the drought was broken and that day it rained cats and dogs. One busload headed for the Inglenook and Martini wineries while the other went to Beringer Brothers and Charles Krug. They then reversed their visits so that all the wineries were visited. As we disembarked from the bus, we were greeted with a glass of sherry wine which, of course, put us in the proper spirit. We then congregated in the sampling room for an assortment of the winery's best vintage red and white wine. There was no limit to the sampling. When this phase was completed, we then went through the winery in small groups to be indoctrinated into the mysteries of the wine world. Lunch took place at one o'clock at Bothe's Paradise Inn located between St. Helena and Calistoga in the Napa Valley.

We were greeted by the Calistoga Chamber of Commerce holding a huge banner with the inscription, "Thanks, M.E.A., for bringing us this million dollar rain." As chairman of our group, I replied, "Thank you. Think nothing of it, gentlemen. This is what San Francisco does to improve our urban-rural relations."

Prior to our luncheon, I had developed a program of wine sampling. We selected only the experts, the ones who bragged and showed-off their knowledge of wines. My co-partner in this program was Phil Hiaring, a public relations man. He eventually became publisher of the prestigious *Wines and Vines* magazine, which today is considered the voice of the wineries and vintners, and is an authoritative and well-read publication.

Phil and I kept a secret for 30 years, which I am now revealing for the first time. At the wine sampling, we selected five bottles, drawing the wine out of the same barrel. Each bottle was labeled one through five. No one else was ever in on our Machiavellian scheme. The experts were blindfolded and given a small glass in order to taste and determine the quality (good, fair or poor), color (red or white), and possible age (over ten years, about five years, or one year). It was amazing and rather amusing how these self-appointed experts varied their classifications. Most of the time, they were off. However, we never embarrassed them. Phil and I generally rated them with a high score. Then, at the table during our program, I announced the results. After a few years of this, I always stated that the city fathers, through their annual visits to the wine country, were considered the best-educated and most knowledgeable public officials in the world on wine. Incidentally, no one has ever challenged this statement. I also stated that they had learned the basic principle and correct way of drinking wine: "Wine is to be sipped and not gulped."

Louis M. Martini was an old friend. Louie, as he was called, was one of the patriarchs of the wine world. Besides his winery and vineyard in the Napa Valley, he owned an additional 500-acre vineyard in Sonoma called Monte Rosso Vineyards. He was very civic-minded and was particularly involved with the San Francisco Opera. It was a privilege to be invited to a barbecue at the Monte Rosso Ranch. This was where he entertained society and others in what was known as the most deluxe of Italian barbecues. There were three groups who were entertained there annually: The Opera Association, the *IL Cenacolo* Club, and our M.E.A. We had the privilege of visiting Monte Rosso on six different occasions.

Joe Vercelli had a small vineyard and winery in Alexander Valley. He was also a chemist and later became manager of Italian Swiss Colony at Asti when sales were low and management was at a low level. Joe made a great success, brought the winery to its heights, and in time retired. He was then called out of retirement to resurrect the ailing Souverain Winery. We were able to make several visits to Italian Swiss Colony where they really rolled out the carpet for our group.

One memorable visit was to Korbel Champagne Winery in 1955. It was the year of the famous Yuba City floods that occurred in December with an encore in February. We had to cut short our winery visit as the Russian River was at flood stage and still rising, and we were taken to a restaurant in Guerneville for lunch. No sooner had we sat down when the sheriff came through the door stating in a loud voice, "All right, boys, grab your chicken legs and get the hell out." We sure moved fast. The street was now under a foot of water and with expert maneuvering by our bus drivers, we took a hill road that got us out of the danger area. It was quite an experience. At our next meeting, I remarked, "Where else could you visit a winery, grab a quick lunch, and see a river out of control with houses, barns, and animals floating before your very eyes?"

In 1984, I reached the point where I felt that I would promote my last seminar. It was time for someone else to take over. The oldtime wineries were gone. Most of them were now in the hands of conglomerates and new generations. I felt that the warmth and intimacy were lost over the years with the oldtimers gone to their heavenly rewards. The conglomerates were cold. They were all businesspeople who lacked the warmth and compassion that made my programs so successful.

On February 13, 1984, I announced the last annual wine tour under my direction. My selection was the Sebastiani

Winery in Sonoma. Gus Sebastiani was my close friend up until his demise, which was a great loss to the wine world. His family continued the operation of this well-known pioneer institution. Fortunately for me, I dealt with Sylvia Sebastiani, Gus' widow, who graced our luncheon and made my day a successful one. Bill Blake, former San Francisco supervisor and a close neighbor of the Sebastianis, added color to my greatest achievement. We dined at the famous Swiss Hotel, which was noted for its fine food. When the program was completed, my fellow city executives gave me a rising ovation. It was indeed my last hurrah.

The M.E.A. found it rather difficult to appoint my successor. They did not follow my recommendation to start at least six months ahead and waited until the last minute to make arrangements, and found most of the wineries to be too businesslike and rather cold.

During these thirty years, I made a lot of friends and really enjoyed my responsibilities. Now, they will go down in my file on Memory Lane. My favorite toast at our annual wine seminar was:

> "The Frenchman loves his native wine,
> The German loves his beer
> The Englishman loves his 'alf and 'alf,
> Because it brings good cheer.
>
> The Irishman loves his whiskey straight,
> Because it brings him dizziness.
> The American has no choice at all,
> So he drinks the whole damn business."

Chapter 49

Events and Happenings in My Lifetime

I recently spoke to a group of teenagers in Millbrae, California. It was a get-together seminar of neighborhood youngsters who I watched grow up over the years. Why did I do this? First of all, the 12 boys and girls assembled were between the ages of 17 and 21. They were above-average students and quite informed about electronics, computers, mechanics, and rock n' roll. What really shocked me was that they had little knowledge of geography, history, literature or the classics. In school, they merely scratched the surface in what they called political science and current events.

A recent revealing story in *National Geographic* strongly emphasized the ignorance of our youth, particularly in geography and history. I had a close relationship with these youngsters and it was no problem in getting them together. I was amazed at their willingness to discuss this problem. Their feeling was that these subjects were no longer taught and if they were, it was only on a limited level. I stressed that we, as a nation of immigrants, cannot go on in this fashion. We must do something about it.

Perhaps I can best describe my point in referring to an article in the *Washington Post* which appeared in 1985. It was a story about fifteen American and fifteen Soviet students who met in Washington, D.C. to discuss the threat of nuclear war. The Americans were gifted students from local schools. The Russians were children of Soviet diplomats and journalists who attended an embassy school. During the meeting, Alexei Palladin pointed out that the Soviet Union and the United States were once allies and friends. ''What do you know about the Second World War?'' Alexei asked the Americans. There was no answer. He nodded smugly. ''Nobody even knows that we were allies fighting Nazism together.'' What a revelation. No wonder we speak of our students as ''educated illiterates.'' Not even one of the American students out of the fifteen had been knowledgeable enough to bring up the Nazi-Soviet Pact that helped usher in World War II, or the Gulag where uncounted men, women and children of conscience had suffered or disappeared.

The Nazi-Soviet Pact was the joint invasion of Poland. The Nazis took the western half and the Soviets grabbed the eastern half of this long suffering country. Then, at the opportune time, the Nazis made an about-face and took the balance of Poland from their Soviet allies, who now became the enemy, and World War II exploded into all its *blitzkrieg* fury.

Our students seemed to have forgotten or were just never taught of the confused nature of our societies. They are unaware of the special freedom we enjoy, because they were never taught the principles of our democracy. To go further into the ignorance of our educated students would require a volume of words. Suffice to say, we do have a problem, a very serious problem.

In 1984, the National Endowment for Humanities commissioned a study of seventeen year-old students to measure their knowledge of American history. Two-thirds couldn't place the American Civil War in the correct half of the century. One-third didn't know that the Declaration of Independence was signed between 1750 and 1800.

Seventy-two percent of the nation's colleges do not require a study of American literature and a similar percentage of university teachers never studied this most important subject. The average American tourist does not have an idea of what country he visits or where it is on a map.

I would like to relate a few happenings which have taken place in my lifetime that have carefully been swept under the carpet. The ends justify the means as Machiavelli points out in *The Prince*.

During World War II, there was a Navy cover-up where they enlisted the help of the Mafia to solve the problem of sabotage on the New York waterfront, which was damaging the war effort, especially in the forth coming invasion of Africa. The Navy-Mafia alliance secured the waterfront so that it was possible to commence the African shipments, making it safe for shipping, for American lives, and for the control of sabotage by enemy agents and the heavy pilferage on the docks. Unfortunately, the Navy began a considerable cover-up at war's end and most of the files were secretly destroyed.

It all began because 21 American and allied ships were torpedoed off east coast ports in January of 1942, followed by 27 in February and 50 in March. The *S.S. Normandie*, converted to a troop ship and able to outrun any submarine, burst into flames and capsized at her Hudson River pier. Spies and saboteurs flooded the New York waterfront. Naval Intelligence sought the help of the Mafia. The contributions of "Lucky" Luciano and other Mafia members were enormous in ending the sabotage. He was transferred to Great Meadows Prison from Dannemora so that he could more easily meet with Navy Intelligence. Luciano was eventually deported to Italy after serving ten of his twenty-year sentence for tax evasion.

Who was this "Lucky" Luciano? He was America's most notorious gangster. Born Salvatore Luciano in the poverty-stricken village of Lercara Friddi in Sicily in 1906, he was brought up in the lower east side of New York. By the time he was twenty, he had recruited the partners who were to dominate the rackets for the next thirty years — Frank Costello and two Jews, Meyer Lansky and Benny Siegel. They operated by discipline, careful planning, and expansion, similar to the methods of big business. Prohibition transformed the underworld from a tangle of small family businesses into a smooth operating and fabulously profitable, illegal empire. As the "Boss of Bosses," Luciano killed off the rule of the "Mustachio Pete" godfathers and made the Mafia a modern corporation. He was prosecuted by Thomas Dewey in the 1936 trial. The deal was finally made when Dewey, as governor of New York, signed the extradition order releasing him from Dannemora and exiling him to Italy, never to return to the United States.

"Lucky" Luciano continued ruling his empire from Italy until the end of his life. Together with Lansky and Costello, he made a deal to help secure Franklin Delano Roosevelt's presidential nomination by raising millions of dollars. Later, F.D.R. double-crossed them.

Maranzano and Masseria were eventually eliminated, ending the numerous killings between the Castellamare and the Termini Imeresi wars. The old-style Mafia and the "Moustachio Pete" era had come to an end. "Lucky" Luciano became the *Capo* and was respected by the underworld.

Meyer Lansky established casinos in Havana, Cuba by taking Fulgencio Batista in as a partner. When Fidel Castro took over, Lansky transferred Batista's $300 million to a Swiss bank. The money was used to establish casinos in the Caribbean, London, Beirut, and other locations.

During his exile in Italy, Luciano lived in Sicily in the cities of Palermo and Taormina. However, he spent most of his time in Naples. Many have tried to kill him, but never succeeded. In the end, he died of a heart attack. "Lucky" Luciano never did return to the United States.

This brings us to the Meyer Lansky story and the influence of the underworld in legitimate business. The new crime syndicate now consisted of politicians, businessmen, and the underworld. Legitimate businessmen were wiped out in the Crash of 1929. The underworld came into its own through the genius of Meyer Lansky and Johnny Torrio. The only cash money available was controlled by the crime syndicate. In order to survive, big business got its cash and financing from the underworld. The Mafia was only part of the big crime syndicate controlled by Lansky. Franklin Roosevelt broke up the big city political machine and inadvertently put the gangster in business. Political power with economic influence made the national crime syndicate possible. This is the problem society faces today.

Because I lived in this era, I became engrossed in its happenings. I was also deeply involved in the economics of the time, particularly with regard to Libya, which today is threatening the peace and safety of our world. It was once one of the poorest, but now it is among the wealthiest. There are three regions of Libya: Tripolitania, Cyrenaica, and Fezzan. Once a Garden of Eden, agriculture degenerated after the Romans, and the Arabs and Turks did little. Italy invaded Libya in 1911 and defeated Turkey. It was not until 20 years later did Italy consolidate its authority under Fascism with Italo Balbo as the prime mover. Mass colonization from Italy introduced irrigation, agriculture, buildings and roads. With massive planting, the sand wastes were turned into a garden spot. This ended abruptly by World War II. Italy lost a valuable colony that was quite costly. Libya, again, degenerated in industry and agriculture after Italian rule. The war had almost totally destroyed all the improvements.

King Idris was the first ruler of the Kingdom of Libya. The

first ten years of independence were difficult because of the distrust of the many factions and jealousies. Until 1950, the presence of oil in North Africa was barely suspected. Professor Ardito Desio, an Italian, actually found the first traces of oil in 1938. Oil was struck at Edjeleh in 1955, starting the oil rush. By 1970, Libya became the third largest producer. In 1966, the *Giornale Della Sicilia* headlined, "We Never Knew It — Billions of Barrels of Oil Literally Under Our Feet."

Professor Desio was actually drilling for water. He represented the University of Milan and a group of Italian scientists and agriculturists. As a follow-up to his oil discovery, the *Azienda Generale Italiana Petroli*, known as AGIP, drilled its first hole which turned out dry. Indications, however, showed that they were on the verge of hitting pay dirt when suddenly the Italian invasion of Egypt began, ending further exploration.

The Libyan campaign, while it was for the Middle East oil fields, took place on top of the undiscovered oil deposits, large enough to have sustained the combined Allied and Axis war efforts. Italy and Germany lost the war. Italy also lost Eritrea, Somaliland, and the biggest prize of all, Libya. Then came King Idris, followed by the army coup in 1969 and the world's biggest terrorist, Mohammar Khadafy. When he came to power, he called the bluff of the major oil companies which had previously dictated prices and distribution. They did not stand together as they should have, because they were too greedy. Khadafy proved that Libya's strength was not her own power, but the weakness of others. The members of OPEC were not too happy with this upstart, but Khadafy had the nerve and guts to defy everyone, particularly the Western powers, and led the way to the nationalization of the oil wells and whatever industries were foreign-controlled. Libya, thanks to Khadafy and the support of Syria and Iran, became the center of the world's terrorism. This now leads me to the Seven Sisters and the Arab World.

The Seven Sisters are Exxon, Gulf, Texaco, SOCAL, Mobil, British Petroleum, and Shell. For years, the Sisters told the Arab countries what to do and the Arabs were glad to get ten to eighty cents per barrel. They became conglomerates, monopolizing the production and distribution by products and sales. They were above all government. After shortages caused by the Arab-Israeli wars and with the prices generally rising, the Arabs learned from the oil conglomerates. Eventually, the

OPEC was formed by these producers. It became a question of nationalization or participation, and the Sisters chose participation. This then became a marriage between the sovereign oil producers and the oil companies. They both contrived to create shortages and boost prices. The question of loyalty to what country became a reality.

During the shortages, the companies were told by OPEC to distribute the supply equally to the world. The United States was not a favored country and the national security was threatened. The loyalty, it is noted, was where they made their money. Both the Arabs, particularly the Sisters, produced record-breaking profits.

Enrico Mattei successfully fought the Seven Sisters. He was head of the Italian state-controlled AGIP. He worked with the Arabs in developing new sources to safeguard Italy's supply of oil. He hurt the Sisters so much that it was rumored that his plane was sabotaged when it crashed in Sicily, killing the man who really beat them.

There are nine countries on the Arabian peninsula. Six have oil, lots of oil, while the other two, North Yemen and South Yemen, have none. Saudi Arabia, Iraq, Kuwait, Bahrain, Qatar, United Arab Emirates, and Oman are the big oil producers.

King Abd Al-Aziz Ibn Saud of Saudi Arabia signed a historic agreement in 1933 with an American oil company to extract oil from the desert sands of Saudi Arabia for a couple of chestfuls of gold coins. The king was delighted. The Great Depression had severely drained the royal exchequer. In granting the concession, he had nothing to lose. He cared not for oil as he had no idea as to its potential. The king prayed that this worthless sand would perhaps yield water in sufficient quantities to wet his arid land and raise crops that could somehow feed his nomadic subjects.

On 1928, Standard Oil of California (SOCAL) acquired a concession on the Persian Gulf island of Bahrain. In the meantime, Ibn Saud was unapproachable until a 73 year-old American millionaire, Charles R. Crane, heir to a family fortune that manufactured baths, sinks and toilets, broke down the barrier. He was persistent and the king finally agreed to meet him in Jidda. After a sumptuous banquet, the king asked Crane to supply him with a list of names of engineers and surveyors who could possibly find a source of underground water. Soon after, he sent a list from which the king chose one at random, Karl Twitchell.

Twitchell was a mining engineer from Vermont. The king took a ready liking to him. He informed his majesty that the oil recently found in Bahrain could be in the same geological strata found in Saudi Arabia. Through Twitchell's efforts, SOCAL was able to negotiate an agreement. At this point, Harry St. John Philby became SOCAL's representative. The initial payments to the king were a pittance. He received an advance payment of 30,000 and the first year's rent of 5,000 (English pounds) for the exclusive rights to drill oil. Three years of repeated frustration forced SOCAL to sell half-ownership to Texaco for $21 million. Max Steineke, their chief geologist, was confident that there was oil in the ground. In one final effort, his most promising well went down to 4,320 feet and got its reward. The well flowed at the rate of 3,800 barrels a day. Because of the outbreak of World War II in 1939, the flow of oil was delayed. However, in 1948, it turned into a bonanza. The flow went from 21 million barrels to 143 million barrels a year, with the production increasing at the rate of twenty percent. It was not unexpected.

The Arab mind began to figure that the nation producing the oil was entitled to a bigger share of the profits. The Seven Sisters eventually became the Arabian American Oil Company (ARAMCO). The Arabs were not happy with the pricing, which was determined by foreign oil companies that controlled the concessions throughout the Middle East. The Seven Sisters settled prices in conjunction with one another and in total disregard of the oil countries whose oil they drew. The major oil-producing countries (Saudi Arabia, Kuwait, Iran, Iraq, and Venezuela) created the Organization of Petroleum Exporting Countries, OPEC. They immediately started to flex their muscles. To this, the president of ARAMCO, Bob Brougham, stated, "We don't recognize this organization of outsiders." This was a major error.

Ahmad Zaki Yamani, a Harvard-educated lawyer born in Mecca, took over as Saudi Arabia's oil minister. He played hard with the price-fixing Seven Sisters. The turning point for OPEC came in October of 1973 when Egypt went to war with Israel. Suddenly, oil became a political weapon of unexpected clout. Meeting in Vienna, OPEC proposed raising the price of oil from $3 to $5 a barrel. The oil companies balked, offering only a 15 percent increase. Two weeks later, the United States announced a massive appropriation of $2.2 billion in aid to Israel. This was the straw that broke the camel's back. The

Arabs were outraged, naturally siding with Egypt. They declared a worldwide embargo on oil. The result was an oil panic that changed the economic structure of the civilized world. What the oil companies spurned at $5 a barrel suddenly looked like a bargain. The price of oil jumped to $11 and then to $17 a barrel.

The majority of people who follow our news media today must surely be confused as to the rapid-fire developments in this part of the world.

The Arab World consists of Egypt, Jordan, Syria, Lebanon, Iraq, Saudi Arabia, Algeria, Morocco, Tunis, Sudan, and Libya. These are Mohammeden countries. Who was Mohammed? He was born in 570 A.D. in Mecca, and was first a merchant, then a prophet. He received the Word of God in his fortieth year, 610 A.D. Having little success in the first decade, he went to Medina where he organized and the religion spread rapidly.

Mohammed taught that Christian and Jew should be tolerated, but not treated as equals. "God's design had been partially revealed to the prophets of the Old Testament and to Jesus. He, Mohammed, received the full revelation."

Islam is a reformist religion and "the perfection of previous Jewish and Christian misinformation of the truth." It means, "Submission of the will to Allah." It is impossible to think of the Arabs without Islam or Islam without the Arabs. Islam is the majority religion in the Middle East; the minority being Christian, Jew, Baha'is, Druzes, etc. There are five hundred million Moslems in the world. They do not drink alcohol or use tobacco.

Arab knowledge helped preserve culture while Europe was in the Dark Ages. The Arabs excelled in medicine, optics, astronomy, mathematics and science. In fact, they developed the science of algebra. *Palermo was the jewel of the Arab world.* It was here that the potentates built their palaces and developed their knowledge while Europe slept and did not awaken until the Renaissance. Their glorious period ended with internal bickering, followed by the invasions of the Mongols, Turks, Western powers, and Arab subservience.

There are 21 Arab nations in the world. With Iran, which is non-Arab, they are all Moslem totaling 222 million people. Their common enemy is Israel with a population of four million. Tiny Israel is a powerful unifying force, and a surprisingly divisive issue. It is a blessing — and a curse. Israel's existence demonstrates how ineffective the Arabs have been. No Arab country has met the test of political maturity. Regular, honest elections are not held because of the Israeli-Arab tension. This also favors the autocratic Arab rulers.

Both Arabs and Jews are Semites. The main issue is control of land and Jerusalem's holy places. Jerusalem, now capitol of Israel, is sacred to the Jews, Moslems and Christians. In five wars since Israel became a nation in 1948, it has convinced most Arabs that it will not be driven into the sea.

The Arab mentality is "The friend of my enemy is my enemy." He also believes that "Democracy, American style, is viewed as akin to decadence, allowing 'rabble' to dictate the shape and content of a government." Americans are viewed as easy marks for souvenir sellers, but they are also respected for the Arab schools, clinics and research centers they sponsor.

Chapter 50

Israel and the Jews

I was always interested in the Jewish people and their struggle to become a united nation. Being brought up with Jews in Brooklyn, I felt that we were all immigrants and neighbors who had the same problems. We were a downtrodden minority and it was a struggle to survive.

The Jews have suffered much in their long history. You can hate them or you can love them. With a few exceptions, I can say that I have always held them in high esteem. They earned their new homeland in Israel. (Actually, they returned to what was once their homeland.) Recently, Israel celebrated its fortieth anniversary as a united nation. Some say that at forty, it is a nation in turmoil.

On May 14, 1948, Great Britain gave up its mandate over Palestine. England had seized control over this region in 1920 after the defeat of the Turks in World War I with the collapse of the Ottoman empire. Over the next twenty-five years, Great Britain maintained an uneasy balance between Arab nationalism and the increasing desire of Jews to return to their historic homeland. After World War II, the survivors of the Holocaust demanded a haven from persecution. The ancient dream of a Jewish state in Palestine was rekindled, but thwarted by Arab insistence that Jewish immigration be limited. The British were caught in the middle and were ready to accept any agreement, so they let the United Nations in Flushing, New York fight it out. It lasted seven months as the Jews demanded that Palestine be partitioned into separate Jewish and Arab states. The Arabs objected to any partition. Neither side could prevail with the support of a two-thirds majority of the United Nations. World leaders tried to work out a compromise. England and France warned the Jews that they could not win a military conflict, but Jewish leaders disagreed. Abba Eban, a 73 year-old former foreign minister for Israel said, "The trouble with the Egyptian army is that the officers were too fat while the soldiers were too thin."

The Jewish lobby played political hardball while the Arabs had no lobby at all. They had little diplomatic experience and there was also a great deal of jealousy between them. The Syrians stated that they would never recognize a strong Jewish state. Eban further stated: "We knew that the Moslems would be against us. Even the Vatican State was not willing to recognize a Jewish state."

The biggest surprise came when the Soviet bloc suddenly supported the partition. President Harry S. Truman strongly supported a homeland for the Jews. Except for England, most of the western European nations joined in voting for partition. Opposed to partition were five Arab countries as well as India, Pakistan, Yugoslavia, Turkey, and countries with large Moslem populations.

The Arabs proposed that the new Jewish state be established in Tanzania, an area in the heart of Africa. The Jews needed 32 countries to support the creation of a new Jewish state. In the final manuevering, Haiti, Siam and Chile made their moves.

In the meantime, Eban was concerned over the delaying tactics and the many speeches, so in an expression of utter frustration he shouted, "What the hell am I doing here? Iceland deciding the fate of my people?" After meeting with Eban, Thor Thors, representing Iceland, stood before the assembly and demanded a decision with no more procrastination. General Assembly President Oswaldo Aranha began the roll call on the partition of Palestine. At its conclusion, Aranha announced that "Partition was approved with 33 votes to 13, and ten abstentations." One by one the Arab delegates, with wounded pride and honor, denounced the decision and walked out of the General Assembly.

On May 15, 1948, Israel declared its independence. The next day, the armies of Egypt, Jordan, Lebanon, Iraq and Syria invaded the new state of Israel. This was inevitable. The newly created state of Israel, disorganized as it was , fought with the courage of lions, remembering the Holocaust where millions of Jews died in the gas chambers and furnaces as they were determined not to let this ever happen again. Israel fought for its new homeland and soundly defeated the invaders, the Arabs, who clearly stated, "We will drive them into the sea, the Mediterranean Sea. Palestine belongs to us."

Eight years later in 1956, the Sinai War was fought, followed by the Six Day War when, by right of conquest, the Israelis seized the west banks of the Jordan, Golan Heights, and the Sinai peninsula. Egypt, blistering on the loss of the Sinai, attacked the Israelis on Yom Kippur in 1963. Again, they were soundly defeated. Israel, however, returned the Sinai desert to Egypt including the Gaza Strip. Egypt did not want this troublesome spot nor did the other Arabs. Today, it is the sore spot almost without a solution.

After the fortieth year as a nation, Israel is faced with many new problems. Can she overcome these that now threaten to divide this proud nation of determined people? They now have a leadership crisis. The days of the giants, David Ben-Gurion, Golda Meir, Moshe Dayan, and Menachem Begin, are gone. The men who run Israel today are of smaller stature and less inspiring. Israel is here to stay. We cannot overlook this strategic country or the nation of Israel. Somehow, they will find a leader.

Today, the Jew is an important fixture in our everyday lives. I have loved them and despised them, but all in all, they are a great people who have suffered much and have been scattered all over the world. The "Diaspora" is no more. Now they have their own home. It is a world surrounded by Arabs — four million Jews surrounded by thirty-five million Arabs.

The Jews founded their state with the blessing of the United Nations. When this was contested by force, especially by the Egyptians, they established themselves by right of conquest as had been done before by the Turks, Crusaders, Arabs, Romans, Greeks, Egyptians, Babylonians, and others before them to the dawn of history.

Herzl, the founder of Zionism, sacrificed his life for an ideal. "It is amazing how many people now pretend to be his friend. He had a dream and he paid his price." These were the words of Clemenceau who further stated, "It was his own people he fought." Israel was founded on May 15, 1948, forty years after Herzel's death.

The Jewish community in America is under seige. On an international level, there is the threat to Israel and the plight of the Russian Jews. There is increasing anti-semitism, the concern over Black-Jewish relationships, the internal problems of intermarriage, alienation of the young, and uncertainty with Judaism and the Jewish identity. The divided Jews in America present a problem for the future. They are traditionally Democrat, but voted for Richard Nixon based on his promise to aid Israel.

The Blacks turned against the Jews following the Yom Kippur War in 1963. They sided with the Arabs because of the color line. The Jews in Russia faced a questionable future. This, however, is being resolved. Most of the Jewish concentration is in Lithuania, Polish Russia, and the Ukraine. They are now free to travel to Israel. They have come by the thousands.

The West Bank and Golan Heights are Israel's security. There should be no question about that. If Israel is to survive, there can be no compromise. My feeling is that the Jewish nation will prevail. They have no place to go, but Israel.

Chapter 51

The Emerald Isle

The first impression approaching Shannon Airport is the greenness of the grass. I have never seen grass so green and so attractive.

Joan and I checked in at the famous Dromoland Castle at Newmarket-on-Fergus and had a room in the main round turret. Pat Clark, as Irish as Irish can be, was our chauffeur for our week's stay in Ireland. He awaited to take us on our first tour of Galway Bay. However, an incident occurred that almost brought our trip to an end. While Joan was descending the very steep stairs from our second floor suite, she tripped and almost went down the full twenty-two steps. Fortunately, I was able to stop her fall by being at the right place at the right time. She suffered only a very slight swelling.

Galway Bay was interesting to me because this was one of the points where the Spanish Armada, following its annihilation by the British Navy, landed its many hundreds of Spaniards who were able to swim or paddle ashore. Most of them remained, settled down, and eventually married the blond, blue-eyed Irish beauties that gave to the world the so-called "Black Irish." As a matter of fact, Eamon de Valera, one of the great leaders of Ireland, was a Black Irish. The combination of the dark Spaniard and the light-colored Irish girl produced some of the most beautiful of Irish beauties.

Dromoland Castle was made famous by the O'Brien clan, whose portraits adorned the walls. I didn't sleep well that first night as I had nightmares of the dashing O'Brien clan in their armor running up and down the halls destroying their hated rivals. I'm not sure whether they were the Houlihans or the

McGillicuttys.

I was greatly impressed with the Irish countryside. The farmland was rich in pasture, ideal for cattle and dairy, and, of course, lots of sheep. I immediately saw the similarity of Ireland and my native Sicily. We saw the oldtime Irish farmer plowing his field with a one-horse plow, while in a neighboring field, a young Irish farmer drove a modern tractor pulling modern plowing and cultivation equipment. Another similarity was the Irishman driving a one-horse, two-wheel cart with several cans of milk going to the creamery. In the same breath, there was the young man driving a semi-truck loaded with many cans of milk.

We stopped overnight at the Dunloe Castle. Because of the heavy influx of German tourists, we got the impression that we were in West Germany instead of the Emerald Isle. The language spoken was German and the food had a German flavor.

One of the reasons we went to Ireland was to find out about Joan's grandfather's birthplace. We were searching for a turn in the road called Kilmacow, located south of Kilkenny. Her grandfather's name was Costello. Well, we soon found ourselves in "Costello country." It seemed that every farmhouse we stopped at was named Costello. We were finally directed to this pub, which was all there was to Kilmacow. Our driver was well acquainted with the area and we soon found out that the pub was where Grandpa Costello, like all the other Costellos, spent his free time. We entered this historic meeting place, introduced ourselves, and soon found nine young men all named Costello. The only woman in the pub was the bartender and I quickly named her Molly McGuire. She kept bringing the dark stout ale, which had a rather bitter taste. After the third or fourth one, the taste left me.

Everyone was employed at Kilmacow. There was a big meat-packing plant close by that was working two shifts a day packing beef for shipment to the United States. In 1973, there was a beef shortage in the U.S. and who was supplying the deficit, but poor little Ireland and Israel. However, Ireland was no longer the poor little Ireland of the past. We were told that the pay was good, families owned one or more cars, the homes were well-equipped with the latest gadgets, and people were eating well. In other words, there seemed to be an era of modest prosperity. They could not have cared less about North Ireland.

We sat around the Costello clan for about four hours. After

sitting around with the black ale flowing freely, there came a time when nature called for relief. Having learned where the little boys'room was, I became rather puzzled when I entered this small 10 x 10 room with nothing but tin walls and a gutter. The plumbing was non-existent and I was forced by necessity to face the tin wall and allow whatever to flow down the gutter. I thought I had already spent too much time trying to figure out the Kilmacow plumbing system and returned to my seat around the barrel. I turned to one of the Costellos and inquired as to how they flushed out the system. He did not reply to me immediately, but about ten minutes later I heard a swish followed by another swish. On the third swish, he finally gave me my answer. Without raising his head, he calmly told me that "the plumbing was now working." I gathered at this point that Molly McGuire, besides tending bar, periodically filled a bucket or two of water and quite professionally watered down the tin wall.

When it was time to leave, we all promised to keep in touch by correspondence. We raised a glass for Ireland and we toasted one another for the good old U.S.A. where the plumbing was just a bit different.

Dublin became our headquarters as we stayed at the fashionable Gresham Hotel on O'Connell Street. (Why the cathedral bell started bonging every morning at 6 a.m. remained a mystery.) We enjoyed Dublin with its Trinity College, ancient library, the headquarters of the Irish Sweepstakes, and the Dublin horse show grounds (Ascot).

Perhaps one of the most notable things while passing through the various towns was the thorough Irishness of the store names and places of business. All we saw was Lynch, O'Reilly, O'Houlahan, McCormack, O'Leary, but never a Rosenbaum or a Bacigalupi. As an aside, Joan's solution to the Irish cooking would be to import some good Neopolitan, Florentine and Sicilian cooks, changing their names from "Chelli" to "Kelly" and "Romano" to "O'Roman," and coming out with Irish spaghetti, Irish pizza, or some good Irish ravioli.

In my research on Irish history, I came across various clues as to the origins of the Irish. The province of Elam in what is now Iran-Iraq was in constant warfare with the Babylonians under Hammurabi, the famous emperor. The Elams were eventually driven away. It is said that they migrated through Egypt, North Africa, and eventually found their place in Ireland. As the centuries rolled on, they came back and settled in Egypt. There is an old song that was popular during the Tin Pan Alley days in the Roaring Twenties that dealt with the "Hooligans and the Dooligans." Perhaps it had something to do with the Irish immigration.

> "It must have been the Irish who built those pyramids,
>   for no one else could carry up the bricks.
> It must have been a Doyle who dug the River Nile,
>   for no one but an Irishman could fight the crocodiles.
>
> I think those micks were Turks, Mohammedans
>   and Ghurks.
> They speak of Irish Turkey till today.
>
> Cleopatra was a Colleen who came from Connemara,
> She lost her nationality while roaming in the Sahara,
> So all the Hooligans and the Dooligans must have
>   been Egyptians long ago.
>
> And when Moses went to Egypt and saw those
>   Irish faces,
> He took the name of Flanagan and changed it to oasis.
> So all the Hooligans and the Dooligans must have
>   been Egyptians long ago."

Lo and behold, it is now 1988, just fifteen years later and what a change has taken place. Ireland is in serious economic trouble. Back in 1973, this beautiful land was booming industrially and economically. Now she is hurting badly. There is a serious exodus of youth from this fair land with no work or opportunity for them, particularly the educated. Unemployment has passed the twenty-percent level. The brunt of it is borne by the young. Ireland has the youngest population in Europe due to its high birth rate.

In one year, 31,000 people have emigrated and the number is rapidly increasing. In one small community, not a single resident in a block-long row of houses was employed. They were all on welfare. Most of the exodus is to the United States, Canada, Europe, and particularly the United Kingdom and West Germany. What has caused this great turnabout? What has happened to the large-scale investments by foreign countries during the booming seventies? Is it the leaderless government? The Reverend John Gavin remarked on the Irish situation: "Ireland is like a rudderless boat. It isn't completely sunk, but it is damned near sunk."

Before I close this chapter on the Emerald Isle, I must say a few words on this beautiful, but unlucky, land that has suffered so much under the yoke of its oppressor over the many decades. We must go back to the year 1600 when Ireland was a rebellious English colony. The English Parliament approved the Articles of Plantation in 1610. The English secured the land by planting loyal citizens to the Crown. They brought in Scottish Presbyterians to northern Ireland while the remainder was occupied by the English. This method was cheaper than maintaining a garrison. It was just plain confiscation. As a matter of fact, in 1714, the Catholics owned only seven percent of the land.

The plantation owners fortified their holdings against the deprived Irish peasants, who had been reduced to a nation of serfs constantly facing starvation, unemployment, and a bleak future. What generally happens to people who are confined to a ghetto-like existence? They fought. In 1641, thousands of Protestants were slaughtered. Then came Oliver Cromwell in 1649 when he killed two thousand Catholics in Drogheda and two thousand more in Wexford, not to mention his reign of terror throughout the land. Survivors were shipped to the West Indies. Brutality was shown on both sides and morality was blown to the winds.

In 1688, the natives joined James II, the ex-Catholic King of England, who was supported by the French troops. He was defeated at the Battle of the Boyne in 1688 by William of Orange, the Dutchman who deposed him. James fled to France as did thousands of Irishmen from their native soil. The conquest of Ireland was now complete. Parliament quickly enacted the new Penal Laws, which banned Catholics from holding public office, working in the legal profession, voting, teaching, maintaining the schools, joining the military, and buying land. Every year on July 12th, the Battle of the Boyne is celebrated in Protestant North Ireland by the Orangemen, an organization that claims over 100,000 members.

This unfortunate land and these plucky people were subjected to the potato famine of 1840, one of the first of many such scourges that ravished the Emerald Isle. Many of the Irish fled to Belfast for work. It was noted for its shipyards and many industries. Quite a few were fortunate to get jobs there, although they were subject to long hours, low pay, and miserable working conditions.

In 1916, the Easter Rebellion took place in Dublin and they

were crushed with heavy losses. In 1919, the Irish Republican Army (IRA) and the Sinn Feiners came alive. Many of the IRA wound up in jail. There was terrorism on both sides. The Protestants drove the Catholics from their jobs in Belfast. There seemed to be no end to this senseless fighting.

In 1921, the Republic of Ireland was born while in North Ireland, Ulster was created. The terror continues. Only time will tell if there is ever to be a united Ireland. Perhaps the answer lies in patience. The change will come slowly as each new generation learns to live with each other, and as economic and employment conditions improve. The Irish have tried it before, they can and will do it again. This time, they will march in peace — together.

Chapter 52

The Sleeping Giant and a Typical Mexican-American Family

There are two countries with a common border. One is fabulously wealthy and the other is poor. That country is Mexico.

Before the *Mayflower* landed in New England (Plymouth Rock) and the Dutch came to New Amsterdam (New York), the Spanish explorers, known as the 16th century *conquistadore*, baptized this vast southwest into Christianity. The early Spanish recognized the similarity between the old country and the new world. They brought the seeds appropriate to this virgin country including citrus, nuts, dates, olives and wheat. They also brought the secrets of irrigation for this dry, fertile land. Horses and livestock were transported in large numbers.

The greatest trademark of the early Spanish was the naming of our states, cities, rivers, mountains, and streets in honor of their saints, which remain with us today. How can you translate such names as Sierra Nevada, Santa Barbara, Sacramento, San Francisco, Los Angeles? It is impossible because there is no translation.

We, Americans, cannot overlook the fact that it was the *Mestizo* (part Indian, part Spanish) and the Indian who did the digging, planting, pruning, and the dirty work during the transformation that took place for the three centuries that represented the Spanish occupation.

Mexico proclaimed its independence in 1821. By this time, non-Hispanics began coming into this new territory. They adopted Hispanic ways, so there was compliance and co-existence. However, this peaceful transformation was short-lived. The United States was steadily unfolding its future and

Mexico just happened to be in the way. The fireworks began as the Americans annexed Texas in 1845, leading to a war against Mexico. History must judge this development as less than noble. The American victory yielded a spectacular bounty. In 1848, a peace treaty was signed and Mexico, which was larger than the United States, became smaller. In the Treaty of Guadalupe Hidalgo, Mexico signed away nearly half of all its land. They lost and the Americans gained Texas, New Mexico, Arizona, California, Nevada and Utah by the stroke of a pen.

Defeat left bitterness. Mexicans who ventured into what once was their land became an immigrant people. In fact, they became foreigners in the new American southwest. Although the Treaty of 1848 guaranteed American citizenship to the Mexicans already in the southwest, they no longer governed the land they had named and settled. Even wealthy ranchers lost control of their land as their property was sold, parceled and gone. Confiscation is a dirty word. This happened in too many cases.

We learned much from the Mexicans. Much of its colorful vocabulary found its way into English: siesta, bonanza, fiesta, rodeo. Then, there was mesa, arroyo, canyon, and rio just to name a few. The Spanish sense of leisure and celebration took hold.

The other side of the story of the Mexicans in the southwest was often violent and involved rape, murder, robbery, and lynchings by *bandidos* and vigilantes. According to Richard Rodriguez, a writer, lecturer and author of the book, *Hunger of Memory*, the *gringo* was mean, pale, and quick as a snake. The "greaser" seemed lazy, superstitious and dirty.

The Mexicans were never a free people. They became accustomed to dictatorship, corruption, greed, and mismanagement. In this respect, the few who were in control prospered, and the majority suffered in poverty, unemployment, and lack of hope for the future in their own country. Where else was there to go but to the United States, which was once their country.

They came by the millions. All they had to do was cross the Rio Grande. Most of the time, it cost them everything they owned. Many died and many succeeded. The wetbacks, illegals, and green card holders were welcomed by the farmers who needed them for stoop labor work, which the Americans could not do. The Mexicans had no choice, for it meant work and money. Poverty and unemployment lured them across the border. They came to build our country, the railroads, highways, mines, fields, and the sweatshops. The cities became the centers of crime for those who could not find work and were forced to use illegal means as a way of survival.

No one can deny the Mexican contribution to this country. During World War II, 350,000 Mexican-Americans went off to fight in Europe and the Pacific. There are many famous Mexican-Americans including Ricardo Montalban, Anthony Quinn, and Pancho Gonzales just to name a few. Cesar Chavez had done much for the Mexican farm laborer. He believed in non-violent opposition to those who kept the Mexican farm laborer on his knees. He organized non-violent strikes for an increase in wages received and better working conditions. No longer were the hard-working peasant farm laborers treated as non-human beings. As a result of Chavez's efforts, they gained respect and fair treatment.

The Mexican is a fun-loving person. He is friendly and very family-oriented. His greatest consolation is his family and his child is the hope for the future. It is these children who will develop in the next few generations and that is when the sleeping giant will rise up and demand his rightful title and place in our society as an American. It is only through these coming generations that he can elect his own kind to political office, advance in business and technology, and say, ''Wait a minute. You must listen to me.'' When this time comes, the politicians will come charging in to seek their support. It will be a whole new ballgame.

I will tell the story of a typical Mexican-American family, the Kottas, who became a part of my early California life. William Kotta came from a German background and settled in Mexico. He met and married a native of Mexico, Gregoria, who was of French, Spanish and Indian ancestry. Will, their oldest son, married Mary Scafidi, and it was through her that I came to know the Kotta family. My brother, Frank, was in business in San Francisco prior to my first visit in 1925 when I enrolled in a postgraduate course at the University of California at Davis. He knew the Scafidi family in Brooklyn; thus, began my connection in San Francisco when I met Will and Mary Kotta.

''Poppa'' and Gregoria Kotta lived in a flat on Broadway near Mason Street. At that time, the area on Broadway west of Columbus Avenue was mainly occupied by Italians and Hispanics. (Today, it is part of Chinatown.) Whenever I was in the city, my first visit was with the Kotta family. We ate, sang, played poker, and enjoyed happy evenings. As the years went by, I married and eventually moved to San Francisco. Josephine, my first wife, became very close friends with Mary.

During this time, we met many Mexican-Americans. We lived on Thirtieth Avenue in the Sunset District for eighteen years. The Kottas had a home not too far away. There was an interchange of homes during the many years of our acquaintanceship, entertainment that is. Will was an accomplished pianist. Together with Dan and Lolita Arzac, we joined in the musical and fun weekends. Dan Arzac was also an accomplished pianist, so they both played duets while everyone sang. There was a mixture of Neopolitan and Sicilian folksongs and operas, only to be balanced by the warm, romantic Mexican ballads. David "Dink" Kotta, Will's brother, specialized in jazz and songs of the day. The piano was seldom idle.

Will Kotta was office manager of Coty's in San Francisco and Dink retired from a high position with the telephone company. His other brothers included Henry, who was in real estate, and Ray, a top civil engineer and an all-American in football at St. Mary's College. The youngest was Gus, now retired and living in Millbrae. He had held a top-rank position with a cash register company and was a former all-state basketball player at San Jose State University. During their earlier years, Dink and Henry starred as basketball players for the Salesian Boys' Club in San Francisco's North Beach.

There was nothing real outstanding in the lives of the Kottas except that they were part of the American mainstream. Whenever their presence was felt, they were accepted, respected and well-liked. They didn't marry Hispanics, but girls of Irish, German, English or Italian descent. They, too, realized and were greatly concerned about the "mañana" type of Hispanics. By the example of their everyday lives, they converted many Hispanics to the American way of life.

The Hispanic problem will go away only if we have more people like the Kottas and the Arzacs. Now, we have the Asians. Together with the Blacks and the many other minorities, America will become greater by the tolerance for one another. There is room for all of us.

Chapter 53

Events and People in My Lifetime — Part II

I have searched for answers to many questions that appear to be unanswered. I can't help it. That's my nature.

What really bothered me was why the Bolshevik Revolution in 1914 was permitted and encouraged to expand its evil teachings throughout Europe and later under Communism throughout the world. It is true that Russia suffered much under the Czars. The Cossacks were ruthless and the peasants never had a chance.

I was impressed by a book by Anthony Sutton and others who studied the Bolshevik Revolution who did something about it. They put their research and a gathering of facts in writing.

Perhaps I should start this dissertation under the title, "Wall Street and the Bolshevik Revolution." The Wall Street bankers were definitely linked with the Bolshevik Revolution. The American Red Cross mission to Russia in 1917 contained more financiers than medical doctors. They were more interested in the future Russian market and didn't care whether they were dealing with the Kerensky government or the Bolsheviks. The bankers also didn't care less for the victims of war or the revolution. They subverted the nation's laws in order to import Russian gold. Some Wall Streeters were leading advocates of the Soviet cause in the backroom of politics while supporting the anti-Bolshevik movement. One American financier even donated a million dollars to the Bolsheviks during the first shaky days of their regime.

Western technological assistance to the Soviet Union helped create a military apparatus which threatened the survival of the western world; thus, recalling Lenin's cynical prediction, "The Capitalists will fight amongst themselves over who would sell the Communists the rope with which the Communists would hang them."

President Woodrow Wilson was in sympathy with the Soviet form of government as that best suited for the Russian people. The Bolshevik Revolution could have been nipped in the bud in 1917 had it not been for the Wall Street interests. The American International Corporation was headquartered at 120 Broadway in New York City. This group was heavily financed for the purpose of fomenting revolutions in many parts of the world in the interests of American business.

Wall Street generally donated to both sides, fighting Communism and encouraging it. Then, the inevitable happened. Peace began to break out all over. The Communist ideology, which was spreading its tentacles in all parts of the suffering world, was beginning to spring leaks and signs of its own decadence due to its many failures and a complete breakdown of its internal economic front. It affected those who no longer wanted to deprive themselves of the necessities of life. The western world took this for granted and enjoyed it. Along came Mikhail Gorbachev, who embarked on his policy of *perestroika* (restructuring) and *glasnost* (more open discussion).

Before we get into these two changes, it must be remembered that since the beginning of the Bolshevik-Communist Revolution, the Soviet leadership always talked about changing the economy, but shrank from any fundamental change. Instead, they tried to rescue themselves by begging, borrowing and stealing everything they could from the West.

In 1921, after the Bolsheviks reduced their land to ruin, Lenin proclaimed a new economic policy of "co-habitation with capitalism." He made it clear within the Communist councils that "as soon as we are strong enough to overthrow capitalism, we shall seize it by the throat." He held out the big carrot to the western world. The West thought it was good business and Lenin got what he wanted — aviation, steel industries, textile plants, automotive and tractor industries, and just about everything that the Soviets did not have. Once the foreigners were no longer needed, they were thrown out or in some cases, jailed on charges of industrial espionage.

The West never learned its lesson. In 1970, the Soviets, with their *detente*, again opened up the vast, untapped Soviet market. <u>By 1976, Westerners had erected nearly one thousand factories across the Soviet Republic. So gullible was the West that the Free World banks advanced billions of dollars which paved the way for the Soviets to become the world power that it is today.</u> As a prime example, German, British, Italian, and American firms built the world's largest truck factory on the Kama River. With their Machiavellian thinking, the Soviets undertook the greatest military buildup in peacetime history. We can blame ourselves for what eventually took place. They pushed into Africa, Central America and Southeast Asia. Then, in 1979 they invaded Afghanistan. <u>The trucks carrying Soviet troops and weapons that murdered thousands of civilians *rolled out of the Kama River plant*.</u>

Every uprising and almost every civil war in all parts of the world were financed and supplied with military arms. The use of Cubans as mercenaries in the Angolan War was bankrolled by the Soviets. In the meantime, there developed a restless movement amongst the people in the Soviet Republic and in their many satellite countries still ruled by the iron hand of this communistic society.

The struggle for supremacy had begun to take its toll. Edward Shevardnadze, the Soviet foreign minister, had stated that forty percent of the gross national product went towards the military or as it is now called, defense. By contrast, the United States' figure for the same purpose is almost six percent of the gross national product. Billions of dollars went to support Cuba, Vietnam, Nicaragua, Angola, Ethiopia, and the many other spheres of Marxist domination. Suddenly, the mighty Soviet empire found itself engulfed in economic mismanagement. The collective farm system was a disaster. Millions of tons of grain had to be imported from the West. The U.S.S.R. could no longer feed its people. Food was rationed in many areas. Even in Moscow, milk, fresh meat, fruits and vegetables are often unavailable. It was said that Soviet sausages were so repulsive that cats refused to eat them.

Light industry was decaying with over forty percent of its machinery obsolete. Everyday products that we so freely enjoy and take for granted here are either scarce or non-existent such as aspirin, toothpaste, vacuum cleaners, refrigerators, etc. Only nine out of a hundred Soviets had telephones. The quality of whatever they produced was poor. Spare parts for tractors and power machinery were non-existent. Soviet television sets were so poorly made that they burst into flames. While they received free medical care, the Soviets acknowledged that it was woefully deficient. In Moscow, according to the minister of health, only twelve of their hospitals met modern sanitation standards. Many outlying hospitals lacked not only hot water, but even rudimentary sewage treatment. The list was too long to continue.

Does all this give us a clue as to why Gorbachev was seeking a bailout? Indeed, it does. The Soviets could no longer continue on this self-destructive course. That is why they took the initiative to reduce arms and slowly withdrew from Afghanistan, Angola and the many troubled spots throughout the world where they sought to spread Communism. They are now paying the price they face in their own country — economic disaster.

Of course, we should cooperate in reducing armaments, military build-ups, and the threat of world suicide. But let us not be too naive and make the same mistake that President Woodrow Wilson made when he urged the world, through the League of Nations, to disarm after we came out triumphant in World War I. As it turned out, the only nation to completely disarm was our beloved United States. The other powers did the opposite, particularly Hitler, and the end result was World War II.

Yes, peace is just around the corner. What a glorious word. By the grace of God, I hope I will live long enough to see peace in the world.

Perhaps this peace may come about soon. The Soviet is no more. Russia and the many new republics created from the former Communistic Soviet Federation are struggling to become democracies. The road to becoming a democratic republic will not be easy. Peace in our time? Perhaps.

Chapter 54

Tidbits and Machiavelli

My mind keeps wandering about certain people who left imprints on the world during my lifetime.

Richard O'Connor, in his illuminating book, supplied much fuel to the fire. He pointed out that the pillars of society and the financial world were also human - notably, William Rockefeller, father of John D., who deserted his wife and family. John D. Rockefeller, controlling the vast Standard Oil empire, bought out those who opposed him. He was a strong Baptist. His gifts, although tainted, became sanctified when given to the Baptist Church.

High Episcopalians believed that "God has designated that wealth is for Episcopalians." Commodore Vanderbilt believed that "a secret shared by three persons meant 111 persons were in on it." The Third World now supplies the cheap labor for the manufacturing of capitalistic goods. My inquisitive mind keeps wandering.

We speak of Machiavellianism, the diabolical use of his name. Surely, most people become a bit confused when this name is mentioned. Who was Machiavelli? What did he do? What did he stand for? Why do we use his name today, although he was a product of the 15th century?

I will attempt to give a thumbnail description of this unusual man. Niccolo Machiavelli was one of the most brilliant and versatile intellects of the human Renaissance. He was born in Florence on May 3, 1469 and was employed in diplomatic missions to other countries. When the Medici returned to power in Florence, Machiavelli lost his position, was imprisoned and tortured. In his retirement, he wrote *The Prince*. His motive was patriotic. By the exclusion of moral consideration in the treatment of politics even in his own country, his name became a synonym for all that is diabolical in public and private policy. The book remains a most vivid and suggestive picture of political conditions in Italy of the Renaissance. Some have beheld in it, a manual for tyrants.

Machiavelli was sincere, though too supple a Republican, and by no means desired the universal prevalence of tyranny throughout Italy. His aim was how to build up a principality capable of expelling a foreigner and restoring the independence of Italy. With all his faults and oversights, nothing can deprive him of the glory of having been the modern Aristotle in politics, and the first considerable writer who derived a practical philosophy from history and exalted statecraft into a science.

"Politics are outside morality" and "The end justifies the means" are just some of the examples of Machiavellian ideals in *The Prince*. It was the antithesis of the American founding fathers and of Mazzini in Italy. Machiavellianism played a tragic role in Italian life for centuries. His book was a story of the times in his day. Today, many politicians include *The Prince* as a source on which to base their thoughts.

Chapter 55

A Call From a Computer

I was summoned to serve for regular jury duty only to witness a historic event take place on July 14, 1977. For the first time in the history of San Mateo County, all 15 Superior Court judges agreed that a Criminal Grand Jury should be created in addition to the Blue Ribbon Grand Jury, whose members were nominated and selected by the Superior Court judges for the combined civil and criminal matters.

Sitting in the jury assembly room and waiting for my name to be called, the county clerk announced that the first 30 names called would be selected to qualify for the county's first new Criminal Grand Jury. Four hundred names were thrown into a giant computer from which 30 were to be randomly selected. Out of the 30, only 19 would be chosen to serve. A thorough spinning of the bowl holding the 400 names took place. Placing his hand inside, the clerk came up with the first name, my name. After the first 30 were called, the selection of the final 19 to serve on the jury began. I was the third to be chosen, qualified, and became part of the first San Mateo County Criminal Grand Jury.

Superior Court Judge Thomas Jenkins impaneled this first-time Criminal Grand Jury with the powers of investigation and indictment, thus, began an unusual service to the community in which we were to witness some of the most hair-raising, unbelievable, and most exciting situations for which we were to be paid five dollars each day on duty.

Our first assignment was to inspect the county jail. Our immediate reaction to the overcrowded conditions was one of horror and surprise. Cots were full and half the inmates were sleeping on mattresses on the floor. (As we learned later, this is the situation that exists in practically all the prisons in the state.) No wonder crime has jumped to record levels. Here was where a young offender, probably jailed on a minor offense, was thrown into the company of hardened criminals, resulting in the schooling of crime.

The biggest problem facing the county was drugs. Most of the heavy dealing was in the east Palo Alto area, Menlo Park, San Mateo, and Daly City. It was unbelievable how deep in narcotics the community was. Drug raids were headlined in the newspaper week after week.

I developed a great deal of respect for the undercover agents who risked their lives to make an arrest under the most dangerous of circumstances. The jury sat through hours of detailed reports including bacteriological analyses proving that narcotics were involved. The most interesting part, however, was the appearance of the suspects. After several months, we began to notice that the dealers and users were becoming familiar faces. We inquired as to why the same ones were being brought back time and time again. Evidently, the convicted narcotics peddlers were merely getting a slap on the wrist. The judges did not like our inquisitive remarks and we never received any direct answers.

Another issue we raised was the fact that we were never told of a prisoner's past record. We were told to mind our own business. Again, the jury was admonished to judge the suspect on "this case only." No wonder these criminals were back on the streets after serving only a light sentence for their crimes. Some of them, as we later learned, had from several to many convictions.

It seemed that the Grand Jury was faced with all kinds of roadblocks. The most serious of all was best described in an article which appeared in the *San Mateo Times* on March 24, 1978 entitled, "Prosecution Dealt Blow in Drug Case." The story stated:

"The prosecution of fifty-three alleged narcotics dealers named in a secret Grand Jury indictment and arrested last month in what was the biggest coordinated drug bust in San Mateo County was dealt a severe blow Thursday. Superior Court Judge Gerald E. Ragan ruled that each of the suspects is entitled to a post indictment-probable cause 'hearing' to determine if there is enough evidence to bind them over for a trial. The effect of the ruling, according to District Attorney Keith Sorenson, was to 'render the Grand Jury impotent, clog an already crowded criminal calendar, and to jeopardize the safety of undercover officers and informants.' "

The members of the Grand Jury were furious. Deputy District Attorney William Amideo, who was handling many of the drug cases, stated that the Grand Jury issued indictments after only two days of testimony, whereas the "said preliminary hearings" of all 53 suspects could take months. In the final analysis, the District Attorney publicly stated that Judge Ragan's decision rendered our Grand Jury impotent.

We were very unhappy in our efforts to stamp out the drug dealers in San Mateo County. I supposed the reason why this experiment of a Blue Ribbon Criminal Grand Jury lasted only one year was probably because we were too outspoken. The 15 Superior Court judges weren't very thrilled about our inquisitive behavior.

There was another interesting case that came before us dealing with the tampering of automobile odometers. Eight employees of a prominent wholesale auto dealer were accused of rolling back the mileage on the odometers on over a thousand vehicles. They were charged with grand theft and conspiracy. The alleged, operating in San Jose, were involved with at least ten dealers in San Mateo County alone. Evidently, this was a common practice as these were cars sold to the dealers believing that they were being offered with lower mileage to consumers. The indictment must have scared the hell out of other unscrupulous manipulators as the practice seemed to have ended.

This reminds me of a story about my favorite old-time comedians, the Gaylords. The scene took place in a small town in Sicily. Carlo was visiting his friend, Mangiapane, who was trying to sell his Fiat but to no avail. "No one wants to buy my Fiat," he said, "Because it has over 100,000 miles." To this, Carlo replied, "Why don't you go see Roberto at Bacigalupi's garage? He will set your mileage back for a handful of *lire.*" Two months went by and Carlo met up with his friend again. He asked about the Fiat. Roberto, with a surprised look, said, "Why should I sell my Fiat when it has only gone 10,000 miles?"

We had many different types of cases which we heard

throughout the year. As it turned out, we did too good a job, we were too inquisitive, and we asked too many questions. The judges in San Mateo County decided to return to the single Blue Ribbon Grand Jury in which members were nominated and selected by the Superior Court judges, combining the civil and criminal into one. I believe the judges were in error when they made that decision. In the meantime, the drug problem in San Mateo keeps getting worse.

Chapter 56

Do Americans Work Too Hard?

They say that Europeans really know how to live. They also say that Americans, in the pursuit of the almighty dollar, don't take enough time to relax and enjoy themselves.

In the struggle to become wealthy, we sometimes overlook certain basic facts. How can you spend a million dollars? How do you spend five million dollars?

The average American seeks to avoid hard work. At one time in our early days when America was pushing the frontiers westward, it was a known and accepted fact that "If you don't work, you don't eat." We have come a long way since those colonial days of early America.

The formation of the unions in America was definitely necessary, because there was too much exploitation of the middle-class working people. The early days of the march of labor saw many bitter disputes, killings, and destruction of property. America had to be unionized.

At present day, the average American worker no longer shows any loyalty to his job. He is not interested in what he is producing, punches the clock, goes home at 5 p.m., and is back the next morning. His union protects him from getting fired and the weapon of a strike can always be waved at his employer. Our civil service system leaves much to be desired. We are forced to hire a certain percentage of minorities. Examinations are watered down to interviews. Loyalty and pride in a job no longer exists. The oldtimers took pride in their crafts and aimed for perfection. We don't see that anymore. Today's average American wants to start at the top. I am speaking of the "average American." Does he work too hard?

Let's take a look at the Europeans. In France, they get five weeks of paid vacation on the theory that they will spend it at the beach or in the mountains. In West Germany, there is six weeks of paid vacation. The wonder of the European world is why do the Americans get only two weeks of paid vacation. (I am speaking only in generalities as a great number now get four weeks.) Europeans visiting the United States during their one-month vacation have expressed, "You Americans work too hard."

I recall an incident in a southern Italian village where on one morning shops opened at 10:30 a.m. Upon inquiry, I was told, "We have to open in time to close at noon for our four-hour *siesta*." What a nice way to live, I thought. We, Americans, must be crazy. Why are we killing ourselves? How many cars can we drive? How many television sets or VCRs do we really need? How much of anything can we consume?

The French seem to be well organized in how to enjoy life. Their five weeks of vacation is a national law. Their thirteenth month of pay is not only customary in France, but in Italy and other European countries as well. Another practice, which is quite appealing, is the routine holiday weekend lasting three to four days.

We need a drastic change in our automated society. Too many people hate their jobs and their work. This is because we have been reduced to numbers instead of individuals. Our identities are now sorted by social security numbers, credit card numbers, and driver's license numbers.

Another major problem facing American families is the lifetime accumulation of money, lots of money. They lavish money on their children, and keep accumulating estates to be left to them (many of whom don't deserve it) and to relatives (many of whom were merely strangers during one's lifetime). The injustice here is that the ones who will inherit are usually blood relatives. There are many of these in the undeserving class. This calls to mind a real instance that took place. A wealthy man died and the attorney read the will before his relatives: "Being of sound mind and body, I spent it all myself." Of course, this is a bit drastic, but it makes for good reading and something to think about.

Our immigrant forebears knew what hard work was. They did the menial, stoop labor work — the dirty work that we despise today. He had high hopes, but his dream of easy wealth in the New World quickly faded. As a young Italian immigrant wrote to his family at the close of the century, "After I came here, I learned three things: The streets were not paved with gold; the streets were not paved at all; and they expected me to pave them."

Chapter 57

My Favorite Language — Brooklynese

This story is about a remarkable woman who devoted much time and effort in writing about the strange people from Brooklyn. Being one of them, I was rather excited about the recognition that Margaret Flynn gave to the place of my youth during my growing up days.

I never realized that we, Brooklynites, were a strange people, although I always thought the language was a barrier to my future, particularly with my accent, which to this day is slightly recognizable at times. My grandchildren will ask me from time to time to say "these," "those," "girl," "bird," and "third." I would go along with their requests by saying "dese," "dose," "goil," "boid," and "toid." I love it when they tease me. Only a guy from Brooklyn can pronounce these words the Brooklynese way.

I spent 18 years of my youth in "the greatest city's greatest borough," the borough of Brooklyn. Brooklynites are a breed apart. Most of those in my day were either immigrants or descendents of immigrants. Life wasn't easy back then. One had to start from scratch and pull himself up from his own bootstraps to get ahead. Brooklyn supplied the world with many entertainers, comedians, and celebrities during the era of Tin Pan Alley and the Roaring Twenties.

I recently came across the interesting story by Margaret Flynn that caught my attention and I thought this was a good opportunity to shed some light on these strange people she referred to.

"Ya got dese guys. Dey live in Brooklyn wit dere muddahs and fadduhs, see. People dink dey tawk funny." "Nah," says

400

Margaret Mannix Flynn, "It ain't funny. It's wunnerful." Mrs. Flynn has listened to thousands of people in Brooklyn and as a lecturer at the Department of Speech at Brooklyn College, she put together a study of the dialects and accents of the borough that called itself the nation's fourth largest city. "Most people believe that coming from Brooklyn is some kind of joke," the Brooklyn native said. "It always gets a laugh. You know, the guy in the World War II movie who is played by William Bendix and says he is from Flatbush . . . He always says, 'Toity-toid Street and Toid Avenue' or 'woik' for 'work,' and 'earl' for 'oil.' "

That changing, living dialect is the culmination of wave upon wave of immigration, starting with the Dutch and continuing right up to today's influx of Russian Jews. "Very few places have the rich cultural diversity of Brooklyn and thus, Brooklyn's dialect is especially rich." "We learn to speak from the people around us," Mrs. Flynn said in a recent interview. "Say you have a second-generation Italian child. All around him, he hears relatives who speak an Italian dialect. But then, he's three years-old and goes out to play. He may meet an Irish-American kid or a Jewish-American kid, and he adopts some of the way they speak. Before you know it, his speech is a conglomerate."

And so it goes. New Englanders who came to Brooklyn after the Revolution changed "Mother" to "Mothah"; the Germans changed "where" to "ver" and "so" to "zo"; the eastern Europeans added a melody that made declarative sentences sound like questions; and the Italians made the word "last" sound like "le-ast." The Irish changed "going" to "goin" and "this" to "dis." Mrs. Flynn said the Irish spoke an archaic form of English because of their isolation. The early part of this century marked the arrival of the Blacks who had been similarly isolated and made similar changes in Brooklyn speech.

Even now, Brooklyn's new immigrants are changing the speech of the borough. Puerto Ricans make "ship" sound like "sheep" and "very" like "berry." West Indian, Asian and Russian Jewish newcomers are also having their effect. Mrs. Flynn stated, "Brooklyn is not a peculiar place where people speak a peculiar language. Brooklyn really represents a multinational heritage. I think we deserve a little respect." She makes some interesting points and I, as an ex-Brooklynite and one who has acquired somewhat of a Brooklynese dialect, must agree with the learned lady.

As an interesting tidbit, the word "fanatic" was coined in Ebbets Field, home of the Brooklyn Dodgers. It was here that the rabid — and I mean rabid — fans cheered their heroes when they won, but when they lost, the team was referred to as "dem bums." The fans were such a good-natured, but unruly bunch that one of the Brooklyn sports editors nicknamed them "fanatics." That name stayed with them.

Over the years, I have enjoyed the chiding from my grandchildren of my Brooklynese. Of course, they can poke fun at me all they want, but I'll always be the only one who can speak the language. I am sure that Margaret Flynn will agree with me, as far as Brooklynese is concerned, that to have lived in Brooklyn has been a most interesting experience.

Chapter 58

I Call It Faith

I don't consider myself a religious person and I don't always agree with some of the teachings of my church. I believe that my faith has made me what I am today. If you read the contents of this book, you will agree that I have led quite a diversified life. Some of it has been controversial, but not because I am a controversial person. I have fought for causes and have taken on some powerful opposition. Because I always believed in what I was doing, I had no fear of them no matter who they were.

In my many involvements, I, at times, became angry with certain people. No matter what they did to me, I never hated them. I always believe that if you are angry with a person, you can forgive him, but if you hate a person, it is difficult to forgive him.

A turning point in my life occurred when Frank, my brother, died and Peter, my other brother, developed a series of heart attacks. I was left alone to operate the complicated business of running a bonded winery. There I was with thousands of unfinished bottles of champagne that had to complete their process so as to make them saleable. With Peter unavailable, I was beginning to not only be greatly concerned, but was slowly reaching the heights of desperation. What was I to do?

Holy Name, my parish church, was holding weekly services to Our Lady of Perpetual Help. I was taught at an earlier time that ''he who seeks Her help will never be turned away.'' That was what brought me to these particular services in which the recitation of the Rosary was the major part. (For the benefit of the non-Catholic, I will mention that we do not ''worship'' the Blessed Mother. We merely seek Her help in interceding with Her Son for us.) Somehow, I began to feel that my problem was not getting any worse. Slowly but surely, I saw some daylight. I didn't make any promise or vow to our Blessed Mother. It seemed that the daily recitation of the Rosary eased the tension I was undergoing.

Peter was able to return and take an active part in the business. Just about the time we completed the champagne that was in process, we were able to sell the winery. He got out of the business and eventually went into real estate. I passed my civil service examination and became manager of the agricultural and land division of the San Francisco Water Department, a post I held for over twenty-one years. Was it my faith in the Blessed Mother? I never argued or questioned the point. All I know was that I got into the habit of saying my Rosary every day.

I had three offices during my managerial tenure of the city's lands. One was in San Francisco, one in Millbrae, and the other in Sunol. I didn't have a radio in my car at that time, so reciting the Rosary while traveling was not a problem. It helped pass the time. When I mentioned this to my pastor, Father Richard Ryan, I did say to him that I would count the beads on my fingers. He said nothing in this regard. One week later, he presented me with a pair of beads that I have to this day, which is slightly worn by over 39 years of reciting the Rosary without missing a single day. How I ever managed to do this, I really have no answer. It came naturally, automatically, and without plan.

Most of the time, I would say the Rosary in bits and pieces, and very seldom knelt down. If I were walking, I might say a decade or two, but I always manage to complete it by the end of the day. The Rosary contains five decades of ten "Hail Marys" and one "Our Father" per decade. This is preceded by an introduction consisting of the Credo, one "Our Father" and three "Hail Marys." Each day represents one of three mysteries: The Glorious, The Sorrowful, and The Joyful.

I have found comfort, inspiration, and peace of mind, regardless of the circumstances, in the daily recitation of the Rosary. Those of you who are not of my faith may think that what I have just recited is just another story. You may think as you wish, that is your prerogative. All I can say is I believe that our Blessed Mother will never let you down if you are sincere and ask for Her help.

Perhaps I should end this chapter on the Rosary by reciting

a poem that an old Jesuit priest gave to me many years ago:

"If Christ should come on earth some summer day,
And walk unknown upon our busy street,
I wonder how t' would be if we should meet,
And being God — if he would act that way.

Perhaps the kindest thing that he would do,
Would be just to forget I failed to pray,
And clasp my hand forgivingly, and say,
'My child, I've heard my mother speak of you.' "

Chapter 59

My American Family

In my octogenarian years, I look back and try to analyze what I have done with my life and what have I accomplished. How much wealth does one accumulate? Does that bring joy and happiness? Perhaps to a certain degree.

The wealth I speak of is not material wealth. We all strive to accumulate money, property, and materials of all kinds. So be it. My wealth lies in my family and friends, which has been accumulated through love and understanding, particularly love that comes naturally and from the heart. What else is there in this valley of tears, this life with so much violence and human suffering? To me, the love of my family and their love for me is all I need. It rejuvenates my batteries and gives me added strength to forget the aches and pains that come with age.

I will talk about my two American families, relating only the pleasant memories that stand out in my mind which refuse to deteriorate. I can never overlook the sad happenings (loss of beloved ones) in my life. They remain as my secret loves, the ones I always remember in my prayers.

There they were, six of them, perched on the broad limbs of my beautiful maple tree that made an attractive addition to my Millbrae garden. Whenever any of them visited Joan and me, they made a beeline for their favorite hangout. These were my grandchildren, ranging from five to ten years of age (1966). The site of Kathy, Linda, Kenny (my son Jack's children), and Eileen, Karen and Tom (Joan's grandchildren) in their outdoor clubhouse made a pretty picture. They perched on those limbs for hours chatting away, solving their little problems, laughing, singing, and having fun. One day I mentioned to Joan, "You know, Joan, they look like a group of monkeys." This was the nickname that was given to them at that time and to this day, I still call them monkeys. Years later, I also nicknamed my two young nieces in Palermo, Francesca and Carla, *scimioni* (monkeys). My other two grandchildren, Michelle and Sherie, were not born yet, but they, too, inherited and liked the idea of being called monkeys (but only when Grandpa said it).

My younger son, Peter, married Joyce Moresi, who is of Italian Swiss and Genovese background. Jack's wife, Mary Ellen Herrick, is of Irish-English background. With this combination, you can readily realize why I always boast about the beautiful children produced from these racial backgrounds.

The celebrated maple tree was located on our Sequoia Avenue property in Millbrae. We then moved to Green Hills Estates in a new development there. When we held our first open house, we found no joy or expression on the faces of our grandchildren. "How do you like our new home?" Their unanimous reply was, "What about our maple tree?" Needless to say, time has erased all this and looking back, we think of all the fun the children enjoyed in their early years.

The Brucato and the Elam families were joined together when Joan and I were married in April of 1967. Jack and Peter are my two sons by my first wife, Josephine, who passed away in 1966. Joan has a daughter, Jeanne, who married Jim Elam. They had Eileen, Karen and Tom. Jim was my adversary in our continuous cribbage competition. We were evenly matched and the game was always played in a pleasurable fashion. This was also true with our bocce ball tournaments, which was the feature of our many family picnics. Unfortunately, we lost Jim on Christmas Day in 1985. His passing was a shock and a great loss to all of us. I always considered him as one of my closest friends. I loved that man, my son-in-law.

In an earlier chapter, I talked about the biggest family get-together which is our annual five-day Thanksgiving celebration at Lake Tahoe. Now going into its twentieth year, it was definitely the highlight of our family reunions with all of twenty-two people. I was appointed quarter-master for these gatherings. My job was to organize the five-day expedition and assign each family as to what they should bring, especially in the line of food. Joan's job was to cook the turkey with all the stuffing, assisted by Jeanne, Joyce, Mary Ellen, and Kathy. We had a lot of fun enjoying each other's company.

During the twenty years, we seldom had an absentee. No

matter where the clan was scattered, they always came at all costs because this was our one real family reunion. Time has changed in many ways. The grandchildren are now grown up. Some have married, some have graduated from college and are in the process of seeking their new adult future, and the others are still in school. Despite the fact that we begin to see less of them as they mature, we still see all of them at Thanksgiving.

I live for my family and I know they enjoy me for who I am — natural, warm and loving. My girls are beautiful and charming. They always receive a kiss on both cheeks when we meet. This is my way, Italian-style, of extending greetings to everyone. I always say, ''You see, an Italian really gets his money's worth — two kisses.''

Then, there are my two lovely nieces, Rosalie and Louise, Peter's daughters. Of course, I am their favorite uncle. I have always said that if I ever really needed someone for any reason, they would be there. These two were always inseparable and very close to their mother, Marie, and their father. After Peter's passing, Marie married Dick Cullen, their neighbor who had also been recently widowed. He and his wife were very close to the Brucatos. They lived adjacent to each other and the gate on their fence was never closed. Marie Cullen always remained as my favorite sister-in-law.

Rosalie married Harold Balzer (we call him ''Babe''), who added Lisa and Debbie to our family. Lisa is the image of Frances, my sister, while Debbie is the comedienne of the family, and so lovely. I will always remember when we were entertaining Monsignor Daniel Walsh (now Bishop Walsh) one day at dinner. Engaged in a spirited conversation with the Monsignor, I was emphasizing my point by moving my hands (typical of Italians). Debbie, 11, was seated next to me and enjoying some of my choice olives. Whenever I extended my hand in her direction, my palm would be the recipient of an olive pit. I paid no attention to this at the moment when I was trying to get my point across to Monsignor Walsh. When I suddenly realized what Debbie was doing, we all burst into laughter.

My other niece, Louise, married Steve Hall who was immediately initiated into the Brucato clan. They have two boys, Timothy and Mark. Tim became a star athlete on his high school team, while Mark was student, athlete, and school president. The biggest surprise came ten years later when lo and behold, Louise gave birth to twins, Stephanie and Stacy.

Today, at the age of 14, they are the most gifted and talented of any children I know. Over the years, I have taught the children a little repertoire of songs, ditties, and comical poems as they were growing up. Teaching the twins was a cinch. After the first recitation, they had the lines down perfect by the second time around.

My granddaughter, Linda, made me reach a new plateau last January when a seven-pound bundle named Brian John made me a <u>great</u> grandfather. *Mama Mia*, now I can start all over again with my little ditties. But it doesn't stop here. Linda just announced that the second one is due in the spring. I pray to God to give me enough energy and strength so that I will be able to keep up with this new lease on life in my octogenarian years. What a thrill! I wonder now who will be next. Life sure has a way of going on.

Chapter 60

Update: My American Family

I began this autobiography when I was 80 years old. Now, at the age of 87, seven years have gone by. During this period, my granddaughter Linda has added Gretchen to my collection of beautiful great-granddaughters, now two years old, while Brian has passed his fifth birthday.

Michelle recently received her degree from San Diego State University, while Sherie has added another great-granddaughter, Cassandra, to my collection. *Mama mia!*

Then there is Kathy, my first-born granddaughter, married to Daniel Aliotti who owns and operates one of Carmel's most famous restaurants, L'Escargot.

Marie Cullen, my former sister-in-law and mother of my two nieces, Rosalie and Louise, recently passed on to her heavenly reward, followed by her husband Richard, a most wonderful person.

My talented Eileen, who besides being a top equestrian, is making her mark in the business world. When the time comes, I am slated to escort her down the aisle to join Terri, as I did for Karen, who with her Mark, have set up housekeeping in San Carlos. Tom, so tall and handsome that I am afraid he could wind up in Hollywood, is busy designing tunnels, bridges and whatever is required of him by his employers, the prestigious Guy F. Atkinson Construction Company. My daughter-in-law, Jeanne, recently sold her home in Los Altos and moved close by, inasmuch as her brood has left their nest in order to carry on with their lives, but nevertheless they keep in close touch with her.

Rosalie and Babe remain very close to me while my two

lovely nieces Lisa and Debbie have responsible positions in the family lithographic business.

Louise and Steve carry on in Saratoga, while their Tim graduates from U.C. Santa Barbara and Marc, the scholar in the family, will be going to a school of higher learning, Georgetown University in Washington D.C. And, oh yes, my favorite twin nieces, Stephanie and Stacy, are now grown up - two lovely and adorable young ladies, so lovable and attentive, which is no doubt one of the reasons that keeps me young in spirit and otherwise.

Who could ask for more? Jack and Mary Ellen, Peter and Joyce. What a blessing to have such a family. Here is where I have my wealth, not in material things, but my wealth of family. It is they who give me their love and I, of course, give them my love and affection, which spells happiness and contentment. Most of all, there is Joan at my side who shares these Golden Years with me.

When I look back and see what is happening to the many mixed marriages that are taking place in this melting pot of nationalities in my beloved America, I will try to sum up my feelings in this way: My blood line is thinning through the marriages of my children and grandchildren as with each generation they marry non-Italians, but regardless of how this blood line becomes in the many generations to come, I am happy to say that my Sicilian blood will never go away.

Chapter 61

My Italian Family

What adds to my happiness and joy is that I am not limited just to my American family. There is another part of my family living in *La Mia Bella Sicilia*, my Italian family. Joan and I have visited them on ten occasions in the past twenty years and we have enjoyed their warmth and affection.

It was one of those balmy Sicilian nights. We were enjoying a refreshing glass of Asti Spumanti in the company of a large number of members of the Palermo Rotary Club, who were celebrating their annual *villigiatura* (get-together) at the famous Mondello Palace Hotel Resort where Joan and I were staying. Surrounded by acres of the most beautiful and exotic, semi-tropical landscaping that made one think of this as a possible heaven on earth, we were seated alongside an outdoor, stage-like setting and enjoyed a most entertaining display of gypsy-like dancing by a talented group of Hungarian ballet dancers. It was towards their finale when the lead dancer suddenly stopped and looked around for a partner from the audience. He quickly grabbed my niece, Carla, by the arm and lo and behold, they put on one of the most exciting Hungarian dances that brought the audience to their feet. When she returned to her seat, she was immediately surrounded by the many dignitaries present including the American consul general, and the many bejeweled and well-wishing ladies with their black-tie escorts. Carla grabbed me in fright and said, "*Zio*, I feel so embarrassed." I said, "Brace up, Carla, you are now famous." (She did confess to me later that she had taken up ballet in school.) From that moment on, I nicknamed her "*La Ballerina*."

Mondello is a picture-card resort situated on the Mediterranean with a beautiful sandy beach, a Fisherman's Wharf-type village, and hundreds of villas where the Palermitani spend their summers. We had discontinued going to the Hotel De Palme and the Villa Igea because of the traffic and congestion that plagued Palermo. The other reason why we stayed in Mondello was because my cousins, nephew, and other people we knew all had villas nearby which made visiting easier.

Filippo Zito, my nephew, was six years-old when my sister, Frances, his mother, passed away. We first met in 1972 and subsequent get-togethers gave me an opportunity to tell him about his mother. During our first visit to Palermo, we had dinner at his home. His wife, Giovanna, was born in Rome, but she is strictly Sicilian and is a wonderful cook, producing a plate of pasta that is a combination of a Roman and Sicilian masterpiece. Having learned that I was a lover of *pasta con sarde*, a true Sicilian dish that escaped my taste buds for years, she served enough to supply the Sicilian Navy. Would you believe that this course came after the antipasto and the minestrone and before the *pasta alla bolognese*? The balance of the meal was veal piccata, salad, and a healthy assortment of those Sicilian delicacies, especially *cannoli*. She really wanted to please us. Our dinner lasted close to four hours. Well, this was our initiation into my Sicilian family.

Both my nieces, Carla and Francesca, were brilliant students at the University of Palermo, very attractive and affectionate. Joan and I were immediately adopted not only by them, but by all the relatives we soon came to know. The girls learned English in school as this was the required language. This, of course, made it easier for Joan. We met quite a few people through my nieces.

One day, while having lunch at Filippo's home, there were six of their friends all enjoying the Sicilian pastry, amarettos and comparis when I engaged in some lively discussion on one of my favorite topics. "Now that you are about to take your place in the adult world, what is your approach or possible solutions to the many problems facing us today?" I added, "We, oldtimers, have tried to make this a better world and I don't have to remind you that the problems still exist. What would be your program or ideas?" I was floored when the almost-unanimous reply rang through my unbelievable ears. "We want more rock n' roll."

Filippo has been with the *Cassa di Risparmio* for practically all of his adult years. It is a savings and loan with 230 branches all over Sicily. When we first met him, he was the manager of the Alcamo branch and lived in an attractive apartment in Alcamo. Throughout his banking career, he managed quite a few of the branches in various parts of the island with its main office in Palermo.

Alcamo is famed for its wineries and vineyards, and up to recent time, it was the headquarters of the infamous Mafia. The "Dons", however, have practically annihilated each other in their well-known family squabbles. This was also where Danilo Dolce fought against the Mafia and made efforts to improve the economic conditions of these unfortunate people. We attended mass one Sunday morning in Alcamo. While Joan and I were walking down the aisle, we couldn't help but notice that most of the women wore black. (The old-fashioned mourning period was one year. I presumed that most of them wore black for most of their lives.)

When we returned to Filippo's apartment, there was a steady stream of visitors, most of them close friends of his. As is the custom in Sicily, each brought a gift, usually pastry or cookies. They all wanted to meet the *Americanos.* By the time it was evening, I believe we had enough goodies to open up a *pasticeria* (pastry shop). This gesture of friendship gave me a warm feeling for these people.

A few years later on one of our visits, Filippo informed us that he had risen to one of his bank's top positions. He became the controller of *Cassa di Risparmio* for all of Sicily. With this promotion, he was headquartered in Palermo and was finally settled down in his new condominium. Filippo was a workaholic, Giovanna was a true Sicilian housekeeper, and my two *scimioni*, Francesca and Carla, were my two lovely nieces. They were only a part of my Italian family.

My link to the past were my cousins, Carlo and Franca Columba. Franca was ten years my senior as would be my sister, Frances, had she lived. We were entertained at their beautiful *Isola Verde* (green island) villa in Mondello during our first visit in 1972. Franca escorted Joan and I to the guestroom and insisted that we nap for an hour or two. After ten minutes, we decided that we would stroll around the beautiful one-acre, landscaped estate containing horticultural plants and vegetation from practically all over the world. We followed interesting paths, fish ponds, nooks, and scenery that was unbelievably well planned and carefully executed.

Carlo is a retired engineer and was one of the architects of the many beautiful *autostradas*, or garden parkways, and the many public works that made him in big demand as a consultant to a number of foreign countries. He is also an author and one of the most likeable persons I have ever met. We enjoyed many hours of conversation with this learned and hospitable individual.

Carlo and Franca's son, Mario, a noted physicist and president of the College of Physicists of the University of Palermo, is also an authority on solar energy. During the energy crisis, the University of Palermo and the University of California at Berkeley were engaged in mutual solar energy experiments. He has made several trips to Berkeley, and on one occasion was able to meet practically all of his American relatives at a reception at our home. His talented wife, Lucia, teaches at the University of Palermo. They have three very talented children.

Three years ago, Mario was selected by the Educators of Italy and other groups particularly interested in the unemployment of many degree-holding students without jobs, to run for the House of Deputies representing western Sicily. He was elected by a large vote and served in Parliament in Rome. We were very proud of him.

In 1986, Franca passed away at the age of ninety-two. She and I had become very close, and she told me many things about my family that I didn't know. She was my link to the past.

Rosanna Messina is Filippo's aunt and we regard her as one of the family. She speaks perfect English, but with a slight British accent. Rosanna has been associated with the American Consulate in Palermo for many years. One of her duties was to educate Americans in their diplomatic service in Italy as to Italian customs and protocol. Ino, her husband, was another interesting person. Her father, who recently passed on, was associated with the lemon business. He lived in England and was closely tied in with my father before he came to America. He was our connection with my nephew and cousins during World War II when Sicily was under Allied occupation.

In the twenty-five years of our marriage, Joan and I managed to make ten visits to Palermo. While we traveled to many parts of Europe and northern Africa, we always wound up in Palermo for about a week's time. We were always treated royally and there was always a big farewell upon our departure. They certainly made Joan feel she was part of the family, and

Joan in turn acknowledged her love for them.

I have two wonderful families. Who could ever wish for more? Now, if I could only bring them all together.

Chapter 62

P. S.

Writing a book is like writing a letter. There is always some space left at the bottom of a personal or business letter. This space is usually reserved for a forgotten thought or anything that comes to mind before the envelope is sealed. We generally take care of this after-thought by simply writing two letters, ''P. S.,'' which of course means postscript.

I suddenly realized that I have passed my eighty-seventh birthday. Where has all the time gone? I haven't been successful in holding back the clock and at this writing, I must bring this episode of my life to a rapid conclusion before I go on to greener pastures.

I've spent one-third of my life in bed by sleeping eight hours a day. Waking up earlier than usual, I keep saying to myself, ''What am I doing in bed when there is so much to do and so little time left?'' Translating this into simple numbers, it means that if I reach the age of ninety, I would have only been ''alive'' for sixty years. One morning, while I was halfway through my shredded wheat, I suddenly decided that five to six hours of sleep is all that I needed. I was always an early riser, so my new schedule created no problem.

So many things have happened since I passed the ''80'' mark. When I meet a senior citizen, we usually speak about our aches and pains. I was greatly encouraged the other day when I ran across an article in my morning *Chronicle.* It stated that more people are now living past the age of 85 than ever before. That really made my day. With this kind of encouragement, I can hope to try for ninety. As I have stated in my philosophy of life, middle age begins at 85 while old age starts at 95.

I read in the *San Francisco Examiner* about a couple who will be celebrating eighty years of married life. What is more remarkable is that the husband, Salvatore Caito, recently celebrated his 104th birthday while Providenzia, his wife, claimed to be 96. They were both born in Sicily. What I am attempting to point out is that the possibility of reaching the century mark becomes more feasible with each passing day.

People have remarked how young Joan and I appear despite our age. They ask what our secret is. Really, there is none. We live normal, but active lives. In this respect, we keep unusually busy just so long as we don't have to do things under pressure.

When I retired from my city job in 1970 after managing the public utilities properties for twenty-one years, I vowed that I would avoid pressure at all costs in the future. I had to suffer all those years of procrastination, frustration, and the incompetency of my superiors. If I had another year of this, I would not be telling my story today.

In May of 1985 when I passed my eightieth birthday, Joan and I decided that perhaps we should slow down a bit. I guess it was just a passing thought. Joan, who has been very active with the Children's Home Society and having served as president of one of its auxiliaries, was asked if she would accept the presidency of the Coast County Council. She asked for time to consider this most important development. After discussing in detail the change that would be taking place, I suggested that she accept the position. The enormity of her new responsibility involved the supervision of ten auxiliaries in the Bay Area, their ever-increasing problems and workload, and dealing with neglected, abused and abandoned children.

I always felt proud of Joan in whatever undertaking she was involved in. Everything she did was done with dignity, sincerity, and accomplishment. I never had to be concerned as to the outcome of her many activities. Her legion of friends was perhaps the highest compliment I could pay to her.

It seems that there is no rest for an active person. I do have my responsibilities as director of a successful growing bank. I also have my continuous activity in the historical society and the museum, plus many others which I have taken in stride.

There was rumor that Mary Griffin might run for supervisor of San Mateo County. On two previous occasions, I served as her treasurer when she was successfully elected to the Millbrae City Council and as mayor. It bacame a reality when one of the

Celebrating the 41st anniversary of the Farmers' Market with my lovely wife, Joan — 1983.

A personal interview with the San Mateo Times on the 48th anniversary of the Farmers' Market — August 1991.

supervisors, Jackie Speier, was successful in her bid for the California State Assembly, thus, creating a vacancy on the five-member board. Mary asked me if I would accept the position as her treasurer once more. After discussing the matter with Joan, we said, "Here we go again." Being a countywide race, this became a challenge. I was confident that she would win and she did by a most emphatic plurality.

I believe that one should keep busy not just physically, but mentally, and get involved. In this respect, a political campaign is not only exciting, but you meet all kinds of people. You come to life with each day's developments, good or bad. The important thing is that I have always enjoyed a good fight and in the political world, that is what it's all about.

The other day, one of our bank employees, a very attractive brunette, celebrated her twenty-fifth birthday. In the spirit of fun, I asked her if she would trade her twenty-five years for my golden years. I didn't wait for her reply, but immediately answered my own question by saying that I would rather keep my golden years. I don't believe I would want to start all over again in this topsy-turvy world of violence, computers, and rock n' roll.

Life is a merry-go-round. You can't just sit in your comfortable rocking chair waiting for the next meal. You have to try for the gold ring and don't get off that merry-go-round until you grab it. If you keep missing the ring, so what? At least you are alive and you keep trying. It is better to have calluses on your hands than on your fanny from waiting for the mailman to bring you your social security check.

Another piece of advice for senior citizens is not to retire to a senior citizens' compound where you will be confined to people of your own age group. Your conversation will be limited to the aches and pains that will constitute most of your daily dialogue. What I am trying to convey is that we need young people about us, so that we can keep our minds sharp and our bodies agile. I practice this philosophy with my grandchildren and the younger generation at every possible opportunity. We, senior citizens, are the real sleeping giants. We don't take advantage of the fact that people are living longer, and it will not be too long when senior citizens will approach the majority of the population. Have you ever realized the power that we have in the palms of our hands? I'm not implying that we, as senior citizens, desire to take over and run the government. Hell no! That's not the point. The power that we are assuming, the political power, is to have a more prominent voice in whatever is going on. With all our experience, we should not file our knowledge and know-how on the shelf. The youth of our land needs us. They may not realize or agree with it, but as long as we are a country for, of, and by the people, for God's sake, senior citizens, don't throw away your life. The future needs you, especially the future of this great land of ours.

The city of San Francisco, evidently not caring, leased land in the Sunol Valley that eventually destroyed the city's "million dollar walnut orchard" by uprooting 140 of the 200 acres. The walnut orchard is gone. What will happen to the remaining sixty acres remains to be seen. Tears come to my eyes when I think of the destruction of one of the great beauty spots of the Sunol Valley, the city's walnut orchard, my "million dollar walnut orchard" all for the sake of a few more dollars paid to the city.

The Spring Valley Water Company planted the original one hundred acres and I planted an additional forty acres, followed by another sixty later on. Where the hell were the environmentalists, the Sierra Club, or the city officials who permitted the desecration of these beautiful walnut trees? Now, there are only sixty acres left and they will soon be pulled out. Why? Because they are overrun with ground squirrels, disease, and just plain neglect. I say pull them out. No self-respecting walnut tree would want to be a part of a system noted for its inefficiency and stupidity. (Note: At this writing, the 60 acres of walnuts are gone.)

I can no longer dwell on what has and hasn't been done. I am enjoying my golden years every day, every hour. How much time do I have left? I really don't know. First of all, I have found complete happiness with my family. They know how much I love them and I know the great love they show for me. Would I want more?

There have been two beautiful women in my life. Josephine gave me two wonderful sons and left many memories. Yes, we went through the struggling period of our lives. Who doesn't? Needless to say, we had many friends and many good times until tragedy struck with the untimely death of my loving partner. Joan came into my life and brought a wonderful family with her including her daughter, Jeanne, and Jim, who we lost a few years ago. My adopted grandchildren, Eileen, Karen and Tom, became my own.

I don't believe Joan and I have ever had a serious argument in our twenty-five years of married live. We always discuss things whether they are problems or just everyday happenings. I always jokingly mention to my friends that we follow a democratic process in my family. We even vote on whether we're going to have chocolate or vanilla ice cream for dessert. I vote for chocolate and Joan votes for vanilla. According to the democratic process, the majority rules and we have vanilla. Around Christmas time, I will vote for a white tree and Joan votes for a green one. We will wind up with a green tree. What the hell? It's all in fun and this is the way we conduct our happy and successful marriage. In other words, don't always try to win an argument or discussion. You generally come out ahead when the other side wins.

It is a strange and mixed-up world we live in today. There is so much to do and so little time left to do it, and I fear that my time is up, that is, as far as this autobiography is concerned. How do you come to a conclusion and end with a punchline? I believe that the great composer, Ruggero Leoncavallo, came up with a most proper ending in his opera - *Pagliacci: "La Commedia e Finita."*